Previous studies of the Partition of India have concentrated on the negotiations of the transfer of power at the all-India level or have considered the emergence of separatist politics amongst India's Muslim minorities. This study provides a re-evaluation of the events of 1946–47 focusing on the political and social processes that led to the demand for partition in a Mulsim-majority province, Bengal, and tracing the rise of Hindu communalism. In its most startling revelation, the author shows how the demand for a separate homeland for the Hindus, which was fuelled by a large and powerful section of Hindu society within Bengal, was seen as the only way to regain their influence. The picture which emerges is one of a stratified and fragmented society moving away from the mainstream of Indian nationalism, and increasingly preoccupied with narrower, more parochial concerns.

In this original and thoughtful interpretation of the history of Bengal, Joya Chatterji shows herself to be one of a new generation of scholars prepared to access a wider range of source materials and to question the conventional assumptions of earlier historians.

Cambridge South Asian Studies

Bengal divided

Bengal divided

Hindu communalism and partition, 1932–1947

Joya Chatterji

Trinity College, Cambridge

PUBLISHED BY THE PRESS SYNDICATE OF THE UNIVERSITY OF CAMBRIDGE
The Pitt Building, Trumpington Street, Cambridge, United Kingdom

CAMBRIDGE UNIVERSITY PRESS
The Edinburgh Building, Cambridge CB2 2RU, UK
40 West 20th Street, New York NY 10011–4211, USA
477 Williamstown Road, Port Melbourne, VIC 3207, Australia
Ruiz de Alarcón 13, 28014 Madrid, Spain
Dock House, The Waterfront, Cape Town 8001, South Africa

http://www.cambridge.org

First published 1994
First paperback edition 2002

A catalogue record for this book is available from the British Library

Library of Congress Cataloguing in Publication data
Chatterji, Joya.
Bengal divided: Hindu communalism and partition, 1932–1947 / Joya Chatterji.
      p.   cm. – (Cambridge South Asian studies (no. 57))
Includes bibliographical references and index.
ISBN 0 521 41128 9
1. Bengal (India) – History – Partition, 1947.
2. Communalism – India – Bengal – History.
I. Title. II. Series.
DS485.B493C49 1994
954'.140359–dc20   93-30544   CIP

ISBN 0 521 41128 9 hardback
ISBN 0 521 52328 1 paperback

Contents

Maps

Tables

Acknowledgements

This book first took shape as a fellowship dissertation submitted to Trinity College in 1989. A more finished version was presented as a doctoral thesis to the University of Cambridge in 1990. At each stage, its author incurred many debts of gratitude, and it is a pleasure to be able to thank all those who assisted in its creation.

Generous funding by the Master and Fellows of Trinity College sustained me, first as a graduate student and later as a Fellow, through five years of research, writing and travel. The Smuts Fund made it possible for me to make trips to archives and libraries in India and Bangladesh.

My supervisor at Cambridge, Dr Anil Seal, took an interest in the progress of this work that went well beyond the call of duty. His constant encouragement spurred me into writing it more quickly than I might otherwise have done, while his thorough supervision and eye for detail prevented many errors of style and argument from entering the final version. Dr Rajnarayan Chandavarkar, Professor Ravinder Kumar, and Dr Tanika Sarkar read through early drafts. Their advice was most helpful. Professor Tapan Raychaudhuri and Dr Gordon Johnson examined both the fellowship and doctoral dissertations on which this book is based. Their critical suggestions were valuable and encouraging.

Discussion and argument with friends not only enlivened the process of writing this book, but also stimulated new ideas and helped to make old ones clearer. I am especially grateful to Samita Sen, Subho Basu and Sujata Patel for the many hours spent debating various aspects of my argument. Subho and Samita also assisted me with translation, and shared with me their knowledge of Bengali literature. Samita shared her equally formidable knowledge of the word processor, and took a great deal of time off her own work to help me out of tricky processing problems.

The staff of various libraries – the Nehru Memorial Museum and Library, the National Archives and the Jawaharlal Nehru University Library in Delhi, the West Bengal State Archives, the Centre for Studies in Society and History and the National Library in Calcutta, the Bangla Academy and the Asiatic Society of Bangladesh in Dhaka, the India Office Library and Records in London, the Bodleian Library in Oxford and the University Library in Cambridge – gave me ready access to the materials upon which this research is based. I owe special thanks to Dr Lionel Carter of the Centre for South Asian Studies, Cambridge, Mr. M. Mujadded of the Bangla Academy, Dhaka, and Mr Kanai Lall Sardar of the Special Branch Record Room, Calcutta, who went out of their way to assist me in every possible way.

In Dhaka, Mr and Mrs Ata-ul Huq welcomed me into their home. Professor Taluqder Maniruzzaman, Professor Abdur Rezzak and Shiraz Mannan shared with me their knowledge of the history of Bengal. I am particularly grateful to Badruddin Umar and Feroze Ahsan for making available to me materials from Mr Umar's private collection.

A special word of thanks to Tina Bone and Laura Cordy at Trinity College, and to Marigold Acland and Mary Richards at Cambridge University Press for their invaluable assistance in the production of this book.

My family has indulged and supported my passion for history for several years, and has followed my progress as a research student with great interest (and not a little bemusement). Sara and Peter McManus and Jhupu and Shona Adhikari made my long stays in Calcutta very pleasant by providing me with a most congenial home environment. My grandfather, Frederick Sawyer, and my mother, Psyche Abraham, read through the manuscript with great care, and pointed out many typographical and stylistic errors. Miti and Ramona Adhikari, and Joy and Zygmund Warwick helped me in innumerable ways during my years at Cambridge. Vandana and Arun Prasad have been a constant source of encouragement. Archana Prasad assisted me with archival research when pregnancy and motherhood restricted my movements.

My greatest debt is to my husband, Prakash. Without his constant interest and involvement in my work, this book would have been a much poorer effort. He shared all the burdens of child-care and domestic life willingly and cheerfully, and took time off his own research to allow me to pursue mine. Our son, Kartik, was always cooperative and put up with his mother's academic preoccupations with unfailing good humour.

My father supported and encouraged me at every point. His own lively interest in modern Bengali history and strongly-held (if controversial) views first aroused my interest in the subject. This book is dedicated to him.

Abbreviations

AICC	All India Congress Committee
AIML	All India Muslim League
BPCC	Bengal Provincial Congress Committee
BPHM	Bengal Provincial Hindu Mahasabha
CC	Congress Committee
CPI	Communist Party of India
DCC	District Congress Committee
DIG	Deputy Inspector General
DM	District Magistrate
FB	Forward Bloc
FR	Fortnightly Report
FSR	Fortnightly Secret Report
GB	Government of Bengal
HCPB	Home Confidential Political Branch
INA	Indian National Army
IOLR	India Office Library and Records
IPP	Independent Proja Party
KPP	Krishak Praja Party
LOFCR	Local Officers Fortnightly Confidential Reports
MLA	Member of the Legislative Assembly
NAI	National Archives of India
NBPS	Nikhil Banga Praja Samity
NMML	Nehru Memorial Museum and Library
OT	Oral Transcript
PS	Police Station
RSS	Rashtriya Swayam Sevak Sangha
UMP	United Muslim Party
SB	Special Branch
SP	Superintendent of Police
SSR	Survey and Settlement Report
TKS	Tippera Krishak Samity
WBSA	West Bengal State Archives

Glossary

abhadra	vulgar, crude
abhijata	notable
abwab	traditional, arbitrary exaction above the formal rent
acharan	character
ail	landmark distinguishing two plots of land
aimadar	intermediate tenure holder, particularly in Burdwan
akhara	gymnasium, physical culture club
amal	revenue collector
anushilan	practice
apamaan	insult
ashraf	(Muslim) nobility
ashram	hermitage
atrap	(Muslim) commoners
atyachar	cruelty, oppression
babu	traditional (Hindu) title or respect, Anglo-Indian term (pejorative) for educated Hindus
Bania	member of a trading and money-lending Caste
baralok	lit. 'big people', elites
bargadar	sharecropper
bari	home
barkandaz	messenger
basha	lodgings
bhadra	polite, cultivated
bhadralok	gentle-folk
bhagchashi	sharecropper
bhakti	devotion
biplab	rebellion
boniyadi	traditionally propertied, aristocratic
bratachari	traditional form of physical culture, dance

brittibhogi	professional
bustee	slum, settlement
byayam	exercise
chakuri	service
chaukidar	watchman
chash	cultivation
chashadi	cultivation et cetera
crorepati	multi-millionaire
dadni	moneylending
dal	party, faction
dalan-bari	brick-built pucca house
dalil patra	certificate, document
dar-patnidar	intermediate tenure-holder
Dar-ul-Islam	Islamic state
desh	nation, native place
dewan	manager
dhal	shield
dharma	religion, duty
dharmaablamban	religious practice
dhoti	lower garment
dhyana	meditation
fatka	speculation
gaddi	seat, throne
gamcha	towel used by Brahmins
go korbani	cow sacrifice
goalas	caste of milkmen
gomasta	landlord's steward
goonda	hoodlum
grihastha	householder
hartal	strike
ijaradar	leaseholder
itarta	lit. otherness; pop. baseness, meanness
jabana	foreigner (pejorative)
jalachal	intermediary caste from whom Brahmins may accept water without being 'polluted'
jati	caste, race
jotedar	tenure-holder
khansama	cook
khas khamar	personal demesne
khas mahal	government land
khas	personal
kooli-majur	labourers

korbani	sacrifice (of cows on Bakr-Id)
korfa	under-tenant
krishak	peasant
kutcheri	lower court
lakh	hundred thousand
lakhpati	millionaire
lathi	bamboo stave
lathial	zamindari servant, one who wields a bamboo stave
madhyabitto	middle classes
madrassa	traditional place of Islamic education
mahajan	moneylender
matbar	village leader
maulana	Islamic scholar
maund	measure of weight roughly equivalent to 82 lb.
maulvi	Muslim priest
mela	fair
memsaheb	white woman
mlechha	untouchable
mofussil	district, countryside
mohalla	neighbourhood/locality
mukarari	permanent holding with fixed rent
mullah	(Muslim) learned man
naib	landlord's employee, accountant
nazar-salami	landlord's transfer fee
paik	footman, peon
panchayat	village council
pandal	marquee
para	neighbourhood
patnidar	intermediate tenure-holder
peepul	sacred tree (for Hindus), *ficus religiosa*
pir	Muslim saint
pourasha	manhood, manliness
praja	tenant
puja	prayer, Hindu festival for goddesses Durga and Kali
Rabindra-sangeet	songs by Rabindranath Tagore
raiyat	peasant
rajdrohi	traitor, enemy of the state
rashtrapati	president
sadar	headquarters
sadhubhasha	formal and literary language

sahebi	anglicised
saheb	European
Sakta	tradition of worship of the energy/power symbolised by the mother goddess
salami	landlord's transfer fee
samiti	association
sampraday	community
sanatan	eternal
sangathan	organisation
sangeet	music
sangram	struggle
sannyas	a life of renunciation
sarbajanin	open to all (castes), universal
sarki	arrow
sarva	all
satitva	chastity
satyagraha	quest for truth
shikshita/shikkhito	educated
shraddha	funeral ceremony
shuddhi	ritual purification
srijukta	honorific title (Hindu)
tabligh	conversion (to Islam)
taluqdar	rent-receiving small land-holder
tanzim	(Islamic) organisation
tarun	youth
tatsama	derived from Sanskrit
tazia	(symbolic) bier, carried in procession by Muslims at Moharram
thana	police station
ulema	persons versed in Islamic religious canon
varnashramdharma	scriptural fourfold division of Brahmanical society, caste system
vishayi bhadralok	respectable salaried class
vyavasa	trade or business
zamindar	landlord
zilla	subdivision, district

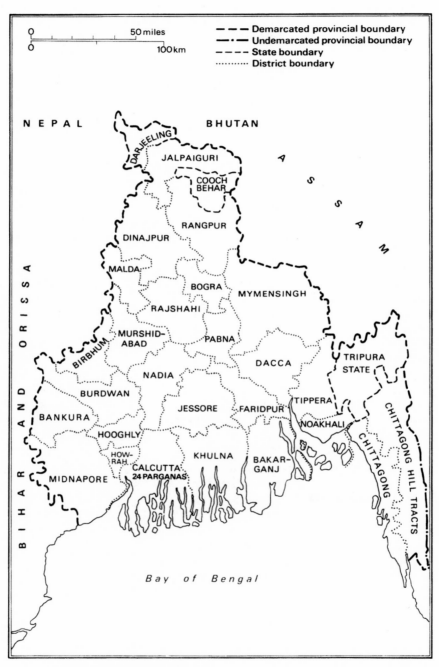

Map 1. Bengal districts

Introduction

When Curzon partitioned Bengal in 1905, this elicited a storm of protest which forced the government to rescind his decision within six years. Indeed, Bengal's reputation for being in the vanguard of Indian nationalism owes much to the agitation which upset the 'settled fact' of partition, and which introduced new techniques of mobilisation to Indian politics.[1]

In 1947, Bengal was partitioned again, following horrific clashes between Hindus and Muslims. On this occasion, however, hardly a voice was raised in protest. On the contrary, the second and definitive partition of Bengal was preceded by an organised agitation which demanded the vivisection of the province on the basis of religion. This movement was led by the very same section of Bengali society that had dominated its nationalist politics since the time of Bengal's first partition: the so-called bhadralok or 'respectable people'. In less than forty years, bhadralok politics had come full circle, moving away from nationalist agendas to more parochial concerns. The central purpose of this work will be to explain these changes in bhadralok politics and to interpret their apparent shift from 'nationalism' towards 'communalism'.[2]

The relationship between Indian nationalism and communalism is complex and ambivalent, both in terms of ideology and political practice. Recent studies have argued that nationalism in India cannot be regarded as the 'other' of communalism.[3] The opposite of communalism is secularism, which separates politics from religion.[4] Admittedly, many aspects of

[1] See Sumit Sarkar, *The Swadeshi Movement in Bengal, 1903–1908*, New Delhi, 1973.
[2] The word 'communalism' is widely used in the Indian context to describe mutual hostility between communities based on religion.
[3] Gyanendra Pandey, *The Construction of Communalism in Colonial North India*, New Delhi, 1990, pp. 2, 241. Also see Mushirul Hasan, *Nationalism and Communal Politics in India, 1885–1930*, New Delhi, 1991.
[4] For an early discussion of the term 'secularism', see G. J. Holyoake, *The Origin and Nature of Secularism*, London, 1896. Also see Bryan Wilson, *Religion in a Secular Society. A Sociological Comment*, London, 1966.

1

Indian nationalism were not in this sense secular:[5] nationalist campaigns often manipulated religious imagery and issues to win popular support.[6] Nor did Indian nationalism have truly secular ideological and philosophical underpinnings. Nationalist thought tended to share the colonial view that the basic unit of Indian society was the community as defined by religion.[7] The 'secular' nationalist ideal was *sarvadharma sambhava*, that is, the equality of all communities and the spirit of accommodation between them.[8] Yet most nationalist thinkers tended to describe national identity in religious terms, and to equate being an Indian with being a Hindu. This was particularly marked in Bengal, in the writings of Bankimchandra Chattopadhyay, Aurobindo Ghosh and Swami Vivekananda and in the brand of 'extremist' nationalism they inspired.[9]

But if nationalist thought was not truly secular, nor was it 'communal'. The main thrust of the national movement was directed against British colonialism. When it appealed to religion, it did so to mobilise religious sentiment against British rule. Communal parties and ideologies, on the other hand, always defined the community based on religion as a political unit in a permanent adversarial relationship with other communities. In theory, therefore, communal ideologists owed more to the colonial wisdom about India than the nationalist. Not only did they see India as a society dominated by communities, just as the colonial civil servants did,

---

[5] See, for instance, the discussion of the relationship between religious and nationalist politics in India in Dumont's essay: 'Nationalism and Communalism', Appendix D, *Homo Hierarchicus. The Caste System and its Implications*, Chicago, 1980. Of course, this relationship was in no sense exclusively Indian, as Dumont suggests. On the role that religion has played in national and proto-national movements in western Europe, see John Breuilly, *Nationalism and the State*, Manchester, 1985, pp. 45–50.

[6] Religious issues could, of course, serve other purposes, which had more to do with the interests of particular groups than with the nationalist cause. There is a large body of literature demonstrating these and other dimensions in the use of religion in nationalist politics. See, for instance, Barbara Southard, 'The Political Strategy of Aurobindo Ghosh. The Utilisation of Religious Symbols and the Problem of Political Mobilisation in Bengal', *Modern Asian Studies*, vol. 14, 1980, pp. 353–376; Anand Yang, 'Sacred Symbol and Sacred Space in Rural India, Community Mobilisation in the "Anti-Cow Killing" Riot of 1893', *Comparative Studies in Society and History*, vol. 22, 1981; John R. McLane, 'The Early Congress, Hindu Populism and Wider Society', in R. Sisson and Stanley Wolpert (eds.), *The Congress and Indian Nationalism. The Pre-Independence Phase*, New Delhi, 1988.

[7] See Ravinder Kumar, 'Class, Community or Nation? Gandhi's Quest for a Popular Consensus in India', in his *Essays in the Social History of Modern India*, Calcutta, 1986.

[8] Prakash Chandra Upadhyaya, 'The Politics of Indian Secularism', *Modern Asian Studies*, vol. 26, 4, 1992, pp. 815–853.

[9] Partha Chatterjee, 'Transferring a Political Theory: Early Nationalist Thought in India', *Economic and Political Weekly*, vol. 21, 3, 18 January 1986; Barbara Southard, 'The Political Strategy of Aurobindo Ghosh'; Swami Vivekananda (edited by Eknath Ranade), *Utthishtat! Jagrat! Hindu Rashtra ka Amar Sandesh*, ('Arise! Awaken! The Immortal Message of the Hindu Nation'), Lucknow, 1972.

they also regarded the two main communities as being irreconciliably opposed to each other. It followed that communal parties were by no means necessarily hostile to the Raj and frequently enjoyed its patronage.[10]

It is in this sense that the idea of a shift from nationalism to communalism will be discussed in this study. It will concentrate upon the Hindu bhadralok of Bengal, who dominated nationalist politics in the province. These politics always had a narrow social base in Bengal, and support from the masses, even in the heydey of Gandhi's influence, was limited and sporadic.[11] Except for a brief interlude during the Khilafat agitation, the Muslims of Bengal, who were more than half the population of the province, shunned the movements led by the bhadralok. But despite being overwhelmingly bhadralok in character, the Bengal Congress remained a political force to be reckoned with until well into the 1920s, and during the first three decades of the twentieth century exerted a powerful influence over the mainstream of Indian nationalism.

But in the last decade and a half of British rule in India, Bengal lost its position of pre-eminence in all-India politics, and was edged out of the nationalist mainstream. During these years bhadralok politics tended to draw inwards, focusing increasingly upon narrow provincial concerns. Preoccupied as they were with defending their interests against challenges posed by other groups in Bengal society, the bhadralok perceived politics more and more in communal terms. The Hindu communal ideology which they now came to construct turned away from and inverted the nationalist tradition in subtle and interesting ways.

This book will look at these processes in the context of the changes in Bengali society and the position of the Hindu bhadralok within it. Although the term 'bhadralok' is widely used and well understood in Bengal, scholars outside it have come to use it in various and sometimes

[10] Jinnah and the Muslim League were given far greater significance than their electoral strength merited and were cultivated as a counterweight to the Congress at least until the end of the Second World War. See Ayesha Jalal, *The Sole Spokesman. Jinnah, the Muslim League and the Demand for Pakistan*, Cambridge, 1985; and Anita Inder Singh, *The Origins of the Partition of India, 1936–1947*, New Delhi, 1987. In Bengal, as this study will try to show, British governors clearly preferred to deal with overtly communal organisations, such as the Hindu Mahasabha and the Muslim League, rather than with Congress or the Krishak Praja party. For their part, the Mahasabha and the League were careful to stay on the right side of the Raj; both parties, for instance, were active in the war effort of the 1940s, a point worth recalling today, when communal organisations which regard Shyamaprasad Mookerjee as a patron saint also claim to be 'true' nationalists.

[11] Sumit Sarkar, *The Swadeshi Movement*; Tanika Sarkar, *Bengal 1928–1934. The Politics of Protest*, New Delhi, 1987; Bidyut Chakrabarty, *Subhas Chandra Bose and Middle Class Radicalism. A Study in Indian Nationalism*, London, 1990.

contradictory ways. In the sixties, John Broomfield used it to describe a westernised caste elite, viewed as a Weberian status group;[12] the term was taken up by another historian to characterise the dominant 'upper crust of Bengali society' who enjoyed a 'despotism of caste, tempered by matriculation'.[13] More recently, the analysis of nationalist politics in terms of the grievances of the Presidency elites has come under critical scrutiny,[14] and with it the use of the term bhadralok has become suspect.[15] But the alternative term offered in its stead – 'the middle classes'[16] – is capable of being as misleading as the term it is intended to replace. Derived as it is from the study of western industrial societies, 'middle class' suggests essentially urban groups, consisting in the main of traders and entrepreneurs, and coming in due course, in advanced industrial societies, to include the salaried professionals.[17] Members of the bhadralok often chose to describe themselves in just this way, taking as their model the prosperous and influential middle classes of Victorian England.[18] But in so doing they, and historians after them, were drawing false analogies between society in Bengal and in Britain.

The basis of bhadralok prosperity was neither trade nor industry,[19] but

[12] J. H. Broomfield, *Elite Conflict in a Plural Society. Twentieth-Century Bengal*, Berkeley, 1968, pp. 5–14.
[13] Gordon Johnson, 'Partition, Agitation and Congress: Bengal 1904–1908', *Modern Asian Studies*, vol. 7, 3, 1973, pp. 534–535.
[14] For an account of the debates that have dogged this school of historiography, see Michelguglielmo Torri, '"Westernised Middle Class" Intellectuals and Society in Late Colonial India', *Economic and Political Weekly*, vol. 25, 4, 27 January 1990, pp. PE 2–11.
[15] See, for instance, the discussion of the term by Sumit Sarkar in *The Swadeshi Movement*, pp. 509–512.
[16] See, for instance, the use of the term 'middle class' to describe this social group by Himani Bannerji in 'The Mirror of Class: Class Subjectivity and Politics in 19th Century Bengal', *Economic and Political Weekly*, vol. 24, 13, May 1989; and by Bidyut Chakarbarty in *Subhas Chandra Bose and Middle-Class Radicalism*.
[17] See Guglielmo Cardechi, *On the Economic Identification of Social Classes*, London, 1977; Nicos Poulantzas, *Classes in Contemporary Capitalism*, London, 1975, and 'The New Petty Bourgeoisie' in Alan Hunt (ed.), *Class and Class Structure*, London, 1977; Anthony Giddens, *The Class Structure of Advanced Societies*, London, 1973; and Raymond Williams, *Keywords. A Vocabulary of Culture and Society*, New York, 1976, 51–59.
[18] Surendranath Banerjea, for instance, described Bengal's 'new middle class' as the standard-bearer of 'enlightenment, freedom, progress and prosperity' in *The Bengalee*, 17 February 1921. Cited in Rajat Ray, 'Three Interpretations of Indian Nationalism', in B. R. Nanda (ed.), *Essays in Modern Indian History*, New Delhi, 1980, p. 1. For a discussion of Victorian influences on bhadralok culture and society, see Sumanta Banerjee, *The Parlour and the Streets. Elite and Popular Culture in Nineteenth-Century Calcutta*, Calcutta, 1989, and Nilmani Mukherjee, 'A Charitable Effort in Bengal in the Nineteenth Century. The Uttarpara Hitkari Sabha', *Bengal Past and Present*, vol. 89, 1970, pp. 247–263.
[19] The few families which had amassed their fortunes as *dewans* and middle men of the East India Company were not able to reproduce their wealth by investing it profitably in trade or productive enterprise: most chose, instead, to buy up landed estates which, certainly by

land.[20] The Bengali bhadralok were essentially products of the system of property relations created by the Permanent Settlement. They were typically a rentier class who enjoyed intermediary tenurial rights to rents from the land. There were many differences within the bhadralok,[21] reflecting the variety in size and quality of their holdings in the land, and in part the result of subinfeudation and the proliferation of intermediary tenures.[22] But from the landed magnate down to the petty *taluqdar*, this was a class that did not work its land but lived off the rental income it generated. The bhadralok gentleman was the antithesis of the horny-handed son of the soil. Shunning manual labour, the 'Babu' saw this as the essence of the social distance between himself and his social inferiors.[23] The title 'Babu' – a badge of bhadralok status – carried with it connotations of Hindu, frequently upper caste exclusiveness,[24] of landed wealth, of being master (as opposed to servant), and latterly of possessing the goods of education, culture and anglicisation.[25] The vernacular term

the beginning of the nineteenth century, promised to be a more secure and lucrative investment. See John McGuire, *The Making of a Colonial Mind. A Quantitative Study of the Bhadralok in Calcutta, 1857–1885*, Canberra, 1983, pp. 1–20; S. N. Mukherjee, 'Caste, Class and Politics in Calcutta' in his *Calcutta: Myth and History*, Calcutta, 1977, p. 15; and Benoy Ghosh, 'Some Old Family-Founders in 18th Century Calcutta', *Bengal Past and Present*, vol. 79, 1960, pp. 42–55. As Sumit Sarkar has pointed out, 'a single Dwarkanath did not herald a bourgeois spring'. 'Rammohun Roy and the Break with the Past' in Sumit Sarkar, *A Critique of Colonial India*, Calcutta, 1985, p. 12.

[20] Indeed, the bhadralok shared (and largely continue to share) a contempt for traders and shopkeepers that reflects the social attitudes of a landed class.

[21] Sumit Sarkar has therefore remarked that 'the trouble with this term ... is that it is much too broad, ranging presumably from the Maharaja of Mymensingh to the East Indian railway clerk'. *The Swadeshi Movement*, p. 509.

[22] Subinfeudation was particularly marked in the districts of Eastern Bengal such as Bakarganj, where there were sometimes as many as fifteen intermediary tenure-holders between the zamindar and the *raiyat*. Tapan Raychaudhuri, 'Permanent Settlement in Operation. Bakarganj District, East Bengal', in R. E. Frykenberg (ed.), *Land Control and Social Structure in Indian History*, Madison, Wis., 1969, pp. 163–174. Not surprisingly, Bakarganj was a district that had a particularly high number of bhadralok Hindus.

[23] In Sarat Chandra Chattopadhyay's novel *Palli Samaj* ('Village Society'), for instance, Masima asserts her bhadralok status to the hero Ramesh with the declaration 'My father was not your father's *gomasta* (steward), nor was he a landless labourer who worked your father's private estate ... Ours is a bhadralok household'. Sukumar Sen (ed.), *Sulabh Sarat Samagra*, vol. II, Calcutta, 1989, p. 137.

[24] S. N. Mukherjee notes that the word 'babu', of Persian origin, was 'always used as a term of respect for Bengali Hindus of the higher orders'. 'Bhadralok in Bengali Language and Literature. An Essay on the Language of Caste and Status', *Bengal Past and Present*, vol. 181, 1976, p. 233.

[25] The dictionary definition of the word is interesting: 'a title affixed to the name of a gentleman; a proprietor; a master; an employer; an officer; a landlord ... given to luxury, daintiness, fastidiousness, foppishness, foppery, dandyism'. *Samsad Bengali–English Dictionary* (2nd edn), Calcutta, 1988. Mukherjee points out that to begin with, the word babu was used by the British as a respectful form of address to Hindu zamindars, and that it only acquired its disparaging connotations at the end of the nineteenth century.

'bhadralok' is useful not only because it expresses this sense of exclusiveness and the social relations that produced it, but also because it carries with it overtones of the colonial origins of this class and its overwhelmingly Hindu composition. Yet neither 'bhadralok' nor 'babu' describe straightforward communal or caste categories.[26] These terms reflected, instead, the social realities of colonial Bengal, the peculiar configuration that excluded, for a variety of historical reasons,[27] the vast majority of Bengali Muslims and low-caste Hindus from the benefits of land ownership and the particular privileges it provided.

Some bhadralok took enthusiastically to the new western education that was available from the early nineteenth century. This 'modern' intelligentsia was drawn, in the main, from the middle and lower echelons of the rent-receiving hierarchy, who recognised that western education was an avenue for advancement under their new rulers.[28] Most belonged to families that were traditionally literate, whose forebears, in another age, had worked as scribes at the Mughal and Nawabi courts, or had formed a part of the traditionally literate caste elite.[29] Some were recruited into the bureaucracy by which the British ruled Bengal, typically at the lower levels reserved for Indians. But even as they established themselves in Calcutta and the district towns, the western-educated bhadralok retained strong links with the countryside. Nirad Chaudhuri, son of a small-town pleader, describes his childhood at the turn of the century and the visits to the family's ancestral village during the Puja vacations

'Bhadralok in Bengali Language and Literature', pp. 233–235. Christine Baxter has argued that the first steps in this direction were taken in the 1820s, when Bhabanicharan Bannerji published his satirical essays portraying the 'babu' as a 'Persianized upstart'. The association with imitative anglicisation came later. Christine Baxter, 'The Genesis of the Babu: Bhabanicharan Bannerji and the *Kalikata Kamalalay*' in Peter Robb and David Taylor (eds.), *Rule, Protest, Identity. Aspects of Modern South Asia*, London, 1978.

26 Many of the richest bhadralok families of Calcutta, such as the Seals and the Basaks, were drawn from the lower rungs of the caste ladder. S. N. Mukherjee, 'Caste, Class and Politics', p. 31.

27 See Shila Sen, *Muslim Politics in Bengal 1937–1947*, New Delhi, 1976, pp. 1–30; Jayanti Maitra, *Muslim Politics in Bengal 1885–1906. Collaboration and Confrontation*, Calcutta, 1984, pp. 9–44; and S. N. Mukherjee, 'Caste, Class and Politics'.

28 'Nobles' like Raja Peary Mohan Mookerjee found 'no charm in formal education. "They looked upon it in open scorn as a thing by which humbler people got their bread"'. P. C. Mahtab, 'Bengal Nobles in Politics: 1911–1919', *Bengal Past and Present*, vol. 92, 1973, pp. 23–36. An analysis made in 1871 of the annual report of the Director of Public Instruction of Bengal thus found that of the total number of 'upper and middle class' pupils in schools, those from the titled aristocracy formed only 0.97 per cent, while the overwhelming majority were sons of lesser land-holders and professionals. Sumanta Banerjee, *The Parlour and the Streets*, pp. 215–216, n. 79.

29 In Bengal, these literate castes included not only Brahmins, but also Kayasthas and Baidyas. Premen Addy and Ibne Azad, 'Politics and Culture in Bengal', *New Left Review*, vol. 79, May-June 1973; and S. N. Mukherjee, 'Caste, Class and Politics'.

and for family weddings.[30] He writes of the emotional bonds that linked town and country:

The ancestral village always seemed to be present in the mind of the grown-ups. Most of them had acquired extensive properties in [the town of] Kishoreganj. They had also acquired ... some sense of citizenship. Yet I hardly remember a single adult who thought of his Kishoreganj life as his whole life ... In our perception of duration Kishoreganj life was the ever-fleeting present, the past and the future belonged to the ancestral village ... [31]

This relationship between town and country found expression in the use of different words to describe the village home and the base in town. The town house was merely a *basha*, a temporary lodging, whereas the village was the *bari*, the home. The sense of belonging to the village was so strong that during Chaudhuri's childhood, 'neither child nor adult at Kishoreganj ever applied to his Kishoreganj house the Bengali equivalent of the word *home*'.[32]

The ancestral village home continued to be occupied by relatives, some of whom managed the family property, while others found employment as *naibs* (accountants) and *amals* (revenue collectors) on neighbouring estates, or as tutors in zamindari schools.[33] By no means all branches of bhadralok families, even amongst those who had received a western education, settled in the towns and joined the professions or services. The Palchaudhuris of Mahesganj were a case in point. Of the two heirs to a large estate in Nadia, Nafar Chandra stayed in the *mofussil* (country), managed the family estates with the help of his *lathials* (servants), held court at the *kutcheri* (lower court), tended the family deities and ran a caste association. His brother Biprodas, on the other hand, graduated from Presidency College in Calcutta and went to England for higher education. On his return, he 'adopted western lifestyle', settled in Nadia

---

[30] Nirad C. Chaudhuri, *The Autobiography of an Unknown Indian*, London, 1988, p. 48.

[31] Stressing the importance of the village, Chaudhuri writes that 'the feeling which our elders had of the relative importance of their existence at Kishoreganj and in their ancestral village cannot be described even by bringing in the parallel of the tree and its roots, a house and its foundations ... for even in these cases, the buried parts exist for the superficial, or at all events are not more important. The immensely greater importance of the absent life was of the very essence of the matter of our life at Kishoreganj placed against our life in the ancestral village'. *Ibid.*, pp. 49–50.

[32] *Ibid.*, p. 50. Also see S. N. Mukherjee, 'Caste, Class and Politics'.

[33] Nirad C. Chaudhuri, *Autobiography of an Unknown Indian*, pp. 58–59. It was not uncommon for educated young men to return from Calcutta to run the family estate. Rabindranath Tagore is only the most well-known example. Another well-known figure who, as a young man, spent several years managing his family zamindari was Surendra Mohan Ghosh, leading member of the Jugantar group of terrorists and latterly president of the Bengal Congress. Interview with Surendra Mohan Ghosh, Oral Transcript No. 301, Nehru Memorial Museum and Library, (henceforth NMML).

town, joined the Congress and sat on the Nadia District Board for two decades.[34] While Biprodas fits easily into the familiar 'western-educated middle-class' model, Nafar Chandra's way of life was no less typical of what might be described as the 'mofussil' bhadralok.[35]

By no means all bhadralok families took readily to western education. Even in the later nineteenth century, many orthodox families continued to have a distrust of the new ideas that was only strengthened by the wild disregard for tradition displayed by the Young Bengal generation.[36] Western education was not in itself a guarantee of bhadralok status. Prafulla Chandra Ray's father was treated as a social outcaste when he returned from Presidency College to run the family estates in Jessore. Indeed, his 'modern' attitudes so offended local zamindari society that the more orthodox families boycotted the *shraddha* (funeral) ceremony of his deceased grandfather.[37] But the early resistance to western education did not survive into the twentieth century. The enthusiasm for English education showed a marked increase from the end of the nineteenth century,[38] a trend that reflected the realities of Empire. The need to master English, the language of power, was keenly felt by ambitious groups all over the sub-continent, and the Bengali bhadralok were no exception.[39] But there were other, more specific, pressures that encouraged the bha-

---

[34] Ratnalekha Ray, 'The Changing Fortunes of the Bengali Gentry under Colonial Rule – Pal Chaudhuris of Mahesganj, 1900–1950', *Modern Asian Studies*, vol. 21, 3, 1987, pp. 513–514. The two brothers Bipradas and Dwijadas in Sarat Chandra Chattopadhyay's later novel *Bipradas* are, similarly, typical of the country-based and the urban bhadralok respectively. Haripada Ghosh (ed.), *Sarat Rachana Samagra* (Collected Works of Sarat Chandra Chattopadhyay), Calcutta, 1989, vol. III.

[35] See the account of the lifestyle enjoyed by P. C. Ray's father as zamindar of Raruli. Prafulla Chandra Ray, *Life and Experiences of a Bengali Chemist*, Calcutta, 1932, pp. 8–12.

[36] P. C. Ray gives an amusing account of the horror with which the local Jessore gentry regarded the antics of the anglicised young men of Calcutta. *Ibid.*, pp. 2, 25.

[37] *Ibid.*, pp. 24–25. Even for the anglicised urban bhadralok, moreover, the sense of family prestige continued to be bound up intimately with the land and the ancestral village. Nirad Chaudhuri thus recalls, 'As soon as we arrived at Banagram we became aware of blood, aware not only of its power to make us feel superior to other men, but also of its immeasurable capacity to bring men together ... At Kishoreganj, our genealogy, like every other boy's, stopped at the father. The story ended with the assertion that Nirad Chaudhuri was the son of Upendra Narayan Chaudhuri. Not so at Banagram. There not only did we know, but we repeated as a catechism: "Nirad Chaudhuri is the son of Upendra Narayan Chaudhuri, who is the son of Krishna Narayan Chaudhuri, who was the son of Lakshmi Narayan Chaudhuri, who was the son of Kirti Narayan Chaudhuri, who was the son of Chandra Narayan Chaudhuri, and so on, to the fourteenth generation".' *Autobiography of an Unknown Indian*, p. 51.

[38] Tapan Raychaudhuri, 'Permanent Settlement in Operation', p. 174.

[39] Bhabanicharan Bannerji in *Kalikata Kamalalay* justified the learning of English thus: 'The necessity of a practical, money-producing education is supported by the shastras. How

dralok to look ever more favourably on 'modern' education. The rentier economy of which they were the beneficiaries began to show signs of strain towards the end of the nineteenth century. Agrarian productivity began to stagnate and land reclamation slowed down, marking the onset of an economic recession.[40] The introduction in 1885 of legislation limiting zamindari powers made the collection of dues more difficult,[41] and rentier incomes began the long process of decline, both in real and absolute terms. In the circumstances, more and more bhadralok families began to see western education as a way of supplementing their incomes and maintaining their influence. In the same period, traditional vernacular education ceased to be an attractive prospect to many high-caste families who still retained an access to it. As Sumit Sarkar has pointed out, the learned persons of high caste who stuck to traditional education had begun to lose their standing and patronage as English education penetrated deeper into rural society at the end of the nineteenth century.[42] The story of one village priest's tragic decline into poverty in Bibhutibhushan Banerji's *Pather Panchali* depicts the typical circumstances that forced an indigent traditional priesthood to turn to the new education for survival.[43]

As western education came to be the choice of most of the bhadralok who could afford it, the prestige attached to it derived not only from the access it offered to opportunities under the Raj, but also from the fact that

can a country be administered without a knowledge of the language of those who happen to be ruling it?' Cited in Christine Baxter, 'The Genesis of the Babu', p. 199. For details on the spread of English, see John R. McLane, *Indian Nationalism and the Early Congress*, Princeton, 1977, p. 4; Gauri Viswanathan, *Masks of Conquest. Literary Study and British Rule in India*, New York, 1989; Tejaswini Niranjana, 'Translation, Colonialism and the Rise of English' in Svati Joshi (ed.), *Rethinking English. Essays in Literature, Language, History*, New Delhi, 1991; and Jasodhara Bagchi, 'Shakespeare in Loincloths: English Literature and the Early Nationalist Consciousness in Bengal' in Svati Joshi (ed.), *Rethinking English.*

[40] Rajat Datta, 'Agricultural Production, Social Participation and Domination in Late Eighteenth Century Bengal: Towards an Alternative Explanation', *Journal of Peasant Studies*, vol. 17, 1, 1989, p. 77.

[41] Rajat and Ratna Ray, 'Zamindars and Jotedars: a Study of Rural Politics in Bengal', *Modern Asian Studies*, vol. 9, 1, 1975, p. 99.

[42] Sumit Sarkar, 'The Kalki-Avatar of Bikrampur: A Village Scandal in Early Twentieth Century Bengal', in Ranajit Guha (ed.), *Subaltern Studies VI*, New Delhi, 1989, p. 15. For further discussion of the theme of the 'indigent Brahmin', see Sarkar's mimeograph, 'The Kathamrita as Text', NMML, Occasional Papers in History and Society, no. 22, 1985.

[43] Bibhutibhushan Banerji, *Pather Panchali* ('Song of the Road'), Calcutta, 1929. Banerji's own experiences followed a pattern similar to those of his boy hero, Apu. Born into a line of village doctors, Banerji's father, like Harihar Ray, earned a precarious living as a family priest. With great difficulty, he educated his son Bibhutibhushan at an English-medium High School. Banerji later went on to graduate with honours from Ripon College in Calcutta, and served variously as a teacher and clerk. See T. W. Clark's 'Introduction' to the English translation of the novel. *Song of the Road* (translated by T. W. Clark and Tarapada Mukherji), New Delhi, 1990, p. 11.

it was still the preserve of the privileged. Western secondary schools and colleges were overwhelmingly dominated by Hindu bhadralok students from families who could afford to pay the price of a protracted and expensive education and of lodgings in far away towns and cities.[44] Indeed, the type of education that became fashionable among the bhadralok reflected not only the needs of the colonial administration but also the attitudes and aspirations of a landed and leisured class. Rammohun Roy's emphasis on practical training and the 'useful sciences' notwithstanding,[45] the choice of Bengal's students was a literary and humanist education,[46] so much so that efforts by an administration worried by the phenomenon of white-collar unemployment to give a more vocational and technological basis to higher education met with angry protests.[47] Such professional education as became popular among the bhadralok, notably in law and medicine, involved long years of training and the prospect of many more years of hardship until professional reputations were established, and inevitably depended upon generous financial support from well-to-do parents. It was thus inherited, typically landed, wealth that under-wrote bhadralok success in education and the professions, and ensured their dominance in these arenas. As bhadralok Hindus came to regard western education as their preserve, they vigorously resisted efforts to broaden the base of a top-heavy educational system, since opening the gates to the lesser sort would undermine its exclusiveness.[48]

Western education was thus a new way of maintaining old pre-eminences in Bengali society at a time when rentierism, the traditional mainstay of the bhadralok, had become less rewarding. In the same period, education became the vehicle by which the bhadralok constructed a new self-image. Towards the end of the nineteenth century, bhadralok authors came to describe their class more and more frequently as the *shikkhita sampraday* (educated community) or as the *shikkhita madhyabitta* (educated middle class) rather than the 'bhadralok', with its conno-

[44] In 1901, Hindus constituted 94 per cent of all students in Arts Colleges, 96.2 per cent of those in professional colleges and 88 per cent of those in high schools. Tazeem M. Murshid, 'The Bengali Muslim Intelligentsia, 1937–77. The Tension between the Religious and the Secular', University of Oxford, D.Phil thesis, 1985, p. 43. Also see Murshid's discussion of the costs and difficulties in securing a western education.
[45] S. D. Collet, *The Life and Letters of Raja Rammohun Roy*, Calcutta, 1962, p. 458.
[46] Himani Bannerji, 'The Mirror of Class', p. 1046. Bannerji's discussion of Tagore's 'Rousseauesque/Reynoldsian' romantic vision of primary education and of his famous Bengali primer *Sahaj Path* ('Simple Lessons') is particularly revealing in this regard. Also see Jasodhara Bagchi, 'Shakespeare in Loincloths'.
[47] Archana Mandal, 'The Ideology and Interests of the Bengali Intelligentsia: Sir George Campbell's Education Policy (1871–1874)', *Indian Economic and Social History Review*, vol. 12, 1, 1975, pp. 81–98.
[48] *Ibid.*, pp. 81–89.

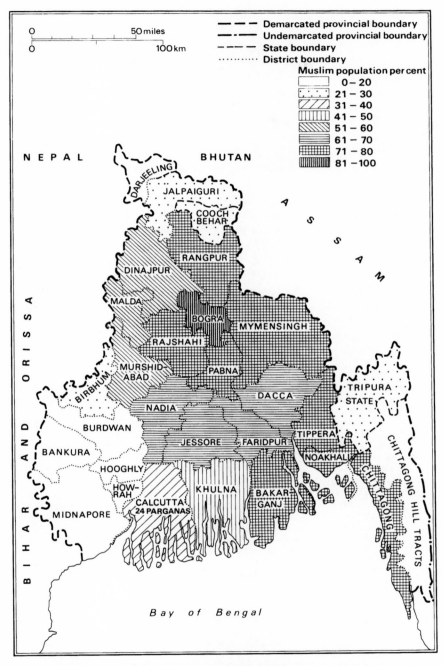

Map 2. Distribution of Muslim population, by district. *Number of Muslims per hundred of the total population, Census of 1931*

tations of a class dependent on landed wealth.[49] An aristocracy of wealth[50] had begun to transform itself (at least in its own eyes) into an aristocracy of culture.[51] In the twentieth century, bhadralok identity came to rest increasingly upon a perception of itself as a cultured and enlightened class, heir to the traditions of the 'Bengal Renaissance', and standard bearer of progress and modernity.[52] This self-image informed bhadralok politics, justifying the claim for representation by early nationalists. In later years, it also served to justify the demand that Hindus should continue to dominate Bengal, and ultimately that Bengal be partitioned.

However, the new bhadralok definition of themselves as a modern, enlightened and cultured middle class was not without its own difficulties. It obscured the extent to which the fabric of bhadralok pre-eminence in Bengali society was made up of a variety of strands, in which their wealth and powers as a landed elite, their position at the top of the caste hierarchy, their privileged access to urban employment and to some measure of authority under colonial rule, all were woven into an intricate pattern of dominance. The contradictions that characterised bhadralok political concerns were a reflection of this. Significantly, one of the earliest political organisations established by the Calcutta bhadralok called itself

---

[49] S. N. Mukherjee, 'Bhadralok in Bengali Language and Literature', p. 233.
[50] The lists of leading bhadralok families in Calcutta published in the early eighteenth century included only the very rich. See, for instance, Bhavanicharan Banerjee's list of the *prathamadhara bhadralok* in his *Kalikata Kamalalaya*, Calcutta, 1823. The list prepared by Radhakanta Deb for H. T. Prinsep in 1822, and later lists based upon it, include the wealthiest but not the most cultured or even the most high born families. It is significant that Rammohun Roy did not find mention in any of these early lists of prominent bhadralok. S. N. Mukherjee, 'Caste, Class and Politics', pp. 16–20.
[51] See Pierre Bourdeiu's use of this concept in *Distinction. A Social Critique of the Judgement of Taste* (translated by Richard Nice), London, 1986, pp. 11–96. Of particular relevance is Bourdieu's discussion of the correspondence between 'economic capital' and what he describes as 'educational' or 'cultural capital'. *Ibid.*, pp. 53–54, 80–83, 303. This argument has been developed further in Bourdieu's recent study of the educational establishment, *Homo Academicus* (translated by Peter Collier), Cambridge, 1988, pp. 47–50. Also see Axel Honneth's discussion of Bourdieu's work, 'The Fragmented World of Symbolic Forms: Reflections on Pierre Bourdieu's Sociology of Culture', *Theory, Culture and Society*, vol. 3, 3, 1986. Also of interest are Raymond Williams' observations on the 'strong class sense' in the modern usage of the word 'educated'. *Keywords*, pp. 95–96.
[52] A classic example is Surendranath Banerjea's famous assertion that 'where you have a middle class, you have enlightenment, freedom, progress and prosperity ... The rise of the middle class in Bengal is therefore the most reassuring sign of the times. It is a certain indication that in this part of India, our faces are set in the right direction, that progress and not retrogression is the order of the day and that the whole tendency of the present conditions make for an increasing measure of prosperity ...', *The Bengalee*, 17 February 1911. Cited in Rajat Ray's 'Three Interpretations of Indian Nationalism', p. 1. Also see

the Landholders' Society.[53] Similar ambivalence was evident in nationalist politics. Just as the bhadralok had one foot in the city and the other in the countryside, so their nationalism, though radiating outward from Calcutta and dominated by urban issues, was strongly committed to zamindari and rent-receiving interests. This commitment reflected the dilemma of an intelligentsia that lived in the towns but remained to a considerable extent dependent on subventions from the countryside at a time when rents were a diminishing asset and the economy did not give them many chances to branch out in new directions.[54] The timidity that characterised nationalist mobilisation in rural Bengal was an expression of the same predicament.[55]

Notwithstanding the fact that it was led by the avowedly 'modern', progressive and anglicised, bhadralok nationalism drew inspiration, to quite a remarkable extent, from Hindu 'revivalist' ideologies.[56] Thus Aurobindo Ghosh, packed off to England at the age of seven and educated in London and Cambridge,[57] developed the philosophy of 'political Vedanta' which preached the identification of the nation with the mother Goddess Kali[58] when he returned home, while Bepin Chandra Pal and Sarala Debi, both from old Brahmo families, introduced Kali Puja and Shivaji festivals onto the nationalist agenda.[59] Bengal's terrorist organisations, though they found their recruits mainly among the western-educated, bound their young followers with religious vows inspired by

Aurobindo Ghosh's comparison of the intellectual 'brilliance' of Bengali Hindus with that of ancient Greece. *Bande Mataram*, 6 March 1908.

[53] This society concerned itself primarily with the protection of landed property from undue government interference, and with issues such as house tax, stamp duties, and the resumption of rent-free land. S. N. Mukherjee, 'Caste, Class and Politics', p. 36.

[54] See Rajat Kanta Ray, *Social Conflict and Political Unrest in Bengal 1875–1927*, New Delhi, 1984, pp. 14–21; and Amiya Kumar Bagchi, *Private Investment in India 1900–1939*, Madras, 1972, pp. 165–170.

[55] This has been demonstrated in several studies of Congress and bhadralok nationalism in Bengal. See, for instance, Sumit Sarkar, *The Swadeshi Movement*; Tanika Sarkar, *Bengal 1928–1934*; Barbara Southard, 'The Political Strategy of Aurobindo Ghosh', and Bidyut Chakrabarty, 'Peasants and the Bengal Congress, 1928–1938', *South Asia Research*, vol. 5, 1, 1985. See also chapters 2 and 3 below.

[56] In fact, the so-called 'revivalist' thinkers were more concerned with the present and creating a sense of cultural identity and national pride in their own society rather than with reviving the past. Tapan Raychaudhuri, *Europe Reconsidered. Perceptions of the West in Nineteenth Century Bengal*, New Delhi, 1988, pp. 8–9.

[57] For an account of Aurobindo Ghosh's rather curious and exceptionally westernised upbringing, see A. B. Purani, *The Life of Sri Aurobindo. A Source Book*. Pondicherry, 1964.

[58] Barbara Southard, 'The Political Strategy of Aurobindo Ghosh', pp. 361–369. Also see Aurobindo's discussion of his philosophy of political Vedanta in *Bande Mataram*, 23 April 1907.

[59] Barbara Southard, 'The Political Strategy of Aurobindo Ghosh', p. 366; Sumit Sarkar, *The Swadeshi Movement*, pp. 304–305.

Sakta philosophy.[60] Even Chittaranjan Das, who gave the appearance of being thoroughly 'anglicised', was deeply influenced by Vaisnavism and has made significant contributions to Vaisnava mystic poetry,[61] while his young lieutenant Subhas Bose was a disciple of Ramakrishna and Swami Vivekananda.[62] This suggests that an uncritical use of the notion of 'westernisation' to explain Bengal's social history has many pitfalls,[63] and that accepting bhadralok descriptions of themselves as the fuglemen of modernity and progress is unwise. Bhadralok lifestyles more usually reflected a mix of 'modernity' and 'tradition', in which outward mannerisms of speech and dress often co-existed uneasily with a deeper 'orthodoxy' in the more private and fundamental concerns of family life and morality.[64] The same ambivalence characterised their political philosophy, which typically asserted the greatness of the Hindu spiritual tradition even as it acknowledged the technological and political prowess of Europe.[65] Interestingly, the first bhadralok association with the trappings of modern politics (a committee with a President, a treasurer and a secretary) was the Dharma Sabha, set up in 1830 to defend the right of Hindu widows to commit Sati.[66] The quest of later generations to create an independent nation state, on the face of it a wholly modern enterprise, was based upon ideologies that equated 'India' with 'Hinduness', and regarded nationalist mobilisation as the awakening and re-invigoration of a long-slumbering Hindu nation. Bhadralok leaders saw themselves as the standard-bearers of Hindu Bengal's destiny. This was a theme that was to re-emerge powerfully in the Hindu propaganda that accompanied the agitation for the partition of Bengal in 1946–47. The description of the bhadralok as a 'westernised elite' is perhaps an uncertain guide to understanding their political preoccupations, or to unravelling the complexities and contradictions of the political philosophies to which they subscribed.

Many of the idioms of Hindu communal discourse were thus recognisa-

---

[60] Rajat Kanta Ray, *Social Conflict and Political Unrest in Bengal*, p. 177.
[61] Prithwis Chandra Ray Chaudhury, *Life and Times of C. R. Das. The Story of Bengal's Self-Expression*, London, 1927, pp. 27–37.
[62] Subhas Chandra Bose, *An Indian Pilgrim* in Sisir Bose (ed.), *Netaji Collected Works*, vol. I, Calcutta, 1980, pp. 39–47.
[63] Some of the problems with this concept have been discussed by M. N. Srinivas in his essay, 'Westernization'. M. N. Srinivas, *Social Change in Modern India*, New Delhi, 1977, pp. 46–88.
[64] As Himani Bannerji points out, family life was an arena where western attitudes were rejected, and bhadralok women were typically entrusted with the task of preserving the 'traditional' world and 'traditional' customs, morality and social codes. 'The Mirror of Class', p. 1044.
[65] Partha Chatterjee, *Nationalist Thought and the Colonial World. A Derivative Discourse*, New Delhi, 1986, p. 58.
[66] S. N. Mukherjee, 'Caste, Class and Politics', pp. 54–55.

ble in nationalist thought, and indeed the thought of the Bengal Renaissance, and had been common currency since the beginning of the twentieth century. But they were subtly reworked in the following decades, their emphasis shifting from anti-British (and anti-western) themes to an anti-Muslim posture. This study seeks to understand this reorientation of bhadralok political perceptions within a context profoundly influenced by changes which transformed Bengali society and politics during the last fifteen years of the Raj. It begins with a discussion of MacDonald's Communal Award of 1932, which dramatically altered the balance of power in the province. At the beginning of the twentieth century, Muslims were a slight majority in Bengal's population as a whole, with a clear preponderance in numbers in the eastern districts (see Map 2). But it was bhadralok Hindus who dominated Bengali society and held most of the levers of power that Indians were allowed to control. The Communal Award, however, allotted Hindus fewer seats in the new provincial Legislative Assembly than even their numbers warranted, and reduced them to a vocal minority in the House. The Award put paid to any hopes that the bhadralok may still have had of real political power when Bengal won provincial autonomy, and gave them the prospect of perpetual subordination to the Muslims. The Poona Pact that followed close on the heels of the Award further reduced high-caste Hindus to a small minority in a House which they had always expected to dominate.

These changes in the political rules of the game would have been less devastating for the bhadralok had they not been aggravated by the impact of the Depression. The sudden and dramatic collapse of agrarian prices and of rural credit placed a tremendous strain upon the system of rent and debt collection that was the mainstay of rentier incomes in Bengal. The rapid decline of the power of the rentiers to extract dues worked to the advantage of more prosperous tenants, who were frequently Muslims. Encouraged by chaotic conditions, these tenants increasingly flouted the authority of their landlords and consolidated their own position in rural Bengal. At the same time, the Government of India Act of 1935 gave the vote to the upper stratum of peasants, and for the first time, a voice in the legislative arena. They were supported by a restless Muslim intelligentsia, which had grown not least because of the Government of Bengal's active promotion of Muslim education and employment in the services, and which had its own grievances against bhadralok Hindus. Both groups were able to make their presence felt in the new Assembly, and to bring the challenge to bhadralok rent-receiving and money-lending interests into the mainstream of Bengali politics. Chapter 2 considers the implications of the rise of mofussil Muslims for the bhadralok and for Bengal politics more generally.

In the process, many traditional distinctions within bhadralok society – between the urban professionals and the rural gentry, between large landlords and petty taluqdars, between the landed aristocracy and the more humble clerics, between the modernists and the traditionalists – were coming to be less distinct. Simultaneously, older political divisions in bhadralok politics – between 'moderates' and 'extremists', between the different terrorist societies, between factions and *dals*, and even between loyalists and nationalists – lost much of their relevance. As essentially bhadralok class interests took primacy over nationalist issues in the political agenda, new political divisions emerged along different ideological axes. Chapter 3, which focuses on the Bengal Congress, examines the declining role of the Bengal Congress in all-India politics, its changing relationship with the central Congress leadership, the emergence within the party of 'right'- and 'left'-wing groupings, and the increasing preoccupation of the Bengal Congress with parochial issues. The eventual capture of the organisation by those on the right who stood for the defence of 'Hindu' interests, and the emasculation of the left within the party, suggested a profound change in the political priorities and perceptions of the bhadralok.

Chapter 4 looks at the ways in which these changed perceptions helped to create a new 'Hindu' political identity. The analysis of literary sources suggests that much of the baggage of nationalist ideology was jettisoned in this period, and its key themes were reconstructed. Significantly, British rule was now looked upon by the bhadralok in a much more favourable light. As 'Muslim rule' came to be regarded as the great and immediate threat to Hindu society, the bhadralok reappraised their past and gave the British the role of liberators who freed Hindu Bengal from Muslim tyranny. Loyalism again became a respectable badge for the Bengali babu: indeed the inglorious history of bhadralok collaboration with British rule was now proudly recalled in order to strengthen the case for special consideration from a Raj which threatened to abandon them to the very tyrants from whom they had been rescued. At the same time, the bhadralok perception of themselves as a cultured elite acquired a new significance: it now promoted a powerful sense of cultural superiority over the Muslims of Bengal. This putative cultural superiority was the central idiom of bhadralok communalism, and ostensibly justified the demand of a minority elite for political power in an era of mass franchise and majority rule. Not only was this argument an explicit rejection of the democratic principles from which Indian nationalism drew sustenance, it also bore a striking resemblance to British legitimations of colonialism, which argued that their racial superiority made Britons more 'fit' to rule India than Indians themselves.

But while the idiom of 'culture' went some way to forge a sense of communal identity among the fractious bhadralok, it had obvious drawbacks as a slogan to rally other Hindus. In the late thirties and forties, the bhadralok relied upon many different tactics to create the semblance of an united 'Hindu' polity, whether by the use of *shuddhi* (ritual purification) or 'caste-consolidation' programmes, which sought to find a place for the lower castes and tribals into an Hindu community. Chapter 5 discusses the ways in which the bhadralok drew upon social aspirations and political grievances at the local level to fortify their communal purposes and looks at the ways in which this contributed to the growing communal violence in Bengal.

From a refusal to countenance being ruled by Muslim 'inferiors', it was a short step to demanding partition and the creation of a separate Hindu homeland. Chapter 6 describes how the bhadralok organised a campaign for the partition of Bengal, deploying the Bengal Congress and the Hindu Mahasabha for this end. It examines why powerful provincial interests rallied behind the movement, where it found its main support and how it was organised. It also considers the reciprocity between all-India imperatives and the demands of the bhadralok. This is not an argument that the determination of Bengali Hindus to see their province partitioned explains the decision to partition India. It suggests instead that the study of a provincial separatist demand may enrich our understanding of Partition, providing the sub-text to a story too often reduced to an account of the priorities of statesmen in Delhi and London.

None of this is intended as an apologia for the much more widely publicised communalism of Muslims, which played a central part in bringing about a division of the sub-continent. Nor does it suggest a fundamental revision in the assessments of the role of imperialism in sowing dissension in many aspects of India's political life. Rather it has been concerned to understand how and why the bhadralok moved away from being the leaders of Indian nationalism and adopted instead a much narrower and less attractive communal stance. It is hoped that this approach will enrich our understanding of communal politics and throw new light on the complex relationship between communalism and nationalism in modern Indian history.

1   Bengal politics and the Communal Award

By 1929, British policy-makers in London and New Delhi could see that the constitutional arrangements devised by Montagu and Chelmsford ten years before would have to be reviewed. The pressures of the past decade had brought constitutional change back upon the political agenda. 'Provincial autonomy' was devised as a measure to fend off pressure at the centre by nationalist politicians, while at the same time broadening the base of Indian collaboration with the Raj. While 'devolving' some power to Indians, the reforms restructured British control over India by a strategic retreat to the centre, where the Raj continued to hold on to the levers of power. At the same time, a number of safeguards were designed to limit the scope of the greater 'autonomy' which was being offered to the provinces. The Communal Award of 1932 was an integral part of this strategy.[1]

The Communal Award was the result of London's decision to divide power in the provinces among the rival communities and social groups which, in its view, constituted Indian society. British administrators saw India as 'essentially a congeries of widely separated classes, races and communities with divergences of interests and hereditary sentiment which for ages have precluded common action or local unanimity'.[2] In fact, the categories into which the administrators classified Indian society reflected British assumptions rather more closely than the social realities of the sub-continent. The British 'essentialist' understanding of India, as Inden points out, 'was committed to a curious and contradictory mixture of *societalism*, in which Indian actions are attributed to social groups – caste, village, linguistic region, religion and joint family – because there are no

[1] Other such safeguards included the role of the Governor (in Council) in the proposed ministries, and the Section 93 provisions under which representative government could be suspended and provinces brought directly under Governor's rule. As we shall see in later chapters, both these safeguards were called into play by the British Government in Bengal. For a discussion of the safeguards built into the 1935 Act, see Sumit Sarkar, *Modern India 1885–1947*, Delhi, 1984, pp. 336–338.
[2] See Lothian to Willingdon, 8 August 1932, in IOLR L/PO/49 (ii).

individuals in India, and *individualism*, in which Indians' acts are attributed to bad motives'.[3] The decennial censuses built up a picture of Indian society as a congeries of 'special interests' and 'groups'. For over a century, the British had ruled India by coming to terms with the interests of those whom they identified as the 'natural leaders' of Indian society, balancing one against another and subordinating them all to their paramount purpose of maintaining British rule in India. At the same time, the British had reservations about these 'natural leaders', and distrusted their motives in relation to the 'people' they claimed to lead. Through this contradictory construction, British rule sought to justify itself in theory and to sustain itself in practice: the colonial civilians claimed to act both as arbiters between the conflicting interests in Indian society and, at the same time, as the guardians of the people against the rapacity and corruption of their leaders.[4]

The Communal Award reflected both the morality and the self-interest of this tradition. The legislatures both at the centre and in the provinces were to be carved up between various 'communities' and interests: Muslims, depressed classes, Sikhs, Europeans, and the 'General' population of Hindus, as well as the 'special' constituencies of landholders, workers, women and dons. The seats allotted to each of these groups were intended to reflect 'importance' (which tended to be defined in terms of loyalty to the Raj) more than mere numbers. So in Bengal, of the 250 seats in the proposed Legislative Assembly, the European group, less than one per cent of Bengal's population, was allotted 25 seats in all, or 10 per cent of the total[5] (see table 1). Elections to the Assembly, in addition, would be by 'separate representation': Muslims alone would elect Muslims, Hindus would elect Hindus, and Europeans would elect Europeans.

The most striking feature of the Communal Award was its distribution

---

[3] Ronald Inden, 'Orientalist Constructions of India', *Modern Asian Studies*, vol. 20, 3, 1986, p. 403.

[4] Interesting examples of this perception may be found in the memoirs of British administrators. For instance, P. D. Martyn, ICS, recalls of his tenure in Kalimpong in 1930: 'The paternalistic attitude of Government, and therefore of me as its representative, towards the hill people was highly developed. The Lepchas and Bhutias had to be protected against the more intelligent and assertive Nepalis and all three against the Plains' folk – notably the ubiquitous Marwaris, the moneylenders of India'. P. D. Martyns's Memoirs, IOLR MSS Eur F/180/13.

[5] Benthall's dissatisfaction as the representative of the Europeans in Bengal, was therefore a little misplaced. Bidyut Chakravarty, in his discussion of the Award seems to have taken Benthall's word for it that the Europeans would be reduced 'to a nonentity' under the Award. Bidyut Chakravarty, 'The Communal Award of Bengal and its Implications in Bengal', *Modern Asian Studies*, vol. 23, 3, 1989, p. 503. In the Bengal Legislative Council, the European bloc had held nine seats in a house of 139, just over 6 per cent. The proportion of seats held by this section therefore *increased* by a margin of 4 per cent under the Award.

Table 1. *The Communal Award in Bengal*

Constituency	Number of seats
Muslims	117
Muslim women	2
General	70
Depressed classes	10[a]
General women	2
European	11
European commerce	14
Indian commerce	5
Landholders	5
Universities	2
Labour	8
Anglo-Indians	3
Anglo-Indian women	1

[a] Of the total number of 'General' seats, at least ten were to be reserved for the depressed classes.
Source: N. N. Mitra (ed.), *Indian Annual Register*, July–December 1932, vol. II, p. 236.

of Hindu and Muslim seats. Hindus, including the depressed classes were given 80 seats, only 32 per cent of the total, although the 1931 census recorded them as numbering 22.2 million people, or 44 per cent of Bengal's population. Muslims were also underrepresented, albeit less obviously, in terms of their population. Numbering 27.8 million in all in 1931, they comprised 54 per cent[6] of Bengal's total population, and more than a third of the total Muslim population of the Indian sub-continent. But the Award gave them 119 seats, or 47.8 per cent of the total seats in the Assembly.

The significance of this distribution lay in its allocation to Hindus of far fewer seats than they might have fairly expected, and in the fact that the Muslim share exceeded the Hindu share by a substantial margin. Under dyarchy Hindus had 46 seats to the Muslims' 39 in the Bengal Council:[7] an arrangement that had reflected and reinforced Hindu bhadralok dominance in Bengal. Now, the positions were to be reversed at a single stroke. Moreover, of the 80 Hindu seats, at least 10 were to be reserved for the depressed classes. The effect was to bring down further the number of caste Hindu seats to 70 in a house of 250, that is, a mere 28 per cent. The

[6] *Census of India 1931, Bengal and Sikkim*, vol. V, part 1. Report by A. E. Porter, pp. 381–388.
[7] Parliamentary Papers on the Montagu-Chelmsford Reforms, Command 812, pp. 295–299.

Communal Award in effect reduced the Bengali bhadralok to being an impotent minority in a Legislative Assembly which they had hoped to dominate in the new era of provincial autonomy. By contrast, for the first time in the history of Bengal's legislatures, Muslims were placed in a position of strength relative to the Hindus.

The Award's distribution of Hindu and Muslim seats in Bengal was a reflection of Delhi's all-India priorities. The Viceroy was convinced of the urgent need to placate Muslims in the aftermath of the Khilafat agitation and would not be persuaded by John Anderson, Bengal's Governor, to consider a more representative distribution of seats for his province. Willingdon explained that it was not possible for him 'to [approach the] problem solely in its provincial aspect in the light exclusively of Bengal conditions. Our own responsibilities compel us to take a wider view. We cannot afford to ignore reactions outside Bengal ... [The] Governor's proposals ... will alienate from us Moslem support not merely in Bengal but throughout India'.[8] The India Office went along with Delhi, but only after some hesitation.[9] Zetland, recently Governor of Bengal, had a fair idea of 'Bengal conditions' and warned of the possible consequences of Delhi's disregard of Bengali Hindu interests. He listed his objections to the Award as follows:

(1) It is putting an advanced people in a position of subordination to a backward people;
(2) It will enormously increase communal bitterness;
(3) It will create a sense of injustice which will not easily be forgiven or forgotten;
(4) It will give rise to increasing agitation and will inevitably give an immense stimulus to subversive movements.[10]

---

[8] Willingdon to Hoare, telegram, 14 June 1932, IOLR L/PO/49. Also cited in J. A. Gallagher, 'Congress in Decline: Bengal, 1930 to 1939', *Modern Asian Studies*, vol. 7, 3, 1973, p. 617.

[9] For a discussion of the differences between Samuel Hoare and Lord Zetland at the India Office and the Viceroy Willingdon in Delhi over the terms of the Award, see Helen M. Nugent, 'The Communal Award: The Process of Decision-Making', *South Asia* (NS), 2.1 and 2.2, 1989.

[10] Note by Lord Zetland on the Communal Award, Zetland Collection, IOLR MSS Eur D/609/22, p. 22. The 'subversive movements' to which Zetland was referring were the activities of the terrorists in Bengal. He evidently feared that the Award would spark off another phase of terrorism, and this was a worry that Bengali Hindus played upon in an attempt to influence Zetland to alter the terms of the Award. Thus N. N. Sircar, the Advocate General of Bengal, warned that 'if the Bengali Hindus feel that justice has been done to them, and their future lies in the working of the proposed Constitution, the bulk ... will turn away from the Terrorists. Whereas under the proposed composition there will be every incentive for turning away from the Legislature in the spirit of aggrieved resentment.' Memorandum by N. N. Sircar, Zetland Collection, IOLR MSS Eur D/609/21 (h)/a.

Zetland was particularly worried about the position of the caste Hindus under the proposals in the Award, and correctly gauged that their reaction to its terms would be extreme. He warned that 'however the elections to these seats work out, the caste Hindus must find themselves in a serious permanent minority in a Presidency in which they play an outstanding part in the intellectual and political life of the people. And I am very much afraid that if the idea gains ground amongst them that they are not being given a fair chance under the new Constitution, they will turn from it in despair'.[11]

Zetland's fears were justified. The Award was seen by the bhadralok as a frontal attack upon their position, and they reacted with indignant outrage. Such unanimity had been rare in bhadralok politics since the death of Chittaranjan Das in 1925. Das had appointed no successor, and his death had been followed by an unseemly struggle for the three famed 'crowns' of Calcutta (the Bengal Congress, the Council and the Calcutta Municipal Corporation) between his two favourite lieutenants, Jatindra Mohan Sengupta and Subhas Chandra Bose. The Bengal Provincial Congress Committee (BPCC) split into two warring factions behind Bose and Sengupta, and the organisation that Das had built up fell into disarray. Even Gandhi's call for Civil Disobedience failed to bring unity to the ranks of the Bengal Congress and each faction launched its own, somewhat half-hearted, campaign.[12] But where Gandhi failed, the Award succeeded. The bitter internecine rivalry that had reduced the Bengal Congress to a cipher was now suspended, as all factions and groups joined together to denounce the Award in the strongest possible terms. *Advance*, the mouthpiece of the Sengupta faction, with unconscious irony described the Award as 'a shameless surrender to the communalists', in which 'the claims of the Hindus have been ignored completely and perhaps deliberately'. It warned the Government that the Hindus would not 'submit to such a sweeping, almost revolutionary change'.[13] *Liberty*, representing the Bose group, was no less vehement in its denunciation: 'The Award amounts to a slur on Indian nationhood ... Unfair is not the word to characterise the terms of the Award. They are insulting and positively mischievous. The Hindus are rendered politically impotent, and the reaction of this process on the cultural, economic and political life of the province will be disastrous.'[14] The Bengali vernacular daily, *Ananda*

11 'Bengal and the Poona Pact', a note by Lord Zetland, IOLR MSS Eur D/609/21 (h)/a.
12 For details of Bengal Congress politics in these years, see Rajat Kanta Ray, *Social Conflict and Political Unrest in Bengal 1875–1927*, New Delhi, 1984; Bidyut Chakrabarty, *Subhas Chandra Bose and Middle-Class Radicalism*; Tanika Sarkar, *Bengal 1928–1934. The Politics of Protest*, New Delhi, 1987; and J. A. Gallagher, 'Congress in Decline'.
13 *Advance*, 17 August 1932.   14 *Liberty*, 17 August 1932.

Bazar Patrika, condemned the Award for its lack of foresight,[15] while the *Dainik Basumati* argued that it was not binding on Bengalis as the 'Premier has not been requested by real representatives of communities to give his Award.'[16] The *Amrita Bazar Patrika*, the most widely circulated nationalist daily, made a scathingly sarcastic attack on the Premier, comparing his justice with that meted out by the village headman in a Bengali fable:

A farmer's sheep having thrust its head into a long-necked earthen jar full of paddy lying in the courtyard, could not get it out. The whole family was non-plussed and the headman was sent for ... He surveyed the situation and cried, 'For a simple thing like this, have you sought my help? How will you get on when I am no more? Just bring me a sword.' Then with one hard stroke of it he severed the body of the sheep from the head. The villagers stood wondering at the keenness of the headman's intellect, but a mischievous young fellow interjected, 'But there is the head of the sheep still inside the jar.' The headman turned towards him with a scornful look and said, 'Dolt that thou art, it may baffle thy wit, but not mine', and with a piece of stone he smashed the jar, scattering the paddy all around the courtyard, and the head of the sheep came out. The farmer's family was relieved. They all felt that they would have been dumb-founded had the headman not come to their rescue ...[17]

Given the decline of bhadralok fortunes, the vehemence of the Hindu reaction is hardly surprising. By the twentieth century, structures that had long sustained the privileged position of the bhadralok had visibly begun to crumble. Pressure upon zamindari interests on the one hand, and the shift in Government policy towards promoting Muslim interests in the services and professions on the other, had cut at the roots of bhadralok influence. Until the Award, however, the bhadralok had held on, if somewhat precariously, to their position of dominance in the political and legislative institutions which mattered. They were still relatively well placed in the Legislative Council; they dominated the Calcutta Corporation, and although Gallagher has argued that their hold over Local and District Boards had begun to weaken,[18] they still had a considerable grip over many of the localities, controlling more seats than their population warranted, particularly in the Muslim-majority districts of East Bengal. In the Hindu-majority districts of the west, however, Muslims had, from the mid-twenties, done somewhat better.[19] But, as a rule, dominant

---

[15] *Ananda Bazar Patrika*, 17 August 1932.   [16] *Dainik Basumati*, 17 August 1932.
[17] *Amrita Bazar Patrika*, 20 August 1932.
[18] J. A. Gallagher, 'Congress in Decline', pp. 601–607. Local and District Boards were elected by joint electorates, with no reservation of seats.
[19] In Burdwan division, where they formed 14.14 per cent of the total population, Muslim membership in Local Boards increased from 11.8 per cent to 15.4 per cent over the period between 1923–24 and 1931–32. Similarly, in the Presidency Division, where Muslims

Hindus of the locality continued to hold sway over the institutions of local self-government throughout much of Bengal.[20] Once the Communal Award had been made, however, this local dominance could never be translated into control at the provincial level. By settling for separate electorates and reservation of seats, the Award made impossible the adjustments and alliances by which the Hindu bhadralok might have been able to convert local influence into provincial power, thus shattering the political ambitions of the most articulate and organised section of Bengali society.

Their reaction to this blow was understandably extreme. More surprising, however, were the grounds on which they rejected the Award, and the terms in which these were expressed. The bhadralok did not invoke standard nationalist critiques of British policies. In all the sound and fury of newspaper editorials, petitions, memorials and speeches denouncing the Award, little was heard about separate electorates and the old imperial game of 'divide and rule'.[21] Nor was there much clamour about the weightage given to Europeans in the Assembly, or indeed, about the discretionary powers of the Governor. While the rest of nationalist India was rejecting the 'autonomy' outlined in the Government's White Paper as a sham, the Bengali bhadralok – Congressmen and non-Congressmen alike – were concerned only with its disregard of their own provincial political ambitions. After the first scathing indictments of MacDonald and the Viceroy, the bhadralok press was curiously muted in its criticism of the British officials who had been the authors of the Award.

comprised 47.2 per cent of the population, their membership increased from 38.83 to 45.4 per cent over the same period. On the other hand, in Dacca Division, where the Muslim population was approximately 71 per cent of the total, Muslims had not been able to catch up in the Local Boards; by 1932 they had captured only 63.5 per cent of the seats. In Rajshahi, too, they were still far behind, for although they numbered 62.24 per cent of the population, by 1932 they had won only 54.9 per cent of the seats in the same year. Chittagong Division formed an exception to this general rule: it was the only Muslim-majority division where Muslims were adequately represented in the Local Boards. Appendix G, *Resolution Reviewing the Reports on the Working of District Boards in Bengal during the year 1923–24 until 1931–32*, Calcutta, 1924–32.

[20] Gallagher overlooked this point. He argued instead that it was in the districts of West Bengal that Hindus would gain from joint electorates, while in East Bengal they would lose. On the contrary, however, in the late twenties and early thirties, while Muslims improved their position in local government all over Bengal, it was primarily in the Hindu heartland of West Bengal that Muslim representation in these bodies actually began to exceed their proportion in the population as a whole. It was in these predominantly Hindu areas that Muslims actually began to challenge Hindu dominance. The significance of this trend will be examined in chapter 4.

[21] Subhas Bose may in retrospect have recognised that the Award was an 'imperial device ... dividing the Indians still further, so that the effect of the meagre constitutional reforms may be sufficiently neutralised'. But even his 'objection to the Award was not to its basis but to its effect. He would have approved the seat distribution under the Award,

Instead, their anger was directed against the group that they regarded as the Award's greatest beneficiaries, the Bengali Muslims. Two days after the Award was announced, the *Amrita Bazar Patrika* reported that Muslim politicians, gloating at the discomfiture of the Hindus, had celebrated their victory by 'throwing a large party'.[22] Stories such as these created an atmosphere of suspicion and hostility, providing the breeding ground for the notion that the Award was a devious Muslim (rather than British) trick, by which they had cleverly succeeded in trapping the Hindus of Bengal into perpetual political subservience. This notion encouraged bhadralok Hindus to claim for themselves the rights of an aggrieved minority, and to demand minority safeguards. A widely publicised memorial to Lord Zetland, signed by all the good and great of Bengal, thus began with the assertion that 'your memorialists belong to the Hindu Community of Bengal, which constitutes a Minority Community, and as such, is entitled to the same protection that is guaranteed to Minorities of the other Provinces.' It went on to declare that 'the Hindu minority of Bengal claim their due weightage of representation as a recognised Minority right'.[23]

This was a curious position for bhadralok nationalists to adopt. It rejected the spirit of nationalist ideology, with its emphasis on the unity of the Indian people against British rule and on the need for Hindus to demonstrate generosity towards Muslims and other 'backward' sections of society.[24] Indeed, several themes that emerged in the anti-Award rhetoric clearly broke with the main currents of nationalist thought. At a meeting at the Calcutta Town Hall presided over by Rabindranath Tagore and attended by many luminaries of the bhadralok world, one speaker's recommendations had much in common with the two-nation theorists':

Let the Hindus and Moslems be organised as separate nationalities in the matter of their separate cultural interests, their education, personal law and the like, and then they can without any discord come together on terms of Equality, Equity and

had it recognised Hindu representation according to the population in Bengal'. Bidyut Chakravarty, 'The Communal Award of 1932', p. 519.
[22] *Amrita Bazar Patrika*, 18 August 1932.
[23] Memorial by the 'Hindus of Bengal' to Lord Zetland, 4 June 1936. Reproduced in a pamphlet entitled *Bengal Anti-Communal Award Movement. A Report*, Calcutta, 1936, p. 4. The pamphlet was signed by Rabindranath Tagore, Prafulla Chandra Ray, Brajendranath Seal, Tulsi Charan Goswami, Ramananda Chatterjee and Raja Debendra Lall Khan of Narajole, among others.
[24] A strong current in nationalist thinking was that the 'backwardness' of a community was the only legitimate ground for demanding safeguards. It also emphasised the need for Hindus, as the majority, to display emotional generosity and understanding towards Muslims and other minorities. See Sarvepalli Gopal, 'Nehru and Minorities', *Economic and Political Weekly*, vol. 23 (Special number), 45–47, 1988, pp. 2463–2466.

Brotherhood in an all-Bengal Federal Assembly. It is the federal idea which alone can suit Bengal.[25]

On other occasions, bhadralok rhetoric against the Award inverted nationalist symbols in interesting ways. B. C. Chatterjee of the Hindu Sabha denounced the Award as a 'betrayal', arguing that 'the outflowering [sic] of the Bengalee Hindu genius, and the upbuilding of Bengal's new civilisation and culture has been the outstanding phenomenon of British India', and that British rule had enabled Bengali Hindu civilisation to flourish. Placing the Muslims on the gaddi would return Bengal to the dark age before Plassey. This, he argued, would be 'to repudiate all that the British have brought about in Bengal since 1757; it would be to initiate a new chapter of Bengal's history headed "The Betrayal of Britain and Bengal"'.[26] The symbolic significance accorded by nationalist historiography to the Battle of Plassey as the first degrading step in the progress of imperial rule in India was turned on its head. Plassey was now reconstructed as a moment of liberation, when the British freed Hindu Bengalis from the dark despotism of Muslim 'tyranny', and British rule, the butt of nationalist hatred, was seen as providing a creative environment for the 'Bengalee Hindu genius'. From this standpoint, British rule was regarded as the lesser evil to 'Muslim rule', whether in the distant past or the immediate future. By jettisoning the anti-British focus of nationalist historiography, a vocal section of bhadralok Bengalis took another significant step away from the mainstream of nationalism.[27]

In the face of the Award, older differences of ideology and political alignment that had divided the bhadralok lost some of their significance. Their shared fury against the Communal Award not only prompted Congressmen to forget their factional rivalries, but persuaded them to join die-hard loyalists and Hindu communal leaders on the same platform. A meeting of Hindu citizens held at the Albert Hall 'to discuss the needs and requirements of the Hindus of Bengal in view of the coming Reforms' was attended not only by Sarat Chandra Bose and J. L. Banerjee of the Congress, but also by Bejoy Prasad Singh Roy, the highest

[25] Radhakumud Mookerji's speech as reported in Bengal Anti-Communal Award Movement, p. 22. This speech was made in support of Mookerji's resolution condemning the Award and was carried unanimously by the Assembly. Ibid., pp. 20–26. There are obvious and interesting parallels between Mookerji's espousal of a 'federal' relationship between the Hindu and Muslim 'nations' of Bengal and Jinnah's call for Pakistan less than a decade later. For a discussion of the federal basis of Jinnah's thinking on the Pakistan question, see Ayesha Jalal, The Sole Spokesman, pp. 174–175, 552–558.
[26] The Betrayal of Britain and Bengal, by B. C. Chatterjee, undated. Zetland Collection, IOLR MSS Eur D/609/21/(h)b.
[27] See chapter 4 below for a more detailed discussion of this point.

ranking Indian civilian in Bengal who was fiercely loyal to the British, Dr Radha Kumud Mookerji of the Hindu Sabha and the Raja Bahadur of Nasipur.[28] The office-bearers of the 'Bengal Anti-Communal Award Movement' included among their ranks prominent Bengali Congressmen such as Nalinakshya Sanyal, Tulsi Charan Goswami and Debendra Lall Khan, Hindu Sabha leaders such as Radha Kumud Mookerji and B. C. Chatterjee, along with the odd loyalist Maharaja.[29]

Another theme with which the propaganda against the Award made play was of a monolithic Bengali Hindu community. The signatories of the memorial to Lord Zetland, all with impeccable bhadralok credentials, had not the slightest hesitation in claiming that it expressed 'the profound disappointment and resentment of the entire Hindu Community of Bengal', and represented the 'national protest of the Hindu Community against the utter iniquity of the Award'.[30] The notion of a monolithic Hindu community with common 'national' interests found increasing currency in the propaganda against the Award. The Award, it was argued, was an outrageous attack on the Hindu community as a whole. Using emotive language and imagery, petitions and speeches painted a picture of an internally coherent and culturally vigorous Hindu community, which had led Bengal to greatness, but was now threatened with destruction. The Award would leave this great community as perpetual serfs of its cultural and intellectual inferiors, the despised Muslims of Bengal.

Of course, the 'culture' to which this hyperbole referred was the culture of bhadralok Bengal. No matter that it was a cultural tradition that hardly touched the lives of the nominally Hindu castes and tribes on the margins of polite society, such as the Santals, Bagdis and Bauris, and was far removed from the practice of the lower and intermediary castes, such as the Namasudras, Rajbangshis, Mahishyas, Sahas, Sadgops and Kaibarttas, who in fact, made up the vast mass of Bengal's Hindu population.[31] The variety of cultural traditions that actually co-existed and competed in Bengal was glossed over in a construction that played upon the theme of

---

[28] In his opening speech, the President, a retired judge of the Calcutta High Court, outlined the purpose of the meeting: 'In view of the coming reforms, the Hindus were faced with a very critical period of their political life with regard to their needs and requirements'. Report of a meeting of Hindu citizens of Calcutta on 28 July 1932 at the Albert Hall, Government of Bengal, Special Branch [hereafter GBSB], File No. 6218/31.

[29] Office-bearers as listed in *Bengal Anti-Communal Award Movement*, title page.

[30] Press statement issued by the memorialists on 25 June 1936. *Ibid.*, p. 9.

[31] The three most numerous castes in Bengal were the Mahisyas, Namasudras and Rajbangshis. Together they constituted almost 30 per cent of the total population of Bengal; Brahmins and Kayasthas, on the other hand, constituted only 13.5 per cent. *Census of India*, vol. V, p. 453.

the homogeneity of 'Hindu Bengal',[32] an idea that was constructed by the bhadralok in its own image. One widely read memorial drew the Government's attention to:

> the enormously predominant part [the Hindus of Bengal] ... have played under the British in the intellectual, the cultural, the political, the professional, and the commercial life of the province ... The Hindus of Bengal, though numerically a minority, are overwhelmingly superior culturally, constituting as much as 64 per cent of the literate population ... while their economic preponderance is equally manifest in the spheres of the independent professions.[33]

Its signatories included some of the most prominent members of the cultural world of the bhadralok: the poet Rabindranath Tagore, the novelist Sarat Chandra Chattopadhyay, the President of the Asiatic Society, the philosopher Brajendra Nath Seal, the chemist Dr P. C. Ray, and the Vice-Chancellor of Calcutta University, Dr Shyamaprasad Mookerjee. Another memorial, the 'Hindu Leaders' Manifesto', declared that:

> The superiority of the Hindu community in educational qualifications and political fitness, their contribution to the growth of civic and political institutions and their record of past services to the State in every branch of administration are too well known to need recapitulation. The achievement of the Hindu Bengalis stand foremost in the whole of India in the fields of Art, Literature and Science, whereas the Moslem community in Bengal has not so far produced a single name of All-India fame in these fields ...[34]

The memorialists to Lord Zetland also 'begged leave' to make the claim that 'the Hindus of Bengal, though numerically a minority, are overwhelmingly superior culturally'.[35] The implication was that the 'cultural superiority' of the Hindus more than outweighed the numerical majority of the backward Muslims, and entitled Hindus to a share of power far in excess of their numbers. The idea of Hindu 'cultural superiority' was thus the central argument through which bhadralok Hindus backed their claims to greater representation in the proposed Provincial Assembly, and gained wide currency in the years to come. Developed in counterpoint to the theme of the 'intellectual backwardness' of Bengali Muslims, this notion was to provide one of the central idioms of Hindu communal identity in Bengal. The further development and politicisation of this

[32] For a glimpse of the variety of competing cultural traditions in the purely urban sphere, see Sumanta Banerjee, *The Parlour and the Streets Elite and Popular Culture in Nineteenth Century Calcutta*, Calcutta, 1989.
[33] Memorial by Hindu leaders, forwarded by the Maharaja of Burdwan to Lord Zetland, 4 June 1936. Zetland Collection, IOLR MSS Eur 207/6.
[34] 'Hindu Leaders' Manifesto', undated, circulated by the Bengal Provincial Hindu Sabha in 1932. GBSB File No. 6218/31.
[35] *Bengal Anti-Communal Award Movement*, p. 5.

identity, and its implications for the politics of Bengal, will be discussed in later chapters.

The response of Muslim politicians to the Award was not as clear-cut as that of Hindu leaders. Many Muslim Congressmen had left the Congress in the late twenties, after the death of Chittaranjan Das and the breakdown of the Hindu–Muslim Pact.[36] The comradeship that had characterised the Non-Cooperation and Khilafat movements had worn thin, and several Muslim nationalists, shocked by the ugly scenes that had accompanied the rescinding of Das' Pact, had come to feel that the Bengal Congress could no longer be trusted to safeguard Muslim interests. Where once there had been 'a general warmness on the part of Muslims with regard to the Congress',[37] there was now a growing feeling that

Congress is nothing but a Hindu institution. An analysis of its activities will demonstrate that it is another manifestation of the Hindus' Muslim-crushing mentality ... The net of intrigue being spread throughout India by this crowd of Hindu Congressites, Swarajis [sic] and revivalists in a united effort to wipe Muslims off the face of India is perilous in the extreme ... So unless the Muslims put up a fair fight for themselves, their religion and their community ... no one will be able to save them.[38]

For younger and more radical Muslims, the moment of disillusionment with the Congress came with the discussion of the Bengal Tenancy Amendment Bill in 1928, when all sections of the Congress/Swarajya party united to oppose legislation which aimed at strengthening the position of tenants against zamindars. As they saw it, 'Congress could now claim to represent merely the rich, the landed gentry and educated

---

[36] The Pact, engineered by Chittaranjan Das, was in essence a compromise between Hindu and Muslim politicians in Bengal about the distribution of power in local bodies. The Pact accepted separate electorates, and conceded that in each district 60 per cent of the seats on local bodies would go to the majority community. It would have given Muslims absolute control over local bodies in the sixteen districts where they were in a majority, leaving Hindus in charge only in nine districts in western and central Bengal. But a groundswell of Hindu opposition both within and outside the Congress ensured that the Pact was never implemented and that it died with its author. For details, see Rajat Ray, *Social Unrest and Political Conflict in Bengal*, pp. 310–316; and Ujjwalkanti Das, 'The Bengal Pact of 1923 and its Reactions', *Bengal Past and Present*, vol. 99, I, 188, 1980, pp. 29–45.
[37] Tamizuddin Khan toured the districts to campaign for the Swarajists in the run up to the elections in 1924. He makes this observation in his memoirs: see *The Test of Time: My life and Days*, Dhaka, 1989, p. 122.
[38] *'Dhakar danga'* ('Dacca Riots'): an editorial in the orthodox Muslim paper *Sariyate Eslam*, Year 5. no. 2, Falgun, 1336 B.S. Cited in Mustafa Nurul Islam, *Bengali Muslim Public Opinion as Reflected in the Bengali Press, 1901–1930*, Dhaka, 1973, p. 99.

minority. It had still not earned the right to lead the workers and peasants.'[39]

But while most Muslims had left the Congress, they had not, by 1932, organised themselves into one party. The old Khilafat Committees were no longer active, and no alternative forum had been established for the mobilisation of Muslim political opinion. Nor was there a single Muslim leader with the authority or standing to speak for Bengali Muslims, let alone the Bengalis as a whole. The Award therefore evoked a variety of reactions from Bengali Muslim politicians. Everyone could see that there were obvious benefits in the Award for the Muslim 'community' but some leaders regretted the emphasis on community, since they could see that the possibilities of supra-communal alliances dominated by Muslim interests were being prejudiced by the Award. Other Muslims wanted more than the Award offered. A not inconsiderable number still retained their allegiance to nationalist politics even after leaving the Congress and they criticised the Award for dividing the Legislature on communal grounds. In this broad spectrum of response, ranging from tempered satisfaction to outrage, there was, to begin with, little unanimity. It was only gradually, in response to the vehemence of the Hindu bhadralok reaction to the spectre of Muslim rule, that Muslim opinion began to range itself more solidly behind the Award.[40] On 17 August, immediately after the Prime Minister's announcement, Fazlul Huq, the mercurial barrister from Barisal, denounced the Award in no uncertain terms:

The much-advertised communal award ... will ... take the breath of the country away ... it has not fallen to our lot for a long time to come across such a preposterous document ... the worst suspicions of the nationalists have been confirmed by what has transpired ... if the new constitution of India embodies this communal settlement ... (Macdonald) may rest assured that all that is good and true in the country will refuse to touch it even with a pair of tongs.[41]

But the very next day, Huq retreated to an equivocal position. He added his name to a petition from a group of young politicians, many of whom had in the past been associated with nationalist organisations, which confessed:

---

[39] *'Kangres o mantritva'* ('Congress and Ministries') in *Saogat*, a journal that hitherto had a pro-Congress profile. Year 6, no. 11, Jyaistha, 1336 B.S. Cited in Mustafa Nurul Islam, *Bengali Muslim Public Opinion*, pp. 99–100.

[40] This is a point that Bidyut Chakravarty had overlooked in his recent study of the Award. He argues that 'in Bengal, the Muslim response was favourable' and quotes Bengali Muslim politicians selectively to prove his point. According to Chakravarty, Fazlul Huq regarded the Award as a '"distinct advance" and was therefore pleased with it'. Bidyut Chakravarty, 'The Communal Award', pp. 503–504.

[41] *Amrita Bazar Patrika*, 17 August 1932.

We have read the Award with mingled feelings. While we appreciate that it is a distinct advance on the present situation it is disappointing to note that the unanswerable claims of the Musalmans of Bengal to majority representation in the provincial legislature have not been recognised. With the Musalmans in the position of a permanent minority in six provinces and of practically political insignificance in the Central Legislature, it was only just and fair that the claims of the Musulmans [sic] of Bengal to a majority representation . . . should not have been ignored. We however appreciate the difficulties of the situation.[42]

This statement was also signed by Huseyn Shaheed Suhrawardy, a member of one of the most prominent Muslim families of Bengal and a former Swarajist who had once been appointed the Deputy Mayor of the Calcutta Corporation by Chittaranjan Das. Huq and Suhrawardy, rivals in most other fields, made common cause in their response to the Award. Other signatories included Abul Kasem, Azizul Huque, Tamizuddin Khan and Musharraf Hossain, who belonged to a variety of different factions and camps.

A. K. Ghuznavi, on the other hand, did not disguise his disappoint- ment with the award. The wealthy zamindar from Tangail, who had twice held office in Bengal ministries and had been a member of the Simon Commission, had evidently hoped that the Award would give Muslims a clear statutory majority. Comparing the Award with the annulment of the partition in 1911, he stated that the Muslims of Bengal were 'bitterly reminded of their betrayal in December 1911 by His Majesty's Govern- ment'.[43]

However, it was not only the question being guaranteed a statutory majority that divided Muslim opinion. Many Muslim politicians had accepted separate representation, albeit as a 'necessary evil',[44] but some still preferred joint electorates. In early August 1932, when the Minister of Local Self-Government, B. P. Singh Roy, introduced a Bill in the Council proposing joint electorates with no reservation of seats in the Municipalities, a number of Muslim members supported him. Abdus Samad, for instance, argued: 'From my experience in local bodies, I am of the opinion that under a system of joint electorate without any reservation of seats we would be able to return members of our commu- nity in overwhelming majority'.[45] As another Muslim councillor explained:

---

[42] *Ibid.*, 18 August 1932. *Amrita Bazar Patrika* responded to this moderate statement by accusing Huq of 'pandering to the taste of his perverted co-religionists'. *Ibid.*

[43] *Amrita Bazar Patrika*, 18 August 1932.

[44] Mujibur Rahman, *Mussalman*, 25 December 1925. Cited in Kenneth MacPherson, *The Muslim Microcosm. Calcutta, 1918 to 1935*, Wiesbaden, 1974, p. 86.

[45] *Amrita Bazar Patrika*, 6 August 1932.

For instance there are 37 U(nion) B(oard)s in the Feni subdivision, but the Presidents are all Muslims. Out of the 8 elected members of the Feni L(ocal) B(oard) as many as 7 are Muslims and only one is Hindu. What would have been the state of things if a certain percentage of seats, say 48, had been allocated for the Muslims. Could we become masters of these boards as we are at present?[46]

Several Muslim councillors welcomed Singh Roy's motion, including Fazlul Huq. Eight Muslim Councillors voted for the Bill, and twenty against. But as Samad explained, of the twenty who had opposed the Bill 'as many as twelve ... were prepared to accept the motion on certain conditions viz, the introduction of universal adult suffrage and the discontinuance of representation of special interests. This clearly shows that the mentality of Muslim members has considerably changed in favour of joint electorates'.[47]

The debate among Muslim leaders over separate electorates reflected their growing confidence that Muslims would be able to hold their own in open elections. This confidence, whether well founded or not, stemmed from the mofussil, where Muslims, both in East and West Bengal, had begun to challenge Hindu bhadralok domination of Local and District Boards. The Bengal Village Self-Government Act of 1919 limited the electorate to the substantial men of the localities. Voters in these local elections included

Every male person of the full age of 21 years and having a place of residence within the Union, who during the year immediately preceding the election has paid a sum of not less than eight annas as Cess (or alternatively, six annas of chaukidari tax) ... in respect of the lands situated wholly or in parts in such Union ... (or) is a graduate or licentiate of any university or has passed the matriculate examination of the Calcutta University ... (and) pleaders and medical practitioners.[48]

In other words, the Act gave the vote only to those with some property or education. Although some commentators attributed the growing strength of Muslims in local bodies to a 'communal awakening' among mofussil Muslims,[49] the fact was that more Muslims in the districts were getting enfranchised because they now possessed the requisite amount of land and education.[50] These advances in the locality encouraged some Muslim politicians to believe that separate electorates and reservation of seats were no longer necessary to safeguard Muslim representation in the Assembly. On the contrary, they were confident that Muslims could stand

[46] Statement by Maulvi Fazlur Rahaman, *ibid.*, 16 August 1932.
[47] *Ibid.*, 7 August 1932.
[48] Bengal Village Self-Government Act of 1919, *Union Board Manual*, vol. I, Alipore 1937.
[49] Subhas Chandra Bose to Motilal Nehru, 12 July 1928, in AICC Papers, File No. 2/1928.
[50] The wider processes that enabled this advance will be discussed in later chapters.

their ground in open contest and that they would, through joint electorates, eventually be able to translate the growing prosperity and numerical
preponderance of their community into provincial power. For this
reason, many were willing to give up these safeguards: they pressed,
instead, for universal manhood suffrage, which would give members of
their community many more votes. This explains why several Muslim
leaders were so half-hearted about the 'advantages' they were supposed
to have gained from the Communal Award.

It was only after sustained political agitation on the part of Hindu
leaders threatened to reverse the Award, that Muslim leaders rallied
around its defence. Thus in September 1933, A. K. Ghuznavi, who had
months earlier condemned the Award as a betrayal, presided over a
meeting which protested against re-opening the communal settlement as
'ill-advised and fraught with grave danger both to the Muslim community and to the country at large'.[51] A month later, Abul Kasem, a
signatory of Huq's guarded and equivocal acceptance of the Award,
presided over a meeting of Muslims in Howrah Town Hall which strongly
opposed any tampering with the Award.[52] In the next few years, as
bhadralok opposition to the Award mounted, the fury with which
Hindus reacted to the prospect of 'Muslim rule' hardened Muslim
opinion in favour of the Award. A little over a year after the Award was
announced, Fazlul Huq was driven to declare: 'I am prepared to be
hanged if I cannot demonstrate to the satisfaction of any judge that the
Hindus of Bengal constitute the very personification of communalism
based on intense selfishness'.[53] In this way, reactions to the Award came
increasingly to be divided along communal lines, with Hindus taking the
lead in denouncing the Award with one voice, and Muslims in reaction
coming increasingly to unite in its defence. The Award thus became a
focus of bitterness and discord, driving a wedge between Hindu and
Muslim politicians and increasingly dividing Bengal politics into two
separate, communally defined groups which were pitted against each
other.

The Poona Pact

While the furore over the Award was still raging, a new dimension was
added to the debate by the signing of the 'Poona Pact'. The Pact owed its
origin to Gandhi's refusal to countenance the creation of separate

---

[51] *Indian Annual Register*, 1932, vol. II, July–December, p. 9.   [52] *Ibid.*, p. 11.
[53] *Statesman*, 12 October 1933. Also cited in Kenneth MacPherson, *The Muslim Microcosm*, p. 126.

electorates for the Scheduled Castes.[54] Gandhi took the view that the problem of untouchability was a religious not a political question which could only be addressed by Hindu society itself through religious reform.[55] At the Round Table Conference in 1931, when the subject of separate electorates for the Scheduled Castes was first broached, Gandhi had made his objections known, threatening 'with all the emphasis that I can command that if I was the only person to resist this thing I would resist it with my life'.[56] This threat was disregarded and the provision of separate electorates for Scheduled Castes was included in the Award. On 20 September 1932, Gandhi undertook a 'fast unto death' in protest against this aspect of the Award.

Gandhi's views on the question of caste and untouchability ran counter to the convictions of those increasingly articulate politicians from the scheduled castes, who, in the late twenties, began to challenge the premise that the scheduled castes were an integral part of Hindu society, and to resist their integration into a political community dominated by high caste Hindus.[57] The most outstanding among these was B. R. Ambedkar, the Mahar leader from the Bombay Presidency. Ambedkar was convinced that the position of the lowest castes could improve only once they were out of the Hindu fold, both in matters of religion and politics. He argued that:

The chasm between the Hindus and the Muslims, between the Hindus and the Sikhs, between the Hindus and the Christians is nothing as compared with the chasm between the Hindus and the Untouchables. It is the widest and the deepest. The chasm between the Hindus and the Muslims is [religious] and not social. That between the Hindus and the Untouchables is both religious and social ... Since power is being transferred into the hands of the Hindu majority they must have political safeguards of the same sort, or if not better, than those conceded to the Muslims and the other minorities.[58]

Ambedkar held out for a few days against Gandhi's 'coercion', but, when the Mahatma continued his fast unto death, he relented, and with the

---

[54] The term 'Scheduled Castes' was coined by the Bengal Government in 1932 to describe the lowest of the low in Hindu society, the untouchables. For details see S. K. Gupta, *The Scheduled Castes in Modern Indian Politics: Their Emergence as a Political Power*, New Delhi, 1985.

[55] Gandhi's views on the question of untouchability and the genesis of the Poona Pact have been discussed in Ravinder Kumar, *Gandhi, Ambedkar and the Poona Pact*, Occasional Papers in History and Society, no. 20. Nehru Memorial Museum and Library, New Delhi, February 1985. A contemporary account may be found in Pyarelal, *The Epic Fast*, Ahmedabad, 1932.

[56] *Indian Round Table Conference (Second Session), Proceedings of the Federal Structure Committee and the Minorities Committee*, Calcutta, 1932, vol. III, p. 1385. Also cited in Ravinder Kumar, *Gandhi, Ambedkar and the Poona Pact*, p. 16.

[57] For a detailed history of the emergence of Scheduled Caste politics, see S. K. Gupta, *The Scheduled Castes*.

[58] B. R. Ambedkar, *Gandhi and Gandhism*, Jullunder, 1970, pp. 57–58.

greatest reluctance, put his signature to the agreement that has come to be known as the Poona Pact.[59] The Pact was a compromise effected by senior Congressmen with another group of scheduled caste leaders, led by M. C. Rajah, who felt that his 'community had been let down by other signatories of the Minorities Pact, and should now throw in its lot with the majority community in joint electorates with reservation of seats'.[60] Signatories of the Pact agreed to reserve a certain proportion of Hindu seats for Scheduled Caste candidates. Elections to these seats would be held on the basis of joint electorates: all Hindus and Scheduled Castes entitled to vote would jointly elect caste Hindu and Scheduled Caste candidates. Different arrangements for the division of Hindu seats were reached for different provinces; for Bengal, it was decided that of the total of eighty Hindu seats, thirty were to be reserved for Scheduled Caste candidates. No Bengali caste Hindu was present when the agreement was signed.

In Bengal, the effect of the Pact was drastically to reduce the caste Hindu proportion of seats in the proposed legislature from about 32 per cent to exactly 20 per cent. Bhadralok Hindus reacted with disbelief, shock and anger. In the Council, N. C. Sengupta characterised the Pact as 'a monument of political folly', while J. L. Banerjee described it as an 'unfair and monstrous injustice committed on Bengalis'. Challenging the legality of the Pact, they argued that it was not binding on the caste Hindus of Bengal because they had not been party to the arrangement. They declared that the Pact was particularly unjust in the case of Bengal, where, they argued, untouchability did not exist. If seats had to be reserved for the low castes, then the number of such seats should not exceed four, because, they declared, there were at most four hundred thousand untouchables in the province. In sum, they denounced the Pact as being 'far worse than the Premier's Award'.[61]

For bhadralok Hindus, the Pact represented a greater threat than that posed by the Communal Award. It was not simply that the number of seats reserved for upper caste Hindus in the proposed Legislature was now substantially reduced, itself a great blow; the Pact also challenged the notional 'Hindu' identity which had begun to emerge as a central idiom of

---

[59] It has been suggested that one of the reasons why Ambedkar succumbed to the growing pressure as Gandhi's fast rapidly became the central issue of Indian politics, was his fear that if Gandhi died, untouchables and low castes might be the victims of 'large scale violence' all over the country. In the circumstances, there was little else that he could have done against Gandhi's unique political methods. See Ravinder Kumar, *Gandhi, Ambedkar and the Poona Pact*, p. 21.

[60] Government of India (GOI), Home Political File No. 41/4/1932.

[61] N. N. Mitra (ed.), *Indian Annual Register*, 1933, vol. I, January–June, p. 3.

bhadralok politics. If, as the Pact suggested, almost half of Bengal's Hindus were 'depressed classes', whose members were, if not untouchable, then at least 'socially and politically backward',[62] this exposed the hollowness of bhadralok claims to represent a single Hindu community, unified by a superior cultural tradition.[63]

Bengali Hindu politicians responded to the Pact by denying that Bengal had a 'caste problem'. Their claim had some substance, for, as the Census Commissioner noted in 1931, 'Bengal in some ways has one advantage over some parts of India in that its caste system is not so rigorous'.[64] Yet by the Commissioner's own assessment, there were more than six million persons who might be classified as untouchables in British Bengal. Other than the sweepers and scavengers, including the Doms, Bhuinmalis, Haris and Kaoras, he listed as many as forty other castes, 'contact with whom entails purification on the part of high caste Hindus'. This list included occupational castes such as Chamars and Muchis, who were traditionally tanners and workers in leather, Sunris, who dealt in liquor, and Patnis and Tiyars who were boatmen and fishermen, 'all well recognised functional castes following occupations regarded with contempt by Hindu society'. It also included aboriginal groups, such as the Bagdis and Bauris of western Bengal and the Dalus, Hadis and Hajangs of Mymensingh. In addition to these 'untouchable' groups, the Census Commissioner listed eighteen aboriginal tribes and forty other castes, who, though not technically untouchable, were categorised as depressed classes,[65] 'whose

62 The list of 'Scheduled Castes' in Bengal was prepared on the basis of 'social and political backwardness' as it was felt that the criterion of untouchability 'would result in a definition unsuitable to the specific conditions of the province'. On the basis of this definition, the Government of Bengal prepared a list of eighty-six such 'backward' castes. Government of Bengal, Appointment Department. Reforms, Resolution 122 A. R., Zetland Collection, IOLR MSS Eur D/609/21(h)/a.
63 Yet paradoxically, the Pact was itself an assertion of the political and religious unity of Hindu society. Gandhi's fast was not so much intended to influence MacDonald to reconsider the question of separate electorates for the Scheduled Castes, but to persuade Scheduled Caste leaders themselves not to insist on a separate political identity. Lothian, the Franchise Commissioner, had found that 'more feeling has been aroused by the depressed classes problem than by any other problem in India ... The Hindu community has been torn from top to bottom between the depressed classes themselves who are demanding separate electorates on the ground that it is the only way in which they can get representatives of their own choice in the legislature, and caste Hindus who are desperately afraid that the great mass of Hindu society is going to be split by the breaking away of the depressed classes into a separate political entity, thereby endangering their majority in India as a whole ... and producing a situation in which the Moslems, depressed classes and other minorities may be able to combine to make a majority against them'. Lothian to Anderson, 4 May 1932. John Anderson Collection, IOLR MSS Eur F/207/3. It was to repair this breach that Gandhi undertook his fast.
64 *Census of India*, vol. V, p. 289.
65 *Ibid.*, appendix to chapter 12, pp. 494–501. Of course the enumeration and categorisation of castes in Census volumes and Gazetteers must be used with care, for inevitably these

Table 2. *Caste and economic differentiation in rural Bengal*

	High castes	Nabashaks[a]	Mussalmans	Harijans	Santals
Literate (%)	50	33	18	4	3
Landless families (%)	18	13	25	87	92
Average assets (in rupees)	2823	1528	1083	73	76
Average value of land (in rupees)	2220	1340	1098	38	39
Average annual income (in rupees)	436	236	172	84	76

[a] Nabashaks is the name given to the intermediate castes, originally nine in number, from whom the high castes may accept water without incurring ritual pollution.
Source: 'Summary Table for Village Economic Surveys', in Hashim Amir Ali, 'Rural Research in Tagore's Sriniketan', *Modern Review*, vol. 56, 1–16, July–December 1934, pp. 42–43.

social, economic and other circumstances are such that [they] will be unable to secure adequate representation of [their] political views or adequate protection of [their] interests without some form of franchise concession'.[66] These were the *chhotolok*: the 'small people' who worked in the fields and homes of the bhadralok[67] but who lived beyond the boundaries of *bhadra* (polite) society. For the first time in Bengal's history, the Award and the Poona Pact hinted at the possibility that the closed world of institutional politics, so long dominated by bhadralok groups, might be opened up to include the *chhotolok*.

Of course, the impact of these new arrangements was limited by the franchise qualifications, which gave the vote only to those who had some property. Very few members of the lowest castes had the necessary qualifications. Village studies conducted in the 1930s demonstrated that 'groupings on a purely economic basis corresponded closely with social

accorded more closely with the administrator's understanding of caste as a 'concrete and measurable' entity with definable characteristics. For a discussion of some of the problems involved in using census material, see Bernard Cohn, 'Notes on the history of the study of Indian society and culture', in M. Singer and B. S. Cohn (eds.), *Structure and Change in Indian Society*, Chicago, 1968, and Rashmi Pant, 'The Cognitive Status of Caste in Colonial Ethnography: A review of some literature on the North West Provinces and Oudh', *Indian Economic and Social History Review*, vol. 24, 2, 1987, pp. 145–162. But these lists, if interpreted critically, provide interesting detail on the variety of jatis and sects and the competing cultural religious and cultural traditions that coexisted under the broad label of 'Hinduism' and 'Hindu society'.

[66] *Census of India*, vol. V, p. 499.
[67] Out of 1,570,000 labourers in Bengal in 1911, 1,442,000 were from the 'depressed classes'; they also constituted almost 60 per cent of the total number of cultivators in the province. S. K. Gupta, *The Scheduled Castes in Modern Indian Politics*, p. 99.

groupings according to caste and religion'. Reporting on a survey of 'some 447 families' conducted in five different villages and three small Santal *bastis* (settlements) in Birbhum, Hashim Amir Ali noted that:

as soon as we saw what caste a particular family belonged to and noted whether that caste was among the high, middle or low castes of Hindu society or whether he is a Mussalman or Santal, we could with a fair degree of certainty, indicate in what economic station his family was likely to fall ... The economic level of the high castes was higher than that of the middle castes. Third in order followed the Mussalmans ... while the low castes such as Hadis, Domes, Muchies were far below with only Santals occupying a still lower economic place.[68] (See table 2.)

There were, of course, variations in this general pattern. Some low castes had, over a period of several decades, improved their economic position and ritual status. Prominent amongst these were the Namasudras of eastern and central Bengal and the Rajbangshis, who were concentrated in the northern districts. Both groups owed their rise up the ladder of success to cultivation of jute in the fertile areas of the north and east. The Namasudras claimed Brahmin status in the 1931 Census, while the Rajbangshis since 1911 had demanded that they be registered as Kshatriyas. Both these castes had made their presence felt in local politics. The Rajbangshis, 'since the inauguration of the Reforms in 1919 ... have succeeded without interruption to get themselves returned to the Legislative Council ... Since [1923] in every election, both the Hindu seats in Rungpore were captured by Rajbangshis, to the exclusion of higher castes. In the Local Boards too, they are getting elected'.[69]

It was groups such as these who were likely to take advantage of the terms of the Poona Pact and the Award to improve their standing in provincial politics, a prospect that Hindu bhadralok politicians did not welcome. Namasudra and Rajbangshi caste associations had stayed aloof from the mainstream of nationalist politics, calculating that a loyalist stance was likely to give them better returns. In his presidential address at the All-Bengal Namasudra Conference of 1928, Rai Saheb Rebati Mohon Sircar (Member of the Legislative Council) had 'emphasized that without the British Government his community [of Namasudras] would have got no chance of gaining their own position back and hence his community should not join in the present political cry [against the Simon Commission] as that course would be suicidal'. *Amrita Bazar Patrika*, the popular

---

[68] Hashim Amir Ali, 'Rural research in Tagore's Sriniketan', *Modern Review*, vol. 56, 1–6, July–December 1934, p. 42. This article collated the findings of several village studies conducted by a group from Santiniketan.

[69] *Who are the Depressed Classes in Bengal? What is their number?* A note circulated at the instance of the Hindu Sabha, the British Indian Association and the Indian Association. Zetland Collection, IOLR MSS Eur D/609/21/HB.

nationalist daily, reacted to the Rai Saheb's speech with characteristically heavy sarcasm: 'We agree that without the British Government "Rebati Babu" would have got no chance of affixing a "Rai Saheb" to his name but fail to understand how the British Government have helped [the Namasudras] to "power"'.[70] The same issue of the *Patrika* reported that at a Namasudra Conference held in Faridpur on 28 and 29 December 1927, resolutions had been passed declaring the loyalty of the Namasudras to the Crown. The hostility and suspicion with which the bhadralok press greeted the activities of the emerging caste associations of the lower orders suggests an underlying anxiety that low caste leaders might follow the same route towards 'minority' or separatist politics pursued by Muslim leaders. Even more worrying were the incidents of rural conflict involving Namasudra share-croppers who joined together with their Muslim fellows against their Hindu landlords. In February 1928, for instance, Muslim and Namasudra *bargadars* of Jessore went on strike against high caste Hindu landlords, refusing to cultivate their lands unless they were offered better terms of remuneration. [71] It was not clear, therefore, that Namasudra and Rajbangshi representatives, once elected to the new Assembly through joint electorates with caste Hindus, would accept the whip of their 'Hindu' brethren.

In contrast, bhadralok nationalists had made some headway in organising a following among the less prosperous and successful low castes and aboriginal tribes. During Non-cooperation, the Congress had encouraged Santals in the Jungle Mahals of Midnapore to confront the Midnapore Zamindari Company, a private British concern.[72] After the agitation was suspended, Gandhians in and around Arambagh launched anti-untouchability campaigns at local Khadi centres in the villages.[73] A few years later, some Swarajists launched a programme of 'reclaiming' aboriginals and untouchables to bring them into the Hindu fold through ritual purification or *shuddhi.* [74] But these efforts did not add up to a challenge to the institution of caste itself. Prominent Gandhians such as Satish Chandra Dasgupta, who led the campaign against the practice of untouchability from *ashrams* in rural Bengal defended the *varna* system, arguing that in its pristine forms, it captured the essence of socialism. Contempt for untouchables and low castes, he argued, was not a feature

[70] *Amrita Bazar Patrika*, 1 January 1928.
[71] Tanika Sarkar, *Bengal 1928–1934*, pp. 39–40.
[72] Swapan Dasgupta, 'Adivasi Politics in Midnapur, *c.* 1760–1924', in Ranajit Guha (ed.), *Subaltern Studies IV*, New Delhi, 1985.
[73] Tanika Sarkar, *Bengal 1928–1934*, pp. 26–27.
[74] Tanika Sarkar, 'Jitu Santal's Movement in Malda, 1924–1932: A Study in Tribal Protest', in Ranajit Guha (ed.), *Subaltern Studies IV*, p. 136.

of *varnashramadharma*,[75] but a distortion of the system that was introduced to Hindu doctrine only after the Muslim invasion.[76] Even so, Dasgupta spoke to a limited audience. In the early thirties, the upper castes in Bengal were, with some notable exceptions, committed to preserving the hierarchical structure of caste society: there is little evidence to suggest that in this regard they were any less conservative than their counterparts in other parts of the subcontinent. On the contrary, when M. C. Rajah moved the Untouchability Abolition Bill in the Central Assembly in 1933, every Hindu member from Bengal reacted violently against it. Pandit Satyendranath Sen took the view that ' ... these untouchables owe their origin to serious violations of marital laws ... [and] by their avocation, by their habits and by their culture they can never come up to the standard followed by the caste Hindus ...'. Amar Nath Dutt declared: 'Let these people be more clean, more pure and cherish better ideals of life and ... then I shall associate with them ...'.[77] The Law Member from Bengal, B. L. Mitter argued that as 'no sovereign political authority established castes ... legislative interference should not be permitted', and B. P. Singh Roy denounced the Bill as 'a direct encroachment on the religious rights of the Hindus and an attempt to undermine the foundations of Hindu society'. This reaction led M. C. Rajah ironically to observe: 'It is surprising ... that the bulk of the opposition comes from a province, Bengal, where they say there is no untouchability'.[78] The Bill was later circulated to various bodies in the province to gauge public opinion. The Governor of Bengal consulted all Divisional Commissioners and district judges, fifty-six 'well known and prominent persons of Bengal representing various schools of thought', thirteen Bar Libraries, and twenty-six recognised associations and religious bodies. He concluded that in Bengal, 'an overwhelming preponderance of opinion is against the Bill'.[79]

Notions of purity, pollution and hierarchy appear, therefore, to have been deeply entrenched in Bengali society.[80] Village studies conducted at

---

[75] The term 'varnashramadharma' describes the philosophy of duties of the four stages of life enjoined in the Vedas.

[76] Satish Chandra Dasgupta, *Bharate Samyavad*, Calcutta, 1930. Also cited in Tanika Sarkar, *Bengal 1928–34*, pp. 27–28.

[77] Legislative Assembly Debates on the Untouchability Abolition Bill, in Government of India, Home Political Files 50/7/33 and 50/11/34.

[78] Legislative Assembly Debates on the Untouchability Abolition Bill, 1 February 1934. In GOI, Home Political File No. 50/7/33, NAI.

[79] 'Opinions on the Untouchability Abolition Bill,' no. 1, *ibid.*

[80] For a discussion of purity, pollution and hierarchy and the caste system, see Louis Dumont, *Homo Hierarchicus. The Caste System and its Implications* (translated by Mark Sainsbury), London, 1970.

the time suggest that caste distinctions were rigorously observed. The author of one such study describes his experience of caste in the village of Goalpara in Birbhum. On his arrival there, he was advised to keep

two servants – one to bring me water and the other, an 'untouchable', who would do the other menial work. The caste of people from whose hands I may be allowed to take water is too high for other kinds of menial work, which only the 'depressed' classes do ... But I ... said, 'We of Viswa Bharati have no caste ... Touchable or untouchable, anyone will do'. But, said [my friend], 'that's not the point. An untouchable is not allowed at most village wells ... and secondly, if you take water from the hands of these people, the villagers won't accept you.'[81]

The Brahmins of the same village, Tarakrishna Basu reports, produced plenty of milk and eggs,

but thanks to their own sense of prestige, the Brahmins would never sell them even when there were too many to be consumed. They would get rotten and be thrown away. One of my elderly Brahmin friends called me in a corner and whispered to me that ... he will be able to supply me half a seer [of milk] every morning; 'But please see,' he cautioned me, 'that this news does not leak out.'[82]

The bhadralok claim that Bengal was free of untouchability was, therefore, greeted with some scepticism. One young student from Viswa Bharati described an incident in Benuria village:

A man belonging to the Dom caste was waiting on one side of the road, but he could not cross it because, he thought, that would mean an affront to us. [My friend] ... understood his difficulty and told him to cross the road. He did so, but with such hesitating steps and timid looks that they cut my mind to the quick. That is what the caste Hindus have made of us, and yet their leaders say that Bengal is free from the sin of untouchability. Bravo![83]

But while untouchability existed throughout the province, it was not practised in Bengal in as extreme a form as in other parts of India,[84] and the number of untouchables was relatively smaller. Bengal's late entry into the process of Aryanisation is widely believed to account for the fluidity of its caste system.[85] It has also been argued that 'Muslim conversion has a great deal to do with the rather unique caste structure in

[81] Tarakrishna Basu, 'Goalpara Notes', Appendix A in Hashim Amir Ali, *Then and Now (1933–1958) A Study of Socio-Economic Structure and Change in Some Villages near Viswa Bharati University Bengal*. New Delhi, 1960.
[82] *Ibid.*   [83] Jiten Taluqdar, 'Benuria Notes'. Appendix B, *Ibid.*
[84] S. K. Gupta, *The Scheduled Castes in Modern Indian Politics*, pp. 99–100. H. H. Risley did not place any caste of Bengal in the category of 'those whose touch pollutes'. H. H. Risley, *The Tribes and Castes of Bengal. Ethnographical Glossary*, Calcutta, 1891.
[85] Sekhar Bandopadhyay, *Caste, Politics and the Raj. Bengal 1872–1937*, Calcutta, 1990, p. 18.

Bengal',[86] since many of the lowest castes had converted to Islam in earlier times. The survival among Bengali Muslims of hierarchical divisions and ritual ranking reminiscent of caste,[87] lends credence to this view. In some districts of Bengal, sufi *pirs* (saints) had won many converts to Islam; in Dinajpur, for instance, where the *pir* tradition was strong, many Rajbangshis had converted to this variant of Islam and were known as nyasas.[88] Another factor which may have influenced caste practices in Bengal was the proliferation of heterodox sects, which, since the seventeenth century, had attracted large followings among the low castes.[89] Vaisnavite cults provided an alternative form of worship that was open to all castes; they also cut a channel for caste mobility. The Manik Kali cult, for instance, established by Hedaram Das of the rising Kaibartta caste, observed no caste distinctions,[90] while large numbers of Rajbangshis in Dinajpur had converted to Vaisnavism.[91] Adherence to Vaisnavite cults, could, over a period of time, obscure the lowly origins of upwardly mobile caste groups. In 1931, when the Census Commissioner attempted to list the different Hindu sects, 30 per cent of all 'Hindus' were found to be members of heterodox sects, chiefly of the Vaisnava and Sakta variety.[92] The emergence and proliferation of such sects and cults in the nineteenth and early twentieth centuries[93] obscured, on the one hand, many of the rigidities of the caste system, giving rise to a uniquely complex pattern of caste practices and relations. On the other hand, it made for a rich variety of competing religious traditions which undermined the hegemonising efforts of orthodox Brahmanic Hinduism in Bengal.

[86] Partha Chatterjee, 'Caste and Politics in West Bengal', in Gail Omvedt (ed.), *Land, Caste and Politics in Indian States*, New Delhi, 1982, pp. 88–101, n. 2.

[87] For an account of hierarchy and rank among Bengali Muslims, see, Carol Prindle,'Occupation and Orthopraxy in Bengali Muslim Rank', in Katherine P. Ewing (ed.), *Shariat and Ambiguity in South Asian Islam*, New Delhi, 1988.

[88] F. W. Strong, *Eastern Bengal District Gazetteer – Dinajpur*, Allahabad, 1912, pp. 36–37. Also cited in Gautam Bhadra, 'The Mentality of Subalternity: *Kantanama* or *Rajdharma*' in Ranajit Guha (ed.), *Subaltern Studies VI*, New Delhi, 1989.

[89] Chaitanya's sect was only the most famous of these. For detailed accounts, see J. N. Bhattacharya, *Hindu Castes and Sects*, Calcutta, 1973; Ramakanta Chakrabarty, *Vaisnavism in Bengal*, Calcutta, 1985 and S. Dasgupta, *Obscure Religious Cults*, Calcutta, 1969. See also Sumit Sarkar, 'The Kalki-Avatar of Bikrampur: A Village Scandal in Early Twentieth Century Bengal', and Partha Chatterjee, 'Caste and Subaltern Consciousness' in *Subaltern Studies VI*, for interesting accounts of the variety of ways in which low caste groups interacted with both the dominant Brahmanic tradition and with heterodox cults.

[90] S. K.Gupta, *The Scheduled Castes in Modern Indian Politics*, pp. 99–100.

[91] Gautam Bhadra, 'The Mentality of Subalternity', p. 60.

[92] *Census of India*, 1931, vol. V, p. 393. The Census Commissioner was disappointed with the 'weak response' that these enquiries met: evidently he suspected that an even higher proportion of Hindus subscribed to one or other of the heterodox sects and cults.

[93] A total number of fifty-six such sects are listed in Ramakanta Chakrabarty, *Vaisnavism in Bengal*, p. 349.

To speak of a single 'Bengali Hindu community' was, therefore, to 'invent' an 'imagined community'.[94] The Poona Pact, by raising the enormously complex issue of caste in Bengal, drew attention to the fractures and cracks that this construction was designed to paper over. It also questioned the claims of bhadralok politicians and their organisations to speak for every section of Hindu society. It represented, therefore, a serious threat to the very basis of bhadralok politics.[95]

One immediate result of the Pact was to create a rift between Bengali Hindu Congressmen and the architects of the pact at the all-India level, the Congress High Command and Gandhi himself. The Bengalis argued that the Pact was 'injurious to Bengali Hindu interests and subversive of their solidarity'; it was viewed by many as a betrayal of Bengal. J. L. Banerjee echoed this sentiment, when, in a highly charged speech in the Council, he declared: 'That the apostle of Nationalism should have proved to be the greatest enemy of Nationalism in Bengal is one of the tragedies of the situation'.[96] Most Bengali Congressmen were irate at the fact that they had been ignored in the discussions that preceded a Pact which had been made 'without consulting the Hindus of Bengal and [so the critics thought] without any knowledge or consideration for the social and political conditions in the Province'. As a result, 'the number of seats reserved [for] the Depressed Classes was out of all proportion to the real needs of the Province'.[97] This was a slight that Bengalis, whether inside or outside the Bengal Congress, could not easily forgive. Time was when the patriots of Bengal had been at the centre of the Congress movement and organisation, and when Bengal had wielded her influence over both the ideology and the leadership of the party. Now the very same Congress had failed to consult Bengal on a question that profoundly affected her future. Few Bengali Congressmen had ever been ardent disciples of Gandhi,[98] and since Chittaranjan Das had engineered Gandhi's defeat on the question of Council entry, most had paid no more than lip-service to his leadership. Gandhi's settlement of the internal succession dispute

[94] These concepts are borrowed from the work of Eric Hobsbawm and Terence Ranger (eds.), *The Invention of Tradition*, Cambridge, 1984, and Benedict Anderson, *Imagined Communities. Reflections on the Origin and Spread of Nationalism*, London, 1990, respectively.
[95] Later chapters will examine the response of bhadralok politicians to this challenge.
[96] J. L. Banerjee's speech in the Bengal Legislative Council, 14 March 1933. Reported in *Indian Annual Register*, 1933, vol. I, January–June, p. 12.
[97] Resolution passed by a meeting of Hindus in Calcutta, held under the auspices of the British Indian Association. *Ibid.*, p. 329.
[98] Gitasree Bandopadhyay, *Constraints in Bengal Politics 1921–41. Gandhian Leadership*, Calcutta, 1984, and Leonard Gordon, *Bengal: The Nationalist Movement*. Both discuss aspects of this conflict between certain Bengali Congressmen and the Gandhian leadership at the centre.

following Das' death, which gave Jatindra Mohan Sengupta all three of Calcutta's crowns and left Subhas Bose out in the cold, had alienated more Bengali Congressmen than it had pleased.[99] The Poona Pact added further fuel to the fire of Bengal's discontent with Gandhi's leadership. This conflict between the provincial organisation and the High Command was to be a central theme in Bengali Congress politics in the period after the Poona Pact.

Centre and Province: the Congress High Command and Bengal

When the second phase of the Civil Disobedience Movement ended in 1934 and senior Congress leaders were released from gaol, the All-India Congress Committee began to hammer out its official stance on recent constitutional developments. The question of whether or not the Congress would work the reforms within the broad framework of the Communal Award was the single most important issue to be decided. Early in 1933, a Government White Paper had set out London's proposals for provincial autonomy,[100] and pressures had built up inside the Congress party to fight elections and accept the terms that were on offer.[101] In 1933, Gandhi had to sanction an attempt to revive the Swarajya Party,[102] while at the same time rejecting the terms of the White Paper which the High Command had already been persuaded to accept. The following year, Gandhi continued to equivocate in his reaction to the Communal Award, and in June, the Working Committee adopted its controversial resolution which showed that it was still sitting firmly on the fence:

The White Paper lapsing, the Communal Award must lapse automatically ... Since, however, the different communities in the country are sharply divided on the question of the Communal Award, it is necessary to define the Congress attitude towards it. The Congress claims to represent equally all communities composing the Indian nation and, therefore, in view of the division of opinion can neither accept nor reject the Communal Award so long as division of opinion lasts.[103]

The need to placate Nationalist Muslims and to keep them within the fold of the Congress party influenced Gandhi's decision, leading him to

---

[99] For details of the succession struggle and Gandhi's role as arbiter, see Rajat Kanta Ray, *Social Conflict and Political Unrest in Bengal*, pp. 345–50.
[100] Proposals for Indian Constitutional Reform, Command 4268 of 1933.
[101] J. B. Kripalani, then General Secretary of the party, recalled: 'Nobody could have imagined that there was such a strong opinion for accepting office ... Excepting Punjab and Bengal, all other provinces were for acceptance of office'. Kripalani to Rajendra Prasad, 15 February 1936. In B. N. Pandey, *The Indian Nationalist Movement, 1885–1947, Select Documents*, London, 1979, p. 98.
[102] B. C. Roy Papers, Part II, Subject File 33/1933.
[103] N. N. Mitra (ed.), *Indian Annual Register*, vol. II, July–December 1934, p. 207.

override the objections of prominent men in his party such as Madan Mohan Malaviya, who vehemently opposed the Award.[104] One of Gandhi's close confidantes had told him, only a few days before this decision was taken, that 'Pandit Malaviyaji is against the Communal Award. Half the Nationalist Muslims are in favour [of it] and there is likely to be opposition in the (Parliamentary) Board. Only if a formula acceptable to Malaviyaji is produced can the ship be saved from sinking.'[105] In the event, however, Gandhi was more concerned to preserve the secular credentials of the Congress party than to smooth ruffled feathers within the party.

If Gandhi hoped that his formula, which neither accepted nor rejected the communal settlement, would be acceptable to all parties, he was mistaken. Bengali Congressmen could hardly afford to let such equivocation pass, and reacted immediately with predictable outrage:

The Communal Award by the Prime-minister is unjust, unreasonable, anti-nationalistic and anti-democratic. This meeting is of the opinion that the indifferent and unsympathetic policy regarding this award adopted by the Congress working committee in their last Benares sitting as extremely derogatory to the nation and as such requests the working committee to reconsider the same.[106]

This sentiment was echoed by Congress committees all over Bengal.[107] In the two years after the Poona Pact, the Working Committee's *de facto* acceptance of the Award confirmed the suspicion of most Congressmen in Bengal that the leaders at the centre cared nothing about their local problems. At an All-Bengal Hindu conference organised in Calcutta early in 1935, Tushar Kanti Ghose, editor of the *Amrita Bazar Patrika*, gave voice to bhadralok opinion when he declared that 'the educated Hindus of Bengal had built the Indian National Congress, they had always obeyed its mandate ... What a pity that the very (same) Congress failed to do anything for Bengal at the time of crisis'.[108]

The High Command's 'betrayal' of Bengal's interests made it legitimate

---

[104] Gandhi's concern for the view of nationalist Muslims was welcomed by many Congress-minded Muslims in Bengal. Abul Mansur Ahmed, for instance, felt that 'By passing this moderate resolution, the Congress saved the nation from imminent catastrophe'. Abul Mansur Ahmed, *Amar Dekha Rajnitir Panchash Bachhar*, p. 41.

[105] K. M. Munshi to Gandhi, 8 June 1934, in K. M. Munshi, *Indian Constitutional Documents, vol. I, The Pilgrimage to Freedom*, Bombay, 1967, p. 375.

[106] Resolution passed by the Pabna DCC, AICC Papers, F. No. G-24/1934–36.

[107] Resolutions protesting against the Working Committees resolution were received from Congress offices in Jhenidah (in Jessore district), Pabna, Birbhum, Burdwan, Calcutta, Hili, Barisal, Chittagong, Mymensingh, Brahmanbaria and Khulna. These and several other documents expressing Bengali Congressmen's distress may be found in AICC Papers, File No. G-24/1934–36.

[108] N. N. Mitra (ed.), *Indian Annual Register*, vol. I, January–June 1935, p. 12.

in the eyes of many Bengalis for the Bengal Congress to defy the centre. Subhas Bose and his supporters had been in constant conflict with Gandhi and the Working Committee since the succession disputes that followed the death of Chittaranjan Das. Interminable squabbles had continued to divide the Bengal party, and the central Congress leadership, called upon repeatedly to act as referee, was drawn deeper and deeper into BPCC affairs. But the High Command had its own axe to grind: it was anxious to tame the fractious Bengalis and was more concerned to establish its hold over the provincial organisation than to act as an impartial arbiter in byzantine disputes.[109] Gandhi's appointment of Sengupta as president of the Bengal party in 1927, and his continued support of Sengupta's faction against Bose until Sengupta died in 1933, was intended to bring the Bengal Congress under the control of men who would toe the centre's line.[110] This was a policy that Subhas Bose and his followers could not stomach and from 1927 onwards, they had gone their own way, refusing to accept the jurisdiction of the High Command.[111] Now, by pointing out the cavalier manner in which the High Command subordinated Bengali bhadralok interests to all-India considerations in the Poona Pact and the Communal Award, the Bose group was armed with a just 'cause'. It enabled them to rally a large following, creating a nucleus of supporters which was more than a faction. The Bose group now claimed the right to speak for Bengal, portraying itself as David heroically challenging the Goliath of the Centre in order to protect the interests of the province. This struck a responsive cloud among many Bengalis who now threw their weight behind the Bose brothers.

When Madan Mohan Malaviya and M. S. Aney parted company with the Gandhian leadership on the question of the Award and set up a new party, the Boses and their group were quick to join them. On 18 August 1934, the Nationalist Party was established in Calcutta, 'with the object of

---

[109] Ten years later, the Congress central leadership was still trying to get to the bottom of some of the BPCC disputes. In one such case, J. B. Kripalani, then the General Secretary of the AICC had obviously reached the end of his tether when he wrote to an appellant from Bengal: 'I am afraid this office can render you very little protection. Only a Bengali can catch a Bengali'. See J. B. Kripalani to J. K. Dhar, 18 July 1939. AICC Papers, File No. P-5 (Part I)/1939–40.

[110] Instead of trying to effect a compromise between Bose and Sengupta, Gandhi in 1927 decided to give Sengupta all of the three disputed crowns of Calcutta: the Presidentship of the BPCC, the Mayoralty of Calcutta and the leadership of the Swarajya party in Council.

[111] Thus for instance, Kiran Sankar Roy, representing the Bose group wrote to the Working Committee's arbiter, P. Sitaramayya, in 1929, 'We are convinced that you are absolutely incapable of being a judge and we are doubtful of your capacity to make a fair report of the facts.' Kiran Sankar Roy to P. Sitaramayya, AICC Papers, File No. G-120/1929.

carrying on agitation against the Communal Award and the White Paper, both in the Legislative assembly and outside and of setting up candidates for election to the legislatures for the promotion of that object.'[112] The formation of the Nationalist Party forced another division upon an already divided Bengal Congress. Although most Bengali Congressmen were sympathetic to the stand that Malaviya and Aney had taken, not all were willing to come out openly against the High Command. Internal factional differences, which had receded into the background in the aftermath of the Communal Award, now re-emerged with a vengeance, threatening the fragile unity of the Bengal Congress.

Behind this lay the fact that the rivals of the Bose brothers owed their position in Bengal politics to the support of the High Command. When Sengupta died suddenly in 1933, his mantle was taken over by Dr Bidhan Chandra Roy, a well-known Calcutta physician. In the late twenties, Roy had been an ardent Swarajist and a disciple of Chittaranjan Das. After Das' death, he had been one of the 'Big Five' of Calcutta, a caucus of wealthy and well-connected individuals who enjoyed considerable influence in Congress circles in the late twenties and who backed Subhas Chandra Bose against Sengupta and Gandhi.[113] However, in the course of the Civil Disobedience Movement, with much of the Congress leadership in gaol, the factional lines of the Congress leadership had been redrawn: the Big Five split up, and B. C. Roy, in alliance with Kiran Sankar Roy and Nalini Ranjan Sarkar, broke away from the Bose brothers. Roy now drew closer to Gandhi and the central leadership and gradually came to occupy the role that Sengupta had played before his death: that of Gandhi's man in Bengal. But unlike Sengupta, who had an organisational base in Chittagong, and a wider constituency in the eastern districts where he had led strikes during the Non-Cooperation movement, Roy in his own right had no following in the province. He had never been involved in agitational politics and had little support inside the Bengal Congress party organisation. As one of his most loyal supporters recalls,

B. C. Roy was not in touch with the younger generation, with the [party] workers all over Bengal. He was an aristocrat. He was a prominent member of the Congress, very influential, a competent man in the Legislative Council and the [Cal-

---

[112] Resolution passed at the Nationalist Conference, Calcutta, 18 August 1934. N. N. Mitra (ed.), *Indian Annual Register*, vol. II, July–December 1934, p. 212.

[113] Other members of the Big Five included Sarat Chandra Bose, elder brother of Subhas and leading barrister, Tulsi Goswami, the son of Raja Kishori Lal Goswami, who returned from Oxford to take over a considerable zamindari and who had substantial interests in the jute business; Nirmal Chandra Chunder, a wealthy solicitor, and Nalini Ranjan Sarkar, one of the first Bengali financiers to make a fortune in insurance.

cutta Municipal] Corporation. We used to give him a prominent place in those spheres, but not in the working of the organisation.[114]

Once the Big Five ceased to work together, B. C. Roy owed such authority as he came to have in Bengal largely to his close relationship with Gandhi. So, when the High Command took its controversial stands on the Poona Pact and the Award, 'Dr Bidhan', as he was affectionately called by his mentor, found himself in the unenviable position of having to defend the centre's unpopular decisions. The Bengal Congress once again split into two camps. The group led by Subhas and Sarat Bose stridently denounced the Poona Pact, the Communal Award and the High Command, while a second section led by Bidhan Roy remained obedient and somewhat sheepishly accepted the decisions taken by the centre.

By the end of 1934, Dr B. C. Roy began to receive reports that 'the general trend seems to be in favour of the Nationalist Party but people who are within the official Congress circle are hesitating to identify themselves with the Nationalist Party'.[115] With elections to the new Provincial Assembly in the offing, even the most loyal men of the centre were loathe to associate themselves with the High Command's refusal to sanction agitation against the Award. So, in the hope that the central leadership would take a lenient and sympathetic view of his problems in Bengal, B. C. Roy supported a motion proposed by Sarat Bose that 'inasmuch as the Communal decision, apart from being an all-India problem, is one of the gravest and most vital problems affecting the province of Bengal ... it is the duty of the provincial Congress organisation to carry out an agitation both in and outside the legislature for the rejection of the Communal decision'.[116] The resolution was passed unanimously in a vote that reflected the extent to which the strength of feeling on the question of the Communal Award cut across the factional differences within the Bengal Congress. Sarat Bose's resolution on the question of the Communal Award was seconded by Kiran Sankar Roy who had crossed over to Bidhan Roy's camp.[117] Forwarding the resolution to the Working Committee, Roy expressed the hope 'that this put an end to the differences between the Nationalist Party and that of the Congress towards the Award'.[118]

[114] Interview with Surendra Mohan Ghosh, NMML Oral Transcript No. 301, pp. 125–126.
[115] R. Pal Choudhuri to B. C. Roy, 4 October 1934. B. C. Roy Papers, Part II, File No. 36 (Part I)/1933–34.
[116] Enclosure in Sarat Bose to Jawaharlal Nehru, 19 September 1936, AICC Papers, File No. G-24/1934–36.
[117] BPCC Report, AICC Papers, File No. P-6 (Part I)/1936.
[118] Bidhan Chandra Roy to Govind Ballabh Pant, 4 December 1936, ibid.

But the High Command would not allow the Bengal Congress to bend the rules so blatantly, even in the interests of promoting the new-found unity in the provincial party. Congress leaders at the centre feared that any agitation against the Award would make its relations with nationalist Muslims more difficult and would intensify communal conflict. Nehru drove the lesson home:

It may be that an agitation, say carried in the main by Hindus leads to a rival agitation in favour of the 'Award' carried in the main by Muslims. This results in creating a situation in favour of the retention of the 'Award', for such a conflict is inevitably exploited by the British Government against us. Therefore the idea of one-sided agitation is not favoured by the Congress.[119]

By 1934 it was clear that any agitation in Bengal against the Award would be a 'one-sided' affair, involving only Hindus and that it would be opposed by most Muslims. In consequence, Bengali Congressmen could expect no concessions from the centre. The Mahatma rebuked Roy 'for suggesting that Bengal could be treated as a special case' with regard to the Award:

I understand that dispensation from adherence to the Working Committee resolution on the Communal Award is being given to Bengal Congress candidates on the ground of conscientious scruples ... until the dispensation becomes part of the Working Committee resolution, no one can grant it. And it cannot be granted even by the Working Committee if the Nationalist Party continues to function. Those therefore, who want dispensation have simply to belong to the Nationalist Party.[120]

The Working Committee insisted that all Congress candidates in the coming elections should stand by its resolution on the Award. When, for instance, Bhabendra Roy, a candidate approved by the Bengal Congress Parliamentary Board, asked to be allowed to oppose the Award, he was immediately dropped by the Centre.[121] B. C. Roy hastily backed down: the BPCC passed a new resolution which left out all references to agitation against the Award.[122] Dr Roy had hoped that the High Command would look the other way while the Bengal Congress bent the rules, but once the central leadership made it clear that they had no intention of allowing the Bengal party to go its own way, Roy and his followers quickly returned to the safe path of obedience and toed the centre's line.

[119] Jawaharlal Nehru to Jagat Narayan Lal of the Nationalist Party, 30 September 1936, in AICC Papers, File No. 24/1936.
[120] Gandhi to B. C. Roy, 30 August 1934 in B. C. Roy Papers, Part II, File No. 36 (Part I)/1933–34.
[121] Statement issued by Maulana A. K. Azad, 4 October 1934, *ibid*.
[122] BPCC Secretary to all members of the Working Committee, 13 November 1936. AICC Papers, File No. 24/710/1936.

Sarat Bose, on the other hand, was spoiling for a fight with the High Command. The elder Bose, with a monthly income of 10,000 rupees, was one of Calcutta's leading lawyers and his enormously successful practice had won him high standing in bhadralok society.[123] His involvement in politics did not, at the outset, go much further than financing the activities of his fiery younger sibling. Gradually, however, Sarat Chandra Bose was pulled into the maelstrom of Bengal politics, and his patronage began to exert its influence beyond the family circle and extended to a network of young Jugantar terrorists,[124] who in turn supported the Bose group in BPCC disputes.[125] The elder Bose had been a member of the Big Five in the twenties and consistently supported his brother, Subhas, against J. M. Sengupta. He had taken over as the Managing Director of *Forward*, the paper started by Chittaranjan Das and had used it as the mouthpiece of the Bose group. Sarat Bose had also been involved in the defence of the Chittagong Armoury Raid prisoners, and in 1932, had been arrested on the charge of being the author of a plot to assassinate Charles Tegart, the Chief of Police, who, understandably disenchanted, described him as 'the power behind his brother'.[126] In the course of the twenties and early thirties, therefore, Sarat Bose had built up a wide circle of supporters and clients, both among the terrorists, who occupied an important place in the rank and file membership of the Congress, and with leading Calcutta politicians. Unlike Bidhan Roy, who owed his position in Bengal to the goodwill of Gandhi, Sarat Bose was a man who mattered in his own right.

In 1936, the elder Bose was released from prison. With Sengupta dead and Subhas in Europe, the High Command, needing someone of authority and stature to take the Bengal Congress through the elections, put

---

[123] He is reported to have lived in a style 'not in any way different from that of an English barrister or judge'. GOI, Home Political File No. 31/27/32.

[124] The Police Commissioner reported that in 1928, Sarat Bose met Monoranjan Gupta and other terrorists in order to discuss the management of the 'Bengal Insurance and Real Property Company' with a view to improving the financial position of the 'revolutionary party' and making provisions for its workers. History sheet and synopsis of Sarat Bose's activities by Charles Tegart, GOI, Home Political File No. 31/27/32.

[125] Kalpana Dutt, one of the principal figures in the famous Chittagong Armoury raid recalls: 'In [the] 1929 Congress election, this [Jugantar] group of Surjya Sen voted for Subjas Chandra Bose in the provincial election and themselves captured the [Chittagong] district Congress with Surjya Sen as secretary.' Kalpana Dutt, *Chittagong Armoury Raiders, Reminiscences*, New Delhi, 1979, p. iii.

[126] History sheet and synopsis of Sarat Bose's activities by Charles Tegart, GOI, Home Political File No. 31/27/32. For details about the career of Sarat Bose, see the *Sarat Bose Commemoration Volume*, published by the Sarat Bose Academy, Calcutta, 1982, and Sisir Kumar Bose, *Remembering my Father*, Calcutta, 1988. The private papers of Sarat and Subjas Bose are an important source for any political analysis of Bengal in this period. The Netaji Research Bureau has published some useful information, but it is a

the past behind them and appointed Sarat to the most important position in Bengal, at the head of the Parliamentary Board. He shared this post with Bidhan Roy. But Dr Roy was no match for Sarat Chandra, and if the High Command hoped that Roy would check the growing influence of the elder Bose, it was to be disappointed. Sarat Bose used his position in the Parliamentary Board to launch himself into active politics and effectively used the issue of the Communal Award to make for himself a dominant position in Bengali politics.

Sarat Bose soon demonstrated that he was willing to do battle with Gandhi and the High Command. On his release, he denounced the Working Committee's stand on the Award and made it plain that he would throw his weight behind the Nationalists if this decision was not revoked. Since Sarat Bose was, at the same time, the acting president of the BPCC,[127] the central Congress leadership could not ignore this challenge. Nehru, therefore, demanded:

to know what your Committee's position is vis-à-vis the Nationalist Party in Bengal. The matter should be cleared up to avoid complications in the future. We want, of course to cooperate with all groups but obviously organisationally we cannot have overlapping and the Provincial Congress Committee can only represent the general policy of the Congress and the AICC.[128]

In reply, the BPCC under Bose's leadership explained that 'the postponement by the Congress Working Committee at Wardha of its final decision in regard to a settlement with the Congress Nationalists on the question of the rejection of the Communal Award was proving to be 'detrimental to the best interests of Congress work in the province [e]specially in connection with the ensuing election to the legislatures.'[129] Public opinion in Bengal, the Secretary of the Bengal Congress pointed out, was firmly against the Award, and he went on to explain that:

For the Provincial Congress Committee, as a representative body, to function democratically, it cannot but have sufficient regard for public opinion, particularly, on such a fundamental issue. Lest there be any further misunderstanding, we have no hesitation in stating that in fighting the grave menace, as the award, there can be no question of the BPCC ignoring public opinion in Bengal ... The anomaly that seems to have been created in the situation is, obviously, due to the Working Committee turning a deaf ear to our cause.[130]

pity that the papers are regarded as family property rather than a resource for all scholars.
[127] BPCC list of office-bearers: AICC Papers, File No. P-6 (Part I)/1936.
[128] Jawaharlal Nehru the BPCC Secretary, 13 July 1933, AICC Papers, File No. P-6 (Part II)/1936.
[129] BPCC Resolution dated 12 July 1936. Enclosure to BPCC Secretary to Jawaharlal, 18 July 1936, AICC Papers, File No. P-6 (Part I)/1936.
[130] Ibid.

Nehru, anxious to avoid an open split in the Bengali Congress at this critical juncture in the election campaign, attempted to placate Bose and his followers, assuring them that:

all of us, or nearly all of us, in the Congress want to reject, and what is more, put an end to this communal decision ... I shall repeat, to prevent any possibility of doubt, the Congress policy in regard to the 'Award'. It dislikes it, does not accept it and rejects it and can never reconcile itself to it, because it is a barrier to our progress to unity, freedom and independence, and is a part and parcel of the British imperialism which it combats ... We all know how hard Bengal has been hit by the Congress decision.

'But,' he added, 'the question has to be tackled on an all-India basis ... I can further assure you that the Working Committee have as great a dislike of the communal decision as anyone in Bengal. But the wider aspects of the problem demand attention.'[131]

But Nehru's reference to 'the wider aspects of the problem', in other words the 'all-India' priorities of the centre, touched a sensitive nerve in Bengal. As the champions of Bengal against the centre, the Bose brothers reacted against Nehru's conciliatory attempt with biting sarcasm:

It is indeed, very gratifying to notice you categorically rejecting the Award ... But then we cannot help feeling somewhat apprehensive when you state that 'the question [of the Award] has to be tackled on an all-India basis'. It may be no news to you that here the opinion has gained ground particularly in connection with the Poona Pact and the Congress policy relating to the Award, that Bengal has been made a pawn in the chess-board of the All-India politics [sic]. There is nothing surprising about it considering the supreme callousness with which public opinion in Bengal has hitherto been treated in the higher circles of the Congress. We naturally, therefore, feel hesitant about the solution of what is peculiarly Bengal's problem being made subservient to all-India politics.[132]

Here again was the strident justification for the increasingly narrow provincialism of Bengali Hindus: the claim that Bengalis were the founding fathers of the Indian National Congress, the architects of Indian nationalism and now the victims of the very organisation they had created. Unable to influence the course of affairs at the centre, the politics of the bhadralok increasingly turned inwards, concerned to counter the threat to their position in Bengal. With their power uncertain in Bengal and their influence at the centre severely eroded, Bengali Congressmen found themselves divided on what their best strategy should be. One section, led by the Bose brothers, wanted a war on two fronts, a fight

[131] Jawaharlal Nehru to the BPCC Secretary, 6 August 1936, *ibid.*
[132] BPCC Secretary to Jawaharlal Nehru, 13 August 1936, AICC Papers, File No. P-6 (Part I)/1936.

against the centre and a campaign to salvage their position within Bengal. Others, like Dr B. C. Roy, thought it more prudent to ally themselves more closely than ever with the High Command in the hope that influence at the centre would strengthen their hand when they negotiated on behalf of their province. In the late thirties, this fundamental difference of approach tore apart the BPCC, not a seamless web at the best of times; and this new burst of fratricidal strife was to have a significant impact on the last days of undivided Bengal.

The High Command's immediate reaction was to avert an open breach in the Bengal Congress and to impose some order upon these rival factions. When the Nationalists in Bengal set up their own candidates against the Congress candidates in the Assembly elections and produced an election manifesto which pledged to fight the Award,[133] Vallabhbhai Patel, the iron man at the centre, stepped in. As president of the Central Parliamentary Board, he made it clear that he would not tolerate such indiscipline, warning that:

The interpretation that has been put by the Bengal Executive Committee on the AICC ... statement about the Communal Decision is entirely wrong and unless the candidates whose recommendations are forwarded by you agree to accept the policy and programme of the (AICC) Manifesto, it would not be possible for the Central Parliamentary Committee to accept the recommendations.[134]

This set the centre and the province on collision course. But in the end, it was the Bengal tigers who backed away. On 8 November, the Nationalist-controlled BPCC changed its election manifesto, taking out every reference to the Communal Award. The Congress High Command, it seemed, had won the first round. In the run up to the general elections, the leaders of the BPCC realised that they needed the support of the all-India Congress for the time being if their party was to make a showing in the ballot-box. The history of interminable factional squabbles in the Bengal Congress since the death of Chittaranjan Das and its failure to take the lead during Civil Disobedience did not augur well for the Congress' success in provincial elections. As one disillusioned Congressmen noted, 'the so-called Congress leaders in Bengal kept themselves hidden in their homes and did not stir out ... I ask you where was Dr B. C. Roy or Mr J. C. Gupta during the Civil Disobedience Movement in Bengal? Certainly nowhere near the Congress.'[135] Another critic pointed out that it

---

[133] Jawaharlal Nehru to Sarat Chandra Bose, 3 September 1936. *Sarat Bose Commemoration Volume*, pp. 226–227.
[134] Vallabhbhai Patel to B. C. Roy, 9 October 1936, AICC Papers, File No. G-24/710/1936. Also cited in J. A. Gallagher, 'Congress in Decline', p. 641.
[135] BPCC Secretary to the members of the Working Committee, 13 November 1936, *ibid*.

was only 'the glamour of the Indian National Congress as an all-India organisation with its wide outlook [which] has to some extent saved the Bengal Congress from being utterly unpopular.'[136] The Nationalists in Bengal were well aware of these unpalatable facts of their political life, and when Malaviya set up the new party in 1934, they had insisted that it should remain, as the Swarajists had remained in the twenties, a splinter group in the Congress. They had argued then that 'without having the word "Congress" attached to this new party it was not likely to excite much interest in Bengal'.[137] For pragmatic reasons of this sort, the Bengal Congress decided to give way to the Working Committee. But the reconciliation was to be short-lived, and in the years that followed, the Bose brothers made much, in their campaigns in Bengal, of the wicked 'imperialism' of the High Command.

[136] Sunil Kumar Bose to Dr Syed Mahmud, 5 May 1934, AICC Papers, File No. G-25/ 1934–35.
[137] Amulya Prasad Chandra to Jawaharlal Nehru, 23 November 1937, AICC Papers, File No. P-5 (Part I)/1937.

2   The emergence of the *mofussil* in Bengali politics

It has been remarked that 'no other Indian city dominated its hinterland as completely as Calcutta dominated Bengal'.[1] In the 1930s, however, the countryside emerged as a major arena of political activity, and, as urban preoccupations began to give way to rural issues as the focus of debate and conflict, Calcutta lost some of its former pre-eminence. The rise of the mofussil in Bengal politics was associated with two major developments of the thirties. The first was the Depression and the crisis of agrarian production relations that followed it; the second was the impact and growing influence of a rural electorate newly enfranchised by the reforms of 1935. While the Depression and the agrarian crisis fuelled unrest and conflict in the mofussil, the 1935 Act served to bring this conflict into the provincial legislature. The politicisation of the countryside was associated with the growing polarisation of politics around 'communal' lines and was to play a central role in shaping the course of Bengali politics in the following two decades.

Despite the big city of Calcutta, Bengal was a predominantly rural society. Criss-crossed by the rivers of the Gangetic delta, it had once been a highly fertile region, exporting rice to other parts of India. Gradually, however, the decay of Bengal's river systems, exacerbated by the construction of embankments and roadways and by the rise of parts of the delta above the level of inundation, reduced the fertility of the soil, particularly in western and northern Bengal.[2] The eastern districts remained fertile, but by the twentieth century, demographic pressures and the splintering of family plots into uneconomic holdings cut back agrar-

---

[1] J. A. Gallagher, 'Congress in Decline', p. 596.

[2] Rajat Kanta Ray, 'The Crisis of Bengal Agriculture, 1820–1927, The Dynamics of Immobility', *Indian Economic and Social History Review*, 10, 3, 1973. Tamizuddin Khan, for instance, recalls that his family estate, 'in the close vicinity of the great erratic river Padma ... which has the habit of annually eroding', was washed away seven times. 'At the seventh erosion not only our homestead, but also the remnant of the landed estate was gone'. Tamizuddin Khan, *The Test of Time*, p. 2.

ian production even in the east. At the beginning of the century, productivity had began to decline and by the 1930s Bengal had become a net importer of rice.[3]

Much of the land in Bengal was cultivated by smallholding occupancy raiyats (cultivators)[4] but there was no single pattern of agrarian relations throughout the province. The Permanent Settlement had created a complex hierarchy of proprietary and tenurial interests in the land, with a range of intermediary tenures between the cultivating tenant and the revenue-paying zamindar.[5] Despite having to carry the burden of this large and unwieldy structure of rent-receiving interests, some sections of the peasantry had attained a measure of prosperity in the late nineteenth and early twentieth century that placed them a cut above the ordinary raiyat, while others had been reduced to the level of share-croppers (*bargadars* or *bhagchashis*) and agricultural labourers.[6] Prosperous peasants, now known in the literature by the generic term *jotedars*,[7] were, it has been suggested, able to combine to resist the demands of the zamindars for enhanced rents, transfer payments (*salami*) and other cesses (*abwabs*). The enactment of tenancy legislation, from the 1885 Act onwards, which strengthened tenurial 'customary' rights against proprietal privilege, gave defaulting tenants the protection of the law against the demands of their landlords, strengthening the hands of jotedars against zamindars.[8] The

[3] Rajat Kanta Ray, 'The Crisis of Bengal Agriculture', p. 260; Sugata Bose, *Agrarian Bengal. Economy Social Structure and Politics 1919–1947*, Delhi, 1986, pp. 44–45.
[4] In Bengal as a whole, 65.9 per cent of the land was tilled by occupancy raiyats or 'owner cultivators' as they were described in the 1931 Census, 21.1 per cent was cultivated by share-croppers and 13.1 per cent by hired labourers. See Partha Chatterjee, *Bengal 1920–1947 The Land Question*, Calcutta 1984, p. 41.
[5] 'In Bakarganj, for instance ... the tiers in the landholding structure were as follows: a *zamindari* estate of 2,000 acres at a revenue of Rs 200 was subdivided into 4 *talukdaris* each of 500 acres and a rent of Rs 100; 20 *osat talukdaris* at the next level, each of 100 acres and a rent of Rs 50; 80 *haoladaris*, each of 25 acres and Rs 25 rent; and finally, among 320 *raiyats*, each with a holding of 6.25 acres and paying a rent of Rs. 15.' *Ibid.*, p. 12. See also Tapan Raychaudhuri, 'Permanent Settlement in Operation: Bakarganj District, East Bengal' in R. E. Frykenburg (ed.) *Land Control and Social Structure in Indian History*, Madison, Wis., 1969.
[6] This argument was first put forward by Ratnalekha and Rajat Ray in the 1970s. See Ratnalekha Ray, *Change in Bengal Agrarian Society c. 1750–1850*, Delhi, 1979, Rajat Kanta Ray, 'The Crisis of Bengali Agriculture'; and Rajat and Ratna Ray, 'Zamindars and Jotedars: A study of Rural Politics in Bengal', in *Modern Asian Studies*, vol. 9, 1 (1975), pp. 81–102. The 'jotedar thesis' has since been developed and refined by other scholars, and continues to be the prevailing orthodoxy in the study of agrarian Bengal.
[7] The term jotedar was used to describe prosperous cultivators in North Bengal. In other areas, different terms were in use, such as *gantidar* in Jessore, *haoladar* in Bakarganj, and *chakdar* in southern Midnapore. To avoid confusion, the term jotedar will be used here to denote prosperous cultivators throughout the province.
[8] For an account of the ways in which colonial law inhibited the growth of full-fledged proprietorship in the land so as to protect the 'customary' rights of small-peasant pro-

introduction of cash crops such as sugar, jute and betel to the economy in the first decades of this century tended to hasten the process of differentiation amongst the raiyats, creating new opportunities for those peasant families who had a little cash and could hire the necessary labour for the cultivation of these new crops. Poorer peasant families, particularly in the eastern and northern districts, also took to the cultivation of jute, borrowing money from *dadani* merchants or moneylenders; but for these families, accumulating interest on their loans soon swallowed up any profits they might have made from the sale of jute, leaving them poorer than ever and trapped in a spiral of debt.

The extent of differentiation within the peasantry and the pattern of agrarian relations in rural Bengal varied from district to district and from region to region. Andre Beteille argued in 1974 that the jotedar-bargadar (rich peasant-sharecropper) nexus, and the high degree of differentiation it entailed, was limited to particular districts of North Bengal and to the newly reclaimed *abadi* areas of the 24 Parganas.[9] Sugata Bose, building on these foundations, argued more recently that the jotedar-bargadar pattern, in which the jotedar-tenant was powerful enough to resist the authority of the zamindar, was an exception to the general rule. In other parts of Bengal, the pattern was different: in the densely populated districts of East Bengal, the relatively undifferentiated smallholding peasantry was predominant, while in West Bengal, landlords were more closely involved in supervising production, particularly on their own 'demesnes' or *khas* lands, using agricultural labour, which was, Bose argues, a well-developed class in this region. There were no rich peasants, or jotedars, he suggests, except in the frontier areas in North Bengal and parts of the 24 Parganas only recently brought under cultivation. Further, he argues that zamindari power did not decline until the early thirties, for although the value of zamindari rents declined during the first three decades of the century, credit replaced rental income as the major source of wealth and power for a new breed of landlord-moneylenders or *taluqdar-mahajans*.[10]

ducers, see D. A. Washbrook, 'Law, State and Agrarian Society in Colonial India', *Modern Asian Studies*, vol. 15, 3 (1981). pp. 649–721.

[9] Andre Beteille, 'Class Structure in an Agrarian Society: The Case of the Jotedars', in his *Studies in Agrarian Social Structure*, New Delhi, 1974.

[10] Sugata Bose, *Agrarian Bengal*. Bose's model, therefore, contradicts the large body of literature which argues for the differentiation of the peasantry under colonial rule. See, for instance, Hamza Alavi, 'India: Transition from Feudalism to Capitalism' *Journal of Contemporary Asia*, vol. 10, 1980, pp. 359–398, and by the same author, 'India and the Colonial Mode of Production', in John Saville and Ralph Miliband (eds.), *Socialist Register*, London, 1975, pp. 160–197; Utsa Patnaik, *The Agrarian Question and the Development of Capitalism in India*, New Delhi, 1986 and by the same author, 'Class

Bose's 'typology' brings out local and regional varieties in the pattern of agrarian relations in rural Bengal. Moreover, it takes account of the increasingly central role of credit in small-peasant cultivation and the growing vulnerability of that economy to the vicissitudes of the world market. But there is evidence to suggest that he has overstated his case in arguing that a differentiated peasantry was an exception rather than the rule in twentieth-century Bengal, limited to a few pockets in the frontier regions of North Bengal and the Sunderbans. Admittedly, the extremely powerful and wealthy jotedar that Buchanan-Hamilton described[11] was a phenomenon peculiar to these few areas, but even a cursory glance at the literature reveals that more modestly prosperous peasants were to be found all over the province,[12] and that many of them, who had holdings which were too large to be cultivated by family labour, took to settling sharecroppers on their lands. Settlement operations in Pabna and Bogra in central Bengal revealed that 'influential and wealthy jotedars, who claim to be raiyats ... have extensive possessions farmed in barga',[13] and in Burdwan district in the West Bengal heartland, it was observed that share-croppers were used 'to an extent that is rather surprising by those raiyats whose holdings are too large to be conveniently cultivated by their own families'.[14] In Noakhali in East Bengal, the settlement officer remarked that several Muslim cultivators had 'risen to become middlemen *howladars* and *talukdars*, and even a few zamindars, but they are of the same [peasant] stock'.[15] In north Mymensingh, some tenants had 'risen in status by buying taluki shares'.[16] In his study of the Muslim village of Lohagarh in Birbhum, Hashim Amir Ali describes its inhabitants in these terms:

Differentiation within the Peasantry', *Economic and Political Weekly*, vol. 11, 1976, pp. 82–101. For the differentiation argument in Bengal, see Amit Bhaduri, 'The Evolution of Land Relations in Eastern India under British Rule', *Indian Economic and Social History Review*, vol. 13, 1976, pp. 45–58; Atiur Rahman, *Peasants and Classes: A Study in Differentiation in Bangladesh*, London, 1988; Partha Chatterjee, 'The Colonial State and Peasant Resistance in Bengal 1920–1947' *Past and Present*, vol. 110, 1986, pp. 168–204; the studies by Asok Sen, Partha Chatterjee and Saugata Mukherjee, *Three Studies on the Agrarian Structure of Bengal*, Calcutta, 1982; B. B. Chaudhuri, 'The Process of Depeasantisation in Bengal and Bihar, 1885–1947', *Indian Historical Review*, vol. 2, 1975–76, pp. 105–165, and Alan Smalley, 'The Colonial State and Agrarian Structure in Bengal', *Journal of Contemporary Asia*, vol. 13, 1983, pp. 176–197.
[11] Francis Buchanan-Hamilton, *A Geographical, Statistical and Historical Description of the District, A Zillah of Dinajpur in the Province, or Soubah of Bengal*, Calcutta, 1883.
[12] This has been demonstrated by Rajat Ray in a recent restatement of the 'jotedar thesis'. See Rajat Kanta Ray, 'The Retreat of the Jotedars?' *Indian Economic and Social History Review*, vol. 25, 2, 1988, pp. 237–247.
[13] D. Macpherson, *Survey and Settlement Report of Pabna and Bogra (1921–29)*, Calcutta, 1930, (hereafter SSR), p. 54. Also cited in Partha Chatterjee, *Bengal 1920–47*, p. 54.
[14] K. A. L. Hill, *Burdwan SSR (1927–34)*, Calcutta, 1940, p. 32.
[15] W. H. Thompson, *Noakhali SSR (1915–19)*, Calcutta, 1919, p. 27.
[16] F. A. Sachse, *Mymensingh SSR (1908–19)*, Calcutta, 1919, p. 41.

The richest of them has assets worth Rs 34,000 ... There are several others equal in economic status to the majority of Sadgops and Kayasthas. But by no means are all Muslim houses well-to-do. In fact the economic status of about half of them is equal to that of the low castes and untouchables – a third [are] even poorer than the households of these Lower Castes.[17]

Even the district of Faridpur in the heart of East Bengal had its rich peasants. Bose's typology relies heavily on J. C. Jack's study of Faridpur, in which he describes the cultivators as a 'homogenous class'.[18] But the same author in another passage refers to a class of Muslim 'prosperous cultivators', whose sons became 'Muhammedan traders, smaller land-owners and ... clerks'.[19] Tamizuddin Khan of Faridpur describes his father-in-law as being a 'well-to-do' tenant, whose 'superior landlords ... were Brahmins', and who had settled 'low-caste Hindu' under-tenants on his property. [20] Tamizuddin himself as a child went to a primary school whose proprietor 'Jhapu Khan ... was the richest Muslim in our locality. He had more lands than anyone else among his neighbours and was also a petty trader'.[21] The prosperous cultivator, thus, appears to have been a far more ubiquitous phenomenon than Bose's typology allows, and significantly, many of these jotedars appear to have been Muslims.[22]

Moreover, Bose's suggestion that zamindars as a rule had remained prosperous in the first decades of the century by becoming involved in moneylending on a large scale is not borne out by contemporary sources. In Mymensingh, the largest district in Eastern Bengal, the District Gazetteer reveals that the zamindar's share of the rent was less than that accrued by the 'ordinary jotedar': 'Cultivators holding under an immediate tenure holder ... pay a little more than those paying under a big landlord, and korfa ryots, or under-tenants holding under an ordinary jotedar, pay almost double.'[23] Sachse does not suggest that either the

---

[17] Hashim Amir Ali, *Then and Now, 1933–1958. A Study of Socio-Economic Structure and Changes in Some Villages near Viswa Bharati University Bengal*, New Delhi, 1966, p. 45.

[18] J. C. Jack, *Economic Life of a Bengal District*, Oxford, 1916, p. 81.

[19] *Ibid.*, pp. 68–69.

[20] Tamizuddin Khan, *The Test of Time*, p. 58.   [21] *Ibid.*, p. 8.

[22] Note that Jack refers to prosperous 'Muhammedan' cultivators in Faridpur, and the wealthy peasant proprietor of Tamizuddin Khan's primary school was a Muslim by the name of Jhapu Khan, and his 'well-to-do' father-in-law was a Muslim gentleman by the name of Bashiruddin Ahmed. Tamizuddin Khan, *The Test of Time*, p. 70. In Noakhali, the settlement officer noted that it was *Muslim* cultivators who had risen to become middlemen: in Burdwan, most *aimadars* with rent-free tenures were Muslims. See Andre Beteille, 'The Case of the Jotedars', p. 128. Most of the substantial jotedars encountered by F. O. Bell as settlement officer of Dinajpur were Muslims, while a few were Rajbangshis. See Bell's 'Notes on Rural travels in Dianjpur', 1939, in the F. O. Bell Papers, IOLR MSS Eur D/733/2.

[23] F. A. Sachse, *Mymensingh District Gazetteer*, Alipore, 1917, p. 32.

zamindars or the intermediate tenure holders were making a comfortable living out of moneylending: 'The bulk of the Hindu bhadralok are themselves petty *talukdars* and tenure-holders ... Those who cannot live on the rents they collect ... take service with the zamindars ... The great bulk of the land is held by a few big zamindars ... [but] the number of estates whose solvency is beyond question is strictly limited.'[24]

Most big zamindars were 'absentees' living in Calcutta, cheated by their 'corrupt and inefficient *amals*' (revenue collectors), and their estates were 'impoverished by litigation and wasteful expenditure'.[25] The absentee landlord, spending most of his time in the city, was hardly likely to be a prosperous moneylender. Rural usury proved profitable only if the moneylender was present in the village during the lean months of the year when the peasant had exhausted his small supply of rice, and was at hand after the harvest to collect his dues. Acharya Prafulla Chandra Ray, for instance, recalls that his father, who was heir to the considerable zamindari estate of Raruli in Jessore, took up moneylending after he had returned to the mofussil:

[My father] had to give up his studies prematurely because he was the only surviving son of my grandfather ... and there was no one at home to look after the family estates ... [He] was heir to landed estates fetching an annual income of nearly Rs 6,000 a year ... As he also had considerable cash in hand, he opened a moneylending business, which for several years was a profitable concern.[26]

But Roy's father moved back to Calcutta some years later, when his sons reached school-going age:

My father was naturally anxious that his sons should have the benefit of the best education then available ... [It was decided] that my parents should remove to Calcutta so that we might not be deprived of their personal care and healthy influence. But there were almost insuperable difficulties in the way of [this] ... plan. His estates consisted of a cluster of small *taluks* and he had embarked on the career of a miniature banker and moneylender in which capacity he advanced money to several people on mortgage of their landed properties. It was, therefore, incumbent on him that he should be on the spot in order to conduct his own affairs and not be away in distant localities for any length of time.[27]

The move to Calcutta may have had a beneficial effect on the boys' education: P. C. Ray grew up to become one of the most distinguished scientists of his time. But it evidently had a less salutary effect on the family's fortunes. By the time young Prafulla took his university entrance

---

[24] *Ibid.*   [25] *Ibid.*
[26] Prafulla Chandra Ray, *Life and experiences of a Bengali chemist*, Calcutta, 1932, pp. 10–11.
[27] *Ibid.*, pp. 23–24.

examinations, his father was 'now becoming involved in serious pecuniary embarrassments. His estates began to be sold one after another. From a creditor to a debtor is but one step ... My parents went home to the mofussil and resided there while my brothers and I went into lodgings.'[28]

For the many ambitious bhadralok families who settled in Calcutta or in the mofussil towns to seek education or employment, it grew increasingly difficult to ensure a steady flow of rent and interest payments from the family estate. Only resident zamindars and petty *talukdars* who remained in their villages could effectively run moneylending businesses, and even some of these, in Mymensingh at least, turned to salaried employment rather than usury to supplement their declining incomes from rent. The same pattern could be seen in other parts of Bengal, notably in Burdwan district. Here it was reported that 'landlords have become mere annuitants upon the land, taking little interest in their nominal estates beyond ensuring the payment of their rent', and that 'generally speaking the patnidars and dar-patnidars are as a body far wealthier than the landlords from whom they hold their leases'.[29] Similarly in Howrah, again in the heart of West Bengal, 'in rural tracts, the zamindars are mostly absentees living in Calcutta or other towns'.[30] This state of affairs did little to make zamindari estates economically viable and, in some cases, encouraged tenants to challenge the authority of their landlords. In Pabna, for instance:

Many large properties belong to non-resident zamindars, while minor estates have been split up and sublet to a large extent. This had closely affected the position of the tenants, for the power of landlords is greatest under compact well-managed estates and is weakened where estates are sub-divided and there are a number of petty share-holders constantly squabbling. As a result of this state of affairs, combinations of tenants against landlords are fairly common in the district, more especially in Sirajganj sub-division.[31]

Thus, even a cursory survey of contemporary reports suggests that the Sugata Bose model must be treated with caution. Even before the thirties, zamindari estates were getting weaker and poorer, and rentiers were not doing well. This was reflected in the gradual decline in the living standards of many urban bhadralok families in the twentieth century. The zamindars of Raruli, it has been seen, had to give up their Calcutta

---

[28] *Ibid.*, pp. 45–46.

[29] Patnidars and dar-patnidars were intermediary tenure-holders in the land, paying rent to the landlords and often sub-letting their holdings, at higher rents, to cultivators. J. C. K. Peterson, *Burdwan District Gazetteer*, Alipore, 1910, pp. 47.

[30] L. S. S. O'Malley and Manmohan Chakravarti, *Howrah District Gazetteer*, Alipore, 1909, p. 28.

[31] L. S. S. O'Malley, *Pabna District Gazetteer*, Alipore, 1923, p. 41.

establishment and retire to the district at the turn of the century: and even successful zamindars with extensive property, such as the Palchaudhuris of Mahesganj, were forced to diversify their investments and seek alternative sources of income as the value of rents declined in the first decades of this century.[32] But it was the smaller zamindars, the petty *taluqdars* and intermediary tenure-holders who were worst hit. The survey and settlement operations in Dacca revealed that new laws had created circumstances in which rent increases were 'hardly commensurate with the increase in the landed population, [and] the condition of the landlord classes, so far as they are dependent in their interest from land, must continue to deteriorate. The class of landlords which is most affected is the petty landlord, whether proprietor or tenure-holder.'[33]

Of the same group, J. C. Jack wrote in 1915:

Upon this class the rise in prices which has been constant for half a century and always increasing in intensity has had such a disastrous effect that too many live on the margin of starvation ... it is known that the number of unemployed among the bhadralok is large and the circumstances of many families are pitiful and their sufferings very great.[34]

It was from this class of petty landlords and taluqdars that most bhadralok were drawn. Some had stayed on in the mofussil as resident zamindars and taluqdars; others had been lured to the city by the new opportunities. Many of those who left the mofussil for the city began to feel the pinch as high prices and declining rentals hit their incomes. Salaried employment in the city was the way they tried to supplement their declining incomes. But such opportunities were limited and increasingly hard to come by. Only a handful of Indians found their way into the coveted posts in the higher levels of the bureaucracy; and establishing a career in the professions or in trade required resources and contacts which only a few of the bhadralok families possessed. Life in the city was competitive and most bhadralok families had to content themselves with ill-paid jobs in the lower rungs of the administration, in teaching and as clerks in private firms. As prices continued to rise, and as the real value of salaries and rentals declined apace, the economic basis of urban bhadralok society was gradually being eroded. As the previous chapter has suggested, this decline influenced the changing orientations of the politics of the urban bhadralok.

The rural gentry, on the other hand, who had remained in the mofussil living on their estates as resident zamindars and taluqdars, paradoxically

[32] Ratnalekha Ray, 'The Changing Fortunes of the Bengali Gentry', pp. 511–519.
[33] F. D. Ascoli, *Dacca SSR (1910–17)*, Calcutta, 1917, pp. 44–45.
[34] J. C. Jack, *Bakarganj SSR (1900–08)*, Calcutta, 1915, pp. 87–88.

found it easier to maintain their position. Zamindars with large estates could more effectively coerce their tenants to pay the full rental and extract other illegal dues through the employment of *gomastas* (peons), *paiks* (footmen) and *burkandazes* (messengers), and could keep a more watchful eye over their accountants and revenue collectors.[35] Several took to moneylending, charging extortionate interest, and, as most of their debtors were also their tenants, it was easier to enforce regular repayments.[36] In some parts of the province, particularly in the western districts, landlords increasingly began to commute cash rents into produce rents, bringing the lands of defaulting tenants under their own personal *khas* possession, and resettling their former cash-paying tenants into produce-paying *bargadars*, *adhiars* or *korfa raiyats*. This was one effective way of getting around the price rise: ensuring zamindars greater access to increasingly valuable produce in place of cash.[37] Many rural zamindari families had thus found new ways of maintaining their incomes and their hold over rural society.

But the Depression brought disaster even to the most successful resident zamindars and taluqdars. Of course there remains much debate about the extent of the zamindari crisis before 1929, but most observers agree that after the worldwide economic slump of that year, zamindari rents declined drastically.[38] In Bengal, the impact of the Depression was felt when agricultural prices, both of cash crops such as jute, grown in several parts of eastern and northern Bengal, and of the chief food crop, rice, came crashing down. Despite the efforts of some landlords to commute cash rents into produce rents, the rural economy of Bengal remained highly monetised in the 1930s. Most peasants on small and

---

[35] Akinobu Kawai, *Landlords and Imperial Rule: Change in Bengal Agrarian Society c. 1885–1940*, 2 vols., Tokyo, 1986 and 1987, in his study of four large zamindari estates demonstrates that all four estates continued to effectively collect their rental up to and beyond the First World War. Rajat Ray also agrees that some of the larger estates were able to function efficiently until the early thirties, but suggests that the smaller zamindaris were less successful, even before the Depression. Rajat Kanta Ray, 'The Retreat of the Jotedars?', p. 239.

[36] See Sugata Bose, *Agrarian Bengal*, pp. 100–105, for an account of *taluqdar mahajani* among those 'bhadralok' zamindars 'who remained on the land', p. 102.

[37] See Ramakrishna Mukherjee, *The Dynamics of a Rural Society. A Study of the Economic Structure in Bengal Villages*, Berlin, 1957; Partha Chatterjee in *Bengal 1920–1947*, and Sugata Bose, *Agrarian Bengal*.

[38] Rajat and Ratna Ray, 'Zamindars and Jotedars: a Study of Rural Politics in Bengal', and 'The Retreat of the Jotedars?', Sugata Bose, *Agrarian Bengal*, Akinobu Kawai, *Landlords and Imperial Rule*; Partha Chatterjee, *Bengal 1920–1947*; Asok Sen, Partha Chatterjee and Saugata Mukherji, *Three Studies on the Agrarian Structure of Bengal*; and Saugata Mukherji, 'Agrarian Class Formation in Modern Bengal, 1931–1951' *Economic and Political Weekly*, vol. 21, 4, 25 January 1986, pp. PE 11–PE 27, are all agreed on this point, though their emphases, of course, differ.

largely uneconomic holdings paid their rents and other, often more onerous, dues in cash, and tended to bring their crops to the market immediately after the harvest. As the population grew and plots were subdivided, the growing pressure on the land forced most peasant households to rely on credit to pay dues, invest in seeds, tools and cattle, for religious and ceremonial functions, and increasingly, simply to feed, clothe and house their families. In jute-growing districts, loans were often advanced through *dadani* merchants, associated with jute exporting firms in Calcutta. Generally, credit was easily available and debt more deeply entrenched in these districts, since jute was a capital-intensive crop and most peasants relied on advances to cultivate it each year. In other rice-growing areas, too, credit had become an essential part of the rural economy by the early 1930s. Interest on loans was unregulated and extortionate, and the effect was that once a peasant family took a loan, it was unlikely ever to be in a position to repay the principal. In this way the cycle of debt was passed from father to son and from one generation to the next.

The slump in prices in 1930 disrupted the whole precarious system. As jute prices came crashing down, jute exporting firms and *dadani* moneylenders simply stopped making advances. Peasants, receiving less than ever for their crop in the market, were no longer able to service their debts or pay their rents and dues. So professional *bania mahajans* and the resident taluqdars who had taken to *mahajani* or moneylending closed their doors to their erstwhile clients. Rural credit simply dried up. The effect on peasant households was catastrophic:

The crisis came in 1930 when owing to over-production of jute and the unprecedented slump in prices, the cultivators found themselves unable to meet their customary obligations in life. In normal times, they would have tided over the crisis by resorting to village mahajans, but on this occasion the source of supply was practically dried up. The village money-lenders scarcely have much accumulated balances; they deal in fluid cash, lending, realising and lending again. In 1930, the arrangement was reversed, they realised little, then debtors could not pay and prospective borrowers could not get relief.[39]

With the drastic fall in crop prices and the collapse of rural credit, many peasant families lost their access to cash and found themselves unable to meet the cash demands for rents and other dues imposed by the landlords. Zamindars, whose own survival was threatened by the sudden fall in rent and interest payments, responded harshly, and several went to the law to force peasants to pay up. Relations between landlords and their tenants

---

[39] Report of the District Magistrate of Tippera, 26 December 1931, Government of Bengal, Home Confidential Political Department (hereafter GB HCPB) File No. 849/31 (1–9).

rapidly deteriorated, with payments of rent and interest being at the centre of the conflict. More and more peasants began to resist the demands of their landlords, demonstrating what district officials described as a 'non-payment complex' or an unwillingness to recognise any obligation to pay rents or interest on outstanding loans. To begin with, withholding rents and interest payments may have been a spontaneous response to unprecedented hardship. But officials and zamindars began to suspect that the 'non-payment complex' was being encouraged and even organised by some local leaders. The effect was to polarise rural communities between rent-receivers and tenants. In Tippera, a densely populated, predominantly Muslim, riverine region, local Hindu land-owners formed a 'Shanti-Rakshini Samiti' ('association for the protection of peace') in Nabinagar town. The Samiti complained that:

Rank Bolshevism is being spread by a number of persons, who, taking advantage of the general economic distress prevailing in this quarter are taking recourse to various ways, either in mass meetings or in secret conclaves, by which people in general, peasants and cultivators, specially Muhammadans are asked to make a common cause against money-lenders, traders and landlords. The preachings of these designing persons have born fruit. Not only is there a sharp cleavage between capital and labour but suspensions of arrear rents and of payments of dues regarding loan bonds are already in evidence. Information is not lacking with regard to acts of violence perpetrated upon law-abiding citizens wanting to come to law courts for institution of suits against defaulting parties, dispossession of land or cutting away of paddies by organised groups ... The local market, which is owned by the local zamindar has been boycotted and ... general foodstuffs are not so easily available as before.[40]

Very quickly, the fall in rent and loan payments manifested itself in other parts of the province and by 1933, British administrators were commenting upon the spread of the 'non-payment complex' throughout Bengal. It was particularly marked in the jute-growing areas of eastern and northern Bengal, where, according to reports, there was 'no doubt that the cultivators, particularly in the Rajshahi, Chittagong and Dacca divisions [were] taking an interest in their own economic positions'.[41] Other than in Tippera, where a group of Congress workers made an attempt to channel local tenant unrest into the Civil Disobedience campaign, there is little evidence to suggest that there was much active work in the rural areas by the Congress, or, for that matter, by any other political party in the early 1930s. However, while not yet overlaid with any party-political or overtly communal colouring, the 'non-payment complex' was beginning seriously to threaten the economic power and social prestige of Bengal's land-

---

[40] A. B. Dutta to the Political Secretary, 4 December 1931, GB HCPB File No. 849/31 (1–9).
[41] GB HCPB File No. 873/33.

Table 3. *Sale and transfer of intermediary tenures: 1929–37*

District	Number of sales of tenure and mukarari holdings	
	1929–30	1937–38
Burdwan	6,537	14,619
Birbhum	3,914	5,788
Bankura	6,807	8,230
Hooghly	3,183	3,249
Howrah	2,936	6,206
Dacca	2,381[a]	3,038
Faridpur	2,914	3,925
Murshidabad	2,233[a]	3,126
Rangpur	277	1,033
Bogra	625	874

[a] Figures for 1929–30 were not available, so the figures for the following year, 1930–31, have been presented.
Source: Annual Reports of the Registration Department (Government of Bengal), 1929–30 and 1937–38; cited in Saugata Mukherji, 'Agrarian Class Formation', pp. PE 13–14.

owning and rent-receiving classes. Ever since the Permanent Settlement had been made more than a century ago, rent and debt payment had been the base upon which the entire structure of privilege in Bengal had rested, financing the lifestyles of Bengali elites, both Hindu and Muslim. Non-payment struck at the base of the edifice, affecting a large and powerful section of society. Among this section was the group described as the Hindu bhadralok: both the urban bhadralok, westernised, articulate and politically organised but maintaining ties with the land and with the estates that supported their rentier lifestyles and their country cousins, the high-caste Hindu landlords, who had so long maintained local power and status through zamindari, coupled in some cases with moneylending. It was this latter group, the rural gentry, which felt the impact of the Depression most severely. Many had been able to maintain their standard of living in the past decades by enforcing rent payments, by lending money and by commuting cash rents into produce rents wherever possible. But now these devices were meaningless: raiyats were showing a new defiance and were less inclined than ever to pay rents and other dues or to repay loans. Produce rents which could be collected on the threshing floor had very little value once crop prices had collapsed. With the onset of the Depression, several large zamindaris began to default on the payment of revenue, signalling a high 'degree of distress among superior tenure holders'.[42] Urban bhadralok families, already under economic pressure from declining rental incomes and high prices, now found it difficult to maintain their links with the land and large numbers of intermediary tenures were sold and transferred at throw-away prices (see table 3). The rise in the number of sales and transfers of mukarari holdings was particularly dramatic in the districts of the West Bengal heartland.[43] The Depression, therefore, had serious consequences for many bhadralok families, leaving some impoverished and others embittered by their battle to maintain their privileged position in Bengali rural society.

For the bulk of the peasants who struggled to eke a livelihood out of their tiny holdings, and were heavily dependent on credit to maintain their farms and their families, the Depression was an unmitigated disaster. Many of the smallest holdings were sold outright, and large numbers of peasants were resettled on former raiyati holdings as share-croppers.[44] But not all peasant families were so badly affected. For the small number of peasants who were fairly prosperous, the jotedars and substantial raiyats, the Depression created new opportunities for further advancement. As their plots provided them with yields that were more than adequate for family consumption, they could hold on longer to surplus stocks of grain and, either sell them during the lean season when crop prices were high, or alternatively, make loans of grain to their less fortunate neighbours. These loans were claimed back in kind, and with interest, after the harvest. Where the indebted peasant family could not repay these loans, their holdings passed into the hands of their creditors. Some jotedars acquired considerable properties in this way.[45] At the same time, under cover of the 'non-payment complex', these rich peasants could themselves avoid paying rents and dues to their superior landlords, making the most of the panic and confusion that followed the Depression to strengthen their hand against the zamindars. These were the ubiquitous jotedars, who in the thirties and forties 'began to loom large in the countryside',[46] making the most of the weakened position of their local zamindars and taluqdars and the destitution of their neighbours to expand their wealth and influence. The Depression thus created a climate of extreme

---

[42] See Saugata Mukherji, 'Agrarian Class Formation', p. PE-13.
[43] For full details of tenure sales and transfers, *ibid.*
[44] *Ibid.*, p. PE-15–16.
[45] *Ibid.*, p. PE-17. Also see Partha Chatterjee, *Bengal 1920–47*, pp. 142–165, for a detailed analysis of transfers of raiyati holdings and the increasing advance of grain-loans by jotedars.
[46] Rajat Kanta Ray, 'The Retreat of the Jotedars?', p. 240.

instability in agrarian Bengal, threatening the dominance of the rentier and moneylending classes and causing unprecedented hardship to the weakest sections of agrarian society, while at the same time strengthening the hand of the jotedars. These developments brought into being a new degree of social polarisation in the countryside.

In 1935, the Government of India Act set up the institutions through which these agrarian tensions were to be drafted into the mainstream of political activity, introducing party politics into the mofussil. The Act enlarged the electorate which now came to reflect the overwhelmingly rural character of Bengal more closely than before. In the Legislature, only twelve of the seventy-eight 'General' or Hindu seats were allocated to urban areas, the remaining sixty-six seats were reserved for rural constituencies. In the distribution of 'Muhammedan' seats, the rural weightage was even greater; here as many as 111 of the 117 Muslim constituencies were rural. Bengal politics, which had hitherto centred upon the metropolis of Calcutta and had revolved around primarily urban issues were now about to be pushed into the countryside. Until the changes introduced by the 1935 Act, the Bengal Congress had paid little heed to the countryside except for the occasional foray which agitational politics sometimes required. Neither the Non-Cooperation movement nor Civil Disobedience succeeded in penetrating the mofussil. No party had made a serious attempt to create an organisational base in rural Bengal. Now, suddenly, it was rural Bengal that mattered and any party or faction intending to achieve power in the provincial assembly had to win over the countryside.

The 1935 Act was followed by a scramble by parties and politicians of all hues to win the mofussil. Muslim politicians were particularly quick to respond to the challenge. The potential in the sheer weight of numbers that Muslims had in the countryside had long been understood by more perceptive Muslim leaders: the first peasant conference had been held as early as 1914 in Jamalpur in Mymensingh district. It was attended by a group of young Muslim leaders from Calcutta, including, notably, Akram Khan and Fazlul Huq. Neither of these men were of the usual brand of ashraf Muslim leaders, most of whom were scions of old families with old money and an education in old universities abroad. Mohammad Akram Khan of Hakimpur in the 24 Parganas had been born into a Muslim family of modest means, was educated at a local madrassa, and first made his name as a traditional Islamic scholar or *maulana*. In 1905, he had been associated with the formation of the progressive Bengal Provincial Mohammedan Association, was an ardent Khilafatist and went to prison in 1922 for being involved with seditious activities. He also founded several journals, including the *Mohammadi* and the *Azad*, which were widely read by Muslims in Calcutta.[47] By editing these journals, Akram Khan enhanced his standing as a prominent maulana.

Abul Kasem Fazlul Huq had a rather different background. He came from the Barisal subdivision of Bakarganj district in Muslim-dominated East Bengal. Although his family claimed ashraf or high status, they were in fact modest taluqdars,[48] and were Bengali-speakers to boot. Huq was therefore something of a country cousin, an outsider in the sophisticated world of the Persian-speaking notables who dominated Muslim politics in Calcutta. However, he compensated for his mofussil origins by having done exceptionally well in his studies and by his unusual skill in oratory. His life-long rival, Huseyn Shaheed Suhrawardy, himself a scion of one of the foremost Muslim families of Bengal, remembers Huq as 'a man of acutely active intelligence, colossal memory, great erudition and a deep insight into human character and mass psychology, ... [who] swayed the emotions and captured the imagination of the people of Bengal with his remarkable gift of oratory and fluency of language.'[49] Huq's schooling was entirely in Bengal but he did have a famous educationist and lawyer, Sir Asutosh Mookerjee, as his mentor when he turned to the law.[50] His early career in the law was in small district towns where he began to dabble in politics. Later, he joined government service, only to leave in 1912 when he failed to get the promotion he thought he deserved. Now a full-time politician, he was elected to the Bengal Legislative Council from Dacca, the first Muslim to be elected from a bhadralok stronghold by an electorate of Hindus and Muslims.

From the start, Huq's political career followed a convoluted and unpredictable course. He had been closely involved with the Muslim Educational Conference and the birth of the Muslim League in Dacca in 1906. Later, however, he turned up among the young Muslim nationalists and was one of the few Bengalis at the signing of the Lucknow Pact in 1916. The following year, Fazlul Huq held the Presidentship of the Congress as well as that of the All-India Muslim League when they held a joint session. In its early years, Huq had been actively involved in the Khilafat movement in Calcutta. However, he broke away from the main body of Khilafatists when the Non-Cooperation was launched in 1920, arguing that its proposed programme of boycotting government schools and

[47] Humaira Momen, *Muslim Politics in Bengal: A Study of Krishak Praja Party and the Elections of 1937*, Dacca, 1972, Appendix III, pp. 88–89.
[48] Harun-or-Rashid, *The Foreshadowing of Bangladesh. Bengal Muslim League and Muslim Politics 1936–47*, Dhaka, 1987, p. 64.
[49] M. H. R. Talukdar (ed.), *Memoirs of Huseyn Shaheed Suhrawardy*, Dacca, 1987, p. 104.
[50] Rajmohan Gandhi, *Understanding the Muslim Mind*, New Delhi, 1988, p. 190. For full biographical details, see A. S. M. Abdur Rab, *A. K. Fazlul Huq*, Lahore, 1966.

colleges would hit Muslim students in particular. As a member of the legislative council, Huq had been closely involved in the efforts to set up schools and colleges for Muslims which went down well with the Muslim 'middle class ... [who] adored him ... because he had provided them with jobs, established colleges, schools and brought opportunities to life'.[51] Huq's politics were a curious mix of his own brand of secular nationalism, Bengali patriotism and Muslim populism; he gave priority to one or the other according to circumstance. He was an opportunist who managed to believe in what he was doing at any given time, and his fabled warmth and generosity made him one of the best-loved leaders of Bengal.

Both Akram Khan and Fazlul Huq represented a new group in Muslim politics. A growing number of Bengali Muslim families were now taking advantage of the new opportunities that Muslims had been given in education and employment once it became British policy consciously to favour Muslims in these arenas.[52] Many of these families, like that of Fazlul Huq, belonged to the 'lesser' rural *ashraf*,[53] but some were drawn from the ranks of well-to-do peasants or jotedars, whose emergence has been discussed above. In 1914, the Committee on Mohammedan Education was pleased to note that more Muslims were going to school, explaining this by the fact that 'the cultivators have recently profited from the jute trade and this has been accompanied by a growing interest in English education'.[54] In the first four decades of the century, Muslims doubled their share of those at school from just over a quarter to more than half.[55] But more than half the Muslim students did not continue their studies after primary school, and in 1940, Muslims numbered less than one in five of the students in arts colleges and just over one in ten in colleges of professional training. Muslim students from peasant families who came to town in search of further education were often too poor to stay in hostels and stayed with relatives, paying for their board by helping to tutor the children of host familes. This was the system of *jagirthaka* that enabled some poor Muslims to go to secondary schools and colleges

[51] Kazi Ahmed Kamal, *Politicians and Inside Stories: A glimpse mainly into the Lives of Fazlul Huq, Shaheed Suhrawardy and Moulana Bashani*, Dacca, 1970, p. 1.
[52] See Tazeen M. Murshid, 'The Bengal Muslim Intelligentsia, 1937–77. The tension between the Religious and the Secular', University of Oxford, D.Phil. thesis, 1985, for a study of the emergence of the Muslim intelligentsia in colonial Bengal.
[53] The term 'lesser *ashraf*' is used by Rafiuddin Ahmed to describe Bengali-speaking families who could lay claim to foreign ancestry and possibly had some property and wealth to back up their claims. See Rafiuddin Ahmed, *The Bengal Muslims 1871–1906. A Quest for Identity*, New Delhi, 1988, p. 15.
[54] *Report of the Committee on Muhammedan Education*, 1914, cited in Tazeen Murshid, 'The Bengali Muslim Intelligentsia', p. 17.
[55] The figure was 27.7 per cent in 1901/2 and 54.1 per cent in 1939/40. *Ibid.*, p. 43

in the towns.[56] Tamizuddin Khan, for instance, left his village in Faridpur for distant Cooch-Behar to enrol there in the free College. But even though there were no fees to be paid, he would not have been able to study there if a professor of Persian at the College, who 'used to do his best for students' placed in circumstances like Tamizuddin's, had not found his young protégé a place as a 'resident student-cum-tutor' at the house of a Muslim Sub-Inspector of Police.[57] He later won a place at the Scottish Churches College in Calcutta, but was still 'too poor to stay in the Jubilee Hostel. Seeing [his] difficulties, the Superintendent of the hostel found [him] a 'jagir', the position of a resident tutor at [the] house of Mr Hassibuddin Ahmed who was then a Munsiff.'[58] Eventually, Tamizuddin Khan graduated with honours, becoming the first Muslim from Faridpur district to do so.

This story was typical of the struggle of most Muslim boys who reached university. They were 'first-generation' students,[59] the sons of peasants who had ambitions for their children. The young men, who went on to become teachers, clerks, munsiffs and pleaders in mofussil towns, remained culturally rooted in their rustic ways, speaking in the rough vernacular, dressing and eating like the country people that they were. J. C. Jack, in his study of Bakarganj, Fazlul Huq's home district, gave this description of the Muslim educated:

[They] live in every respect in the same way as the cultivators from whom they sprang. This applies to Muhammadan traders, to most of the small Muhammadan landowners and to Muhammadan clerks who are generally sons of the most prosperous cultivators and whose habits and standards of living conform in all respects with those of their fathers.[60]

Not all these would-be scholars were able to get at an 'English' education; some Muslims had to settle for instruction at the local seminaries, the maktabs and madrassas. In 1917, the Director of Public Instruction in Bengal commented on this new trend: that 'the successful Muslim cultivator of these parts who desires to educate his son will send him to a Madrassa to learn Moslem law, literature, logic, rhetoric and philosophy and to study Hadis and Tafsir'.[61] By the beginning of the twentieth century, growing numbers of ordinary rural families without social

[56] Interview with Professor Abdur Razzak, Dhaka, 11–13 February 1990. I am grateful to Professor Razzak for sharing with me his knowledge and insights on the question of Muslim education in Bengal.
[57] Tamizuddin Khan, *The Test of Time*, pp. 63–64.   [58] *Ibid.*, p. 69.
[59] Interview with Professor Abdur Razzak.
[60] J. C. Jack, *Economic Life of a Bengal District*, p. 68.
[61] Cited in Rafiuddin Ahmed, *The Bengal Muslims*, p. 142.

pretensions were getting their sons into such schools and many of these boys went on to become mullahs, gaining status in village society as religious leaders. The education in madrassas was different and lower than that in the English secondary schools, so the madrassa-educated Muslim found it difficult to get to universities or compete successfully for secular employment in the city.[62] In any event, only a tiny fraction of the total number of school-going Muslims went to madrassas.[63]

It was this Muslim intelligentsia, ashraf in its aspirations[64] but usually lowly in its origins, lifestyle and culture which came to the fore in Bengali politics in the 1930s. Until then, a Muslim politician such as Huq had been preoccupied with urban matters. Most leaders had concentrated upon the battle against bhadralok dominance in schools, universities, municipalities and councils, and had pressed for reservations and safe-guards for their community. Now, as the mofussil opened up and large numbers of more prosperous Muslim peasants were given the vote by the 1935 Act, leaders such as Fazlul Huq, Tamizuddin Khan and Akram Khan saw the chance to make their mark on provincial politics. Fluent in colloquial Bengali, familiar with the aspirations and cultural idioms of their rural fellows, they could more convincingly project themselves as the spokesmen of the Muslim peasantry than the notables who had tradi-tionally dominated Muslim politics. They were the men who led the Krishak Praja Party; and they helped to shape the *krishak* (or peasant) movement in Bengal.

The Krishak Praja Party was set up by some Muslims in the Legis-lative Council who were spurred by the Bengal Tenancy Act of 1928 to form a pressure group to protect the tenants and the labourers.[65] Foremost amongst them was Fazlul Huq, who was elected leader of the 'Council Praja Party' as it came to be known, and Tamizuddin Khan, who became its secretary. In 1929, this group formed the Nikhil Banga Praja Samity (the All Bengal Peasant Association) to provide support outside the Council, with Akram Khan as its first secretary and Fazlul

[62] *Ibid.* pp. 27–32.
[63] The proportion of Muslim students in madrassas rose from under 0.81 per cent in 1881/82 to 4.89 per cent in 1926/27. Tazeen Murshid, 'The Bengal Muslim Intelligentsia', pp. 45–46. Rafiuddin Ahmed has tended to overemphasise the popularity of madrassas in Muslim education. Murshid's work suggests that religious education was a second-best option, chosen by many Muslims for its relative cheapness and accessibility rather than in preference to secular vernacular or western education.
[64] Some of the more successful Muslim middle-class families attempted to achieve ashraf status (or ashrafise), by marrying into sharif households and by adopting ashraf-style names and titles: gaining the status of '*atrap-bhalamanus*' (low-born gentleman). See Rafiuddin Ahmed, *The Bengal Muslims*, p. 27.
[65] *The Bengalee*, 3 July 1929; cited in Harun-or-Rashid, *The Foreshadowing of Bangladesh*, p. 32.

Huq as one of its vice-presidents. In the early thirties, the new organisation held conferences in the mofussil on agrarian matters, and began to link up some of the many *krishak samitis* (cultivators' associations) which had mushroomed in eastern Bengal during the Depression.

However, this new organisation did not attract much attention until 1935, when the Government of India Act came out of the statute book.[66] Suddenly, the Nikhil Banga Praja Samity became the focus of much hectic attention, attracting a wide range of Muslim politicians from the city. Abul Mansur Ahmed, a prominent krishak activist, recalls in his memoirs, that 'the Praja Samity was, in 1935, a multi-party affair. It included in its ranks Congressmen and anti-Congress Muslim leaders, loyalists and nationalists. Muslims of all parties, leaders and workers were present within its fold'.[67] As the only Muslim organisation that could claim agrarian leanings, the Praja Samity was the bandwagon upon which Muslims of all colours jumped in order to win the semblance of support to establish their credentials as peasant leaders. In the same year, the Presidential Chair fell vacant, and in no time, the various groups began to compete for the control of the Samity. Two competing groups were formed around Akram Khan and Fazlul Huq to try to win the presidency. Akram Khan's group was backed by powerful urban bosses such as Huseyn Shaheed Suhrawardy, who had little interest in agrarian organisation but recognised the importance of the rural vote. Fazlul Huq's camp included many younger activists, such as Abul Mansur Ahmed of Mymensingh, Shamsuddin Ahmed of Nadia and Syed Nausher Ali of Jessore, all 'English' educated professionals[68] who supported the Congress and saw themselves as a radical and progressive alternative to the old-style leadership.[69] In true Bengali fashion the struggle for the control of the Samity eventually tore it apart: Huq led a breakaway faction which gave itself the title of the Krishak Praja Party or the Peasants and Tenants Party; Akram Khan continued to lead the rump of the Nikhil Banga Praja Samity for the few months that it survived until in its turn it was absorbed by the Muslim League.

When Huq's men left the Praja Samity they took with them most of the existing krishak organisation, and quickly set to work to establish a host

---

[66] Nor did Huq and his coterie take much interest in the Praja conferences held in the mofussil. Thus early in 1935, Huq consented to inaugurate a Praja Conference in Dacca but failed to keep his appointment. Bazlur Rahman Khan, *Politics in Bengal 1927–36*, Dhaka, 1987, p. 31.

[67] Abul Mansur Ahmed, *Amar Dekha Rajnitir Panchash Bachhar*, Dacca, 1970, p. 91.

[68] Harun-or-Rashid, *The Foreshadowing of Bangladesh*, p. 64.

[69] Abul Mansur Ahmed, *Amar Dekha Rajnitir Panchash Bachhar*, p. 92.

of new samitis in those localities of northern and eastern Bengal where they could muster support. In May 1936, a branch was set up in Natore in the Rajshahi district,[70] that month the District Magistrate of Mymensingh reported that many praja samitis had been established in his district, and that 'in most cases this [was] part of an election campaign to the new [Assembly]'. The man providing the drive behind this Krishak Praja Party campaign in Mymensingh was Abul Mansur Ahmed, whose memoirs throw light upon the early days of the krishak movement in Bengal. At the time, Ahmed was 'a young but unsuccessful pleader, a good speaker and a good Bengali writer'. The Mymensingh krishak campaign was financed by Maulvi Abdul Majid, a retired Deputy Magistrate, who, according to the District Magistrate of Mymensingh, was 'such a fool that in the vain hope of becoming the Chairman of the District Board he would readily part with his hard earned money'.[71] The Nawab of Dhanbari and his son Hassan Ali set up a local printing press known as the 'Milan Prem' press, which brought out the Krishak Praja Party's journal, *Chashi* ('The Cultivator').[72] All of this hinted at the beginnings of an ominous trend for the Raj: some of its erstwhile collaborators in the rural localities were beginning to put their toes into the murky waters of electoral politics.

The leaders of the newly organised Krishak Praja Party had varied origins. Some were neither krishaks nor prajas (tenants). Fazlul Huq, just as Abul Mansur Ahmed, had begun his career as a lawyer in a provincial town and Majid had been a civil servant. Shamsuddin Ahmed, another prominent krishak leader and a founder member of the Krishak Praja party, was a lawyer from Nadia district. Others had more humble origins. Tamizuddin Khan's father was a smallholding cultivator who had a tiny three-acre plot in Faridpur,[73] Shah Abdul Hamid came from a family of small jotedars in Mymensingh[74] while Nausher Ali 'had begun life as a process server in the Civil Court in the Narail sub-division'.[75] Most of these men had acquired some education and had made their careers in mofussil towns, while retaining the cultural mannerisms of the countryside. Abul Mansur Ahmed, though a well-educated lawyer, was described as 'a zealous worker who does not aim at self aggrandisement and whose

[70] Report of the Rajshahi Divisional Commissioner, Local Officers Fortnightly Confidential Reports, (hereinafter LOFCR) for the first fortnight of May 1936, in GB HCPB File No. 56/36.
[71] Report of the Dacca Divisional Commissioner, *ibid.*
[72] Abul Mansur Ahmed, *Amar Dekha Rajnitir Panchash Bachhar*, p. 102.
[73] Tamizuddin Khan, *The Test of Time*, p. 3.
[74] Bazlur Rahman Khan, *Politics in Bengal*, p. 27, n. 125.
[75] P. D. Martyn Memoirs, IOLR MSS Eur F/180/13.

humble ways appeal to the ordinary cultivator'.[76] These were men able to win the confidence of the new rural voters: most of whom were jotedars who had acquired enough property to get the vote under the new franchise. Under Huq's leadership, many jotedars of this sort were recruited into the party: by 1937, five jotedars had joined eleven 'professionals' and two former government servants on its Election Board.[77]

The proclaimed objective of the Praja Party was to abolish zamindari without compensation. Its manifesto called for rents to be remitted and debts to be written off. These were prospects bound to please peasants, exciting millenarian hopes among the poor and lowly. But the slogan which dominated the Krishak Praja Party programme, 'Down with Zamindari', was one that reflected the aspirations of the richer peasants, who held occupancy rights direct from the zamindars. It was they who were the most vocally critical of zamindari powers which stood in the way of their economic and social betterment. For the poorer under-tenants, lower down the scale, the oppressors were less the zamindar than the occupancy tenant or patnidar from whom they held the land, and to whom they paid rent, usually at a far higher rate than that paid to the zamindar. However, the 'neo-populist' rhetoric[78] of the krishak leaders glossed over these differences within the peasantry and singled out the zamindar and moneylender as its target. The choice of the zamindar and moneylender as the focus of krishak agitation was designed to make the most of such cultural unity and common purpose that the very different Muslim groups the Krishak Praja Party was trying to bring together possessed. Prosperous cultivators, Muslims of the middling sort, small traders, clerks and petty landowners and 'the cultivators from whom they sprang' who all shared the same 'habits and standards of living',[79] could all rally behind a campaign against the zamindar and moneylender, who were characterised as Hindu oppressors of the Muslim people. As Jack points out, the gulf between ordinary man and the bhadralok Hindu zamindar, rentier or bania was there for all to see:

Landowners, clerks, professional men such as doctors, lawyers and priests form a class apart. They are of the three higher castes and have for centuries lived in a different manner from the *ordinary population*. They have more wants and more ways of spending their money; they eat less but better food with greater variety, their houses are built on a different plan and are better furnished; their clothes

---

[76] Report of the Rajshahi Divisional Commissioner, LOFCR for the first fortnight in May 1936, GB HCPB File No. 56/36.
[77] Harun-or-Rashid, *The Foreshadowing of Bangladesh*, p. 65.
[78] See T. J. Byres, *Charan Singh, 1902–1987: An Assessment*, Patna, 1988, for a discussion of 'neopopulism'.
[79] J. C. Jack, *Economic Life of A Bengal District*, p. 68.

although the same in cut display more quality and colour ... Another class which has a standard of living of its own, different on the one hand from that of the working classes and on the other hand from the 'respectable' classes, is the Hindu shopkeepers ... their families tend to be numerous, they keep several servants, their houses are large, well built and well furnished, they expend a certain amount upon the education of children and much larger sums than the working classes upon domestic events.[80]

The Krishak Praja Party seized the opportunity to present itself as the tribune of the 'ordinary population' against the elites, not only the Hindu bhadralok but even the wealthier Muslims who traditionally had dominated the scene. The stamp of the mofussil had, in the past, relegated men like Fazlul Huq to being country cousins of urban sophisticates who ruled the roost in Calcutta. But now, for Huq and his fellows in the Krishak Praja Party, these rustic origins were coming to prove a valuable asset, which, if skilfully deployed, could give them the means to wrest power from their adversaries. But they had to find the right rural backing: men with local weight and a command over the votes who could be enrolled by the Krishak Praja Party in its battle against the old bosses. There were many jotedars eager in the aftermath of the Depression to capitalise upon their gains and bid for a share of power. The Krishak Praja Party's manifesto in true populist style declared its commitment to 'the needs and requirements of the people',[81] but it was designed to attract the jotedar group in particular. It demanded the abolition of the Permanent Settlement, the reduction and capping of land rent, the annulment of the zamindari right of pre-emption, the abolition of other cesses including *abwab* and *nazar-salami* and the establishment of Debt Settlement Boards:[82] all measures that would strengthen the hand of tenant-proprietors who were pressing up against entrenched zamindari positions. The party leadership and its manifesto failed to address other problems which flowed from the increasing stratification of the peasantry: the expansion of jotedar prosperity at the expense of their less fortunate neighbours, the increasing incidence of transfers and sales of plots by smallholding peasants and the rising number of impoverished share-croppers and agricultural labourers. This laid the Krishak Praja party open to the charge of being a 'jotedar party'. As Abul Mansur Ahmed candidly admitted, there was truth in this allegation:

---

[80] *Ibid.*, p. 69. Emphasis added.
[81] Shila Sen, *Muslim Politics in Bengal 1937–1947*, New Delhi, 1976, p. 79.
[82] Details of the Krishak Praja Party programme and manifesto may be found in Humaira Momen, *Muslim Politics in Bengal*; Shila Sen, *Muslim Politics in Bengal*; Bazlur Rahaman Khan, *Politics in Bengal*; and Harun-or-Rashid, *The Foreshadowing of Bangladesh*.

Bengal's krishak movement was criticised by many as being a jotedar movement. In absolute terms, their accusations held a great deal of truth ... but were, for that era, a kind of ultra-leftism ... According to my knowledge and belief, then the Praja movement was a natural and spontaneous people's movement, appropriate to the needs of the time.[83]

The Krishak Praja Party was thus the agency by which the jotedars, mainly Muslim and newly enfranchised, came out of the wings onto the centre stage of Bengal politics. In the past Muslim jotedars had played little part in provincial politics, though they had begun to make their mark in the localities. Their growing strength on Local Boards throughout Bengal suggests that by the mid-thirties, Muslims had learnt to use joint electorates to their advantage, even in districts where they were in a minority.[84] By 1936, thirteen districts were firmly under Muslim control,[85] and in two others, Murshidabad and Malda, Muslims held exactly half of all the seats on Local Boards. In that year, Muslims held just over half of all Local Board seats in Bengal as a whole.[86]

This increase in Muslim local influence reflected, in turn, the growing prosperity of a section of Muslim cultivators, particularly in the northern districts where 'most union board presidents would be found to belong to the jotedar class with from 30 to 300 acres of land'.[87] Now that these jotedars, hitherto confined in the districts and localities, had been given an entrance into provincial politics, the Krishak Praja Party proved a convenient platform from which they could make their presence felt. In this way, the bitter conflicts that had come to plague the countryside during the Depression had entered the provincial arena. Tensions between zamindars and their tenants, between moneylenders and debtors and between jotedars and share-croppers, which in the past had been both sporadic and confined to the localities now came to spill into the politics of the province. In the past agrarian conflict had sometimes taken on a

[83] Abul Mansur Ahmed, *Amar Dekha Rajnitir Panchash Bachhar*, p. 63.
[84] By 1936, Muslims held 38 per cent of the seats on the Katwa Local Board in Burdwan, 44.4 per cent in the Rampurhat subdivision of Birbhum district, 25 per cent in Uluberia Local Board in Howrah, 46.6 per cent in Basirhat and 50 per cent in Baraset, both in the 24 Parganas. All these localities had large Hindu majorities. *Resolutions Reviewing the Reports on the Working of District, Local and Union Boards in Bengal, 1936*, appendix G.
[85] These were Jessore (60.2 per cent), Dacca (57.8 per cent), Mymensingh (73.4 per cent), Faridpur (59.4 per cent), Bakarganj (64.1 per cent), Chittagong (73.3 per cent), Tippera (63.8 per cent), Noakhali (73.3 per cent), Rajshahi (64.4 per cent), Dinajpur (56.8 per cent), Rangpur (64.8 per cent), Bogra (74.17 per cent) and Pabna (66.6 per cent). *Ibid.*
[86] The figure had risen from 46.8 per cent to 50.8 per cent between 1935–6 and 1936–7. *Ibid.*
[87] F. O. Bell, Dinajpur SSR, pp. 16–17. See also F. O. Bell's 'Notes on Rural Travels in Dinajpur, 1939', IOLR MSS Eur D/733/2, pp. 42, 74.

communal colouring in some local pockets,[88] now it contributed powerfully to the polarisation of the province's politics along communal lines.
As tenancy laws, proprietary rights, interest rates and the Permanent
Settlement itself came under a concerted attack from chiefly Muslim
'krishak' representatives in the new Assembly, the predominantly Hindu
beneficiaries of the zamindari system were forced to join together in
combinations which were increasingly communal in composition and in
tone.[89]

This is not to suggest, however, that the jotedar–zamindar contest was
directly translated into communal terms as a conflict specifically between
Hindus and Muslims. Nor is to argue, in the manner of Rajat and Ratna
Ray, that 'it was the conflict between *zamindar* and *jotedar* in East Bengal
which constantly fed the Muslim separatist movement in the province as a
whole and led ultimately to the partition of Bengal in 1947'.[90] Admittedly
the vast majority of landlords were high-caste Hindus, and most peasants
and many jotedars were Muslims. However, there was a not insignificant
number of Muslim landlords, particularly in East Bengal. Men such as the
Nawab of Dacca and Khwaja Mohiuddin Faroqui owned vast estates
spreading over several districts. Significantly Krishak Praja leaders were
usually keen to play down their communal leanings, and, in the campaign
for the Assembly elections, purposely chose prominent Muslim zamindars as targets to demonstrate their impartiality. Thus, in August 1936,
Fazlul Huq addressing a crowd of 4,000 Muslims in Comilla in Tippera
district launched 'an extremely bitter attack on zemindars [*sic*] in general
and Sir Nazimuddin and Sir K. G. M. Faroqui in particular, whom he
accused of spending public money on their own election campaigns, and
disregarding the interests of the poor'.[91] The programme and style of the

---

88 See for instance, Tanika Sarkar's study of the Dacca and Kishoreganj riots in 1930:
'Communal Riots in Bengal' in Mushirul Hasan (ed.), *Communal and Pan-Islamic Trends
in Colonial India*, New Delhi, 1985. More recently, Suranjan Das has emphasised the
underlying class basis of 'communal' riots in agrarian Bengal in the first decades of this
century. Suranjan Das, 'Communal Riots in Bengal, 1905–1947', University of Oxford,
D.Phil thesis, 1987.
89 Bazlur Rahman Khan's argument that the KPP should be seen 'as a political platform for
a section of the Bengali Muslim middle class from which to attack both caste Hindu and
traditional Muslim leadership', while raising the important question of the nature of the
political ambitions of the middle-class KPP leadership, ignores the vitally significant
rural jotedar component in the party. It was this section that constituted a new force in
Bengal politics, which, by dragging agrarian conflict from the distant mofussil into the
Assembly added a new dimension and gave a new direction to provincial politics. B. R.
Khan, *Politics in Bengal*, p. 29.
90 Rajat and Ratna Ray, 'Zamindars and Jotedars: a study of Rural Politics in Bengal',
p. 101.
91 Report by the Chittagong Divisional Commissioner, GB LOFCR for the first fortnight of
May 1936.

Krishak Praja movement was not couched in religious terms, and even
though the Party contested only Muslim seats in the elections it tried to
maintain a non-communal stance. It was not the Krishak Praja Party but
the traditional Muslim ashraf leaders, both urban and rural, who made
much of Muslim solidarity in an effort to win the new Muslim vote.

In May, 1936, as a result of an initiative of Nawab Habibulla of Dacca,
a new Muslim party was formed 'to fight the election on the basis of a
definite political programme'.[92] Set up at the Calcutta residence of the
Nawab of Dacca, the party was intended to take the place of the provincial Muslim League, which had by this time fallen into decay. Styling itself
as the 'United Muslim Party', its first president was of course the Nawab;
another Nawab, Musharraf Hossain of Jalpaiguri, was its vice-president,
Huseyn Shaheed Suhrawardy was its secretary, and the Calcutta merchant, Hassan Ispahani, its treasurer. The new party was in fact an
electoral alliance between several of the most prominent and powerful
Muslim families of Bengal. If these families were to enter the political
kingdom promised to them by the Communal Award and the 1935 Act,
and fight off the challenge of the new Krishak Praja Party, they had to
bury their own rivalries and unite against their new competitors. As this
alliance was the heart and centre of the new Bengal Provincial Muslim
League and was to play a vital role in political developments, the antecedents of its members must be examined.

The Dacca Nawabs were originally prosperous hide merchants from
Kashmir who had moved first to Delhi and then to Bengal in the
eighteenth century. After the Permanent Settlement of 1793, the family
put its money into land, purchased from the profligate Nawabs of Bengal.
In the years that followed, they married into local families who helped
them to strengthen their hold over new territory. In 1835 they purchased a
dilapidated French factory building, refurbished it in the style of the old
Nawabs and christened it 'Ahsan Manzil'. This palatial residence on the
banks of the river Padma became a hot bed of intrigue: in later times it
was to become a headquarters of the Muslim League, not only for Dacca
but for all Bengal. In 1875, the Government gave Abdul Ghani the title of
'Nawab' in belated recognition for being conspicuously loyal during the
1857 revolt and the title was made hereditary two years later.[93]The family
did well in the next few decades under the patronage of the British, to
whom they remained unswervingly loyal until the partition of Bengal
was revoked in 1912. And although Nawab Salimulla died in 1916

[92] *The Statesman*, 25 May 1936.
[93] An interesting history of the first family of Dacca is provided by Kazi Ahmed Kamal,
Politicians and Inside Stories, pp. 116–117.

disillusioned with his patrons, his descendants stuck to the family tradition of loyalty to the Raj and kept away from the Khilafat agitation.

In the twenties, the family rose to new heights. Khwaja Nazimuddin, a
cousin of the Nawab, showed that the faithful could still expect handsome
rewards from their grateful masters:

Short statured with a bulging pear-like figure, he was known for his insatiable
appetite and his unfailing submission to the . . . Britishers . . . Dressed in 'sherwani'
and breeches-like 'choordiar-pyjamas' with a 'fez' (Turkish) cap and wearing little
shoes, he carried a . . . cane with a knob and represented an age and a tradition.[94]

Educated at Cambridge, Nazimuddin returned to become Chairman of
the Dacca Municipality. In due course he became Minister of Education
in 1929, and finally in 1934, he was appointed to the Viceroy's Executive
Council. His family stuck to its 'Persian' pretensions, married into prominent North Indian Muslim families and made a point of speaking only in
Urdu or English. By 1934, the family estates covered 'almost 200,000
acres and [was] spread over some seven Districts in E[astern] Bengal
together with property in Shillong, Assam, and with a rent roll . . . of some
£120,000 a year'.[95] With its wealth, social status and close relationship
with the Raj, the family of the Nawab of Dacca was the single most
powerful Muslim family in Bengal.

The treasurer of the new party, Hassan Ispahani, was one of the
wealthiest Muslim merchants in the province. The Ispahani family were
originally Persian traders, who had established themselves in Bombay and
Madras in the nineteenth century. The indigo trade brought them to
Bengal at the turn of the century. They set up their headquarters in
Calcutta in 1900, and went on to become a major export house, with a
branch office in London.[96] The family had played a significant part both
in the Khilafat Movement in the twenties, providing leaders and money.
In 1932, the younger Ispahani established the 'New Muslim Majlis' in
Calcutta. Hassan had studied at St John's College, Cambridge, and was
called to the Bar in 1924. On his return to Calcutta, he joined the family
business, 'M. M. Ispahani, Ltd.', and in 1933 was elected to the Calcutta
Corporation.[97] Through Ispahani, the United Muslim Party was able to
forge a connection with Calcutta's Muslim merchants, many of whom
helped to finance the Khilafat Movement.

---

[94] S. Rahmatullah Memoirs, IOLR MSS Eur F/180/4.
[95] P. D. Martyn Memoirs, IOLR MSS Eur F/180/13. Martyn was the Chief Manager of the
Nawab's estate in 1933–34.
[96] Kenneth Macpherson, *The Muslim Microcosm*, p. 121. For full biographical details, see
M. A. H. Ispahani, *Qaid-i-Azam Jinnah as I Knew Him*, Karachi, 1966.
[97] Z. H. Zaidi (ed.), *M. A. Jinnah-Ispahani Correspondence – 1936–1948*, Karachi, 1976.

The third founding member of the new Muslim party was Huseyn Shaheed Suhrawardy. Suhrawardy belonged to the leading ashraf family of Bengal, which claimed an ancestry going back to the first caliph. In the twentieth century, the Suhrawardy family did exceptionally well out of the new opportunities that British rule in Bengal offered adept Muslims. Huseyn's uncle, Hasan Suhrawardy rose to become the first Muslim Vice-Chancellor of Calcutta University. Huseyn himself married into the family of Sir Abdur Rahim, a prominent Muslim leader in the twenties.[98] Huseyn started his political career during the Khilafat Movement and was the secretary of the Khilafat Committee for several years. Like other Khilafatists in the early twenties, he joined the Swarajya Party and was appointed Deputy Mayor of the Calcutta Corporation after the Das Pact had been signed. In 1926, however, after the Calcutta riots, Suhrawardy broke with the Swarajya party and turned his energies to the trade union movement in Calcutta. In the next few years, he 'organised a large number of labour unions and employees unions, some communal and some general, such as seamen, railway employees, jute and cotton mill labourers, rickshaw pullers and hackney carriage and buffalo cart drivers and khansamas [cooks]'. In his memoirs, he recalls that 'at one time I had as many as 36 trade unions as members of a Chamber of Labour I had founded to oppose the Communist labour organisations'.[99] It was in this period, when he defended the Muslims accused of crimes after the 1926 riots (including a notorious slum criminal)[100] that Suhrawardy built up his connections with Calcutta's underworld.[101] By the 1930s, therefore, Huseyn Suhrawardy had developed a large number of different connections, among the elite, among workers and the underworld bosses of Calcutta.

The 1935 Act, however, allotted only six Muslim seats to urban areas, of which four were in Calcutta.[102] So whatever influence Suhrawardy and Ispahani might have had over Muslims in Calcutta, this would have given them a poor reward in terms of seats in the Assembly. If the old Muslim families were to succeed in transforming their social pre-eminence into

---

[98] M. H. R. Talukdar (ed.), *The Memoirs of Huseyn Shaheed Suhrawardy*, pp. 106–107. An account of the history of the Suhrawardy family may be found in Begum Shaista Ikramullah, *From Purdah to Parliament*, London, 1963.

[99] *The Memoirs of Huseyn Shaheed Suhrawardy*, p. 106.

[100] This was Meena Peshawari, wanted for several murders committed during the Calcutta riots of 1926. Suhrawardy undertook to intervene with the police to get him bail. Hamidul Huq Chowdhury, *Memoirs*, Dhaka, 1989, p. 45.

[101] Kazi Ahmed Kamal. *Politicians and Inside Stories*, p. 54.

[102] These were Calcutta North, Calcutta South, Hooghly-cum-Howrah (Municipal) and Barrackpore (Municipal). The remaining two urban constituencies were 24 Parganas

political power it was clear that the United Muslim Party would have to win a share of the rural voters. None of these ashraf gentlemen had the taste or the stomach for muddying their boots in the paddy-fields: so instead, they directed their energies towards trying to win over the krishak organisations and their leaders to the United Muslim party. To begin with, this policy met with some success, when Akram Khan and the rump of his faction in the Nikhil Banga Praja Samiti were persuaded to join the United Muslim Party.[103] However, it was Fazlul Huq's Krishak Praja Party that was making the running in the countryside, so in June, 1936, the United Muslim Party set up a sub-committee to meet representatives of the Praja Party 'to invite their cooperation in running the elections on the ticket of the United Moslem Party'.[104] But Fazlul Huq was not a man to give up easily the rich gains which, he calculated, would now be his with the backing of the rural vote. Huq believed that he was the man to deliver the goods, and wanted these goods for himself. The moment had come for him to claim the countryside as his constituency and he was ready to challenge the Dacca family which he had long despised as 'the self-styled leaders of Bengal imposed by the patronage of the British'.[105] So Huq spurned the hand of cooperation extended to him by the leaders of the United Muslim Party and instead began to campaign against the Dacca Nawabs in their own districts, telling the voters there to back 'the true representatives of the peasants'.[106]

In the past the old ashraf leadership could have ignored a show of independence of this sort but now they could not afford to overlook Huq in his new incarnation as the self-styled leader of rural Bengal. Unable to tame Huq, the leaders of the United Muslim Party looked for help from outside the province. In July, 1936, Ispahani invited Jinnah to Bengal, in the hope that Huq would accept the authority of an all-India leader. Jinnah was busy reconstructing the All-India Muslim League and bringing it under his control, so he welcomed the chance of making an entry into Bengal politics. In August, he arrived in Calcutta, and quickly persuaded the Nawab's party to join the Muslim League. However, Jinnah had less success with Huq. Confident of his position as the proclaimed leader of the krishaks and loathe to surrender his independence, Huq refused Jinnah's terms. Jinnah was more than a little put out by this show of arrogance, and in the years that followed did his best to tame a volatile

(Municipal) and Dacca (Municipal). See Franchise, Elections in Bengal, IOLR L/P and J/8/475.
[103] Shila Sen, *Muslim Politics in Bengal, 1937–1947*, New Delhi, 1977, pp. 74–75.
[104] *The Statesman*, 2 June 1936.
[105] Kazi Ahmed Kamal, *Politicians and Inside Stories*, p. 19.
[106] *The Statesman*, 13 July 1936.

politician whom he always referred to as 'that impossible man'.[107] But for the moment, Jinnah's visit to Bengal had paid some dividends: he had succeeded in re-establishing the Bengal Provincial Muslim League, he had ensured that it would continue to be led by the wealthiest and best-connected Muslim families of Bengal and that it would be, if not under his control, at least in his debt. The Muslim League was thus reborn in Bengal, and Fazlul Huq and the Krishak Praja Party remained outside it.

The two parties, therefore, fought the elections as rivals. One unexpected result of separate electorates was that if there were rival claimants for the leadership of a particular community, they had no alternative but to fight each other at the polls. So in the general elections in Bengal, it was not the Congress that posed a challenge to the Krishak Praja Party or to the Muslim League since the Congress did not contest any Muslim seats. The electoral struggle was between the two major Muslim parties who pitted their rhetoric and programmes against each other rather than against the Congress or the Hindu Sabha. Instead both the Krishak Praja Party and the Muslim League were forced to compete with each other in claiming to represent the 'true' interests of the Muslims of Bengal.

The Krishak Praja Party, however, continued to avoid being overtly communal and kept its focus upon agrarian issues. Huq campaigned mainly on the platform of bread and butter ('*Dal-Bhat*'), demanding the abolition of the zamindari system and calling for 'Swaraj'. His manifesto included the pledge to release political prisoners, a demand usually made by Congress and suggests that Huq still hoped to make a deal with the Bengal Congress. Interestingly enough, in a mirror image of the Congress, the Krishak Praja Party did not contest a single Hindu or Scheduled Caste seat, even though its ranks included both caste Hindus and Namasudras, many of whom were jotedars.[108] Huq's campaign was directed towards winning the Muslim vote. So, at a district conference in Lakshmipur in Noakhali district, the programme 'opened with a procession of volunteers through the town to shouts of "Allah-ho-Akbar" and "Down with Zamindari"'. At the same conference 'an attempt of Hindu members from Calcutta to get a resolution passed denouncing the Communal Award and reformed constitution met with no success'.[109] Another Krishak Praja candidate, Syed Nausher Ali, won applause from the villagers of Narail in Jessore by promising a tube-well in every village; but again, his appeal was directed specifically to Muslims, and 'on one occasion at least, the

---

[107] Nor did Fazlul Huq ever refer to Jinnah by his popular title: 'Qaid-i-Azam'. Kazi Ahmed Kamal, *Politicians and Inside Stories*, p. 18.

[108] Shila Sen, *Muslim Politics in Bengal*, p. 81.

[109] Report of Chittagong Divisional Commissioner, GB HCPB File No. 56/36, LOFCR for the first fortnight of June 1936.

Muslim voters in one area were informed that their prayers flew upwards and could not reach Allah unless they had a good representative in Council'.[110] And although Huq extended feelers to the Congress about a post-electoral alliance, he had no intention of allowing his party's electoral identity to be taken over by the Congress. When Huq arrived in Madaripur in his home district of Bakarganj to find that the Congress Socialist Lalmohan Sen had convened a meeting in his name, he curtly refused to attend it and instead called a separate meeting of his own. Huq thus 'dissociated himself entirely from the (Congress) Krishak Samiti movement' and made it absolutely clear that 'his Party was entirely separate from Lalmohan Sen's organisation'.[111]

The Muslim League campaign, on the other hand, appealed to the simple notion of Muslim unity and the welfare of the Muslim community as a whole. Before its open breach with Huq, the League had taken faltering steps towards the rural Muslim voter. In January 1936, for instance, Nazimuddin had gone to Noakhali, Lakshmipur and Chatkil 'to visit Krishak leaders, to listen to what they had to say ... and to direct the activities of the Krishak samities to the right channels ... He stated that ... the Samitis should seek Government recognition'.[112] A few months later, Suhrawardy voiced the hope that the new party would be recognised by the masses as 'the guardian of their interests'[113] and the League claimed that its 'first aim was to improve the lot of the ryots and labourers'.[114] However, once it became apparent that the main rival to the revived League in the elections was to be the Krishak Praja Party, it adopted as its manifesto the 'uplift' specifically of the Muslim 'community'. Its propaganda glossed over the differences within that 'community' and the huge gulf, social as well as cultural, between the ashraf and the atrap, between well-to-do urban Muslims and the rural poor. For the notables of the League, Islam was the obvious and indeed the only platform from which they could plausibly claim the allegiance of the rural Muslim voter. Suhrawardy himself was hardly a pious Muslim. In the words of a contemporary acquaintance, he 'was totally unscrupulous, but not communal or religious. He ate ham and drank scotch and married a Russian actress':[115]

[110] P. D. Martyn Memoirs, IOLR MSS Eur F/180/13.
[111] Report of the Dacca Divisional Commissioner, LOFCR for the first fortnight of September 1936, GB HCPB File No. 56/36.
[112] Report of the Chittagong Divisional Commissioner, LOFCR for the second fortnight of January 1936. *Ibid.*
[113] *The Statesman*, 26 May 1936.
[114] Humaira Momen, *Muslim Politics in Bengal*, p. 48.
[115] Author's interview with Nikhil Chakravarty, New Delhi, 6 February 1989. Nikhil Chakravarty worked as a secretary for the Muslim League leader, Abul Hashim, and so came to know Huseyn Suhrawardy well.

He kept himself engaged in his off-hours . . . in such things as dancing, company of good-looking young ladies, outings with them, listening to the finest recordings of Western music of which he had over a thousand records [and] . . . making exposures from his small movie-camera.[116]

The same Suhrawardy, and his sophisticated and westernised associates in the League, now sallied forth to fight the elections in the name of Islam. Facing the challenge of an alternative Muslim leadership from the Krishna Praja Party which claimed to be the 'true representatives' of the peasants, the Muslim elite were forced into a more demotic mode. Muslim communal rhetoric, making much of the unities of the Muslim community, was their way of responding to the threat. This sheds a new light on the conflict between jotedars and zamindars; it was as much a civil war within the Muslim 'community' as a straight fight between Muslims and Hindus. Muslim communal rhetoric was as much a product of rivalries between the Muslim establishment and the spokesmen of rising Muslim groups who challenged it, as a response to Hindu bhadralok domination.

The high point of the Krishak Praja Party's electoral campaign came in the fight over the Muslim rural constituency of Patuakhali North, a 'political backwater' that was a part of the Dacca Nawab's personal estate. As the campaign got under way, Fazlul Huq, in a dramatic gesture that was characteristic of his political style, challenged Khwaja Nazimuddin to a straight fight in any constituency of his choice. Rising to the bait, Nazimuddin chose Patuakhali North, the scene of a major communal riot in 1927, calculating that here perhaps his name and an appeal to Islam would sway the rural voters more than Huq's programme.[117] All the power and influence of the Ahsan Manzil were poured into Nazimuddin's campaign, and even the Governor, Sir John Anderson, took the unprecedented step of visiting Patuakhali and urging voters to return the Khwaja.[118] Huq, however, was more than a match for the Dacca family. He informed the voters of Patuakhali that the struggle was 'an all out fight between the zamindars and the peasants', and promised, that in the event of his victory 'by the grace of God, I shall abolish zamindari in the shortest possible time'.[119] This was enough to win over the newly enfranchised voters of Patuakhali, and Nazimuddin was roundly defeated, getting less than half the votes that Huq won (6,308 votes to Huq's 13,742).[120] Flushed

---

[116] S. Rahmatullah Memoirs, IOLR MSS Eur F/180/14 a.
[117] For further details on the Patukhali riot, see Partha Chatterjee, 'Agrarian Relations and Communalism in Bengal, 1926–1935' in Ranajit Guha (ed.), *Subaltern Studies I*, Delhi, 1982, pp. 22–24; Tanika Sarkar, *Bengal 1928–32: The Politics of Protest*, pp. 25–26, and Suranjan Das, 'Communal Riots in Bengal', pp. 181–182.
[118] Kazi Ahmed Kamal, *Politicians and Inside Stories*, pp. 118–120.   [119] *Ibid.*, p. 20.
[120] 'Franchise, Elections in Bengal, 1936–37', IOLR L/P and J/7/1142.

with victory, Huq declared 'in the event of the failure of the Government
to accept the demands of the peasants, I [will] throw the Writers Building
into the Laldighi'. [121]

Patuakhali was a boost to the morale of the Krishak Praja Party and
was a defeat that Nazimuddin was never allowed to forget. Huseyn Suhrawardy had been returned from two separate constituencies in Calcutta. He
surrendered one of these to enable Nazimuddin to be elected unopposed in
a by-election. The Khwaja therefore was able to enter the new Bengal
Legislative Assembly by the back door, but he never again contested an
election where there was the remotest possibility that he could be defeated.
If anything, his association with the Government had worked against
Nazimuddin. The story goes that when a Muslim League worker asked a
Patuakhali peasant why they had voted for Fazlul Huq 'though Nazimuddin has done so much for you', the peasant retorted 'But why has he put
tax on tobacco and increased the cost of the post card?' When informed
that these were taxes imposed by the centre and not by the provincial
government, the peasant replied 'No, he could have solved it if he had just
written to the Viceroy. He is the man of the Viceroy'. [122]

An appeal to Islam by Nazimuddin had failed to win him the support of
rural voters, even in a constituency that had been the scene of a serious
and prolonged communal riot less than a decade before. Patuakhali raises
doubts, therefore, about the 'irrational strength of Muslim identity' which
the East Bengal peasants were supposed to have shared and which is
believed to have been 'channelled into the movement for Pakistan'. [123] It
has been argued that the Muslim peasantry, relatively undifferentiated
and sharing an 'identical set of tenurial credit, and market relations' developed a 'remarkable degree of cohesiveness'. [124] This cohesiveness, it has
been suggested, found expression in a 'communal solidarity'[125] that
enabled 'Muslim rent-receivers, where they did exist, [to be] considered
part of the peasant community'. [126] This 'peasant-communal conscious-

---

[121] Kazi Ahmed Kamal, *Politicians and Inside Stories*, pp. 20–21.   [122] *Ibid.*

[123] Sugata Bose, 'The Roots of "Communal" Violence in Rural Bengal. A Study of the
Kishoreganj Riots, 1930', in *Modern Asian Studies*, 16, 3, 1982, p. 491. More recently,
Suranjan Das has also argued that 'the Muslim masses had a more readily identifiable
communal and religious identity', and that 'the vertical integration of Muslim society . . .
created and sustained the potentials [sic] for communal outbreaks'. Suranjan Das,
'Communal Riots in Bengal', pp. 25–34.

[124] *Ibid.*, pp. 468–469.

[125] Tajul-Islam Hashmi argues that by the mid-twenties 'the communal solidarity of the
Muslim peasants had become stronger than class solidarity'. Tajul-Islam Hashmi, 'The
Communalisation of class struggle: East Bengal peasantry, 1923–29', in *Indian Economic
and Social History Review*, 25, 2, (1988), p. 189.

[126] Partha Chatterjee argues that 'the very nature of peasant consciousness . . . is religious'.
See his 'Agrarian Relations and Communalism', pp. 11, 31.

ness'[127] is said to have furnished the dynamic behind the communalisation of Bengali society. It has been suggested that 'without the agrarian dimension to the Hindu–Muslim problem in Bengal, the politics of separatism would have in all likelihood proved ineffectual and been washed away by the strong tide of a composite nationalism'.[128]

But the Patuakhali election and Nazimuddin's humiliating defeat point in another direction, suggesting that it might be wrong to assume that 'communalism' was available ready-made among the Muslim peasantry. Despite the constituency's history of communal friction, and despite his openly communal campaign, Nazimuddin was unable to convince Patuakhali's rural Muslim voters to support him. The same pattern was repeated all over rural East Bengal, where the Krishak Praja Party secured thirty-three seats, six more than the Muslim League which only won twenty-seven. (Nine of the League's victories were in the Dacca district alone, where the strength of Nawabi influence undoubtedly accounted for the party's success.) Overall, the Muslim League fared best in the urban constituencies, where it won all six seats. It also did well in the more urbanised areas of the mofussil, such as the 24 Parganas and Dacca, and in North Bengal, particularly in Rangpur District where it won five out of seven seats. The candidates of the Krishak Praja party fared best in the East Bengal countryside, sweeping Khulna, Mymensingh, Bakarganj, and Noakhali. The Krishak Praja Party polled 31.51 per cent of the total Muslim vote, but won only thirty-six seats in all, while the Muslim League, though it polled only 27.10 per cent of the vote, won thirty-nine seats in the new Assembly.[129] The remaining thirty-nine Muslim seats were won by independent candidates, who were 'mostly men of local influence, each of whom will command the votes in his own parish. Some candidates are said to stand in the hope of being bought off'.[130]

A second 'Krishak' organisation, the Tippera Krishak Samity, was remarkably successful in Tippera, winning five out of seven seats in that district. The Tippera Krishak Samity was formed in 1919 by Maulvi Emdadul Huq, a member of the Legislative Council, but by the early thirties, it had come under the control of 'more active and energetic men'[131] associated with the local Congress Committee. In 1936, however,

---

[127] *Ibid.*, p. 32.   [128] Sugata Bose, 'The Kishoreganj Riots', p. 463.

[129] 'Bengal Legislative Assembly. Election Results, 1936'. IOLR L/PandJ/7/1142.

[130] Report of the Dacca Divisional Commissioner, LOFCR for the second fortnight of December 1936, GB HCPB File No. 56/36.

[131] These were Mukuleswar Rahman, Kamini Kumar Dutta and Abdul Malek, all with long records of involvement in anti-British 'seditious' activities. Report of the District Magistrate of Tippera dated 23 December 1931, GB Home Poll File No. 849/31 (1–9) .

the party was renamed the 'Krishak O Shramik Samity' ('Peasants and Workers Party') and began to distance itself from the local Congress organisation. It now came under the 'more extreme' and 'communistic' leadership of Yakoob Ali and Wasimuddin Ahmed.[132] The latter was returned from the Tippera Central Constituency in the 1937 election, trouncing Sir K. G. M. Faroqui, Nawab, zamindar and minister.[133]

Here was another instance where rural Muslim voters resisted the communal appeal of a Muslim bigwig and politician and supported instead the local workers of the Krishak movement. The electoral success both of the Tippera Samity and the Krishak Praja Party suggests that for at least those Muslim peasants who had the vote the 'communal' Muslim League was by no means an automatic choice. Indeed, the parties that were most closely associated with peasant and jotedar aspirations – the Krishak Praja Party and the Tippera Krishak O Sramik Samity – were least 'communal' in their activities, programme, membership and appeal; while the party of the Muslim elite, the Muslim League, was blatant in its appeal to Islam and to Muslim identity. The sense of solidarity shared by the relatively undifferentiated peasant communities of Bengal was by no means simply religious, nor was it always automatically drawn behind communal or separatist politics. It could equally be mobilised behind egalitarian (or populist) secular programmes which addressed themselves directly to agrarian issues and other areas of experience and forms of identity shared by peasant societies which had little to do with religion.

Congress and the mofussil

All of this presented the Bengal Congress with an acute dilemma. Land ownership under the Permanent Settlement and the privileges it brought with it had created the social milieu from which the Congress recruited most of its support. The Congress in Bengal was, by and large, a party of the bhadralok, which, in its early days, like the bhadralok itself, had straddled both town and countryside. But since the end of Non-Cooperation and the death of Chittaranjan Das, the party, riven by internal dissension, had retreated to the metropolis and dissipated its energies in the city's municipal politics. Even where it had a presence in the districts, the party had a powerful urban bias. District party offices were invariably situated in the *sadar* subdivision towns which were the seat of administra-

---

[132] Report of the Chittagong Divisional Commissioner, LOFCRs for the first fortnight of June 1936, and the first fortnight of July 1936, GB HCPB File No. 56/36.
[133] Bengal Legislative Assembly. Election Results 1936. IOLR L/P and J/1142.

tion[134] and their members were drawn from the district bhadralok: school teachers, pleaders, salaried employees, and, of course, students.[135] By the early thirties, the Bengal Congress had become a party of the towns, but one that still retained its connections with landed interests. Many of the party's leaders were themselves absentee zamindars who possessed considerable estates in the mofussil, and most had rentier interests of one kind or another. Kiran Sankar Roy was the zamindar of the considerable estate of Teota in Dacca, Tulsi Charan Goswami's father was a wealthy landlord (Raja Kishori Lal Goswami), and Tarak Nath Mukherjee, the grandson of Raja Peari Mohan Mukherjee, had large estates in Uttarpara. Surendra Mohan Ghosh, the Jugantar leader who went on to become President of the Bengal Provincial Congress Committee belonged to a family of zamindars 'with a good deal of landed property in Mymensingh', while his close associate in the Mymensingh District Congress, Babu Bijoy Roy Choudhury, was the zamindar of Tulsi Ghata.[136] Other Congressmen owned more modest rural properties, while most merely held rent-receiving rights in subdivided and subinfeudated estates. Congress activities, moreover, depended heavily on the patronage of landowners and moneylenders in the mofussil. Their funding was crucial, as Tanika Sarkar points out, to Gandhian welfare work in the districts. The ashram at Outshahi village in Bikrampur, for instance, had as its patron the local zamindar, Indubhushan Gupta, and the patron of the ashram at Barisal was the Ramchandrapur zamindar, Kaliprasanna Guha Choudhury. The national school at Gangajalghata was set up by the son of a local zamindar. Gandhian work at Sonamukhi and Patrasayar was begun by the local zamindar and at Simlipil by a wing of the local Raja's family.[137] Babu Brijendra Kishore, zamindar of Gauripur, contributed 50,000 rupees towards the costs of the Tarakeswar satyagraha and was a regular and generous donor to the coffers of the Mymensingh district Congress.[138]

The politics of the Bengal Congress reflected the social conservatism of its predominantly bhadralok membership. Even in the Gandhian era of

[134] The Secretary of the BPCC wrote in 1929 that 'mostly the members are in towns ... the district towns are the headquarters of District Congress Committees'. Kiran Sankar Roy to Motilal Nehru, 14 February 1929. AICC Papers, File No. P-24/1929.
[135] Evidently most were western-educated: much of the correspondence between DCCs and the BPCC was conducted in English.
[136] Interview with Surendra Mohan Ghosh, NMML Oral Transcript No. 301, pp. 1–10, 194.
[137] Tanika Sarkar, *Bengal 1928–1934*, pp. 30–31.
[138] Interview with Surendra Mohan Ghosh, NMML Oral Transcript No. 301, pp. 120, 125. For details of the Tarakeswar Satyagraha, see Rajat Kanta Ray, *Social Conflict and*

greater mobilisation of popular support, the Congress leadership in Bengal displayed an attitude towards the peasantry that was deeply paternalistic. For those Gandhians who worked in the field at 'village reconstruction', the abuses of the zamindars were difficult to ignore. But for Satish Chandra Dasgupta, Bengal's leading Gandhian, these abuses were a symptom of the erosion of the traditional zamindari system. He saw the zamindar as traditionally something of an enlightened despot, who administered justice, protected his tenants and presided benevolently over the religious and cultural life of rural Bengal.[139] If zamindars no longer fulfilled these functions, it was because the Raj had reduced them to being mere tax-collectors. Dasgupta's panacea for all the problems of the countryside was to restore the zamindar to his rightful place at the head of rural society. He perceived no conflict of interests between the good landlord and his tenants and wanted the peasants to be educated in 'such a way that they will contentedly stay on in villages and lead blameless lives'.[140] Chittaranjan Das also professed faith in 'village reconstruction' as the answer to rural Bengal's problems and urged that village panchayats be set up to look after 'sanitation, water-supply, night schools, industrial and agricultural education and to settle petty disputes'.[141] Neither Das nor his successors in the Bengal Congress were willing to face up to the bald fact that the Bengal countryside was riven by conflicts of interest too deep to be amenable to facile solutions such as these. The nationalist press reacted to the Bengal Tenancy Amendment Bill of 1928 with the pious belief that 'there is absolutely no reason why all disputes between the zamindars and raiyats should not be settled in a way satisfactory to both sides'. It professed not to 'understand why there should be any difficulty in adjusting the new demands of the one to the old-enjoyed privileges of the other'.[142] Indeed, the one issue on which different factions of the Congress saw eye to eye was that zamindari rights must be protected. Despite the bitter factional conflict raging in the party, all but one of the forty-odd Swarajist Councillors voted in unison against the provisions of the 1928 Tenancy Amendment Bill.[143] In 1930, they

Political Unrest in Bengal, pp. 333–334, and Buddhadev Bhattacharyya et al., *Satyagrahas in Bengal 1921–1939*, Calcutta, 1977.
[139] Satish Chandra Dasgupta, *Bharater Samyavad* ['Communism in India'], Calcutta, 1930.
[140] *Ibid.*, p. 65.
[141] Rajat Kanta Ray, *Social Conflict and Political Unrest in Bengal*, p. 212. See also Bidyut Chakrabarty, 'Peasants and the Bengal Congress, 1928–38' in *South Asia Research*, vol. 5, 1, May 1985, p. 32.
[142] *Amrita Bazar Patrika*, 10 August 1928. Also cited in Partha Chatterjee, *Bengal, 1920–1947*, p. 81.
[143] *Proceedings of the Bengal Legislative Council*, 3 and 4 September 1928, pp. 823–824, 927–928. For further details, see Gautam Chattopadhyay, *Bengal Electoral Politics and*

combined again against a bill that proposed to place the cost of primary education in the countryside onto zamindari estates. Even after the party retreated to the towns in the late twenties, its leaders had kept intact their commitment to their landed interests in the mofussil which they had left behind but had not abandoned.

The troubles in the Bengal countryside which accompanied the Depression, especially the threat that peasants would withhold their rents, alarmed many Congressmen. As rent payments fell and intermediary tenure-holders were forced to sell their holdings, bhadralok families which had rural sources of income felt the pinch.[144] For those with jobs in the city, falling agricultural prices brought a corresponding rise in the real value of cash earnings which compensated, in part, for the loss of income from the land. But for the rural bhadralok, resident landlords and taluqdars who had stayed on in the mofussil, the Depression brought real hardship. Rent-collection fell off drastically, debts were impossible to recover and crop sales fetched low returns. By 1933, when 'the non-payment complex' had spread all over Bengal, the 'Hindu Community' in the eastern districts began to voice its 'alarm at the growth of the movement'.[145] Some zamindars turned to the courts in the hope of enforcing rent-payments; others relied on extra-legal forms of coercion, employing lathi-wielding paiks to evict stubborn peasants from their holdings. In Hooghly, zamindars were reported to be 'putting undue pressure upon their tenants for rents' by filing 'a large number of ejectment suits'.[146] In Bankura, relations between landlords and tenants deteriorated after incidents in the Saltora thana area where 'the local landlords [had] been employing Barkandgazes [*peons*] to oppose the reaping of paddy by their tenants in order to compel the latter to pay their rents immediately'.[147] Incidents such as these could rapidly assume a 'communal' dimension in cases where the zamindar was Hindu and the tenants Muslim. For instance, in the Labhpur thana of Birbhum district, 'trouble arose when a Hindu zamindar ordered his Muslim peon to assault a

Freedom Struggle, 1862–1947, New Delhi, 1984, pp. 104–115, and Partha Chatterjee, *Bengal, 1920–1947*, pp. 87–95.
[144] Saugata Mukherji concludes from his study of land transfers that 'the evidence seems to suggest that the older class of intermediate tenure holders were finding it more profitable to dispose of their rights in the land'. See his 'Agrarian Class Formation in Modern Bengal', p. PE-13. Much of the urban bhadralok belonged to this class.
[145] GB HCPB File No. 873/33.
[146] Report of the Commissioner, Presidency Division, LOFCR for the second fortnight of May 1936, GB HCPB File No. 56/36.
[147] Report of the Commissioner, Burdwan Division, LOFCR for the first fortnight of December 1937, GB HCPB File No. 10/37.

Muslim tenant' over the question of a paddy-loan';[148] and in Howrah, there was an ugly incident when a Hindu zamindar, having obtained a decree for khas possession against a Muslim tenant, threatened to demolish a mosque on the disputed land.[149]

In the western districts, the most bitter disputes were between zamindars and their tenants, but in the jute-growing districts of North and East Bengal it was the Hindu moneylenders who were the focus of the most violent attack. In Noakhali, Krishak Samiti members were suspected of being involved in a campaign of stealing and killing cattle owned by Hindu moneylenders. In the same district, a raid was mounted on the home of a Hindu moneylender at Ambanagar, in what appeared to be an 'organised dacoity'. The victim was reported to have been tortured.[150] This attack came in the wake of an agitation organised by the local Krishak Samiti for the 'complete remission of arrear rents'. Muslim volunteers circulated printed notices which declared that 'until the peasants are masters of the country and its wealth, no relief will be obtained'. Inevitably, this caused tension between the krishak volunteers and the 'local Bhadralog Hindus'.[151]

There had, of course, been troubles in the past between Muslim peasants and Hindu zamindars.[152] But the violence had not been specifically 'communal' in its orientation.[153] Invariably, however, Muslim peasant violence was interpreted by the bhadralok as being communally motivated. Incidents such as these were portrayed as communal attacks on local Hindus by fanatical Muslim hordes, even when attacks were motivated by economics. This can be seen in the description in a pamphlet of an incident in Kishoreganj in 1930 when Muslim peasants attacked a powerful Hindu zamindar and moneylender, Babu Krishna Chanda.[154]

---

[148] GB HCPB File No. 752/36.   [149] GB HCPB File No. 281/36.
[150] Report of the District Magistrate, Noakhali. LOFCR for the first fortnight of May 1937, GB HCPB File No. 10/37.
[151] Report of the Commissioner, Chittagong Division, LOFCR for the second fortnight of May 1936, GB HCPB File No. 56/36. In another incident in the Nandigram *thana* of Rajshahi district, 'a [Hindu] mahajan in [the] area was murdered in broad daylight'. Local administrators connected the murder to the development of 'a movement for refusal to pay dues to Mahajans ... fostered by designing persons for electioneering purposes'. Report of the Commissioner, Chittagong Division, LOFCR for the second fortnight of May 1936, GB HCPB File No. 56/36.
[152] See Tanika Sarkar, 'Communal Riots in Bengal'; Partha Chatterjee, 'Agrarian Relations and Communalism in Bengal'; and Suranjan Das, 'Communal Riots in Bengal'.
[153] Suranjan Das has demonstrated that in many of these rural riots, the cause of the conflict was economic: the targets of mob violence were usually property and debt-bonds rather than idols or temples, and both Hindu and Muslim moneylenders and shop-keepers were attacked. *Ibid.*
[154] Lakshmi Kanta Kirttana and Kumud Bhattacharya, *Ganer Bahi Loter Gan* (Book of Songs, Songs of Plunder), Mymensingh, 1930.

A crowd of Muslims had surrounded the sturdily built house of the zamindar and demanded that he hand over to them all debt bonds (*dalil patras*) in his possession. This Krishna Chanda refused to do and when the mob continued to threaten him, he and his son fired upon them, killing some and injuring others. When the trigger-happy zamindar ran out of ammunition, one of his servants, himself a Hindu, called the mob back, reassuring them that his master had no bullets left. The avenging crowd returned, killed the hapless zamindar and his family and put his house and his motorcar to the torch.[155] This incident had to do with agrarian, not communal issues, where the zamindar's ostentatious wealth aroused the wrath of the crowd.[156] His total lack of sympathy for his debtors at a time of unprecedented hardship and his brutal attack on an unarmed crowd provoked the fury not only of his tenants who were Muslims but also of his domestic servant who was a Hindu. But the authors of the pamphlet portrayed the incident as a communally-inspired attack:

> To whom shall we tell this sorrowful tale?
> ... Brothers, an unprecedented incident has occurred
> In the subjugated Kishoreganj locality of Mymensingh zilla
> They have looted fifty villages, brothers!
> How many have fled from the cruelty of the Mussalmans
> How many have died of starvation?
> Mobs of Mussalmans descended, and told Hindus
> Give us all the loan-bonds that you have
> The brick built houses of the bhadralok and the rice-urns of the poor,
>   All were destroyed in front of their eyes, nothing was spared ...[157]

With their closed paternalistic vision of peasant society under the benevolent rule of just zamindars, bhadralok Hindus too often failed to see that peasants might have grievances against their rural overlords which had little to do with community. Most Congressmen were equally blind to the acute economic distress which underlay these conflicts and found it more convenient to interpret them simply as Hindu–Muslim riots. Thus, when Muslim and Namasudra bargadars combined against a Hindu zamindar in the Narail subdivision of Jessore, the Bengal Congress insisted that this was a purely 'communal' incident.[158]

But under the terms of the 1935 Act, the Congress had no choice but to

---

[155] The full details of the incident have been recounted by Suranjan Das, 'Communal Riots in Bengal'. This was the only case in which a zamindar was actually killed in the Kishoreganj riot of 1930.

[156] The *dalan bari* ('big, brick-built house') and the newly purchased motor car, seem to have been the particular focus of the wrath of the crowd.

[157] *Ganer Bahi Loter Gan, Tritiya Gan.*   [158] Tanika Sarkar, *Bengal, 1928–1934*, p. 40.

appeal to those very sections of rural society it had long ignored if it was to make a decent showing in the elections. Rural voters were now to fill 178 seats out of the total of 250 in the new Assembly. Even if the party were to contest only the seats allotted to Hindus by the Communal Award, sixty-six of the total eighty Hindu constituencies were rural. In these constituencies agrarian conflict could not be simply explained away as 'communal' friction. By pushing the Bengal Provincial Congress Committee out of its familiar Calcutta environment into the mofussil, in search of precious rural votes, the Act of 1935 forced Congress leaders to rethink their attitudes on agrarian matters.

The new electoral arithmetic and the impact of the Depression on rural Bengal posed a serious challenge to the Bengal Congress. The party had no alternative but to try to cultivate krishak voters at a time when its traditional supporters in the mofussil, the large zamindars and intermediary tenure holders, faced a crisis. Just when its own people felt most threatened by peasant radicalism, the Congress had to contemplate sanctioning krishak agitations under its own banner to win new rural votes. In the past, even at the height of Civil Disobedience, the party leadership had consistently refused to sanction the withholding of rent.[159] Such forays as the Bengal Congress had made into the countryside in the course of agitational struggles had been made on issues carefully chosen to make the target the British Government and not local zamindars or moneylenders. During Non-Cooperation, Birendranath Sasmal had succeeded in persuading prosperous Mahishya peasants in Contai and Tamluk to boycott the Union Boards, and in Birbhum, Jitendralal Banerjee had urged peasants to resist settlement operations.[160] But when local firebrands in the Santal agitation had called for the suspension of rent payments even in British-owned estates such as the Midnapore Zamindari Company, the central Congress leadership would have none of it: it was

---

[159] There were a few exceptions, where local Congress workers encouraged the withholding of rent in certain pockets. But more often than not, where such movements were sanctioned by the BPCC, there was a background of factional in-fighting within the party leadership. For instance, in the case of the Arambag agitation against the Hooghly zamindar by local Gandhian activists, studied by Hitesranjan Sanyal, the zamindar in question was Tulsi Charan Goswami, himself a prominent Congressman, but of the opposing camp in the party. Goswami was forced to resign from the presidentship of the Hooghly District Congress Committee, and the agitation was suspended soon afterwards, before it could 'take on a class line'. See Hitesranjan Sanyal, 'Nationalist Movements in Arambag', in *Annya Artha*, September 1974, and Bidyut Chakrabarty, 'Peasants and the Bengal Congress, 1929–38', pp. 35–36.

[160] *The History of the Non-Cooperation and Khilafat Movements in Bengal*, GB HCPB File No. 395/1924.

not ready to sanction a no-rent campaign.[161] In the thirties, the zamindar lobby was keener than ever before to persuade the Congress leadership to steer clear of no-rent agitations, this at just the juncture when the party desperately needed the votes of the very rent-payers in the countryside who wanted to withhold their payments.

It is hardly surprising, therefore, that the Bengal Congress would rather not have contested the elections at all.[162] It had no prospects of winning the glittering prizes of provincial autonomy. The Award had seen to that. The elections threatened to expose the hollowness of its claims to represent rural Bengal, and the limits of its social and organisational base in the mofussil. But once the High Command decided to contest the election, the Bengal wing of the party had to follow suit and put on as brave a face as it could. By good fortune, the Bengal Congress now contained a small body of men who were willing to try their hand at bringing the peasants into its fold. There had always been some Congressmen who wanted the party to expand its social base and give up its traditional conservatism and now they found their numbers strengthened. Terrorist groups for many years had provided the Congress organisation with an active cadre. Some of their stalwarts had been incarcerated in the detention camps in Deoli and the Andamans and had there been converted to Marxism. Released in the mid-thirties, they returned to the Congress ready to rally workers and peasants with the same enthusiasm with which they had launched their terrorist campaigns. In June 1936, *The Statesman* carried a story entitled 'Red Agents in Indian Villages', which created a stir in Calcutta. The article claimed that:

The minds of the Indian peasants and labourers are being poisoned by the insidious propaganda of Moscow-trained communists ... Former terrorists are now joining the ranks of the Communists and though their present methods are 'peaceful', signs are not wanting that if the agitation is not checked India is faced with a serious revolutionary movement.[163]

Investigating the story, the Governor of Bengal concluded that 'a campaign of socialist and communist propaganda [was] likely to be started in [the districts]' where 'the swing over to communism [was] most

[161] Swapan Dasgupta, 'Adivasi Politics in Midnapur'; Bidyut Chakrabarty, 'Peasants and the Bengal Congress', p. 32.
[162] Early in 1936, J. B. Kripalani found to his surprise that 'there was ... a strong opinion for accepting office ... excepting [in] Punjab and Bengal'. J. B. Kripalani to Rajendra Prasad, 15 February 1936, in B. N. Pandey, *The Indian Nationalist Movement: Select Documents*, p. 98.
[163] *The Statesman*, 12 June 1936. Kalpana Dutt, one of the accused in the Chittagong Armoury Raid case, was one of the more celebrated converts to communism. See her account in *Chittagong Armoury Raiders, Reminiscences*. Also see David M. Laushey,

marked'.[164] In July 1936, the Bengal Public Security Act was extended
from Calcutta to the 24 Parganas and Hooghly districts to deal with the
'increasing frequency' of 'meetings and processions in Calcutta and its
suburbs at which the tenets of communism have been preached and at
which the well-known symbols which are associated with revolutionary
movements have been displayed'.[165] In 1935, the Communist Party of
India adopted the 'United Front' strategy of working with the Congress
and this paved the way for young communists to join the Bengal Congress, forming a radical wing within the party, ready to go out to the
villages and mobilise the peasants in the nationalist cause. But these
radicals formed a small minority in the Bengal Provincial Congress
Committee, and the Party clung to its conservative moorings. The krishak
campaign launched by the Congress in Bengal on the eve of the 1936
elections clearly reflected the contradictory forces that were pulling the
Party in opposite directions during the mid-thirties.

The case of the Tippera Krishak Samiti demonstrates some of the
pressures to which Congress-associated krishak samitis were vulnerable.
The Tippera Samiti had come under the control of local Congress activists in the early thirties, when it had been reconstituted under the
leadership of Mukuleswar Rahman.[166] The revival of the Samiti was the
work of a group of 'more active and energetic men', which included
Rahman himself, Abdul Malek, Abdul Jalil and Babu Kamini Kumar
Datta, each with a long history of anti-British 'sedition'. The District
Magistrate reported that

the last named is the brain of the movement and also finances it. He is a
well-known pleader at Comilla and has considerable social influence ... [He]
addresses meetings [in the interior] declaiming against landlords in general. The
Samity has its headquarters at Comilla town and has got a small office where
Maulvi Mukuleswar Rahman lives. It is interconnected with the local Congress
organisation and in fact all the leading members are members of the local
Congress committee.[167]

*Bengal Terrorism and the Marxist Left. Aspects of Regional Nationalism in India,
1905–1942*, Calcutta, 1973.
[164] Bengal Governor's Fortnightly Report (FR) for the first half of June 1936, GOI, Home
Poll File No. 7/11/36, NAI.
[165] Blandy to Hallett, 31 August 1936, in GOI, Home Poll File No. 6/7/36. In July, the
Bengal administration reported that 'the Commissioner of Police has collected figures
showing that 85 meetings at which the Communist flag was displayed and speeches in
support of Communism were made, were held in Calcutta in the 87 days from 2 April
to 28 June 1936'. Twynham to Hallett, 26 July 1936, in GOI, Home Poll File
No. 7/11/36.
[166] Report of the District Magistrate of Tippera, 26 December 1931, GB HCPB File
No. 849/31, Serial Nos. 1–9.
[167] *Ibid.*

In Comilla town, the samiti's proceedings had a distinctly Congress flavour. At a May Day rally in 1931, red flags were brandished by the crowds, but the resolutions passed by the leaders were far from revolutionary and did not include the demand that the zamindari system be abolished or overthrown. In Comilla, even the most radical Congressmen appear to have been anxious to avoid contentious issues and to keep the krishak movement within the broad framework of the Civil Disobedience programme. But it proved difficult to contain the movement in the countryside. Krishak samitis emerged all over the district, in Chandina, Bunchang, and Laksam in the Nabinagar and Kasba thanas. It was strongest in Brahmanbaria, where it was reported that

Samitis have been started in almost every village ... Almost everybody in the village is a member of the samiti except the mahajans ... The samitis now demand that the mahajans must surrender their documents and that the samitis themselves will decide how and when the debts must be repaid. The mahajans have become panic-stricken and some of them are reported to have returned their documents and put themselves at the mercy of the samiti leaders. The latter have been active against the landlords and are not allowing them to cut paddy in their *khas* land. Local labour is being induced not to serve the local landlords and imported labour has been scared away by the threatened violence. Arbitration courts have been established by the village samitis in many places.[168]

Given the severe economic hardships of the time, krishak activities were likely to go beyond the modest parameters set out by the Congress. Tippera was one district where the Congress had hoped to organise krishaks without upsetting too many local apple carts. Here 'the Hindu high-caste gentry had a relatively weaker presence than in their traditional habitat in Dacca, Faridpur and Bakarganj. In 1911, '[one] man received rent for every 48 who paid in Tippera ... [and] there were fewer landlords agents here than anywhere else in the province'.[169] However, even in this district, krishak politics proved to be socially divisive, setting peasants against landlords and moneylenders, stirring up violence particularly in outlying villages. [170]

So it is hardly surprising that the Congress made no effort to extend the krishak movement outside Tippera to other districts. Krishak organisation had proved to be dangerous and uncontrollable, threatening agrarian interests to which most Congress leaders were committed. It was not until the Communal Award and the 1935 Act made it clear that Congress could not survive in the new Assembly without constructing a broader

[168] *Ibid.*   [169] Sugata Bose, *Agrarian Bengal*, p. 183.
[170] Dr A. B. Dutta, Honorary Secretary, 'Shanti Rakshani Samiti' to the Political Secretary, Government of Bengal, 4 December 1931; in GB HCPB File No. 849/31 (1–9).

base in the countryside, that the party nervously returned to as innocuous an agrarian programme as it could get away with.

In Tippera itself, samiti leaders such as Ashrafuddin Ahmed Chaudhuri and Abdul Malek, who had close contacts with the Calcutta Congress leadership, quickly distanced themselves from the more 'extreme' elements in the organisation. Both men had been associated with the Bengal Congress since the Khilafat Movement. Abdul Malek of the Kasba thana, 'a man of poor means [who] owes a considerable sum to a Co-operative Credit Society' had served a term during Non-Cooperation for 'seditious' activities[171] and Ashrafuddin, a Comilla pleader, was a Bose loyalist of note.[172] Both men had been at the forefront of the Krishak agitation in Tippera, provoking the district administration to conclude that 'nobody in this district is more responsible than this Abdul Malek and Ashrafuddin Chaudhuri for all the mischief and troubles concerning peasants'.[173] But on the eve of the elections, their leadership was challenged by the extreme wing of the samiti

with the result that the movement is at present divided by sharp internal dissensions. A new section has been formed of which Osimuddin Ahmed and one Yakub Ali are among the principal members. They are doing their best to discredit Ashrafuddin Chaudhury with the general body of cultivators by accusing him of being no true cultivator and describing him and his supporters as a group of Zamindars, moneylenders and Pleaders.[174]

As Ashrafuddin Chaudhuri struggled to keep his hold over the movement, the conflict between the two camps grew increasingly bitter, and, at a conference in Shibpur at the end of May 1936, 'there was an abusive interchange of speeches. Eventually, when a riot threatened, the President dissolved the meeting.' Even the District Magistrate could see that the dispute was something more than 'personal rivalry', and reflected upon 'some distinctions in politics, Ashrafuddin's party being in general constitutional and Yakub Ali's party communistic'.[175] Pressures from within the local samiti and the increasingly fierce competition to win the krishak vote forced Ashrafuddin to prove his commitment to the peasant cause and his speeches became more and more 'objectionable from the point of view of the conservative landlord.'[176] Attacks from the left forced Ashrafuddin to resort to more 'vigorous propaganda inviting the support of the

[171] GB HCPB File No. 95/37.
[172] For an account of Ashrafuddin's life and career, see Jalaludin Ahmed Chaudhury, *Rajbirodhi Ashrafuddin Ahmed Chaudhuri*, Dhaka, 1978.
[173] GB HCPB File No. 95/37.
[174] Report of the Commissioner, Chittagong Division, LOFCR for the first fortnight of June 1936, GB HCPB File No. 56/36.
[175] *Ibid.*   [176] *Ibid.*, for the second fortnight of February 1936.

krishaks', and he began to denounce zamindars as 'enemies of the country'.[177] This was dangerous ground for the Congress party and Ashrafuddin tried to take the sting out of his speeches by focusing his attack on Khwaja Faroqui, a loyalist Muslim landowner. As the attacks grew sharper, Faroqui reacted by instituting defamation cases against two of Ashrafuddin's close allies, Abdul Malek and Anwarullah.[178] Nevertheless, Ashrafuddin could not keep up with the anti-zamindar radicalism of his rivals. As a leading Congressman, he had, in the end, to stick to the party line and temper his calls for agrarian reform. By April 1936, Abdul Malek had been 'edged out' by Maulvi Osimuddin,[179] the man responsible for tabling the controversial amendment to the 1928 Tenancy Amendment Bill; and by July, the local administration reported that 'Ashrafuddin's influence appears to be waning before that of his more extreme rivals'.[180] Osimuddin Ahmed contested the election from the Tippera Central rural constituency as the candidate of the Tippera Krishak Samiti, defeating Khwaja Faroqui by a considerable margin,[181] and neither Ashrafuddin nor any of his cronies were returned to the Assembly. The Congress leadership in Calcutta refused to have anything to do with the new 'extreme' leadership of the samiti, and even Kamini Kumar Dutta, the Tippera Congressman who had been 'the brain behind the movement' since its inception was refused a Congress ticket in the Assembly elections. Dutta stood as a 'rebel' against the official Congress candidate,[182] and although he lost the election, he polled over 23,000 votes.[183]

The Tippera experience showed what a double-edged weapon the krishak factor was for the Bengal Congress. Krishak agitation in the localities was impossible to contain within the modest limits set by Congress leaders; Congress-funded samitis were liable to fall into the hands of men who were less amenable to the discipline of provincial leaders and who were keen to take the movement along more 'extreme' lines. So even in the last stages of their electoral campaigns, provincial Congress leaders showed little enthusiasm for the krishak samitis that had begun to emerge in the districts. In May 1936, 'efforts [were] made by

---

[177] *Ibid.*, for the first fortnight of February 1936.
[178] The two were prosecuted for writing and circulating two pamphlets entitled *Nawab Faroquir Karamti* ('Nawab Faroqui's Miracle') and *Faroqui Shaheber Chalbazi* ('Faroqui Sahib's Trickery'). GB HCPB File No. 95/37.
[179] Report of the Commissioner, Chittagong Division, LOFCR for the first fortnight of April 1936, GB HCPB File No. 56/36.
[180] *Ibid.*, for the first fortnight of July 1936.
[181] Bengal Legislative Assembly, Election Results, 1936–37. IOLR L/P and J/7/1142.
[182] AICC Papers, File No. E-5/1936–37.
[183] Bengal Legislative Assembly, Election Results, 1936–37. IOLR L/P and J/7/1142.

members of the Congress Socialist Party to organise a Peasants' Conference in Barisal with the object of starting Krishak Samities in the District', under the initiative of the Socialist Lalmohan Sen and local members of the Jugantar organisation,[184] and in Bankura, 'Jagdish Chandra Palit, a Congressman of Betur' attempted 'to organise Praja Samitis in and around Kotulpur and Patrasyar' in the Vishnupur subdivision to protest against 'the fact that certain zemindari Gomasthas have been evicting tenants for arrears of rent'.[185] But there is no evidence to suggest that any of these samitis received the slightest backing from the provincial Congress leadership; not one senior Congress leader appears to have addressed or attended the rallies they organised.

Even in Midnapore, where its hold was strong, the provincial Congress quickly lost control over the nominally Congress local krishak samitis, and 'by 1933, Congress organisation in Midnapore was very much under the influence of a new radical group which denied its connection with the Congress and expressed dissatisfaction with the doings of Gandhi'.[186] It was only just before the Assembly election, in December 1936, that the district Congress resolved to form krishak samitis. Without undue cynicism, the District Magistrate attributed this belated concern for the peasantry to the fact that 'Congress have been defeated in the establishment of Union Boards and there is no doubt that they anticipate defeat in several constituencies during the election'.[187] And despite the efforts of Sarat Bose and Prafulla Ghosh to 'stir up enthusiasm for Congress candidates', few were taken in. A meeting addressed by these two gentlemen from Calcutta was 'thinly attended despite market day', and the speakers were 'constantly heckled'. After the speeches were over, a local person stood up and bluntly 'said that Congress only came to them when they wanted votes but when there was distress . . . Congress was not to be found'.[188]

The Bengal Congress' campaign to woo the rural voter was, by and large, weak and fragmented. Local krishak samitis too often lacked the support of the provincial organisation, and even where these samitis had some impact upon little local pockets of opinion, their leaders did not get

[184] Report of the Commissioner, Dacca Division, LOFCR for the first half of May 1936, GB HCPB File No. 56/36.
[185] Report of the Commissioner, Burdwan Division, LOFCR for the first half of December 1936, *ibid.*
[186] Governor's Fortnightly Report for the second fortnight in March 1933, IOLR L/P and J/1933; also cited in Bidyut Chakrabarty, 'Peasants and the Bengal Congress', p. 34.
[187] Report of the Commissioner, Burdwan Division, LOFCR for the first fortnight in June 1936, GB HCPB File No. 56/36.
[188] Governor's Fortnightly Report for the first fortnight of January 1937, in GB HCPB File No. 10/37.

nominated to be the Congress candidates in the elections. The Congress ended up by failing to contest a single Muslim seat, even in Tippera, where the Tippera Krishak Samiti had given it strong peasant backing. In the 'general' Hindu constituencies, hardly any prominent krishak activists were given Congress tickets.[189] The Congress bosses had good reason to fear that the krishak connection was alienating many of the party's most loyal supporters. In November 1936, some local Hindu bigwigs told the Magistrate of the Presidency Division that 'there is little support among the Hindus for communism or any subversive policy and that the Congress was entirely out of favour. It was made clear, however, that most Hindus would vote for any vigorous Hindu candidate even if he was a Congressman.'[190]

The mofussil Hindu gentry was clearly nervous about any signs of radicalism in the Congress. With their rents and receipts from debt payments falling off because of wild promises by krishak candidates, Hindu zamindars wanted a sober Congress electoral campaign. For its part, the Congress could ill afford to alienate its wealthy backers in the mofussil when it needed all the money it could get for the elections. More often than not, the party was forced to put up only those candidates who would finance themselves, and would give the party money rather than expecting handouts from it. When the final list of Congress candidates was drawn up, financial considerations were clearly paramount. Dr B. C. Roy, who chaired the Bengal Congress parliamentary board, explained why some candidates had been dropped in favour of others: 'Dr Dhar was not very keen ... as he was not prepared to spend money ... We had to alter the selection for Dacca [and] Mymensingh. Surjya telephoned to say that he could not find the money, so we have selected Sj. Kumar Sankar Ray.'[191] Kumar Sankar, a cousin of Kiran Sankar Ray, was a wealthy Dacca zamindar. In the Jessore general rural constituency, the man who got the Congress ticket 'paid Rs 20,000/- to the Congress Election fund'.[192] In Midnapore, the District Magistrate noted that:

Congress at present seems to be hampered by shortage of funds and it has not even yet been finally decided who will be their nominees for the general constituency. In the Ghatal-Jhagram constituency the original proposal to set up Babu Kisori Pati

---

[189] Thus Kamini Babu of Comilla fought the election as an 'independent' and Jagdish Palit of Betur did not stand at all. Bengal Legislative Assembly. Election Results, 1936–37. IOLR L/P and J/7/1142.

[190] Report of the Commissioner, Presidency Division, LOFCR for the second fortnight of November 1936, GB HCPB File No. 56/36.

[191] Bidhan Chandra Roy to Jogendra Chandra Chakrabarty, 27 September 1934. B. C. Roy Papers, Part II, 36 (Part I)/1934, NMML.

[192] Report of the Commissioner, Presidency Division, LOFCR for the first fortnight of October 1936, GB HCPB File No. 56/36.

Roy has been postponed because Congress is considering whether it would not be better to set up the Raja of Narajole.[193]

Eventually, both Roy, who had been active in the anti-Union Board campaign, and the Raja of Narajole, a wealthy Sadgop zamindar, were given Congress tickets.[194] But in most cases, the Congress parliamentary board, crippled by a shortage of funds, usually preferred candidates with wealth and influence. This was one reason why the big changes in the electorate did not result in a correspondingly dramatic transformation in the sort of persons who fought the elections as Congress candidates: as many as fifteen Congressmen who had been members of the old Council successfully fought the 1936–37 elections on a Congress ticket.[195] In a handful of rural constituencies, the party brought in a few local activists such as Kisori Pati Roy and Ishwar Chandra Mal of Midnapore and Nishitha Nath Kundu of Dinajpur who won their spurs during Civil Disobedience. But in most rural constituencies, krishak samiti workers were left out in the cold and tickets went instead to wealthy members of the bhadralok. Far from being undermined by the weighting in favour of rural voters, this group – local zamindars and taluqdars, smalltown pleaders, merchants and traders – tightened their grip over the Congress organisation. Once the babus from Calcutta had ruled the Congress roost, but now the mofussil gentry began to come into its own.

The mid-thirties thus catapulted two new groups into prominence in the Bengal Congress. One group was the radicals, who were keen to see the Congress take up the krishak cause. The Congress Party's abysmal showing in the rural constituencies, where it won only thirty-five out of sixty-six Hindu seats,[196] simply underlined the need in radical eyes for the Congress to take a new line on agrarian matters. The other group was the mofussil bhadralok, who were against any concessions to the peasantry and were determined to bring the Party back to its traditional conservative moorings. These two groups, each with diametrically opposed views on the way forward, were set on a collision course in the forties. The struggle between them for the control of the Party was to work a subtle but significant transformation in the politics of the Bengal Congress.

[193] Report of the District Magistrate of Midnapore, *ibid.*
[194] Roy was returned from Jhagram-Ghatal, while the Raja won his seat in the Midnapore Central constituency.
[195] They were Pramathanath Banerjee, Sarat Chandra Bose, Surendranath Biswas, Subhas Bose, Jatindranath Chakrabarty, Harendranath Chaudhuri, J. M. Dasgupta, Jogendra Chandra Gupta, Prabhu Dayal Himatsingha, Debendra Lall Khan, Manmatha Nath Roy, Kiran Sankar Roy, Naliniranjan Sarkar, Bidhan Chandra Roy and Nagendra Nath Sen.
[196] Twenty-eight of these victories were in 'general' or caste Hindu constituencies. Bengal Legislative Assembly, Election Results, 1936–37. IOLR L/P and J/7/1142.

3   The reorientation of the Bengal Congress, 1937–45

Scholars are coming to recognise the era of 'provincial autonomy' as a period of heightened communal consciousness, during which organised politics increasingly fractured along lines of community. In the six Hindu-majority provinces where the Congress held office between 1937 and 1939, it has been argued that Congress policies raised, in Muslim eyes, the spectre of a 'Hindu Raj'.[1] In Bengal, where Hindus, a large and vocal minority, were at best junior partners in the exercise of provincial autonomy, developments took a different course. But here too social and political divisions hardened along communal lines. Between 1937 and 1945, four ministries took office in Bengal, each attempting to achieve a stable accommodation between the different political interests. But by 1945, when negotiations began in earnest for the ending of British rule, there was little evidence among Bengal's politicians of a spirit of compromise. These were years of great complexity, as parties and factions variously split, changed sides or regrouped. This chapter will not attempt to provide a detailed narrative of the political manoeuvrings of this period. Instead, it will focus on broad trends in the Bengal Congress so as to identify the shifts and alignments that pushed politics into the communal abyss.

The Congress and the 'left' initiative

On April Fool's Day 1937, Fazlul Huq was sworn in as the first premier of Bengal, at the head of a Krishak Praja–Muslim League coalition ministry. The Congress, which with fifty-two seats[2] was the largest single party in

---

[1] See, for instance, B. R. Tomlinson, *The Indian National Congress and the Raj, 1929–1942. The Penultimate Phase*, London, 1976, for an account of the 'Ministry period' at the all-India level. For an examination of the impact of Congress policies at the level of provincial politics, see Mukul Kesavan, '1937 as a Landmark in the Course of Communal Politics in the U.P.,' Occasional Papers in History and Society, Second Series, No. XI, Nehru Memorial Museum and Library, New Delhi, 1988.
[2] These included two seats reserved for women and four for labour.

the new Legislative Assembly, formed the main opposition. The Muslim League and the Krishak Praja Party had fought the elections as rivals, and Huq would have preferred the Congress as the Krishak Praja's partner in office. The Congress and the Krishak Praja Party had been informal allies in the general elections, with the result that the Congress had contested no Muslim seats and had given the nod to the Krishak Praja campaign in the localities. The pledge in the Krishak Praja manifesto to release the detenus was in its turn meant as an olive branch to the Congress. But early in February 1937, the understanding between the Congress and Krishak Praja Party broke down when the two parties failed to reach an agreement on the agenda of the coalition government. Congress spokesmen (including Sarat Bose, Bidhan Chandra Roy and Kiran Sankar Roy) wanted the release of political prisoners to be the first priority, an issue over which the ministry should be ready to resign if necessary. Krishak Praja leaders, on the other hand, felt that krishak welfare was what mattered most. They argued that a commitment to resigning over the question of detenus might place peasant welfare in jeopardy.[3] In the event, the Congress leadership dithered over whether or not to accept office at all, let alone whether to join a coalition government, and Fazlul Huq, having 'pleaded and pleaded in vain for active co-operation or even tacit support ... [was] ... forced into the arms of the Muslim League'. [4]

The Muslim ministries which took office, first the League–Praja coalition and later the Muslim League on its own, put through the Assembly a series of measures which promoted various Muslim interests at the cost of bhadralok privilege. But the Congress in opposition was powerless to resist this legislative onslaught. The 1937 elections had brought into the Legislature a large number of rural representatives. Many were zamindars and taluqdars, but some were of a new breed of politician. Born and bred in the mofussil, these men had cut their political cub teeth in Union and District Boards, while others were leaders of local krishak samitis, who spoke for peasants and jotedars.[5] As their self-proclaimed leader, Fazlul

---

[3] See Abul Mansur Ahmed, *Amar Dekha Rajnitir Panchash Bachhar*, pp. 134–139. There are several versions of what lay behind the breakdown of negotiations between the Congress and the KPP. It is often argued, for instance, that the talks broke down because Gandhi and the Congress Working Committee refused to allow the Bengal Congress to join a coalition government. Author's interview with Amiya Bose, Calcutta, 4 March 1990. There is, however, no conclusive evidence to support any particular theory.

[4] Humayun Kabir, *Muslim Politics 1906–47 and other Essays*, Calcutta, 1969, p. 27. Kabir was himself a member of the Krishak Praja Party in the thirties, and according to Abul Mansur Ahmed, was present at the meeting at which the KPP–Congress talks broke down. Kabir, however, makes no mention of the meeting.

[5] Commenting on the presence of 'krishak' politicians in the Assembly, the Governor recognised 'the prominent part taken by "Krishak Samitis" and the attacks levelled against the Zamindari system' in the elections. He pointed out that in Noakhali district 'all

Huq was bound to put forward tenancy legislation and the Bengal Tenancy (Amendment) Bill was tabled in September 1937.[6] The Bill proposed to abolish the right of the zamindar to extract *salami* (or the landlord's transfer fee) and also his right of pre-emption, thus enabling his tenants freely to subdivide and transfer their holdings. In effect, the Bill denied the zamindar the freedom to choose his own tenants or to stop larger tenants from consolidating their holdings on his estates. Tenants would now have the power to enlarge and rationalise their holdings without let or hindrance from the zamindars, who would no longer be able legally to curb tenants on their estates. The Bill also sought to abolish the power of the landlords to extract rent through the certificate procedure and slashed the rate of interest payable on arrears of rent by half, while placing a ceiling on the enhancement of rent for a period of ten years.[7] All in all, the Bill seriously inhibited the power of the zamindar to extract rent from his tenants. It threatened to undermine the very basis of the zamindar's power and prosperity in the mofussil, while strengthening the hand of the rich peasant. Since most zamindars were bhadralok Hindus, the Bill was seen as a deliberate challenge to Hindu dominance in the countryside. Hindu zamindars denounced the Bill as a communal measure that was 'utterly revolutionary in character'[8] and predicted that it would 'bring in its train confusion and disaster to the country'.[9]

Next to come under attack were the zamindari *hats*, or local markets for the sale of crops and other produce, which were a vital source of zamindari revenue. In 1939, the Cabinet discussed

a Bill to provide for the establishment of Government markets and licensing of private markets for agricultural products – a very necessary measure with strong Muslim support: clearly, however, the landlord Hindu Ministers are convinced

---

but one of the successful candidates were not even matriculates'. Governor's Fortnightly Report (FR) for the second half of January 1937, GB HCPB File No. 10/37. See also GOI Home Poll File No. 132/38.

[6] Huq's partner in the coalition government, the Muslim League, was, of course less enthusiastic about tenancy reform, and attempted to delay the introduction of the Tenancy (Amendment) Bill in the Assembly. But Huq's party grew increasingly impatient and forced him to take up tenancy reform in the monsoon session of 1937. See Abul Mansur Ahmed, *Amar Dekha Rajnitir Panchash Bachhar*, p. 151, for an account of how members of the Krishak Praja Party exerted pressure on their 'unpredictable' leader.

[7] The Bill was passed in 1938 by 80 votes to 72: the Congress bloc remained neutral. See *Bengal Legislative Assembly Proceedings*, Second Session (1937), vol. 51, 3–4. For an account of the voting patterns on the Bill in the Assembly, see Partha Chatterjee, *Bengal 1920–1947*, pp. 172–182.

[8] See Linlithgow's account of a memorandum received from the Secretary of the East Bengal Landholders' Association protesting against the Bill, in Linlithgow to Zetland, 7 October 1937. Zetland Collection, IOLR MSS Eur D/609/14.

[9] Account of a meeting of the East Bengal Landholders' Association in Dacca, *Amrita Bazar Patrika*, 12 April 1939.

that the real intention of the measure is to give the Muslims the power to expropriate or break up the markets of private land-owners by indirect means.[10]

The Ministry also took steps to give immediate effect to the Bengal Agricultural Debtors Act of 1935, setting up 'debt settlement boards' in three thousand villages within a year of coming to office.[11] These boards were intended to provide a forum where moneylenders could reach a compromise with their debtors. But in fact they encouraged debtors to renege on their debts. This made the credit crisis worse and did nothing to improve relations between creditors and debtors.[12] In 1940, the Bengal Moneylenders Act made it mandatory for all persons in the business of lending money to obtain licences, and fixed the maximum rate of interest at 8 per cent. Moneylending was a business dominated by Hindu professional mahajans, banias, shopkeepers and landowners for whom usury had long been a lucrative trade, and the Act hit them hard.

These measures, of course, equally affected the interests of Muslim zamindars, represented in the Assembly by eleven members of the Dacca Nawab's extended family.[13] Nazimuddin and his zamindar colleagues in the League tried hard to draw the teeth out of the proposed legislation and they had a measure of success. The Governor reported that the final version of the Bengal Moneylenders Bill in 1940 was a shadow of its former self:

Starting as a Government Bill to regulate moneylending, it was twisted under party pressure to a Bill to scale down moneylenders' dues drastically, and in the form in which it emerged from the Select Committee, it would have been an impossible measure. Suhrawardy, though not responsible for the Bill, in fact took charge by arrangement with his colleagues and succeeded during the debates ... in improving it a great deal, partly by widening the scope of the loans to which it would not apply and partly by improving its provisions.[14]

But Muslim League ministers were unable to check the flood of anti-zamindar legislation. They were 'alive to the necessity of keeping the

[10] Brabourne to Linlithgow, 19 December 1939, FR. Linlithgow Collection, IOLR MSS Eur F/125/38.
[11] Azizul Haque, *The Man Behind the Plough*, Calcutta, 1939, p. 169.
[12] At a meeting of District Magistrates and Divisional Commissioners held in 1938, there were several reports that the Act 'was interpreted as a protection against monetary claims' and had encouraged among rural debtors 'a disinclination to meet their pecuniary obligations'. GB HCPB File No. 283/38.
[13] P. D. Martyn, erstwhile manager of the Nawabi estates, recalls that 'the Nawab and Sir Nazimuddin were Ministers, Shahabuddin [the younger brother of Nazimuddin] was Chief Whip and several of the younger members became Parliamentary Secretaries. Mrs Shahabuddin was also in the Assembly ...'. P. D. Martyn Memoirs, IOLR MSS Eur F/180/13, p. 9.
[14] Herbert to Linlithgow, 10 May 1940, FR. Linlithgow Collection, IOLR MSS Eur F/125/40.

masses behind them, at the cost, no doubt, of legislative and administrative concessions',[15] and, much to the disappointment of the Governors, Muslim League ministers in the coalition showed an inclination to 'curry popularity with the agriculturists by promises which they know are incapable of fulfilment, but which they feel they must make or fall behind in the race for votes'.[16] The League had joined hands with the Krishak Praja Party on the understanding that they would support measures to dismantle the zamindari system provided that zamindars were compensated for their losses.[17] For the Muslim elites such as the Dacca Nawabs, economic losses in their estates promised to be amply compensated for by the rewards of office. But Hindu zamindars faced the prospect of further economic loss without corresponding political gains.

The legislative onslaught did not, however, stop at the countryside. Muslim coalition governments used their new political muscle to create opportunities for middle-class Muslims, giving them 'legislative and administrative concessions which, ironically enough, will often bear harder than ever on the Hindu middle class'.[18] In 1938, the Fazlul Huq ministry changed the rules about police recruitment so that 'while enlisting Bengali constables the Superintendent of Police must see that not less than 50% of the recruits are Muslims'.[19] In the same year, the ministry passed legislation that stipulated that 60 per cent of all government appointments be reserved for Muslims.[20] In 1939, the Government instructed local bodies 'not to propose for appointment to local bodies persons who were known to be actively opposed to the policy of the Ministry', and slapped administrative controls on nominations to the Union Boards, which accounted for one third of their total membership.[21] And in 1939, the Calcutta Municipal Amendment Act put an end to Hindu supremacy in that traditional bastion of bhadralok power, the Calcutta Corporation.[22] But the unkindest cut of all came in 1940, when

---

[15] Brabourne to Linlithgow, 5 February 1939, FR. Linlithgow Collection, IOLR MSS Eur F/125/39.

[16] Reid to Linlithgow, 19 April 1939, FR. Linlithgow Collection, IOLR MSS Eur F/125/39.

[17] Abul Mansur Ahmed, *Amar Dekha Rajnitir Panchash Bachhar*, p. 148.

[18] Brabourne to Linlithgow, 5 February 1939, FR. Linlithgow Collection, IOLR MSS Eur F 125/39.

[19] Government of Bengal, Home Police File P 3-1-19, Proceedings A 79–81, December 1938. Cited in Shila Sen, *Muslim Politics in Bengal*, p. 113.

[20] N. N. Mitra (ed.), *Indian Annual Register*, 1938, vol. II, July–December, p. 23.

[21] Government of Bengal, Local Self Government Circular No. 428 (5)–L.S.G., dated 19 April 1939, File No. 20–3 of 1938; cited in Shila Sen, *Muslim Politics in Bengal*, p. 109.

[22] Of the total of 98 seats, 47 were to be reserved for Hindus of which 4 seats were to go to the Scheduled castes, giving Hindus 3 seats less than an absolute majority. The remaining 51 seats were to be divided between elected aldermen (5), Mahommedans (22), Special Constituencies, including the Bengal Chamber of Commerce, Port Commissioners etc.

the Ministry introduced the Secondary Education Bill, taking control of higher education in the province away from Calcutta University and vesting it instead in a Secondary Education Board in which Muslims were to be given a greater say. Higher education was not only a mainstay of bhadralok power and influence; it was also a symbol of their exclusive identity. In threatening their control over this vital asset, the Bill also challenged the very basis of their 'cultural superiority', the main plank of bhadralok communal discourse.

Faced with this unprecedented series of challenges, the Congress Party split apart. The dissensions of the early thirties, temporarily papered over during the elections, re-emerged in a different shape. In 1936, after the reconciliation between the Working Committee and the Nationalists, Sarat Bose had taken over the running of the Congress Parliamentary Board, marginalising his rival, Dr B. C. Roy.[23] Sarat Bose was a formidable politician, whose power and abilities had long been recognised by his adversaries.[24] Bose had helped to ensure that the Bengal Congress did reasonably well in the elections. But he was well aware that the Congress could have done better, particularly in the mofussil, where in nine out of seventeen constituencies they contested, Congress candidates were defeated by independents.[25] When the understanding between the Congress and the Krishak Praja Party broke down and the Krishak Praja Party formed a coalition with the League, Bose saw the folly of the Congress decision not to contest any Muslim rural seats. In his eyes, the elections had proved the point that if the Congress remained tied to its narrowly bhadralok moorings, it would never be able to regain the initiative in Bengali politics. To survive as a political force in the new era

(12), Labour (2), Anglo-Indian (2), and eight nominated members, of which three would be Scheduled Castes. The Act was passed by 128 votes to 65: it was opposed by the Congress, the Independent Scheduled Caste Party, all caste Hindu members of the Nationalist Party, while the KPP remained neutral. N. N. Mitra (ed.), *Indian Annual Register*, 1939, vol. II, July–December, pp. 160–161.

23 See AICC Papers, Files No. P-6 (Part I)/1936 and P-6 (Part II)/1936, for details on the strategems by which Sarat Bose gained effective control of the Parliamentary Board and the BPCC executive.

24 The police, for instance, regarded him as the power behind his brother, and less flatteringly, as 'the real snake in the grass'. The British Government in Bengal saw him as 'a most dangerous opponent of Government and a man who in intellectual attainments is far superior to the majority of Congress leaders in the province ... He is a man with considerable influence and great powers of organisation'. Memorandum by Charles Tegart, GOI Home Poll File No. 31/27/32.

25 In the Murshidabad General Rural Constituency, the Congress Scheduled Caste candidate was defeated by the Hindu Sabha nominee: in all but six of the other Scheduled Caste constituencies which Congress contested, it lost to independents. Independents also won in the thirteen Scheduled Caste constituencies where the Congress had failed to put up a candidate. Bengal Legislative Assembly, Election Results. IOLR L/P and J/7/1142.

of mass politics, the Congress would have to broaden the basis of its support and refurbish its tarnished secular image.

Bose, however, was in a difficult position. He was the leader of the opposition against a ministry which not only represented most Muslims with the vote but which also had some claims to represent the peasant interest. Moreover, he was all too conscious that his own grip on the Congress was far from secure, and that he could not afford to appear to be too conciliatory to Muslims and peasants. A decade before, the Bengal Congress had rejected Chittaranjan Das' attempt to break a similar communal deadlock, and the fate of the Das Pact was not a good augury for an accommodation between Hindu and Muslim politicians.[26] In fact Sarat Bose's options were severely limited. By taking advantage of the recent influx of young socialists and communists into the party, he tried to take the Congress leftwards in a more secular, if populist, direction. His strategy in the House was to oppose the ministry 'from the left'[27] while launching a campaign outside to win the 'masses' to the Congress.

This 'radicalisation' of the Congress in the late thirties has been discussed by Partha Chatterjee, who has linked it to the wider patterns of socio-economic change in Bengal. Chatterjee suggests that changes in the structure of land relations in the province, specifically 'the complete non-viability by the 1920s and 1930s of the overwhelming part of zamindari and tenure-holding landed property ... created the possibility of a large middle class which was ... dissociated from landed property. Now it became a class predominantly urban in its livelihood and social outlook'.[28] However, this process had only just begun in the thirties. The urban radical intelligentsia, which was to play a crucial role in re-shaping Bengali politics after Independence, was only one strand in the warp and weft of Bengal's public life. Losing their roots in landed property did indeed foster a brand of radicalism amongst a few bhadralok; but it provoked a reactionary political conservatism amongst many more.[29] In the conflict between radicals and conservatives, the latter had by far the bigger battalions.

In the first months of the Huq ministry, Bose rallied his motley crew of

[26] For a discussion of the ill-fated Hindu–Muslim Pact of Chittaranjan Das, see Ujjwalkanti Das, 'The Bengal Pact of 1923 and its Reactions', *Bengal Past and Present*, vol. 34, part I, 188, January–June, 1980.

[27] Partha Chatterjee, *Bengal 1920–1947*, p. 172.   [28] *Ibid.*, p. 177.

[29] This is a possibility that has been ignored in studies of Bengali politics. See, for instance, Partha Chatterjee, *ibid.* and Sugata Bose, *Agrarian Bengal*, pp. 190–214. The same is true of Bidyut Chakrabarty's recent more detailed study, which builds upon Chattterjee's thesis and associates 'middle-class radicalism' with 'the formation of a new social class that was less dependent on rent incomes from landed property'. *Subhas Chandra Bose and Middle Class Radicalism*, p. 5.

followers. They included members of the left, disaffected Congressmen, students and krishak leaders. His was a vocal but relatively small group, outnumbered by the conservatives who still dominated the party. Bose appointed as Secretary of the Bengal Provincial Congress Committee Babu Kamal Krishna Roy of Bankura, known to be 'sympathetic to the krishak cause',[30] and later gave the same post to Ashrafuddin Ahmed Chaudhuri, the Muslim krishak leader from Comilla, who was persuaded to return to the Congress fold.[31] But despite the fact that for a few years, left-wingers held key offices in the BPCC executive, their efforts to widen the social and communal basis of the Bengal Congress were hampered by constraints inside the Party itself. Sarat Bose's 'mass contact' campaign never had the full weight of the Congress behind it.

The radical programme thus included traditional nationalist slogans, which put national unity above social change. In Tippera, where Ashrafuddin Ahmed Chaudhuri was active in the campaign, it was reported that 'the local Krishak movement appears to have coalesced completely with the Congress ... Resolutions show change from the purely agrarian outlook to that of the congress socialist party'. Calls for the ending of the Permanent Settlement were lumped together with the familiar Congress demand for the release of political prisoners.[32] Local activists had to be kept from treading on the toes of powerful Congress zamindars. In Midnapore, the Congress restricted its activity to the Government's *khas mahal* estates,[33] leading the Viceroy caustically to remark that 'it is an interesting comment on the sincerity of the Congress agrarian agitation that the Zamindari of one of the most troublesome Congress leaders in Midnapore has been comparatively immune from it'.[34]

There is evidence also to suggest that the Congress mass-contact campaign on occasion sought religious Muslim sanction. One curious document circulated in Rangpur in 1939, defending the Congress Party against the charge of being a Hindu organisation, declared that it was British rule, not the Congress or the Hindus who were 'the only cause of the ruin of

[30] Report from Burdwan Division, LOFCR for the first fortnight of July 1937, GB HCPB File No. 10/37.
[31] Ashrafuddin had joined hands with the KPP in the middle of 1936, after being edged out of the leadership of the Tippera Krishak Samiti. Now he was inducted into the BPCC with the charge of leading a 'mass contact' campaign in Bengal. Abul Mansur Ahmed, *Amar Dekha Rajnitir Panchash Bachhar*, p. 135.
[32] Report of the Commissioner, the Chittagong Division, LOFCR for the first fortnight of June 1937, GB HCPB File No. 10/57.
[33] A 'no-rent' movement in the Contai *khas mahals* was led by the Congressman Babu Ishwar Chandra Mal. GB HCPB File No. 283/38.
[34] This was a reference to the zamindari of Debendra Lall Khan, the Raja of Narajole, Congressman and close associate of Sarat Bose. Brabourne to Linlithgow, 6 January 1939, FR. Linlithgow Collection, IOLR MSS Eur F/125/39.

Moslems'. This was because British rule had 'snatched away the standard of Islam from the hands of the Moslems' and 'prepared the Macaulay scheme in order to deprive Moslems of this country of their religious-mindedness'. It invoked the authority of long-dead Muslim clerics to encourage Muslims to join the Congress:

In 1888 ... the Moslems ... had asked from the Ulemas of those days as to whether it was proper for the Moslems to join Congress and to carry on a struggle for India's freedom unitedly with Hindus ... In reply to that, in that very year of 1888 hundreds of Ulemas such as Enamul Ulema Kutubul Ahtab, Hazrat Shah Rashid Ahmed Gangoli and ... Maulana Mahammadul Hasan ... had proclaimed its propriety.[35]

An effort was also made to approach Muslims through local pirs who could be persuaded to work for the Congress. Nirad Chaudhuri, who was Sarat Bose's secretary at the time, writes that

the idea was to get at the Muslim masses through their traditional religious leaders ... the very set of men who were the most active promoters of Muslim group consciousness. Subhas Babu invited a whole host of them ... to Sarat Babu's house. Whether their travelling expenses were paid by the Congress or not, they came. One day I saw a procession of Muslim divines trooping into Sarat Babu's house.[36]

These features of the Congress mass contact campaign suggest that it was populist in message and style and did not fit easily into the usual mould of radical left-wing political movements. But within the spectrum of bhadra-lok political opinion, which was fast hardening into unbendingly communal attitudes and which clung determinedly to traditional privilege, the mass contact campaigners represented the liberal left.[37] Under the steward-ship of the left, the policies of the Bengal Congress underwent a distinct change. For the first time in its history, the Party was heard to call for the abolition of the Permanent Settlement and to advocate the suspension of rent payments. In December 1937, reports came in from Burdwan that 'the Congress party, helped by Dasarathi Ta, has been enrolling members. The alleged oppression of the Chakdighi Zamindars in realising rents was discussed at one of the meetings'.[38] The estates in question belonged to

[35] Mohammed Ehsanul Huq Effendi, *Bartaman Rajnaitik Sankat O Musalmaner Kartabya*, ('Present Political Troubles and the Duty of Muslims'), Domar, Rangpur, 1939. GOI Home Political File No. 37/30/39.

[36] Nirad C. Chaudhuri, *Thy Hand Great Anarch! India, 1921–1952*, London, 1987, p. 469.

[37] Simply put, the philosophy behind the campaign was that 'the solution of the communal problem lies ultimately in social justice'. Text of Sarat Chandra Bose's statement to the Press released at Calcutta on 15 March 1947, *I Warned my Countrymen. Being the Collected Works 1945–50 of Sarat Chandra Bose*, Calcutta, 1968, p. 182.

[38] Report of the Commissioner, Burdwan Division, LOFCR for the first fortnight in December 1937, GB HCPB File No. 10/37.

the Singh-Roy zamindars, a leading bhadralok family which had good connections with the British, and was therefore an obvious target for the Congress. In Bankura, a local krishak samiti was established under the auspices of the Congress; meetings were organised in different parts of Nadia by Congress workers to urge peasants to enlist as members of the Party,[39] and in November 1937, 'some forty Muslim cultivators' in Dacca division were induced to join the Congress.[40] In 1938, the District Magistrate of Birbhum spoke of a recent agitation against the payment of rent by 'communistic sections of the Congress'. Officials from Midnapore also complained about a 'no rent' campaign, which was 'a part of the movement led by Babu Iswar Chandra Mal' in the Contai khas mahals (government estates) since 1937.[41] The movement showed no signs of abating and the Governor told the Viceroy at the end of the year that

Reports continue to come in, from all sources, of the continued activities by Congressmen, strongly supported by ex-detenus, to stir up discontent and disaffection among the cultivating classes and to promote a rebellious and indisciplined frame of mind among students. Instances of actual preaching of 'no payment of rent' are rare but as one Commissioner remarks, 'No organised campaign is necessary in support of a movement so congenial to the people'.[42]

Sarat Bose is also known to have put out feelers among Muslim students in Calcutta, attempting to win the more radical among them over to the Congress.[43] These efforts met with some success: in March 1938, a police memo alleged that 'Mr. Sarat Chandra Bose has paid money to those leading members of the A[ll] B[engal] M[uslim] S[tudents] League through his agents Kazi Moizudin Ahamed, Abdus Sattar and others'.[44] Later that month, a meeting was held in the Carmichael Hostel by the same group of Muslim students calling for 'the emancipation of toiling peasants and the nationalisation of key industries'.[45] The *mohalla* (neighbourhood) and city Mass Contacts Committees in Comilla in Tippera

[39] Report of the Commissioner, Presidency Division, LOFCR for the second fortnight of July 1937. GB HCPB File No. 10/37.
[40] Report of the Commissioner, Dacca Division, LOFCR for the first fortnight of November 1937, *ibid.*
[41] GB HCPB File No. 283/38.
[42] Brabourne to Linlithgow, 4 December 1938, FR. Linlithgow Collection, IOLR MSS Eur F/125/38.
[43] In April 1938, a Special Branch agent reported that: 'Nazimuddin Ahamad, the Chairman of the All Bengal Students Federation and Abdus Satar, member of the same, are carrying on propoganda amongst the Muslim students of Calcutta and inducing them to join the All Bengal Students Federation the supporter of the Congress. There are very few Muslim students in this organisation ... Mr Kazi Moizuddin Ahamad has been engaged by the Congress leaders to have the Muslim students of Calcutta in their suport by any cost [sic]'. Memo dated 2 April 1938, in GB SB 'PM Series', File No. 13951/38.
[44] Memo dated 16 March 1938, *ibid.*   [45] Memo dated 24 March 1938, *ibid.*

District, and similar committees in Calcutta and in Burdwan, reported some success in recruiting Muslims. By May 1937, over a thousand Muslims were reported to have joined the Party in the suburbs of Calcutta alone.[46] The following year, the party set up three new sub-committees to deal respectively with mass contacts, peasants and the agrarian programme; in 1939, the Congress officially accepted the abolition of the Permanent Settlement as a part of the party programme.[47] In June of that year, the mass-contact initiative had a spectacular triumph when the Krishak Praja ex-Minister, Nausher Ali, signed the Congress pledge.[48] But, as the Governor pointed out, it was not an unalloyed victory:

The left wing elements have been reinforced by the accession of the Muslim ex-Minister, Nausher Ali, who has signed the Congress pledge and has been making rather wild speeches against "Imperialism" and zamindars – but the value of this reinforcement is open to doubt. Muslim feeling has in places run high against him and the welcome which the Amrita Bazar Patrika has given him to the ranks of the Congress has been decidedly reserved.[49]

The hostile reaction which met Nausher Ali's conversion to the Congress reflected some of the obstacles that the mass contact campaign faced. It challenged the hold that Bengal's Muslim politicians had enjoyed over Muslim cultivators, forcing them to realise

how serious are the possibilities of agrarian agitation fomented by ex-detenus, and, what is more important, their Muslim supporters in the Assembly have also begun to take alarm at the prospect of these organised and inveterate revolutionaries getting too much out of control among Muslim cultivators by means of wild promises and skilful exploitation. The threat to their own local leadership no doubt disturbs them no less than the threat to the peace of the Province.[50]

The campaign predictably ran into trouble in the localities, arousing the suspicion and hostility of local Muslim leaders.[51] In November 1937, forty Muslim peasants who had joined the Congress in Munshiganj were

---

[46] *Bombay Chronicle*, 18 May 1937, and Manzoor Ahmed to Ashrafuddin Ahmed Chaudhuri, 13 July 1937 (in Urdu), AICC Papers, File No. 42/1937 (1), cited in Mushirul Hasan, 'The Muslim Mass Contacts Campaign: Analysis of a Strategy of Political Mobilisation', pp. 117–118.

[47] BPCC Annual Report, 18 February 1939, in AICC Papers, File No. P-24 (Part II)/1938–39.

[48] Nausher Ali of Jessore, Minister for Public Health and Local Self-Government in the first Fazlul Huq ministry was dropped in June 1938, when the entire Huq cabinet resigned and reconstituted the Ministry without him. This left Fazlul Huq as the only member of the Krishak Praja Party in the Government. See Franchise, Ministries, 1937–46, in IOLR/L/P and J/8/475 and Shila Sen, *Muslim Politics in Bengal*, p. 119.

[49] Brabourne to Linlithgow, 6 January 1939, FR. Linlithgow Collection, IOLR MSS Eur F/125/39.

[50] Reid to Linlithgow, 5 April 1939, FR. *Ibid.*

[51] The mass-contact movement in the United Provinces provoked a similar response. In the words of one scholar, 'it offered too little too late. Its one perceptible consequence in UP

forced by local *mullahs* to recant.[52] In Nadia, the Congress campaign met
with organised protest from the local Krishak Praja Party who rallied
Muslim tenants against the oppressions of local Hindu zamindars.[53] In
Barisal, at a Praja Samiti meeting organised by the local Congress Committee, a quarrel broke out between Hindu and Muslim members, and all
Hindu Congressmen were forced to leave the meeting.[54] In Noakhali, it
was noticed that 'the visits of Noakhali Krishak leaders ... have given
offence to the local Maulvis, who are now doing counter-propaganda'.[55]
In July 1937, the District Magistrate reported that

The Noakhali Congress Executive are touring systematically in the villages to start
new Congress offices and to enlist members. The office bearers of the new committees are almost all Hindus, and there is no sign at present of their drawing in the
Muhammadan Krishak element on any large scale, as in Tippera. Their activities
in the Lakhimpur–Raipur–Ramganj area are greatly resented by Ghulam Sarwar,
who regards that part of the world as his preserve and does not want his followers
drawn off to another camp. There is bitter hostility at the moment.[56]

Ghulam Sarwar Hossain was an influential Noakhali pir who had led the
extreme wing of the Noakhali Krishak Samiti which called for all rents to
be remitted, the boycott of zamindari markets and the extirpation of
moneylenders from Debt Settlement Boards.[57] He had kept aloof from the
Krishak Praja Party, preferring to fight the election as an Independent,
winning in the Ramganj-cum-Raipur rural constituency by the spectacular margin of over 12,000 votes.[58] When Fazlul Huq took office, Sarwar
flirted with the idea of joining the Congress in order to lead the mass
contact campaign in his area. According to the District Magistrate,
Sarwar had claimed that

the local Congress leaders were trying to get him to join them, and he would be
ready to do so if the Congress took up the Krishak cause and supported an amendment to the Bengal Tenancy Act. At the moment the general Muhammadan popu-

---

was a further closing up of the ranks of Muslim politicians and another spurt of
Hindu–Muslim rioting'. Gyanendra Pandey, *The Ascendency of the Congress in Uttar
Pradesh 1926–34. A Study in Imperfect Mobilization*, New Delhi, 1978, p. 151.
52 Report of the Commissioner, Dacca Division, LOFCR for the first fortnight of November 1937. GB HCPB File No. 10/37.
53 Report of the Commissioner, Presidency Division, LOFCR for the second fortnight in
July 1937. *Ibid.*
54 Report of the Commissioner, Dacca Division, LOFCR for the first fortnight in September 1937. *Ibid.*
55 Report of the Commissioner, Chittagong Division, LOFCR for the second fortnight in
June 1937. *Ibid.*
56 Report of the Commissioner, Chitagong Division, LOFCR for the second fortnight in
July 1937. *Ibid.*
57 Report of the Commissioner, Chittagong Division, LOFCR for the second fortnight of
August 1936, GB HCPB File No. 56/36.
58 'Franchise, Bengal Legislative, Assembly Results, 1936', IOLR L/P and J/7/1142.

lation takes little interest in the Congress, which is weak in the district; but the position would change rapidly if influential leaders thought an alliance with the Congress to their advantage.[59]

But his unrestrained campaign against local zamindars and mahajans led the local Congress to have second thoughts about the merits of having Ghulam Sarwar as an ally. Throughout the summer of 1937, he was reported to be 'stirring up trouble', threatening 'the boycott of Hindu zemindars Hats',[60] and inciting violence against zamindars and mahajans. This was going too far, even for the Congress in its new 'radical' garb. Noakhali's bhadralok panicked; by the end of July, Congressmen in Noakhali came to the rescue of their traditional allies and took action against Sarwar, setting the police upon him: 'the Congress leaders came to the DIG of Police ... to ask (not without some grounds) for the protection of Hindus in that area from Krishak Samiti goondas ... [They] cited a speech by Sarwar containing incitement against mahajans and talukdars as well as defamatory statements against specified persons.'[61] At the same time, the Congress launched a campaign on Sarwar's own patch, a move which turned Sarwar into an implacable enemy of the Congress. Muslim League Ministers had made several efforts to get Gholam Sarwar onto their 'side', so as to 'fight congressits [sic] ... who are trying to capture Noakhali Krishak Samitis'.[62] Now they found him willing to make terms. Sarwar unleashed a virulently communal campaign to pull his peasant followers out of the 'Hindu' Congress and stepped up his attacks on Hindu mahajans and taluqdars. Warning 'his constituents against the congress attempts to win them over', he 'observed that the real aim of the congress was to oust the Muhammadan Ministry so as to establish a Hindu Raj in its place'. On one occasion, he incited local cultivators to stop by force 'a Congress Muslim from presiding over a "Detenu Day" meeting'.[63] Sarwar not only made sure that the Congress efforts to recruit Noakhali's Muslim peasants failed, but by bitter diatribes against specifically 'Hindu' zamindars, he also succeeded in converting agrarian conflict in Noakhali into a Hindu–Muslim issue. He thus helped to lay the

[59] Report of the Commissioner, Chittagong Division, LOFCR for the first fortnight of June 1937, GB HCPB File No. 10/37.
[60] Ibid.
[61] Report of the Commissioner, Chittagong Division, LOFCR for the second fortnight in July 1937. Ibid.
[62] Nazimuddin instructed the DM to 'try and bring about a reconciliation between Gholam Sarwar, Maulvis Abdur Rashid, Ibrahim and Abdur Rezzak. If these four can work together then there is no danger of Krishak Samitis going over to the Congress'. Note by Nazimuddin dated 16 May 1937. GB HCPB File No. 307/37.
[63] Report of the Commissioner, Chittagong Division, LOFCR for the first fortnight in August 1937, GB HCPB File No. 10/37.

foundations for what was to be one of the worst communal riots in Bengal's history.[64]

A similar pattern can be seen in other parts of the province, where Congress efforts to win over Muslim peasants provoked the ire of local Muslim leaders and often led to a perceptible rise in communal tempers. In Tippera, the early successes of Ashrafuddin Ahmed Chaudhuri's campaign[65] sparked off hostile Muslim counter-demonstrations in Chandpur, at which 'most of the speeches tended to disturb relations between the communities by urging the audiences not to buy from Hindu shops, not to employ Hindu lawyers and generally to have as little to do with Hindus as possible'.[66] On one occasion, when Ashrafuddin 'went to a religious meeting in a mosque and started a political discussion, [he was] opposed by another speaker who urged the gathering not to join the Congress'.[67] When Subhas Bose (then president of the All-India Congress Committee) visited the district in 1938, he optimistically claimed that 'the response I received from the Muslim public exceeded my fondest hopes and I have come back with the confidence and certainty that ... the Muslims of Bengal will before long be all inside the Congress'. In fact his procession was met with brickbats by 'a crowd of Muslim Leaguers'.[68] And when, in 1939, Pabna suffered a spate of communal incidents, the Governor took the view that these were linked with 'the efforts on the part of local Muslim Leaguers to compete for popular favour simultaneously against the wild promises of the Congress left wing and the equally wild promises of the Muslim Krishaks: promises alone being insufficient it has probably been found necessary to appeal to fanaticism as well.'[69]

The hostility of local Muslim leaders was, however, only one of the obstacles in the path of the mass contact campaign. In Bengal just as in other parts of India, the campaign depended critically on the backing of district and local Congress Committees, and this backing was often not to be had.[70] In most districts in Bengal, the mass contact initiative created deep fissures within local Congress Committees, a mirror image of the

---

[64] The police believed that Ghulam Sarwar did more than any other leader to incite Noakhali's Muslims into 'avenging' the Muslim deaths in the Calcutta Killing in 1946. GB SB, 'PM Series' File No. 937/46.

[65] Report of the Commissioner, Chittagong Division, LOFCR for the second half of July 1937, GB HCPB File No. 10/37.

[66] Report of the Commissioner, Chittagong Division, LOFCR for the first fortnight of November 1937. *Ibid.*

[67] Report of the Chittagong Division, LOFCR for the first fortnight in September 1937. *Ibid.*

[68] AICC Papers, File No. 39/1938.

[69] Reid to Linlithgow, 22 May 1939, FR. Linlithgow Collection, IOLR MSS Eur F/125/39.

[70] Mushirul Hasan, 'The Muslim Mass Contacts Campaign', p. 214.

splits in the provincial leadership. Local supporters of the B. C. Roy group were suspicious of any cause espoused by the Bose brothers and stayed aloof from the campaign for reasons that had everything to do with traditional factional rivalries. But others were alarmed by the new 'radicalism' of the party. In Birbhum, the Congress Committee split when Babu D. Chakravarti of Bolpur dissociated himself from the krishak conference at which M. N. Roy, Bengal's best-known Communist, was to preside, on the grounds that 'he is opposed to communism and thinks that the spread of communistic ideas ... will be harmful to the interests of the country'.[71] In Bankura, 'the local Krishak Samity and the Abhoy Ashram' were locked in 'a struggle for supremacy', with krishak samiti leaders 'trying to capture all the organisations of the Abhoy Ashram'.[72]

Divisions such as these within local committees enfeebled the mass contact campaign. It was reported, for instance, that a district krishak conference in Patrasayer failed because 'some local people and members of the Congress camp had obstructed [it] in all possible ways by preaching false and wild rumours ... Congressmen privately dissuaded people from attending these meetings ... [at which] the people of Betur Ashram and other Congressmen were conspicuous by their absence.'[73] The men of the Abhoy and Betur Ashram groups were the small but dedicated bands of Gandhians who had consolidated their local position in Hooghly and Bankura through years of sustained work for village reconstruction and the uplift of Harijans. As traditional Gandhian satyagrahis, they resented the intrusion of divisive radicalism into the local Congress. Similarly, in North Bengal, the Bose group could not put their good intentions into practice because the Congressmen on the spot would not take up the krishak campaign. The Governor of Rajshahi Division remarked that

there are no indications at present in the mofussil of rapprochement between the rank and file of the praja party and the Congress. The former are eagerly looking for leadership against the zemindars and the mahajans, and the Congress workers who are Hindus are not prepared to implement this role against zemindars and mahajans who, (particularly the latter) are mainly Hindus.[74]

At the provincial level, too, the Bengal Provincial Congress Committee faced strong internal opposition to what was condemned as a policy of 'pandering to Muslims' and it was reported that 'a number of Calcutta

[71] Report of the Commissioner, Burdwan Division, LOFCR for the first fortnight in July 1937, GB HCPB File No. 10/37.
[72] Report of the Commissioner, Burdwan Division, LOFCR for the first fortnight in July 1937. *Ibid.*
[73] Report of the Commissioner, Burdwan Division, LOFCR for the first fortnight in April 1937. *ibid.*
[74] Report of the Commissioner, Rajshahi Division, LOFCR for the second fortnight in April 1937, GB HCPB File No. 10/37.

Muslim leaders were dismayed by the Bengal PCC's reluctance to pursue the Mass Contacts campaign and enlist Muslim support'.[75] Many in the Bengal Congress feared that the new Provincial Committee line would lose the Party its old supporters and would give too much away to the Muslims. Even in Tippera and Noakhali, where it was strongest, the mass contact movement elicited only equivocal support from the local Congress Committees. As the Divisional Commissioner observed,

There is evidence that even in congress circles the nature of the communist menace is beginning to be understood. Thus one local leader made it clear ... that he was strongly opposed to tampering with special legislation against revolutionaries [because] all these acts would shortly be required against communists, whose activities have been alarming the professional middle classes. The adoption of an extreme socialist policy by the Congress ... must in time alienate a section of the population on which they have hitherto been able to rely for support, both moral and financial.[76]

The successes of the mass contact campaign proved to be more and more illusory as the months passed and even the left wing of the party began to tread cautiously. When the Bengal Tenancy (Amendment) Act was put onto the statute book and conflict between zamindars and tenants escalated, many Congress activists were forced to tone down their campaign. Reports from the districts told of activity by 'communistic sections of the Congress' only in the Balurghat area of Dinajpur and in Birbhum. By now, officials were taking the line that 'Congress was not hostile to the zemindars as far as the reports showed', and from Burdwan word came that 'Congress[men] were declaring that Government were afraid of the raiyat and were afraid to help the zemindars in collecting their money'. In Contai, Iswar Chandra Mal of the Congress led an agitation for rent reduction in the government khas mahal estates, where the krishak cause could be turned against the government rather than against the Hindu zamindars.[77] A similar agitation in Burdwan was directed against the Damodar Canal Tax by Dashrathi Ta. But this tactic was no longer the effective device it had been in the past. By directing no-rent campaigns against the government, the Congress was now challenging the Krishak Praja–Muslim League Ministry, and not the British Raj.[78] This dilemma was brought home to Ashrafuddin Ahmed Chaudhuri, now Secretary of

[75] S. M. Ahmed to Ashrafuddin Ahmed Chaudhuri, 19 August 1937 (in Urdu), AICC Papers, File No. 47/1937, cited in Mushirul Hasan, 'The Muslim Mass Contacts Campaign', p. 214.
[76] Report of the Commissioner, Chittagong Division, LOFCR for the first fortnight in April 1937, GB HCPB File No. 10/37.
[77] GB HCPB File No. 283/38.
[78] Ibid. Sugata Bose has overlooked this point in his discussion of the agitation. See Sugata Bose, Agrarian Bengal, pp. 243–244.

the Provincial Congress Committee, on his tour of his home district. In December 1937

An opposition meeting arranged by [him] at Comilla created local excitement and looked like causing a breach of peace between the convenor's party and minister-ial supporters ... throughout the tour Ashrafuddin Ahmed, though the chief local opponent of the Ministry, protested publicly and privately his respect and admir-ation for the Hon'ble [Chief] Minister.[79]

The Congress mass contact campaign was never more than a patchy and uneven set of local initiatives. In some areas, it failed to get off the ground, whether due to opposition from local Muslim leaders, or indeed from within the Congress itself. At the provincial level, the campaign was opposed by many Congress leaders and those who led it were held back by fears that they would imperil the fragile unity of the Party. Nevertheless, the campaign had some success in recruiting Muslims into the Congress and tempered the pro-zamindar and conservative profile which the Party had traditionally presented. The decision to call for the abolition of the Permanent Settlement was a big departure for the Congress. Mass contact was a strategy which if it had wholeheartedly been implemented might have challenged the communal polarities of Bengal's politics.

But Sarat Bose lost much of his personal credibility as a 'radical' when the Bengal Tenancy (Amendment) Bill was introduced in the Assembly in 1937. As the leader of the Opposition, Bose had to decide the Congress line on a Bill which threatened zamindari powers. This put the spotlight on the Congress attitude to the question of agrarian change and exposed Bose and his policy to the critical scrutiny of the zamindari lobby on the one hand and the krishak leaders on the other. Sarat Bose had no choice but to oppose the Bill if he was to carry his party with him. Yet his commitment to his left-populist policy led him to prevaricate. In what has aptly been described as a 'milk and water speech',[80] Bose sat on the fence, declaring that while 'Congress was definitely not in favour of the perpetu-ation of landlordism ... at the same time it discouraged any attempt on the part of any section of the people to describe another section as exploiters'.[81] To divert attention from Congress opposition to the Bill, Bose dressed up his objections in 'ultra-leftist' terms, criticising the Bill for not going far enough towards protecting the rights of the under-raiyats and introducing an amendment calling for the suspension of rents paid by under-tenants.

[79] Report of the Commissioner, Chittagong Division, LOFCR for the second fortnight in December 1937, GB HCPB File No. 10/37.
[80] Gautam Chattopadhyay, *Bengal Electoral Politics and Freedom Struggle*, p. 156.
[81] *Proceedings, Bengal Legislative Assembly*, 30 September 1937, p. 2093. Also cited in Gautam Chattopadhyay, *Bengal Electoral Politics and Freedom Struggle*, p. 151.

Historians have interpreted this belated defence of the under-raiyat as evidence that the Bengal Congress in the thirties was a radical body.[82] Of course, by taking up the cause of the under-tenant, the Congress exposed the Bill for what it undoubtedly was: a piece of legislation designed to favour rich and middle peasants against zamindars. It is also true that on the whole, under-tenants and share-croppers paid more rent, in cash and kind, to the rich peasants or occupancy tenants from whom they held their small plots than the latter paid to zamindars. Nevertheless, to suggest, as one historian has done, that the Congress Party opposed the amendment simply because it did not go 'far enough in protecting the actual cultivators'[83] is to ignore both the tenuousness of Sarat Bose's control over party policy and its long-standing and still powerful commitment to the protection of zamindari interests.[84] In fact, the Party was deeply divided, both in Calcutta and the localities and the 'left' wing which supported Sarat Bose's initiative was by no means the dominant element within a party which clung to its zamindari moorings. Indeed, zamindari interests within the Bengal Congress emerged from the Assembly elections stronger than they had been before 1937 because the Party had been forced to rely more heavily than ever on the financial and moral support of the mofussil bhadralok to conduct its campaign in the countryside. Sarat Bose's reaction to the Tenancy (Amendment) Bill was a compromise designed to placate his own restless left-wing and the members of the Legislative Assembly from the Krishak Praja Party who supported him,[85] while at the same time trying to retain the support of the conservatives in the Party. Bengal's zamindars were bitterly opposed to any legislation which restricted their rights and promoted the interests of occupancy tenants, but the structure of rural stratification allowed them to take a less self-interested stand on the question of the under-tenants,

[82] Sugata Bose, *Agrarian Bengal*, pp. 210–214; Partha Chatterjee, *Bengal 1920–1947*, pp. 172–80.

[83] Sugata Bose, *Agrarian Bengal*, p. 210.

[84] Chatterjee is more sensitive to the 'strong element of strategic manouevre' involved in the Congress position, but argues for a 'process of general radicalisation of middle-class ideology and culture in Bengal' in the thirties, suggesting that this wrought a dramatic transformation in bhadralok (and, by extension, Congress) politics. He argues that the Congress attack on the Bill from the 'left' was a manifestation of this transformation. Partha Chatterjee, *Bengal 1920–1947*, pp. 172–177.

[85] Tamizuddin Khan and Shamsuddin Ahmed led a band of seventeen rebel Krishak MLAs who lost patience with Huq for not taking up the peasant cause with due firmness. They formed an 'Independent Proja Party' (IPP) in the Assembly, joining the opposition behind Sarat Bose. However, the IPP was co-opted into the ministerial coalition a year later, when Tamizuddin and Shamsuddin joined Fazlul Huq's cabinet as ministers. Brabourne to Linlithgow, 18 November 1938, FR. Linlithgow Collection, IOLR MSS Eur F/125/38, and Pinell to Laithwaite, 7 January 1939, Enclosure I, *ibid.*, MSS Eur F/125/39.

with whom they had few dealings.[86] As Dietmar Rothermund points out with unusual perspicacity:

the *bargadars'* cause could be espoused by the big zamindars who had no direct relation with sharecroppers and could, therefore, adopt an attitude of disinterested benevolence towards them. At the same time, these landlords were concerned about a bargain with the occupancy *raiyats* and the solicitude for the *bargadar* could serve as a useful purpose in the political game.[87]

Particularly after the Depression, defending the rights of bargadars or under-raiyats was another way of challenging the powers of the jotedars and bigger occupancy raiyats, under whom a growing number of sharecroppers held their plots, and contemporary krishak leaders saw the inwardness of this tactic. Abul Mansur Ahmed recalls that in Mymensingh zilla

The influence of zamindars over the Congress leaders was unlimited ... Congressmen did not simply fail to help the krishak movement, they actively hindered it. A small number of Congress workers launched a krishak samiti which preached that the Praja movement was in reality a jotedar movement, which far from helping the poor peasants, would actually increase their oppression ... I was deeply suspicious that certain pro-zamindari Congressmen used this ultra-leftist slogan to hinder the Praja movement.[88]

In the event, the Congress party's stand on the question of the Tenancy (Amendment) Act lost the Party whatever small gains it had made through mass contact. As F. O. Bell's tour diaries reveal, by 1939 the terms of the Tenancy Act were well understood even in the most out of the way parts of the province[89] and Muslim League propaganda made sure that Muslim peasants knew that the Congress had opposed it. One popular ballad declared:

> For all the *gamcha*-wearing [high caste Hindu] zamindars
> The passing of the [Tenancy Amendment] Act brought ruin.
> All the Congressmen said, what destruction!
> They did not allow the pro-peasant bill to be passed.

[86] Voting patterns for the Bengal Tenancy (Amendment) Act of 1928 reveal that some of the bigger zamindars had voted in favour of concessions to under-raiyats, while the Congress-Swarajya camp had voted against. Partha Chatterjee, *Bengal 1920–1947*, p. 87.

[87] Dietmar Rothermund, *Government, Landlord and Peasant in India Agrarian Relations under British Rule*, Wiesbaden, 1978, p. 109.

[88] Abul Mansur Ahmed, *Amar Dekha Rajnitir Panchash Bachhar*, pp. 67–71.

[89] In the course of survey and settlement operations in the northern district of Dinajpur, Bell spoke to several peasants and jotedars in various thanas and villages. His records of these meetings suggest that the terms of the 1938 Tenancy Act were well known in a district where the only leaders many peasants had heard of were Gandhi and Fazlul Huq. In political terms, therefore, there is no doubt that the Tenancy Bill was a master stroke by the first Huq ministry. F. O. Bell Papers, IOLR MSS Eur D/733/2.

> ... All the zamindars are the foster sons of Congressmen
> ... O peasants, look, at all the Congressmen! [They are]
> Oppressive, unjust, malicious and hostile.[90]

The credibility of the mass contact campaign was, therefore, fatally damaged by the party's stand on the Tenancy Bill. The Muslim League saw to it that Congress prevarications on rural reform were brought into the open. Bose's tactic of attacking the Tenancy Bill 'from the left' was an ingenious strategy, no doubt, but one that failed to convince many Muslim members. The Muslim League could now persuasively spread the word among the Muslim peasantry that the Congress was still the party of the zamindars. All that Sarat Bose's repeated calls for the abolition of the Permanent Settlement succeeded in doing was to irritate the conservatives in his own party.

The very fact, moreover, that the Congress happened to be the main opposition party against a ministry controlled by Muslims gave politics in the Assembly a communal dimension that Sarat Bose would have preferred to avoid.[91] Bose was committed to bringing the ministry down, while putting forward the Congress as a secular alternative. He was careful to couch his attack on the ministry in nationalist terms, choosing, as far as he could, issues which he hoped would have no communal implications, such as the demand for the release of the 'detenus' or the under-trial terrorists, many of whom were still in detention camps in Deoli and the Andamans. When the Bengal Government failed to follow the lead of the six Congress ministries, which immediately on taking office released all political prisoners, Bengali detenus in the Andamans threatened to go on hunger-strike. The Jugantar group had backed the Bose faction in the twenties but in the changed political climate their support could no longer be counted upon. Aware that the mass contact programme had made them more enemies than friends within the Congress organisation, the Bose brothers made a bid to win over the two big terrorist groups, Anushilan and Jugantar. With the support of Calcutta's new student organisations, they took up the cause of the hunger-strikers, and launched a campaign to demand their immediate release. In the Governor's opinion

The hunger strike has been seized on as a God-send by the extreme elements who were anxious for some peg on which to hang an agitation. They are utilising the misguided and unnecessary sufferings of the prisoners as a means of galvanising

---

90 *Bangiya Prajaswatwa Nutan Ain O Leaguer Bani* ('The Bengal Tenancy Amendment Act and the League's Message'), Dacca, 1939, in GB HCPB File No. 463/39.
91 Nikhil Chakravarty emphasised this point in his interview with the author, New Delhi, 6 February 1989.

into action the diverse and disunited left wing elements which are as much in opposition to Congress proper as to Government.[92]

But the strike proved to be a serious embarrassment to the Ministry, and in particular to Fazlul Huq, whose election manifesto had promised to release political prisoners. The prisoners eventually gave up their strike and most were released, but the whole affair did little to improve the atmosphere between the parties in Bengal. Bose's involvement in a no-confidence motion against the Ministry in 1938 only made matters worse, causing so much ill will amongst Calcutta Muslims that the rebel Muslim Praja members associated with the move were forced to take shelter among Hindus.[93]

The attempt by the 'left' wing of the Congress to break the communal deadlock in Bengali politics by wooing the Muslim 'masses' was, therefore, far from being an unqualified success. In the Assembly as on the ground, they were constrained by the conservatism of the Bengal Congress. Sarat Bose failed to bring off his double act as leader of the Opposition on the one hand and as champion of secular and progressive nationalism on the other. Nevertheless, Bose (like Chittaranjan Das before him) was able to maintain his personal reputation as a non-communal Hindu and some Muslim leaders continued to trust him. Thus in 1941, he successfully negotiated the establishment of a coalition government between Shyama Prasad Mookherjee's Hindu Mahasabha, his own Forward Bloc group and a number of Krishak Praja MLA's: no mean achievement. But such a spatchcock ministry could not survive. Bose was arrested and detained before it took office. With Bose out of the picture, John Herbert, the Governor of Bengal, who despised Huq and deeply distrusted the 'fifth columnist' Forward Bloc, found it all too easy to play off Shyama Prasad against Huq and to engineer Huq's resignation.[94] Even so, Bose remained one of the few Congressmen with whom Muslim leaders felt they could do business. But for reasons that will be examined below, Sarat Bose and his left-wing allies were never to regain

---

[92] Governor's FR for the first fortnight of July 1939. Robert Reid Papers, MSS Eur E/278/5 (a).

[93] No-confidence motions were tabled against ten ministers by the Bose group supported by the rebel Independent Proja Party. And although Sarat Bose attempted to disarm Muslim opinion by tabling the first motion against a Hindu minister, Sris Chandra Nandy, the move provoked Muslim hostility. Muslim MLA's who backed Bose, including Tamizuddin Khan, Shamsuddin Ahmed and Dr Sanullah received death threats from members of their community, and Tamizuddin was forced to leave his own home and take shelter in a Hindu locality. GB SB 'PM Series', File No. 13951/38, memos dated 21 March 1938 and 1 May 1938.

[94] See Herbert to Linlithgow, 5 December 1941, FR, Linlithgow Collection, IOLR MSS Eur F/125/41, and Herbert to Linlithgow, 8 May 1942, FR, *ibid.*

their leading position in the Bengal Congress and were unable to influence the course of Bengal politics in the crucial years before Partition.

Centre and province: the taming of the Bengal Congress

In the late thirties, the Bengal Congress came to be embroiled in a conflict with the central Working Committee leadership that yet again split the party apart, both at the all-India and provincial levels. The events which led to the dramatic Tripuri session of the All-India Congress Committee and culminated in the expulsion of Subhas Chandra Bose from the Congress Party have been well chronicled[95] and will not be examined here. Instead, this study will analyse the impact of these events on the course of Bengali politics and on the polarisation of party-political affiliations along lines of community.

In 1939 Subhas Chandra Bose took the unusual step of declaring his intention to stand for election to the presidentship of the All-India Congress Committee against the wishes of the Congress High Command. The younger Bose had already spent an unremarkable year as President in 1938; and by now the central leadership felt that they had made enough concessions to placate the party's left wing. Subhas Bose's campaign and eventual re-election to the post in 1939 reflected the strength of the left wing within the all-India Congress and also the inclination of provincial Congressmen to rebel against the dictates of the Working Committee. The rebellion was, however, put down with a firm hand and, with a little moral persuasion from Gandhi, Bose was forced to resign from the presidentship at the tumultuous Tripuri Session of the Congress. Not long afterwards, both he and his brother Sarat Chandra were expelled from the Congress.

In Bengal, the Bose brothers had a not inconsiderable following within the provincial Congress. Their supporters included communists and socialists, several members of the old Anushilan terrorist party and a wing of the Jugantar group[96] as well as representatives from the proliferating student organisations which had taken a prominent part in the agitation for the release of the Andamans political prisoners in 1939.[97] Moreover,

[95] See, for instance, Leonard Gordon, *Bengal: The Nationalist Movement 1876–1940*, New Delhi, 1979; and Gitasree Bandopadhyay, *Constraints in Bengal Politics*.
[96] The Governor reported that 'of the delegates who formed the electoral college to elect the President – 544 in number – over 80 are ex-detenus and 14 are ex-State Prisoners: of this total 544, 300 are probably supporters of Subhas Bose in the Provincial Factions'. Brabourne to Linlithgow, 5 February 1939, FR. Linlithgow Collection, MSS Eur F/125/39.
[97] For an account of the history of student politics in Bengal, see Bazlur Rahman Khan, *Politics in Bengal 1927–1936*, Dhaka, 1987, pp. 92–127. The active role of students in the

the revolt of the Bose brothers against the High Command was 'generally appreciated in Bengal though whether from a genuine dislike of the autocratic methods of the right wing or merely from a sense of local patriotism is somewhat uncertain',[98] and won the support for the rebels from a wide circle of Bengali patriots.[99] These supporters stuck with the Bose brothers for over a year after their expulsion and they formed a parallel 'Congress' in the province which continued to function without sanction from the High Command.

All this was familiar ground for the Bengal Congress, which had a long history of factional divisions and disputes with the centre. What was new was the centre's determination to crush the rebel faction. Shaken by the orchestrated challenge to its leadership, the Old Guard was no longer willing to tolerate indiscipline in the province which had led the rebellion.[100] The Working Committee under its new President, Dr Rajendra Prasad, was clear that 'the issue between the Bengal PCC and its Executive on the one hand and the Working Committee on the other is ... simply of the relations that ought to subsist between them. It is evading the simple issue of obedience and loyalty which the former owes the latter.'[101] Soon afterwards, everyone in the Bengal Congress who remained loyal to the Boses was suspended[102] and those who promised allegiance to the High Command were placed in charge of the new, reconstituted, Provincial Committee. The result, inevitably, was chaos. An enquiry into its affairs revealed that

the Congress organisation of the Province is in a state of great confusion. The Provincial Secretary flouts the Provincial Tribunal, the District President countermands the order of his own Secretary, the Subdivision revolts against the Provincial Secretary and different bodies usurp the function of the Tribunal ... There is no end of disputes regarding the validity of the different Congress

Andamans agitation was underlined by Nikhil Chakravarty in his interview with the author, New Delhi, 6 February 1989.

[98] 'Confidential Report on the Political Situation for the first half of July, 1939', by E. N. Blandy, in the Robert Reid Collection, IOLR MSS Eur E/278/5.

[99] Indeed, this sentiment brought Bose support from unlikely quarters: the Governor noted that 'local patriotism probably explains, to some extent, the fact that the normally hostile group of Dr Bidhan Roy decided at the last minute to support him'. Brabourne to Linlithgow, 5 February 1939. Linlithgow Collection, MSS Eur F/125/39. Needless to say, Dr Roy's show of solidarity was short-lived.

[100] The High Command was evidently determined to put an end to speculation that 'Mr Gandhi has lost his nerve and now cannot even say "go to a Bose"!' Linlithgow to Zetland, 7 February 1939. Zetland Collection, MSS Eur D/609/17.

[101] Rajendra Prasad to Sarat Chandra Bose, 4 February 1940, AICC Papers, File No. P-5 (Part II)/1939–40.

[102] B. N. Palit to AICC Secretary, AICC Papers, File No. P-5 (Part II)/1940.

Committees and the number of parallel Congress Committees is also very great.[103]

This was a situation that Vallabhbhai Patel and the Working Committee were not willing to tolerate. In June 1939 Patel started a campaign to bring subordinate Congress Committees to heel when he introduced a resolution at an AICC Conference in Bombay, prohibiting Congressmen from launching civil disobedience without permission from their Provincial Committee.[104] Less than a week later, the Sardar issued a circular to the secretaries of the Provincial Congress Committees stating that

it had come to his notice that subordinate Congress Committees in various places passed resolutions calling in[to] question the decision[s] of the AICC. If subordinate organisations went to the length of questioning the authority of the superior organisation, there would be no discipline left in the Congress organisation. He therefore requested all Provincial Congress Committees to warn Congress Committees subordinate to them, against all such undesirable action.[105]

Armed with new powers, the Working Committee got down to the task of disciplining the unruly ranks of the Bengal Congress. An 'Election Tribunal' was appointed under the chairmanship of the noted Bengali Gandhian, Satish Chandra Dasgupta, with its Calcutta office at the Khadi Pratishthan premises, thus advertising its status as a client of the central leadership. The Tribunal was told to prepare the electoral rolls for the coming BPCC elections and it used this power to remove from the rolls all members of parallel Congress Committees who were known to be loyal to Subhas and Sarat Bose.[106] The result was that the BPCC emerged from a year of bitter conflict and confusion, purged of all dissidents and a creature of the centre. By May 1940, the Executive Council of the BPCC had 'been turned into a Satyagraha Committee',[107] as had several district and subdivisional Congress organisations in Bengal. Satyagraha had never held much attraction for Bengali Congressmen, and B. C. Roy had once asked Gandhi to exempt Bengalis from having to take the 'satyagraha pledge'. Now as the party came under the firm hand of the centre, hardly a protest was heard when satyagraha was imposed on the province.[108] Whether local Congress organisations liked satyagraha or

[103] Report of the Congress Election Tribunal to the AICC President, 5 October 1939, AICC Papers, File No. G-56/1939.
[104] N. N. Mitra (ed.), Indian Annual Register, 1939, vol. I, January–June, p. 32 (H).
[105] Ibid., vol. II, July–December, p. 2.
[106] See AICC Papers, File No. P-5 (Part I)/1936–37 and P-5 (Part I)/1939–40.
[107] BPCC Secretary to AICC General Secretary, 13 May 1940, in AICC Papers, File No. P-5 (Part II)/1940.
[108] There are only seven letters in the AICC files from individual Congressmen asking to be released from the satyagraha pledge (five from Midnapore and two from Burdwan), and

not, they had to toe the line or face expulsion from the Congress. As one BPCC member from Sylhet complained

The DCC, Sylhet, has converted itself into a Satyagraha committee. The Office Bearers of the DCC belong to the National Front Group (led by M. N. Roy). They have no faith in the Satyagraha technique of struggle and far less in the Charka. But with a view to retaining hold on the congress machinery they have signed the pledge which they never mean to redeem.[109]

Although the Working Committee was powerless to prevent such token obedience, it had the power to keep Subhas Bose's followers out of the Party. The BPCC executive, wanting to restore the depleted ranks of the Party, begged the High Command to allow rebels who repented back into the fold:

We are of the opinion that it will be expedient if some way could be devised to allow the now repentant persons to come back into the fold. Among those who were misled into the revolt by Sj. Subhas Chandra Bose and who have seen the error of their ways there are some who are good enough and the Congress organisation in Bengal will be strengthened if they are allowed to return to the fold.[110]

But, the central leadership, unprepared to forgive and forget, rejected this appeal. By the early forties, therefore, the entire structure of the Bengal Congress had been altered, all traces of rebellion had been erased and the party, once notorious for its fractiousness, had been convincingly tamed. Ever since the death of Chittaranjan Das, the High Command had been sucked into Congress politics in Bengal, first to settle disputes but increasingly in an effort to promote its own men. Some Bengali Congressmen, led by the Bose brothers had fought against the interventions of the Working Committee. Subhas and Sarat Bose made the most of Bengali outrage at what many saw as the high-handedness of the High Command in its treatment of Bengal. Years of opposing the High Command had welded their followers together, united in their antipathy to a 'dictatorial' centre. In the 1930s, the Bose group had also attracted many followers from the left, for Subhas and Sarat Bose had begun to regard 'mass contact' as the only way of breaking the communal deadlock in Bengali politics.

In 1927 the Bose group may still have been little more than a 'faction', whose aim was to get control over the BPCC and the Corporation, but by

---

even in these cases, the reasons stated are not ideological, but on the grounds of illness and family circumstances. See AICC Papers, File No. P-5 (Part II)/1941.
[109] Sailaja Mohan Das to the BPCC Secretary, 13 May 1940, in AICC Papers, File No. P-5 (Part II)/1940.
[110] BPCC secretary to Kripalani, 10 June 1940, AICC Papers, File No. P-5 (Part II)/1940.

the end of the thirties it had become a party with a stable membership bound together by the belief that Bengali solutions had to be found for the problems of Bengal. As they tried to find a basis of agreement with Muslim leaders and to expand the social base of the party, the Bose brothers became convinced that social rather than communal solutions were the answer; and they steered their party increasingly to the left. In the late thirties, the Bose group drew behind it the variety of left-wing organisations that had emerged in the province in the previous decade. These new recruits tried to take the party beyond its traditional bhadra-lok world and reach out to the 'masses'. By the end of the decade, the Bose group had elaborated an alternative strategy in Bengali politics, characterised by a commitment to secular solutions to Bengal's political problems. Had the group survived, it may well have broken the communal mould that was fast setting hard in the province.

But in 1939 this group was expelled bag and baggage from the Bengal Congress and eventually in the forties splintered up into a host of lesser parties. The result was that the Congress organisation in Bengal lost much of its most secular membership. The Bengal Congress of the forties was certainly a disciplined body, chastised by the High Command into perfect obedience. But it was a party more than ever Hindu in composition and conservative in character. In 1940 the All-India Congress Committee instructed its Bengal client that its main duty as 'passive Satyagrahis is to see that they do not foment Labour, Kisan and Student strikes'.[111] This tight control remained even after the end of the Second World War. In the run-up to the elections of 1945–46, the official Bengal Provincial Congress Committee was still weeding out dissidents by denying them Congress membership and Congress tickets. Dr Nalinakshya Sanyal, an important Congress Member of the Legislative Assembly and an outspoken supporter of the mass-contact initiative who had held several public meetings 'advocating that Communists should be allowed to work within the Congress',[112] was denied a Congress ticket in 1945.[113] Several Calcutta committees suspected of having left-wing sympathies were denied receipt books for enlisting their members as paid-up

[111] AICC General Secretary to BPCC Secretary, 16 May 1940, AICC Papers, File No. P-5 (Part II)/1940.

[112] In February and March 1945, Sanyal organised meetings in Kushtia, Burdwan and Midnapore jointly with the Communist Party of India urging communists and Congressmen to work together. Report of the Commissioner, Presidency Division, LOFCRs for the first fortnight of February and the first fortnight of March 1945, GB HCPB File No. 37/45. See also the Report of the Political Situation for the first fortnight of February 1945. *Ibid.*

[113] Dr Nalinakshya Sanyal to AICC Secretary, 23 March 1946, AICC Papers, File No. P-5 (Part I)/1945–46.

Congress members; [114] student groups such as a Nava Yuvak Sewa Samiti who were loyal to the Bose brothers were kept out of the organisation.[115] As A. K. Bhattacharya from Murshidabad complained to the Working Committee:

those at the helm of Congress in Bengal seem no[t] eager for increase of membership ... in the matter of enrollment of members, persons other than the so-called 'Khadi Group' and particularly forward blockists [sic] are being denied elementary facilities. I should also say that 'Khadi Group' is not real Khadi at all in Bengal generally.[116]

But he got short shrift from the High Command. Despite three telegrams and two letters, the Working Committee refused to inquire into his complaint and referred him back to the Provincial Congress Committee.[117] Significantly, the few remaining Congress Muslims, such as Ashrafuddin Chaudhuri, were in effect expelled from the Congress. Released from prison in 1945, Ashrafuddin found that the old attitude of hostility to anyone who had been associated with the Bose brothers still persisted. Writing in December 1945, he observed:

Today amazingly after my release I hardly find any co-operation between the workers and sufferers who were in Jail ... and the present BPCC Executives. I deeply deplore this situation. It appears from the behaviour and conduct of the present BPCC that all of us who were connected with the old BPCC and particularly, the Forward blockists [sic] are intolerable with the present office bearers of the Provincial Congress ... I desire to know from the leaders of the [Working Committee] what they have decided about us. Are we to be turned out of the Congress for what we did in the past?[118]

Fazlul Karim Chaudhuri, the Muslim President of the Gopinathpur Primary Congress Committee in Tippera District, was refused Congress membership. Tippera was a Muslim-majority district where the Congress had established a base in the late thirties. Fazlul Chaudhuri was one Muslim recruited by the Congress who enjoyed the confidence of local Muslims; he had contested the Assembly elections as an Independent and had lost to a candidate of the Tippera Krishak Samiti by a narrow margin

---

[114] Several letters complaining about the irregularities in the BPCC's nomination of candidates for the Assembly Elections are filed in AICC Papers, File No. P-5 (Part I)/1945–46.
[115] The Secretary of the Nava Yuvak Seva Samiti reported that the Ward XIII Calcutta Congress Committee had refused to accept as many as 378 receipts submitted by the samiti; *ibid.*
[116] A. K. Bhattacharya to AICC Secretary, 22 October 1945; AICC Papers, File No. P-5 (Part I)/1945–46.
[117] AICC Papers, File No. P-5 (Part I)/1945–46.
[118] Ashrafuddin Ahmed Chaudhuri to Kripalani, 9 December 1945, in Jamaluddin Ahmed Chaudhuri, *Rajbirodhi Ashrafuddin Ahmed Chaudhuri*, Dacca, 1978, p. 163.

of 863 votes.[119] Now, with his left-wing sympathies, he found there was no place for him in the Bengal Congress and was bluntly told the reason: 'you belong to a group of workers who have carried out the anti-national propaganda in favour of "Peoples War" . . . since the 1942 movement'.[120] In another case, a Muslim candidate nominated by the Bose-controlled Howrah District Congress Committee was rejected by the Working Committee.[121] The result was to give the Congress Party in Bengal, long identified with Hindu interests, an overwhelmingly conservative and Hindu character. It is hardly surprising, therefore, that in the general elections of 1945–46 the Bengal Congress put up only two Muslim candidates. The first, T. A. N. Nabi, standing from Jangipur in Murshidabad, received only 161 votes, while 17,000 votes were cast for his Muslim League rival. The other candidate was Syed Nausher Ali, the speaker of the Assembly who had been won over to the Congress by Sarat Bose in 1939. Nausher Ali stood from two constituencies, Jessore Sadar and Jessore East. In the first he received a paltry 1,616 votes and in the second 5,743, losing in both cases overwhelmingly to his Muslim League rivals, each of whom received more than 30,000 votes.[122]

Gallagher's contention that the Bengal Congress 'declined' in the thirties[123] misses the main point. On the contrary, the Bose group in this period had not only succeeded in tightening their grip on the Party but had also given it a wider social base, a more dynamic organisation and a new political agenda. The Congress in the late thirties was a party capable and willing to take the initiative in challenging the increasing communalism in Bengali politics. But the failure of Subhas' bid for power at the centre in 1939 had dire consequences for Bengal: the expulsion of the entire Bose group from the 'official' Bengal Congress in the early forties meant the secular and progressive elements within Bengal's Hindu leadership were thrown out of the Party, which came increasingly to be identified with dominant Hindu interests.

Bhadralok communalism and the Bengal Congress

After the Tripuri session, the Congress in Bengal adopted a more overtly communal posture, in part due to the intervention of the Working Committee in its affairs. Yet there are indications that pressures internal

---

[119] Bengal Legislative Assembly. Election Results, 1936. IOLR L/P and J/7/1142.
[120] Kalipada Mookherji to Fazlul Karim Chaudhuri, 28 November 1945, in AICC Papers, File No. P-5 (Part I)/1945–46.
[121] AICC Papers, File No. P-5 (Part I)/1945–46.
[122] 'Franchise, Elections in Bengal, 1946', IOLR L/P and J/8/475.
[123] J. A. Gallagher, 'Congress in Decline'.

to the provincial Congress also influenced this reorientation in party policy. The Bengal Congress had always been closely associated with Hindu bhadralok interests, and although these interests had been subordinated during the mass contact movement, their influence over the Party remained strong. Many persons within the Bengal Congress were nervous about Sarat Chandra Bose's efforts to expand the social base of the Party. Once the Tenancy Amendment Act was on the books in 1938, rent collections fell back still further[124] and mofussil zamindars in the party were angered and alarmed by the efforts of left-wing Congressmen to organise peasant no-rent campaigns. The President of the Jessore Congress Committee confessed that he was anxious because 'his party was swinging to the Left and that in consequence, he (and others like him) would be left high and dry'.[125] Similar fears were expressed at a meeting of the Hooghly District Landholders' Association, at which the President declared:

I ... am sorry to say that the Congress in Bengal has been trying to down us by preaching the cult of socialism and communism amongst our tenants, the result of which is a no-rent mentality throughout the greater part of the province. It is a pity that the leaders of the Congress cannot control their left-wing better.[126]

In many local Congress bodies, efforts were made to squash the krishak campaign, and this often split the committees apart. In May 1939, in several Burdwan districts where 'the Krishak agitation still continues as usual', the Governor thus recorded 'the beginning of a split between the [Congress] Krishak agitators and the Congress proper'.[127]

Equally, many Congressmen found Sarat Bose's performance as leader of the opposition deeply disappointing. Leading the opposition from the left had not brought the ministry down. It had also prevented Sarat from doing the job that many felt he should be doing: putting up an effective

[124] District officials meeting in 1938 to discuss the progress of the no-rent campaign noted that the incidence of non-payment had increased, in many cases due to a 'misunderstanding of the legislation passed'. The collection in one estate of the Maharaja of Burdwan 'had fallen from 42% to 24% in the preceding year'. GB HCPB File No. 283/38. In a detailed statement on the situation in Balurghat where the no-rent campaign was strong, the Commissioner reported that 'rent collections have fallen this year inspite of better crops and prices. The Subdivisional Officer states that up to date 80% is usually collected but this year only 30% to 40% has been collected. One landlord told me that so far only Rs. 12,000/- has been collected against a current demand of Rs. 41,000/-. Another told me that Rs. 3,000/- had been collected against a current demand of Rs. 35,000/-. The Dinajpur Raj gave collections so far as 30% to 35%'. A. J. Dash, 'Agrarian Situation in Balurghat Sub-Division', GB HCPB File No. 191/39.
[125] P. D. Martyn Memoirs, IOLR MSS Eur F/125/39.
[126] The Presidential speech of the Maharaja of Burdwan as reported in *Amrita Bazar Patrika*, 2 May 1939.
[127] Reid to Linlithgow, 5 May 1939, FR. Linlithgow Collection, IOLR MSS Eur F/125/39.

defence against the ministry's spate of legislation against Hindu bhadra-lok interests. His party in the Assembly was forced, as one observer pointed out, 'to speak with two voices': 'one when it is attempting to obtain Muslim support and another when it is forced in[to] the position of defending non-Muslim vested interests. Sarat Bose's attempt to reconcile these two irreconcilable attitudes has ... largely nullified the effect of Hindu representation in the Legislature.'[128] This was particularly evident when the Bengal Moneylenders Bill was tabled in 1939. After much 'heated discussion', the Congress Party, 'under pressure from their "wild men"',[129] 'decided not to oppose the consideration of the Bill and not to take any steps that might be interpreted as a dilatory attitude on the part of the Congress members in the interests of the money-lenders'.[130] The *Amrita Bazar Patrika* spoke for many of its bhadralok readers when it declared that this decision 'has taken our breath away':

May we ask if the Congress Party cared to ascertain the views of its constituencies in regard to this matter? Those views could easily be ascertained, and in fact had been most clearly and emphatically expressed. There is not a single nationalist paper ... that supported the Bill ... If [the members of the Congress Party] owed any sense of responsibility to their constituencies ... they should have opposed the Bill with all their might ... In the present case, some of the allies of the Congress Party of the Krishak Praja group have given vehement support to the Moneylen-ders Bill. Is it to placate them, or at any rate, not to forfeit their support, that the party decided to adopt a non-committal attitude?[131]

In the event, the attack against the Bill was led by a Marwari industrialist, Debi Prasad Khaitan.[132] The sweeping provisions of the Moneylenders Bill[133] made it an issue which affected Bengal's urban businessmen and financiers as much as mofussil creditors – the zamindars and professional mahajans. Both these groups had given the Congress crucial financial backing in the past. Now, when the Congress allowed the Moneylenders

[128] Woodhead to Linlithgow, 19/20 June 1939, FR. *Ibid.*
[129] Reid observed that the decision not to oppose the Bill involved the Congress 'in criticism from their own Press, including the Bose Press, which, quite prepared to preach socialist views against the Government or against "Imperialism" ... is far too concerned with middle-class Hindu interests to regard the provisions of this Bill with equanimity'. Reid to Linlithgow, 19 April 1939, FR. *Ibid.*
[130] *Amrita Bazar Patrika*, 5 April 1939.   [131] *Ibid.*, 6 April 1939.
[132] *Ibid.*, 5 April 1939.
[133] The Act made it obligatory for all persons in the moneylending business to obtain trade licences from the Government, which was now under the control of the Praja–League Ministry. It restricted interest rates on secured and unsecured loans to a maximum of 6 per cent and 8 per cent respectively. The Act also stipulated that 'under no circumstances may the amount of interest on a loan, whenever paid, be permitted to exceed the amount of the original loan' to be applied 'retrospectively for an indefinite period'. Herbert to Linlithgow, 10 May 1940, FR. Linlithgow Collection, IOLR MSS Eur F/125/40.

Bill to go unchallenged, monied interests in the town and countryside alike began to recognise that the Congress under the leadership of Sarat Bose might not give them the returns on their investment to which they felt entitled. If the Congress no longer was prepared to look after zamindari and business interests in the Legislature, neither of these 'special interests', with only five seats apiece in the Assembly, would by themselves be able to oppose the measures of the Huq Ministry. It is not surprising that on his accession as Governor in 1939, John Herbert encountered Hindu 'anxiety regarding the position not only of landlords but also of capital and vested interests'.[134]

Alarmed by the mass-contact initiative, zamindari and business groups began to reconsider their support for the Congress Party under Sarat Bose and to cast around for alternatives. In July 1939, the Acting Governor Robert Reid had told Delhi that

There is talk of attempts to form a party outside the Congress that would exclude the Bose brothers and adopt a business-like policy of looking after Hindu interests in a constitutional fashion: it is probably true that Subhas Bose is deeply distrusted and disliked by many Hindus, while his brother, Sarat Bose, though perhaps less distrusted, has forfeited confidence by the failure of his leadership in the Assembly to split the Muslims or to defend the interests of the Hindus as a community – a task he has left to the much abused Hindu Ministers.[135]

Reid was of the opinion that 'the brothers Bose are almost as unpopular on personal grounds as they are in the rest of India',[136] and John Herbert endorsed this when he took over in Calcutta. He informed Delhi that 'Nazimuddin seems convinced that Subhas is increasing his unpopularity with practically every section of Hindu opinion.' and that 'Tushar Kanti Ghosh, the Editor of the *Amrita Bazar Patrika* ... confirmed that impression'.[137]

Disgruntlement with the Congress under the Bose leadership was perceptible amongst an increasingly wide circle of the Hindu bhadralok, both in Calcutta and in the mofussil. In the districts, even the Andamans hunger-strike failed to elicit much enthusiasm or support for the Bose brothers within local Congress Committees. Even in Midnapore, once the epicentre of revolutionary terrorism, local Congress workers denounced the Provincial Congress Committee for supporting the striking detenus.

[134] Herbert to Linlithgow, 23 December 1939, FR. Linlithgow Collection, IOLR MSS Eur F/125/39.
[135] Reid to Linlithgow, 6 July 1939, FR. Robert Reid Papers, IOLR MSS Eur E/278/5 (a).
[136] Zetland thus described Reid's assessment of the situation in a letter to the Viceroy. See Zetland to Linlithgow, 27 June 1939. Zetland Collection, IOLR MSS Eur D/609/11.
[137] Herbert to Linlithgow, 7 June 1940, FR. Linlithgow Collection, IOLR MSS Eur F/125/40.

By now, the Midnapore Congress Committee had become a 'moderate constitutional party', dominated by the 'Right-Wing'.[138] The transformation of the Midnapore party arguably reflects a wider shift in bhadralok political sympathies, away from romantic revolutionary nationalism towards the more practical and matter-of-fact business of defending their own interests.[139]

Not all the bhadralok were equally or indeed, directly affected by the new legislation. But growing numbers shared the sense that their world was rapidly falling apart, that their way of life and values were threatened by the new political order. Some were dismayed by the entry of the 'lower orders' into the hitherto exclusive world of Congress politics. Surendra Mohan Ghosh of the Mymensingh Jugantar group had been an admirer of Subhas Bose in the twenties. But on his release from detention in 1937, he parted company with Bose 'because I thought that he was going the wrong way': 'When I went to [Subhas'] house, I found it full of riff-raffs [sic] and street urchins. There was a crowd of them. I asked Sarat, "Are these your followers and supporters? These are not political workers. These are riff-raffs".'[140] Others were alarmed by the changes in the Congress membership and programme. Members of the Bangiya Brahman Sabha of Calcutta felt that:

The Congress has been swept off its old moorings and changed its character. Its politicians and their followers are now largely ill-educated and ill-informed men, fed on the imported literature of modern Irish history, Italian and Austrian revolutions, French republicanism and Soviet rule. They are anxious to try on India the experiments of Western Civilization ... and to do away with established institutions like Brahmanical hierarchy and zamindari landlordism as one allied system ... which, in the name of social reform, strikes at the very roots of Hinduism.[141]

---

138 LOFCR from Midnapore, for the first fortnight in July 1939, in the Robert Reid Papers, IOLR MSS Eur E/278/5 (a). As in other parts of the province, the Midnapore Congress had been divided internally, since 1933, between the old guard and 'a new radical group which ... openly expressed dissatisfaction with the doings of Gandhi'. By the middle of 1939, this 'kishan' group had 'cut itself adrift' from the Congress. FR for the second fortnight of March 1933, IOLR L/P and J/12/47 and FR for the second fortnight of April 1939, IOLR L/P and J/12/144.
139 The extraordinary success of the Quit India movement in the Tamluk and Contai subdivisions would seem to contradict this picture. But by all accounts, this movement was organised at the grass-root level by local leaders whose connection with the national, provincial and even district arms of the Congress was extremely tenuous. See Bidyut Chakrabarty, 'Political Mobilization in the Localities: The 1942 Quit India Movement in Midnapur', Modern Asian Studies, vol. 26, 4, 1992.
140 Transcript of interview with Surendra Mohan Ghosh, NMML OT No. 301, p. 235.
141 Memorandum of the Bangiya Brahman Sabha, Calcutta, in the Zetland Collection, IOLR MSS Eur D/609/21 (h)/a.

Statements such as these express the profound and widespread sense of disquiet at the loss of the old order and the contempt of an elite for the 'ill-educated and ill-informed' 'riff-raff' who now influenced politics. Subhas and Sarat Bose, far from stemming the tide that was sweeping the old world away, had opened the floodgates still wider and there were many who could not forgive them for this. The Hindu press reflected this mood. The *Amrita Bazar Patrika*, which in the company of many other 'nationalist' newspapers in these years adopted a stance that was uncompromisingly communal,[142] took the lead in orchestrating bhadralok opinion against the Bose brothers for 'neglecting Hindu interests'. Its editor, Tushar Kanti Ghosh, an old enemy of the Bose family, was active behind the scenes in efforts to break the Bose influence in Bengal politics.[143]

This was the context in which the Hindu Mahasabha was re-established in Bengal. On 27 December 1939, Veer Savarkar launched the Mahasabha in Calcutta, flying its saffron flag over Wellington Square.[144] The Viceroy, who happened to be in Calcutta on the day, told London that the Hindu Mahasabha was

gradually emerging, and with considerable vigour, as something approaching a political force. [They] have just held a monster-meeting here [in Calcutta] from which there has emerged a series of resolutions highly communal in character and condemnatory of the Congress ... I will not be surprised, things being as they are, if the Mahasabha were to succeed in stealing a certain amount of Congress thunder.[145]

The Mahasabha movement in Bengal was led by Dr Shyama Prasad Mookerjee, son of the renowned educationist and politician, Sir Ashutosh Mookerjee. Shyama Prasad had entered the Council as a Swarajist in 1929 but had left the Congress two years later, convinced that the party could not effectively represent Hindu bhadralok interests. In the thirties, as an independent member of the Corporation and the Assembly, he devoted his considerable energies to defending what he saw as 'Hindu'

---

[142] Bhola Chatterjee, in his detailed study of the Bengali press, remarks on the 'communal consciousness' that was evident in all sections of the Hindu press: 'Whenever anything had something to do with religion and all that went with it, both *Advance* and *Liberty* made a common cause. All those attractive phrases of revolution and enlightenment were no match for their feeling of reverential awe for the "eternal values" of Hindu religion, its social system [included]'. Bhola Chatterjee, *Aspects of Bengal Politics in the Early Nineteen-Thirties*, Calcutta, 1969, pp. 18–20.
[143] See Reid to Linlithgow, 20 August 1939, FR. Robert Reid Papers, IOLR MSS Eur E/218/5, and Herbert to Linlithgow, 7 June 1940, FR. Linlithgow Collection, IOLR MSS Eur F/125/40.
[144] N. N. Mitra (ed.), *Indian Annual Register*, 1939, vol. II, July–December, p. 52.
[145] Linlithgow to Zetland, 23 January 1940, Zetland Collection, IOLR MSS Eur D/609/19.

interests. But he proved ineffectual, and, as the legislative onslaught against bhadralok power continued unabated, Mookerjee recognised the need for an organisation in Bengal which would back his efforts.[146] The issues which the Mahasabha took up were precisely those that worried the bhadralok, many of whom despaired of any effective remedies from a Congress led by the Bose brothers. Its propaganda took pains to address typically bhadralok concerns:

The Hindu people need no reminding that our situation as a community is deteriorating day by day. In every sphere of life our rights and our interests are being cruelly trampled under-foot. In the sphere of politics the mischievous Communal Award has crippled us, leaving us in a state of helplessness in the Legislative Assembly, and reducing us to slaves in the matter of provincial administration and legislation. In the case of employment in government services, merit and ability are disregarded, and by the miracle of communal favouritism, the door to government employment has been closed for Hindus. In the social and religious spheres, our position is equally difficult. Hindu women are oppressed, Hindu boys and girls are kidnapped ... Hindu temples are polluted and Hindu idols are destroyed ... Due to the Congress mentality, a misguided tendency towards generosity ... has created obstacles in the path of Hindu life and progress and has dragged Hindus towards destruction. Faced with the British bureaucracy's promotion of Muslims on the one had, and with the Congress' conciliatory and yielding mentality on the other, the Hindu race is being strangled to death – economically, politically and culturally![147]

The Mahasabha had made an unequivocal bid to be the alternative to the Congress in Bengal that many were looking for. In the first months of its campaign, the new Hindu party succeeded in attracting support from among the Congress' traditional supporters, who had been disappointed by Sarat Bose's failure to protect their interests in the Assembly and by his flirtation with 'radical' causes outside it. Big business was the first to switch its allegiance. Calcutta's wealthy Marwari families contributed handsomely to the Mahasabha's coffers, and Jugal Kishore Birla, whose family in the past had underwritten many Congress ventures,[148] headed the list of donors who financed the Mahasabha conference in Calcutta. Also on the list were Seth Bansidhar Jallan, Badridas Goenka and Radhakissen Kanodia, while Khaitan and Company made a generous

---

[146] For biographical details, see Balraj Madhok, *Dr. Syama Prasad Mookerjee, A Biography*, Delhi, 1954. See also, J. H. Broomfield, *Elite Conflict in a Plural Society*, 1968, pp. 282–284.
[147] *Hindur Sankatmoy Paristhiti: Netribrinder Ahaban* ('The Hindus' Difficult Position: The Leaders' Call'), Calcutta, 1939; a Mahasabha publication enclosed in GB SB 'PH' Series, File No. 501/39.
[148] For an account of the relationship between the Birlas and the Congress, see G. D. Birla, *In the Shadow of the Mahatma – a Personal Memoir*, Calcutta, 1953.

contribution.[149] Khaitan and Company was owned by the family of Debi Prasad Khaitan, who, like most Marwari entrepreneurs, had made his fortune in the speculative (*fatka*) jute markets.[150] Khaitan had helped Subhas Bose in the past, negotiating on his behalf with different business houses to raise funds for the Congress.[151] But now he reconsidered his position towards Bose and his party and decided to hedge his bets. Khaitan and several of his Marwari business associates felt that paying a premium to the Mahasabha would provide a better insurance in Bengal. The new Hindu party also attracted the support of wealthy Bengalis, who put up 10,000 rupees for the Mahasabha's inaugural conference.[152]

In the mofussil, several big zamindars took up the cause of the Mahasabha, repudiating their traditional ties with the Bengal Congress. Maharaja Sashi Kanta Acharya Choudhury, who had large estates in Mymensingh, acted as host to a Mahasabha conference in his zamindari. In Malda district in North Bengal, a Mahasabha meeting was held at the house of Babu Bhairabendra Narayan Roy, the zamindar of Singhbad.[153] In 1941, another Mymensingh landlord, Babu Hemanta Chandra Chaudhuri, whose estates were under the Court of Wards and who was an Honorary Magistrate, was reported to have 'taken a leading part in a Mahasava meeting recently and was the principal speaker'.[154] Mofussil zamindars, who had been key supporters of the Congress during the Assembly elections, had changed tack and welcomed the new Hindu party which promised to defend their landed interests in a more determined fashion than the Bose Congress.

There were those within the Bengal Congress leadership who took the same view. Prominent among them was Nalini Ranjan Sarkar, the Calcutta financier who had been the Minister for Finance in the Fazlul Huq Ministry. Sarkar, who had made his fortune in the insurance business, was a member of the 'Big Five' in the late twenties; and though he was not himself a popular Congress 'leader', he wielded considerable influence in Congress circles. In the early thirties when the Big Five split up into contending factions, Sarkar had joined that section of the Party which drew increasingly close to the central Gandhian leadership and became in

[149] Memo dated 3 December 1939. GB SB 'PH' Series, File No. 501/39 (III).
[150] For an account of the rise of Marwari business-houses in Calcutta, see Omkar Goswami, '*Sahibs, Babus* and *Banias*: Changes in Industrial Control in Eastern India, 1918–50', *Journal of Asian Studies*, vol. 48, 2, May 1989, pp. 289–309.
[151] GOI Home Poll File No. 4/14–A/40.
[152] Memo dated 3 December 1939. GB SB 'PH' Series, File No. 501/39 (III).
[153] GB SB 'PH' Series File No. 501/39.
[154] District Magistrate, Mymensingh to the Commissioner, Dacca Division, 19 March 1941. GB HCPB File No. 13/41.

time an implacable enemy of the Bose brothers.[155] In 1937, he joined the Huq Ministry as Finance Minister against the wishes of the High Command and forfeited his Congress membership but he remained 'as close a follower of Gandhi and the Right Wing and as bitterly opposed to Subhas Bose as ever'.[156] As minister, 'he secured maximum possible concessions to Hindu interests by hints of a possible resignation'.[157] When war broke out in 1939 Sarkar, following the Congress lead, resigned from the Cabinet. He was not immediately re-admitted to the Congress but continued to exert great influence over what was now the 'official Congress', causing the Governor to remark:

The official ban placed on him by Congress when he joined the Ministry has not yet been lifted. Although he has close connections with Surendra Mohan Ghose, the Jugantar leader, he has a considerable and, probably, steadying influence on him. His connections with that section of the Congress is more by way of using that influence to counteract the moves of the Bose brothers and prevent them from gaining control over a greater section of the Congress. His tendency is to work behind the scenes and he is 'out' of Bengal politics, in rather the same way, though on a smaller scale, that Gandhi is 'out' of the All-India Congress. He has the confidence of the Hindu community in Bengal, with the exception of the section headed by the Bose brothers. He is more truly representative of Hindu nationalist opinion in Bengal than any other leader and he has the support of Hindu vested interests in Bengal.[158]

Like many of his Marwari business associates, Sarkar was not prepared to place all his eggs in the Congress basket so long as his old rival, Sarat Bose, was in command of the party. So when he resigned from the Ministry, Sarkar took up with the Mahasabha whose leaders had been 'attempting to win him over' for some time.[159] According to the Governor, 'Nalini Ranjan Sarkar attended the [inaugural] conference [of the All-India Hindu Mahasabha] for one day, sat on the platform and had a good reception'. But Sarkar was an astute politician and was well aware of the difficulties that would face any Hindu party that challenged the Congress. So he made no move to 'identify himself formally with the Mahasabha'. Indeed the Governor was sure that he would not do so

---

[155] It was rumoured that talks between Sarat Bose and Fazlul Huq for the formation of a coalition ministry broke down over Nalini Sarkar: that Huq was determined to have him as Finance Minister and that Sarat Bose refused to join any coalition of which Sarkar was a member. Shila Sen, *Muslim Politics in Bengal*, p. 93. For Sarkar's version of the split, see *Why Mr. Nalini Ranjan Sarkar left the Congress*, Calcutta, 1937, p. 5. Nalini Ranjan Sarkar Papers, Serial No. 15, NMML.

[156] Herbert to Linlithgow, 6 January 1940, FR. Linlithgow Collection, IOLR MSS Eur F/125/40.

[157] *Ibid.*   [158] Herbert to Linlithgow, 13 August 1940, FR. *Ibid.*

[159] Memo dated 24 December 1939. GB SB 'PH' Series, File No. 501/39 (V).

'unless he were convinced that ... the Mahasabha was likely to become a really effective organisation, or one that could be led back into the Congress fold'.[160]

There is good reason, therefore, to believe that the Presidential Election dispute and the High Command's attack on the Bose group was not entirely unwelcome in Bengal. Several zamindars and businessmen who traditionally had supported the Bengal Congress were so frustrated by the Party under the leadership of the Bose brothers that they had seriously considered shifting their allegiance to an alternative party and many had endorsed the establishment of the Hindu Mahasabha in Bengal. But with the expulsion of the Bose brothers and their left-wing followers from the Party, they realised that perhaps they would not have to look outside the Congress after all. Instead, in the coming years, they could now hope to recapture the Congress organisation in Bengal and turn it back into an instrument of their purposes. A few months after Tripuri, the Governor reported that among 'Hindus'

there has been a good deal of strong talk on very definitely communal lines ... The situation would be entirely altered if there could only emerge a powerful Hindu organisation upon which the Hindu element in the Assembly could rely for practical and consistent support ... I believe that there are many Hindus like [Nalini Ranjan] Sarker (sic) ... who recognise the need of an organisation such as this, but they are perhaps pinning their hopes on eventually gaining the upper hand in the Bengal Congress, which they regard as the only possible Hindu organisation in Bengal. If so, the outcome of the contest between Subhas Bose and Dr B. C. Roy's 'Right Wing' group may be of vital importance in the future development of the province.[161]

Step by step, confidence was gradually restored in the Bengal Congress, once it became clear that the brothers Bose and their followers were firmly to be kept out of the Party. The High Command's purge of the Bengal Congress found strong support in the 'official' Bengal Committee, indeed, there were those who wanted it to proceed further and faster. Thus Satin Sen, hero of the Patuakhali Satyagraha,[162] wrote to Rajendra Prasad urging him to 'ban' the Bose group forthwith:

[160] Herbert to Linlithgow, 6 January 1940, FR. Linlithgow Collection, IOLR MSS Eur F/125/40.
[161] Reid to Linlithgow, 20 August 1939, FR. Robert Reid Papers, IOLR MSS Eur E/278/5.
[162] In 1927, Satindranath Sen, a former Jugantar activist, led a 'satyagraha' in Barisal to protest against the D. M.'s decision that processions playing music should not be allowed past a newly constructed mosque in Patuakhali, in accordance with established local custom. With the support of the Hindu Sabha, Sen, then a prominent local Congressman, organised sankirtan processions past the mosque every day, defying prohibitory orders and courting arrest. The affair sparked off a major communal riot in neighbouring Ponabalia. For further details, see Partha Chatterjee, *Bengal 1920–1947*,

In Bengal Subhas babu has allied himself with the C[ommunist] P[arty] C[ongress] S[ocialist] P[arty] Kisan (and Students Federation etc.) organisation. Even before Subhas Babu had developed his latest desperate and fanatical attitude these organisation[s] had been ... responsible for discrediting the Congress by its attacks on the leadership, the 'reformist and reactionary mentality of the Congress', etc etc. Since the revolt of Subhas Babu, these organisations have developed activities which are outrageously anti-Congress, anti Gandhi; class war is openly preached; of late the Communists have been distributing leaflets ridiculing Non-violence, civil disobedience, Satyagraha etc and advocating violent insurrection etc etc ... It is time that suitable steps are taken immediately. Subhas Babu is exploiting these organisations and these organisations too are exploiting Subhas Babu to their hearts content. With the saddest result on Congress' position, prestige and power.[163]

Once the purge of Subhas and his allies had been carried through, the Bengal Congress was able to take an unabashedly Hindu stand on what the authorities referred to as 'vested interests'.[164] In March 1941, in protest against the provisions of the Secondary Education Bill,

the official Congress Party staged a walk-out from the Assembly ... after Kiran Sankar Roy had read out a carefully worded statement. This left the door open for their return in order to oppose any contentious measures, such as the Secondary Education Bill and the Calcutta Municipal Amendment Bill ... The implication was clear that Congress represented Hindu interests.[165]

The following month, Nalini Ranjan Sarkar was formally re-admitted to the Congress, a step that was 'hailed with delight' by members of the Jugantar party and the official Congress in Mymensingh.[166] Sarkar had earlier made 'public utterances' on the Secondary Education Bill, which, in the view of the Governor, 'rather overstep the mark'.[167] Clearly, the new 'official' Congress was not afraid openly to identify itself with Hindu bhadralok interests in the Assembly, nor were its new leaders careful to maintain a secular image outside it. Nalini Sarkar's return restored confidence in the Bengal Congress that the party would deliver the goods,

pp. 77–78, Tanika Sarkar, *Bengal 1928–1934*, pp. 25–26, and Suranjan Das, 'Communal Riots in Bengal, 1905–1947', pp. 181–187.
163 Satindranath Sen to Rajendra Prasad, 23 February 1940. AICC Papers, File No. P-5 (Part II)/1940.
164 See, for instance, Woodhead to Linlithgow, 19/20 June 1939, FR. Linlithgow Collection, IOLR MSS Eur F/125/39.
165 Herbert to Linlithgow, 7 March 1941, FR. Linlithgow Collection, IOLR MSS Eur F/125/41.
166 Report of the Commissioner, Dacca Division. LOFCR for the second fortnight of April 1941. GB HCPB File No. 13/41.
167 Herbert to Linlithgow, 10 September 1940, FR. Linlithgow Collection, IOLR MSS Eur F/125/40.

and those of its supporters who had abandoned it in favour of the
Mahasabha now slowly began to return to the Congress fold.

But the Hindu Mahasabha was not prepared to give up its ground
without a fight. Launching an aggressively communal campaign which led
to heightened friction between the communities, the Mahasabha tried
hard to keep the support of bhadralok Hindus by denouncing the Congress for its alleged 'appeasement' of Muslims. And, in the early forties,
there were signs that this campaign was beginning to have some effect. In
March 1941, a major communal riot broke out in Dacca, following
months of sustained Mahasabha propaganda on the question of the
Secondary Education Bill. Sparked off by a fabricated report that Hindu
women had been molested by Muslim youths,[168] the violence rapidly
spread through Dacca city and spilled over into the surrounding countryside. In the strained aftermath of the riot, the Mahasabha appeared to
have gained ground at the expense of the Congress. The assessment on the
spot was that

the position of the Bengal Congress has further weakened and the Hindu Mahasava has gained in strength owing to the unfortunate communal riot at Dacca and
strong communal tension in some other districts. Almost every person is found
reluctant to pay in the 'Relief Fund' opened by the Congress but are voluntarily
paying to the fund opened by the Hindu Mahasava ... The responsible officers of
each department [of the Calcutta Corporation] were found sympathetic to the
realisation of the Relief Fund but when the ordinary employees were approached
they refused to pay a farthing to the Congress Relief Fund as the Congress being a
non-communal body would extend their relief to both the Hindus and the
Muslims. This they would not tolerate.[169]

Forced to compete with the Hindu Mahasabha on a communal platform
in order to keep the support of the many bhadralok Hindus who wanted a
hard line against Muslims, the Bengal Congress let it be known that its
relief programme after the riots was for Hindus only. It was decided that
all monies raised by the Congress Relief Fund would be used to finance
the resettlement of Hindu refugees from Dacca who had fled to the nearby
state of Tripura to escape from the riots. As Kamini Dutta, the leading
Dacca Congressman who presided over the Congress inquiry into the
riots, pointed out

the Maharaja of Tripura is ... ready to give [Hindu refugees] all facility for
permanently settling in Tripura State. But the effect of this will be disastrous to

[168] The *Amrita Bazar Patrika*'s story of the harrassment of Hindu women on Holi was
proved false by police enquiries. Suranjan Das, 'Communal Riots in Bengal, 1905–1947',
p. 269. See also the *Statement Submitted on behalf of the Bengal Provincial Hindu
Mahasava before the Dacca Riots Enquiry Committee*, Shyama Prasad Mookerjee
Papers, NMML, File No. 57/1942–43.
[169] Memo dated 7 April 1941. GB SB 'PM' Series, File No. 734/41.

the Hindu Community in Bengal, as this will encourage further attempts to coerce the Hindus to leave Bengal ... Congress workers are ... persuading the refugees to return back. But to enable these refugees to resettle many of them have to be financially helped ... This will be the Relief.[170]

This policy of 'communal relief' pursued by Congressmen in Dacca had the sanction of the Congress High Command. Rajendra Prasad justified it in the following terms:

The Hindu Mahasabha people are not giving help to the Mahomedans and so [Hindus] are not giving the money to Congress workers. They fear that the Congress workers may help the Mahomedans also. They give help only to the Hindus. If Congress cannot be of any help to the public at this critical time, then it may lose its hold on the public.[171]

Similar pressures persuaded the Bengal Congress to represent the Hindu 'community' before the Dacca Riots Enquiry Committee. As Kamini Dutta explained to Nalini Sarkar:

To go unrepresented in this Inquiry would practically have placed the Bengal Congress out of public life in Bengal. But our position there is a very delicate one. We have to maintain the Congress standard and at the same time strongly uphold the Congress position in the eyes of the public ... As to filling any statement in writing on behalf of the BPCC before the Inquiry Committee the matter is a very intriguing one. BPCC cannot in writing commit itself to a communal one-sided standpoint but at the same time we should not by any statement jeopardise the position of the Hindu Community or of any other Hindu organisation.[172]

The 'other Hindu organisation' to which Dutta referred was, obviously, the Hindu Mahasabha. In the event, the two parties worked together closely to put up the case for the 'Hindu community' before the Dacca Riots Enquiry Committee. Once again, Kamini Dutta and Nalini Ranjan Sarkar put their heads together to plot the best course for the Congress. Dutta pointed out that

Congress is in the best position to lead evidence about the incidents in the rural areas but it will not be advisable to take the responsibility for it. The task is a huge one and will require considerable expenditure. Congress may work conjointly with Hindu Sabha in this matter. Hindu Sabha will finance the organisation in this respect. Our help will be of immense value to them. Without Congress co-operation it will be very difficult for them to have the requisite materials from the rural area ... The case in the rural area is the best one for the Hindus. The guilt of

---

170 Intercepted letter from Kamini Dutta to Nalini Ranjan Sarkar, dated 14 April 1941. *Ibid.*
171 Intercepted letter from Rajendra Prasad to Gandhi, dated 16 April 1941. *Ibid.*
172 Intercepted letter form Kamini Kumar Dutta to Nalini Ranjan Sarkar, dated 8 May 1941. GB SB 'PM' Series, File No. 734/41 II.

both the communities is almost on a par [sic] in the Dacca town and the verdict will also be the same.[173]

The terms of the deal between the two organisations are of particular interest. Dutta was clear that the costs of putting a case together would be too heavy for the Congress to bear but seemed confident that the Hindu Mahasabha would be both willing and able to provide the necessary finance. This suggests that the flight of capital from the Bengal Congress during the years of Sarat Bose's leadership had, indeed, been of serious proportions. When the 'official' Congress recaptured the organisation after the expulsion of the Bose group, they had discovered that its coffers were empty,[174] and its new leaders had not found it easy to fill them. According to one secret report,

in order to relieve the financial difficulties of the new Bengal Provincial Congress Committee, several members have promised monthly subscriptions, but have not paid them regularly. The recurring monthly expenditure of the Committee is Rs. 2,500/- approximately so that far more sustained efforts are required to place the Committee's finances on a sound basis. The Provincial Committee does not own any property.[175]

The Mahasabha, on the other hand, had become a wealthy organisation in a few short years. But while it had been able to attract money, and despite the Mahasabha's unconvincing boast that it had as many as fourteen hundred branches in the province,[176] it had not succeeded in establishing an organisation which could compare with the base that the Congress still possessed, particularly in the mofussil. So the Mahasabha was forced to depend upon the Congress infrastructure in order to collect the necessary witnesses and material from the outlying areas where Hindus had suffered heavy casualties during the riots. A pattern of collaboration was thus established between the two organisations which survived well beyond the sittings of the Dacca Riots Enquiry Committee. The two parties continued to work closely together whenever it was necessary to put up a coordinated defence of 'Hindu' interests. Where 'Hindu' interests were believed to be at stake, there was little to

[173] Dutta referred to the fact that while Hindu casualties had been higher in the outlying rural areas, Muslim casualties were heavier in Dacca city itself. *Ibid.*
[174] There were allegations that Subhas Bose had sequestered the funds of the Bengal Congress before his arrest, and that he had ensured that both the party's money and its property were held in his name. See the memo dated 9 March 1939, entitled 'Funds available exclusively to Bose and his left-wing allies', in GOI Home Poll File No. 4/14–A/40 (NAI).
[175] *Ibid.*
[176] Ashutosh Lahiry to Rai Bahadur Surendra Nath Gupta Bhaya, (President, Rajshahi District Hindu Mahasabha), 14 August 1945. Shyama Prasad Mookerjee Papers, II-IV Instalment, File No. 90/1944–45.

distinguish between the politics and policies of the two parties. And, as the Governor observed, it was, more often than not, the Mahasabha that set the tone of the debate: 'The Congress party is finding itself more and more following the Mahasabha lead. Had elections been impending, they would have been opposed; as it is, they are tending to come together and would form an undesirable combination.'[177]

However, Herbert was proved wrong. By the time the next elections came around in 1945–46, the contest he expected between the two parties did not materialise. In the intervening years, particularly after the Congress had been banned in 1942, the membership of the two parties had tended to overlap more and more as many Congressmen joined the Mahasabha to avoid arrest.[178] During these years, the two parties grew closer organisationally and politically, and, as an official report noted, they seemed willing to admit it: 'In the absence of Congress from the field, there has been no hesitation to identify the Hindu Mahasabha more closely with this undoubtedly Hindu body. Indeed, as may be expected, Dr S. P. Mukerjee has been making it clear how near he is personally to the Congress.'[179] Later that year, the two parties went into the elections to the Calcutta Corporation as allies. At an election meeting on 16 March held 'under the joint auspices of the Hindu Mahasabha and the Congress', Mr. N. C. Chatterjee of the Mahasabha announced that his party 'had joined hands with the Congress to oppose [the] combination of the Muslim League and Imperialism' and that 'it was intended to set up a national coalition party'.[180]

The ban on the Congress Party and the flight of its members to the Mahasabha during the War created the misleading impression that the Mahasabha had done better out of the alliance than the Bengal Congress. But when the War ended, the Mahasabha's gains proved to be largely illusory. In fact, Congress had done well out of its relationship with the Mahasabha and the 'Hindu' cause; it had worked to strengthen the hold of the Bengal Congress over its bhadralok constituency. When the ban on

---

[177] Herbert to Linlithgow, 22 March 1942, FR. Linlithgow Collection, IOLR MSS Eur F/125/42.
[178] The entry of members of the Hindu Sabha into the Congress had worried the Bose Congress in the late thirties, and Ashrafuddin Chaudhuri had appealed to the Working Committee to disallow overlapping membership between the two parties. But the High Command had taken the view that 'there is ... nothing in the Congress constitution ... to prevent primary memebrs of such organisations from being office-holders in the Congress organisation', and so there was no way to check this tendency in the early forties. See the correspondence between Ashrafuddin Chaudhuri and Rajendra Prasad, in AICC Papers, File No. P-5/1938.
[179] GOI Home Political File No. 9/1/44.
[180] Memo dated 18 March 1944. GB SB 'PH' Series, File No. 501/44 (I).

the Congress was lifted, the Mahasabha found its ranks sorely depleted, as many of its recruits returned to the Congress. Others, while continuing to maintain close links with the Mahasabha, supported Congress candidates in the election. Indeed, this practice was so widespread that the General Secretary of the Bengal Mahasabha was prompted to ask district branches for 'detailed report[s] about the Mahasabha members who have deserted the Hindu Mahasabha or who have worked against the Hindu Mahasabha candidates during the Central Assembly Election, while retaining their connection with the Hindu Mahasabha'.[181]

In the run up to the 1945–46 elections, the Bengal Congress renewed its commitment to 'Hindu' bhadralok and business interests, firmly distancing itself from the Communist Party and the Forward Bloc. In July 1945, Maulana Azad, the President of the All-India Congress Committee 'asked for collection of evidence of [Communist] "treachery" during the 1942 disturbances and afterwards', marking the beginning of the Congress campaign to denounce the Communist Party as 'anti-national' for taking part in the War effort during the Quit India movement.[182] Interestingly, the Congress leadership made no parallel move against the Hindu Mahasabha which had supported the British war effort since 1939. In Bengal, there were reports that the Congress, which 'now feels stronger on account of the return of its former members ... has begun to attack the Communists'.[183] The Congress also launched campaigns in the districts in the name of 'Hindu unity', appropriating the Mahasabha's message.[184] The Congress had quickly re-established itself as the party that could most effectively protect bhadralok and other powerful Hindu interests. In November 1945, it was observed that all over the province, 'the Congress is gaining ground at the expense of the Mahasabha'[185] and reports from the eastern districts, where the Mahasabha had been strongest, indicated 'a general rallying of Hindu opinion behind the Congress'. News from the constituencies confirmed that the Congress had plumped for a wholeheartedly communal campaign, and that this had the support of the Provincial Congress leadership. The Mymensingh District Magistrate reported that 'the Chairman of the Provincial Congress Committee [had]

[181] Bengal Provincial Hindu Mahasabha (B.P.H.M.) circular to district branches. Enclosed in an intercepted letter from Debendra Nath Mukherjee, General Secretary B.P.H.M. to M. C. Dhiman, dated 17 December 1945. GB SB 'PH' Series, File No. 501/45 (V).
[182] Fortnightly Secret Report on the Political Situation (FSR) for the second fortnight in July 1945. GB HCPB File No. 37/45.
[183] Ibid.
[184] Report of the Commissioner, Dacca Division, LOFCR for the first fortnight in November 1945. GB HCPB File No. 37/45.
[185] FSR for the first fortnight in November 1945. GB HCPB File No. 37/45.

been in the district campaigning effectively on the lines of Hindu unity'.[186]

The Mahasabha tried to fight back by depicting itself as a plausible alternative to the Congress during the elections to the Central Assembly.[187] But the Congress took the wind out of the sails of the Mahasabha by putting up as its candidate Babu Sasanka Sehkar Sanyal, notorious as a powerful spokesman of Hindu causes. Sanyal had represented the Hindu case in local communal disputes in his home district of Murshidabad, in one case refusing to allow the branches of a 'sacred' tree to be cut so as to allow a Muslim tazia to pass,[188] in another insisting that a mosque should not be built within a hundred yards of a Hindu temple.[189] With its vigorous campaign for 'Hindu unity' and its clever choice of candidates, the Congress trounced the Mahasabha, making a clean sweep of all six Hindu seats.[190] Indeed, the Congress had such signal success in appropriating everything that the Mahasabha had achieved and stood for – its membership, its slogans and its programme – that even its own members could see little point in the Mahasabha continuing to exist as a separate organisation. As one group of Calcutta Hindus advised Shyama Prasad,

The question of the existence of the Hindu Mahasabha as a separate Political Organization does not arise anymore after the Congress has thrown out an emphatic challenge to the Muslim League ... The people ... want you to contest in the ensuing elections from a body not narrowly communal ... you are the fittest man in Bengal to lead the Congress to its Great Goal ... [We] appeal to you to join the Congress.[191]

Recognising that it could no longer hope to compete with the Bengal Congress as a champion of Hindu interests, the Mahasabha avoided what would almost certainly have been a humiliating defeat in the elections to the Provincial Assembly. Instead, it took the line of supporting Congress candidates to 'strengthen the national front'. A police informer thus reported with some bewilderment that

[186] Report of the Commissioner, Dacca Division, LOFCR for the first fortnight in November 1945, GB HCPB File No. 37/45.
[187] Thus N. C. Chatterjee of the Mahasabha admitted that 'Bengal's situation is extremely difficult ... The Congress ... will not allow our candidates to go without a contest ... Even if we can capture two seats out of six in Bengal, it will be a great triumph'. Intercepted letter from N. C. Chatterjee to Raja Maheshwar Dayal Seth, 4 December 1945. GB SB 'PH' Series, File No. 510/45 (V).
[188] Report of the Commissioner, Presidency Division, LOFCR for the first fortnight of August 1945, GB HCPB File No. 37/45.
[189] Report of the Commissioner, Presidency Division, LOFCR for the first fortnight of September 1945. *Ibid.*
[190] 'Franchise. Elections in Bengal, 1945–46', IOLR L/P and J/8/475.
[191] Letter to Shyama Prasad Mookerjee signed by several Hindus of Calcutta, 4 December 1945. Shyama Prasad Mookerjee Papers, II-IV Instalment, File No. 75/1945–46.

Table 4. *Commerce and landholders. 'Special interests' and the Congress: 1936–37 and 1945–46*

Constituency	Successful candidate and Party	
	1936–37	1945–46
Commerce and Industry		
Indian Chamber of Commerce	D. P. Khaitan / Independent	D. P. Khaitan / Congress
Bengal National Chamber of Commerce	H. S. Paul / Independent N. R. Sarkar / Independent	B. C. Ghosh / Congress A. K. Ghosh / Congress
Marwari Association	R. Tapuria / Independent	A. L. Poddar / Congress
Landholders		
Burdwan	B. P. Singh Roy / Independent	Maharaja of Burdwan / Independent
Presidency	Maharaja S. C. Nandy / Independent	Maharaja S. C. Nandy / Congress
Rajshahi	Maharaja S. K. Choudhury / Independent	N. S. Singhee / Congress
Chittagong	K. C. Roy / Independent	A. C. Sinha / Congress.
Dacca	S. K. Acharya Choudhury / Hindu Nationalist	S. K. Acharya Choudhury / Congress

Source: Compiled from Franchise Files IOLR L/P and J/7/1142 and L/P and J/8/475 for the years 1936–37 and 1945–46 respectively.

it appears that the B[engal] P[rovincial] Hindu Mahasabha is not showing the same zeal in the forthcoming Provincial elections as it had done in the Central Assembly elections. It has decided to set up prominent and influential candidates only in those general constituencies where the Congress candidates are found weaker and inferior in social status. A contest between the Mahasabha and the Congress candidates is thus expected only in a few constituencies ... According to Dr S. P. Mukharji the activities of the Mahasabha should be directed only on one target, that of strengthening the national front and launching the final attack on British Imperialism ... The Mahasabha must function vigorously and it must occupy a distinct place ... but it should avoid a clash with Congress.[192]

The Mahasabha eventually decided to contest twenty-six seats, but was defeated by the Congress in all but one. Dr Shyama Prasad Mukherjee was returned unopposed from Calcutta University. It polled only 2.7 per cent of the votes in the 'general' constituencies, while the Congress polled 77 per cent.[193] What is more, the Congress was extremely successful in the

[192] Memo dated 5 February 1946. GB SB 'PM' Series, File No. 829/45.
[193] 'Franchise, Elections in Bengal, 1946', IOLR L/P and J/8/475.

'Special' constituencies reserved for business and landholding interests, winning four out of five seats earmarked for Hindu zamindars, and all four seats reserved for Hindu business (see table 4). This was a significant improvement over its performance in the 1936–37 elections, and showed that businessmen and landholders in Bengal had decided to return to backing their clients of old – a sure sign that Congress had recaptured command of the big battalions.

The overwhelming success of the Bengal Congress in the Hindu constituencies, and more particularly in the Commerce and Landholders seats reflects the extent to which the party had been transformed in the forties. Following the expulsion of the Bose group, the Bengal Congress presented a profile that was at once more 'Hindu' and more conservative. In so doing, it had effectively appropriated the Hindu Mahasabha's brief. The result was that the Congress won back the favour of those interest groups which had backed the Mahasabha for a short while. Thus Marwari business-houses, reassured by the presence of the financier Nalini Sarkar at the helm of the new Congress leadership, showed renewed confidence in the Party. Among the businessmen who contested the election on a Congress ticket was Debi Prasad Khaitan, who had contributed generously to the Mahasabha's coffers in 1939.[194]

Equally, many of the big zamindars who had played an active part in Mahasabha politics at the outset had returned to the Congress fold by 1945. The District Magistrate of Mymensingh made an interesting comment on the political sympathies of zamindars in his district:

The Maharaja of Susung, the Senior Maharaj Kumar of Mymensingh, the Acharya Choudhuries of Muktagacha and in fact all Hindu-Zamindars are Hindu Mahasabhaites. The second Maharaj Kumar of Mymensingh proclaims himself as a Congressite but he is a Hindu Mahasabhite at heart. The political creed of most Hindus of the district is a mixture of Congress and Hindu-Mahasabha – more of the Hindu-Mahasabha than of the Congress ... candidates who are strong Hindu Sabhites at heart but will win Congress tickets will have the best chance. I do not anticipate any strong fight between the Congress and the Hindu Mahasabha in Mymensingh district – in fact in many districts of Bengal.[195]

He was proved right in 1946, when four out of five landholders seats were won by the Congress. From his own division, the zamindar S. K. Acharya Choudhury, erstwhile Hindu Nationalist and active member of the Hindu Mahasabha,[196] was returned on a Congress ticket. For Hindu landed interests in Bengal, there was little to choose between the Hindu Maha-

[194] *Ibid.*
[195] Note by the District Magistrate of Mymensingh on the progress of electoral campaigns in the district, GB HCPB File No. 314 A/45.
[196] See GB SB 'PH' Series, File No. 501/39.

sabha and the Bengal Congress of the mid-forties. The Congress could now be trusted to defend Hindu interests as resolutely as the Mahasabha. Not surprisingly, Bengal's zamindars settled for the Congress since the old firm carried greater weight both in provincial and in national affairs.

4   The construction of bhadralok communal identity: culture and communalism in Bengal

Questions of 'identity' have not traditionally been the subject matter of historians. They have generally been viewed as belonging to a sphere far too ambiguous to be studied using the conventional tools of historical method. But recent trends in the social sciences – in particular the critique of empiricism and the growing acceptability of interdisciplinary and interpretative approaches – have encouraged historians to venture into this territory. Social anthropology, hermeneutics, linguistics and literary theory in particular have provided conceptual tools with which they have analysed the sacred and symbolic spheres around which communal identities have been forged.[1]

It is possible to outline, with the help of these resources, the emergence of a bhadralok Hindu communal identity in Bengal in the early decades of this century. This has not been attempted before, not least because this identity has not been immediately visible to historians. There are at least two reasons for this. The first is that studies of communalism in India have tended to have Partition as their point of reference. Because Par-

---

[1] Studies of communal identity in India have been particularly influenced by Michel Foucault's history of 'discursive formations' and Edward Said's critique of colonial constructions of 'otherness' and 'the self'. Michel Foucault, *The Archaelogy of Knowledge* (translated by A. M. Sheridan Smith), New York, 1972; Edward Said, *Orientalism*, London, 1987. Other works that have been influential include Eric Hobsbawm and Terence Ranger (eds.), *The Invention of Tradition*, Cambridge, 1983; Benedict Anderson, *Imagined Communities. Reflections on the Origin and Spread of Nationalism*, London, 1983; Victor Turner, *Dramas, Fields and Metaphors: Symbolic Action in Human Society*, Ithaca, 1974; and Clifford Geertz, *The Interpretation of Cultures*, New York, 1973. Some important and representative studies of communal identity in India include Gyanendra Pandey's, *The Construction of Communalism in Colonial North India*, Delhi, 1990; 'Rallying Round the Cow. Sectarian Strife in the Bhojpuri Region *c.* 1888–1917' in Ranajit Guha (ed.), *Subaltern Studies II*, Delhi, 1986; and 'In Defence of the Fragment: Writing about Hindu–Muslim Riots in India Today', *Economic and Political Weekly*, vol. 26, 11–12, Annual Number, 1992; Sandria Freitag, 'Religious Rites and Riots: From Community Identity to Communalism in North India', University of California, Berkeley, Ph.D. dissertation, 1980 and 'Sacred Symbol as Mobilizing Ideology. The North Indian Search for a "Hindu" Community'; *Comparative Studies in Society and History*, vol. 22, 1981;

tition is widely believed to have been the outcome of a Muslim separatist movement, such studies have focused primarily on the emergence of Muslim separatism and Muslim communal identities.[2] In the case of Bengal, this has led to the common assumption that the Muslims of Bengal were inherently communal and separatist, and that their communal sentiments could be mobilised at will by 'elite' leaders for their own ends.[3] Other historians have drawn attention to the close parallel between divisions of 'class' and 'community' in Bengal, which meant that social conflicts, whether in town or countryside, could quickly assume communal dimensions. But again, the roots of this process of communalisation are seen to lie within Muslim society: Muslim peasants are seen as possessing a ready-made 'peasant-communal' ideology, 'available for mobilization by various rival factions of the Muslim provincial leadership' in the thirties.[4] Another argument locates the dynamic of communalism in Bengal in 'the conflict between zamindar and jotedar in East Bengal'. But here again, this conflict is believed to have spawned a specifically Muslim communalism, which 'constantly fed the Muslim separatist movement in the province as a whole'.[5] While the intricacies of agrarian structure and modes of conflict are themselves the subject of heated debate, it is generally accepted that the 'irrational strength of Muslim identity ensured that the conflict in rural Bengal was channelled into the movement for Pakistan'.[6]

Anand Yang, 'Sacred Symbol and Sacred Space in Rural India'; and David Gilmartin, *Empire and Islam, Punjab and the Making of Pakistan*, Oxford, 1988.

[2] See David Page, *Prelude to Partition. The Indian Muslims and the Imperial System of Control*; F. C. R. Robinson, *Separatism among Indian Muslims. The Politics of the United Provinces' Muslims, 1860–1923*, Farzana Shaikh, *Community and Consensus in Islam: Muslim Representation in Colonial India, 1860–1947*, Cambridge, 1989; Shila Sen, *Muslim Politics in Bengal, 1937–1947*, New Delhi, 1976; and Rafiuddin Ahmed, *Bengal Muslims 1871–1906. A Quest for Identity*, New Delhi, 1981.

[3] Broomfield, for instance, attributes the collapse of the 'Hindu–Muslim nationalist alliance' in the mid-twenties to 'an influential section of the Bengal Muslim leadership ... determined to turn the *separatist tendencies of their community* to political gain'. J. H. Broomfield, *Elite Conflict in a Plural Society*, p. 317. Emphasis added.

[4] Partha Chatterjee, 'Agrarian Relations and Communalism in Bengal, 1926–35', p. 38. In the same vein, Suranjan Das argues that 'the Muslim masses had a ... readily identifiable communal and religious identity', and that 'in their move to turn the separatist tendencies of their community to political gain, the Muslim politicians received powerful help from the *ulema*'. Suranjan Das, 'Communal Riots in Bengal, 1905–1947', p. 51. In his recently published book on the subject, Das admits to 'a particular astigmatism' in his work, in that 'it has much more on Muslim and little on Hindu communal activity', but explains this in terms of insufficient source material on the latter. Suranjan Das, *Communal Riots in Bengal, 1905–1947*, Delhi, 1991, pp. 14–15.

[5] Rajat and Ratna Ray, 'Zamindars and Jotedars', p. 101.

[6] Sugata Bose, 'The Kishoreganj Riots', p. 491. These theorisations, particularly that of Suranjan Das, draw heavily upon the work of Rafiuddin Ahmed, who has argued for the emergence of a powerful sense of community identity amongst Bengal's Muslims in the

All these arguments, whatever their merits, suggest (perhaps unwittingly) that communalism in Bengal was essentially a Muslim phenomenon. This has led historians to assume that a parallel Hindu communalism did not emerge, or that if it did, it was too limited and peripheral to have contributed in any significant way to the conflicts that led to Pakistan.[7] This assumption, in turn, lends credence to the dangerously flawed notion that Muslims, more than other religious communities, are intrinsically 'communal'.[8]

Bhadralok communalism has failed to attract the attention of historians for a second reason. It has too readily been assumed that communal identities are necessarily constructed around specifically religious (or 'sacred') symbols,[9] such as the issue of music before mosques,[10] *go*

late nineteenth century. Rafiuddin Ahmed, *Bengal Muslims*. They ignore the work of Asim Ray, who makes the opposite case. Ray argues for the development of a significant tradition of 'syncretism' in Bengali Islam, and traces the development of an alternative 'Bengali' identity among them in the same period. See Asim Ray, 'The Social Factors in the Making of Bengali Islam', *South Asia*, vol. 3, 1973, pp. 23–35; 'Bengali Muslims and the Problem of Identity', *Journal of the Asiatic Society of Bangladesh*, vol. 22, 3, December 1977, pp. 192–7, and 'Bengali Muslim Cultural Mediators and Bengali Muslim Identity in the Nineteenth and Early Twentieth Centuries', in *South Asia*, vol. 10, 1, June 1987.

7 Shila Sen argues, for instance, that the Hindus 'were opposed to Partition in every form'. *Muslim Politics in Bengal*, p. 227. Also see Suranjan Das' analysis of the Patuakhali Satyagraha and the Ponabalia Riots of 1927, in which he argues that the Patuakhali Satyagraha was not 'initiated' by Hindu communal considerations, but that these might have been its unintended result. 'Communal Riots in Bengal', pp. 181–182.

8 Francis Robinson has taken this view in his debate with Paul Brass on the origins of Muslim separatism. See his articles, 'Nation Formation: the Brass Thesis and Muslim Separatism', *Journal of Comparative and Commonwealth Politics*, vol. 15, 3, November 1977, pp. 215–234, and 'Islam and Muslim Separatism', in David Taylor and Malcolm Yapp (eds.), *Political Identity in South Asia*, London, 1979. More recently, the case for the 'communitarian' (but not 'communal') basis of Islam has been argued by Farzana Shaikh, *Community and Consensus in Islam*, which further made muddy an already confused field of study.

9 The concept of 'sacred symbols' reflects the influence on historical writing of symbolic anthropology. Particularly influential have been the work of Clifford Geertz – his description of religion as a cultural system of symbols – and Victor Turner, and his concepts of 'symbolic action' and 'communitas'. Clifford Geertz, *The Interpretation of Cultures*; Victor Turner, *Dramas, Fields and Metaphors*. Problems associated with the symbolic approach have been raised in Dan Sperber, *Rethinking Symbolism*, Cambridge, 1975; and Pierre Bourdieu, 'The Production of Belief: Contribution to an economy of symbolic goods', in Richard Collins et al. (eds.), *Media, Culture and Society*, London, 1986. Some of the difficulties in Geertz's symbolic theory are suggested by Talal Asad, 'Anthropological Conceptions of Religion: Reflections on Geertz', *Man* (NS), vol. 18, 1983; by Peter Van der Veer in ' "God Must be Liberated!" A Hindu Liberation Movement in Ayodhya', *Modern Asian Studies*, vol. 21, 2, 1987, pp. 283–284, and in a more detailed way, in his book, *Gods on Earth. The Management of Religious Experience and Identity in a North Indian Pilgrimage Centre*, Delhi, 1989, pp. 44–52. For a fuller discussion of the impact of symbolic, semiotic and deconstructionist approaches on the writing of history, see Raphael Samuel, 'Reading the Signs' *History Workshop Journal*, 32, Autumn 1991.

10 P. K. Dutta, for instance, has argued that 'music before mosque had in fact become a consensual system, by means of which one communal formation could dramatise to the

korbani ('cow slaughter') or cow protection,[11] the desecration of idols, clashes over the observance of religious festivals,[12] over 'sacred space' and 'sacred time'.[13] Communal riots have often been sparked off by these issues, and for this reason, they have been assumed to be potent symbols of communal identity. Frietag, for instance, speaks of the construction of communal identity as 'the process by which activists could isolate out of *religious practice* particular symbols and could develop around these symbols an idiom, a specialized vocabulary, to express the vision of community'.[14] This emphasis on sacred symbols derives in turn, from what might inelegantly be described as the predominant 'riot-specific' or 'riot-centric' approach to the study of communalism, in which riots are used as a 'window' (albeit somewhat opaque) into social history.[15] While much has been learned from the study of collective and communal violence, such a 'riot-centric' approach creates difficulties in the study of communal identity. Not least of these difficulties is that this approach tends to take on board uncritically much of the baggage of the colonialists' 'imagined' India, in which the 'riot' is a recurring theme and assumes a view of the Indian psyche in which violence and 'fanaticism' lurk just beneath the surface.[16]

A focus on the 'immediate' and specific causes of violent conflict encourages undue emphasis on the proximate issue that provokes it. And because the issue in question may very often be a violation of a 'sacred symbol', the emotive power of that symbol is often assumed to be crucial to the identity of the community concerned. This assumption is reminiscent of colonial perceptions of India, which viewed popular religion as

other, their mutual antagonism'. P. K. Dutta, 'War over Music: The Riots of 1926 in Bengal', *Social Scientist*, vol. 18, 6–7, June–July 1990, pp. 41–42.

[11] Anand Yang, in his study of the Basantpur riot of 1893, makes the case that 'as with other disturbances which erupted in that year in such disparate cities as Bombay and Rangoon, and in towns and villages of North India, the conflict at Basantpur ... involved religious issues, in particular, the symbolic significance of the cow'. Yang, 'Sacred Symbol and Sacred Space', p. 578. Freitag also concludes that cow protection 'retains special significance ... as an important example of the trend toward the Hindu definition of community.' Freitag, 'Sacred Symbol as Mobilizing Ideology', p. 624. Pandey's examination of the cow-protection riots also analyses the 'symbol', but with different emphasis and different conclusions. See Gyan Pandey, 'Rallying round the Cow'. Also see Peter Robb, 'The Challenge of Gau Mata. British Policy and Religious Changes in India, 1880–1916', *Modern Asian Studies*, vol. 20, 2, 1986.
[12] Nita Kumar's study focuses on festivals and processions in the construction of caste, occupational and communal identities in Banaras. Nita Kumar, *The Artisans of Banaras. Popular Culture and Identity, 1880–1986*, Princeton, 1988, pp. 201–227. Freitag also sees festivals as a 'metaphor of community identification'. 'Religious Rites and Riots', p. 89.
[13] Yang, 'Sacred Symbol and Sacred Space', p. 580; Kumar, *Artisans of Banaras*, p. 222.
[14] Sandria Freitag, 'Religious Rites and Riots', p. 36.   [15] *Ibid.*, p. 6.
[16] See Gyanendra Pandey's discussion of the place of the riot in colonial discourse. Gyanendra Pandey, *Construction of Communalism*, pp. 17–65.

'emotional' and 'animistic',[17] and emphasised the 'mysterious power' of religious symbols over 'superstitious natives', and the irrational force of these 'primordial' attachments.[18] It has, moreover, encouraged historians to overlook two important aspects of these 'sacred symbols'. The first point that they have generally emerged recently: this is itself a point of some significance.[19] The second is that they served primarily as obvious markers of difference, setting out, clearly and publicly, the boundary between one community and its perceived 'rival'. In order to appreciate the power of symbols, this rivalry and the processes, whether social, economic or political, which fed it must be examined, as well as the wider discourses of 'difference' through which this rivalry was commonly expressed. These discourses describe the 'essences' that constitute a community in its own eyes: attributes that are invariably conceived as a cluster of intrinsic 'differences' that distinguishes it from its rival. These descriptions also attempt to impose homogeneity upon one community ('us') while at the same time constructing as a mirror image an equally homogeneous but opposite other: 'them'.[20] In these wider narratives of difference, specifically religious or sacred differences often enter only tangentially.

[17] See Inden's discussion of the Indological view of popular Hinduism as an 'emotional laity', and of folk religion as 'changeless animism'. Ronald Inden, *Imagining India*, Cambridge, Mass., 1990, p. 86.

[18] Gyanendra Pandey, *Colonial Constructions of Communalism*, p. 37; Peter Van der Veer, '"God must be Liberated!"', p. 284. Also see Terence Ranger, 'Power, Religion and Community: the Matabo Case', in Chatterjee and Pandey (eds.), *Subaltern Studies VII*, pp. 221–227. The assumption of racial superiority that runs through colonial literature is not replicated in riot-centric studies, which tend to adopt either a stance of cultural relativism, or one that privileges the 'indegenous' or 'popular' over the 'western' ('rational') or 'elite'. But these studies tend to take on both the 'essentialism' of colonial and imperial narratives, and their implicit denial of the history and the agency of the peoples they described. See Edward Said, *Orientalism* and Ronald Inden, *Imagining India*, for more detailed discussion of these points.

[19] Far from being a 'primordial' attachment, the issue, for instance, of music before mosques, was first raised in Bengal only in the mid-1920s. P. K. Dutta, 'War over Music', p. 40. Datta's researches reveal that the question of music before mosques seems 'to have had no immediate past', and that in the subcontinent as a whole, there were no recorded conflicts on this issue from 1893–1922. Suranjan Das also dates the emergence of the issue to 1926; before then, he argues, it 'had hardly worried the Hindus or Muslims'. He interprets the sudden emergence of this symbol as an expression of a new 'Muslim rigidity'. *Communal Riots in Bengal*, p. 28.

[20] The importance of 'boundaries' in the construction of community identity is stressed in Anthony P. Cohen's *The Symbolic Construction of Community*, London, 1985. The homogenising effect of communal discourse in contemporary India is discussed in Sudhir Kakar, 'Hindutva Harangue', *Sunday Times of India*, 19 July 1992; Gyanendra Pandey, 'Hindus and Others: The Militant Hindu Construction', *Economic and Political Weekly*, vol 26, 52, 28 December 1991, p. 3008; Pradip K. Dutta, 'VHP's Ram at Ayodhya. Reincarnation through Ideology and Organization', *Economic and Political Weekly*, vol. 26, 44, 2 November 1991, p. 2517; Tanika Sarkar, 'Woman as Communal Subject: Rashtrasevika Samiti and Ram Janmabhoomi Movement', *Economic and Political Weekly*, vol. 26, 35, 31 August 1991; and Neeladri Bhattacharya, 'Myth, History and the

The inwardness of communal identities can be understood not only by looking at the internal structure of the discourses, but by identifying the historical processes by which they were constructed.[21] Such an approach may help to 'de-mystify' communalism, and to reveal the communal intention of discourses in which religious or sacred symbols play little part (and which could therefore be mistakenly assumed to be 'secular'). Bhadralok Hindu communal discourse had these characteristics. In its hyperbole, the symbols of the cow, Kali and Durga were peripheral.[22] Yet it was no less powerful in its appeal, and no less communal in its intention, than other more obviously religious narratives.

Culture and Identity

If there was a single unifying symbol of bhadralok identity in the first half of the twentieth century, it was arguably 'culture'. Since the late nineteenth century, the bhadralok had regarded themselves as a group that was 'cultured';[23] by the early twentieth century, they saw themselves, more specifically, as heirs to a particular cultural heritage, the 'Bengal Renaissance'.[24] The extraordinary sense of attachment of the bhadralok Bengali to his 'culture' has often been remarked upon in academic writing.[25] In popular stereotype and literary satire, the Bengali is often parodied as a comic figure spouting *Rabindra-sangeet*, quick to take offence at any real or imagined slur against his cultural heroes.[26] Yet while the Renaissance

Politics of Ranjanmabhoomi', in Sarvepalli Gopal (ed.), *The Anatomy of a Confrontation. The Babri Masjid-Ramjanmabhumi Issue*, New Delhi, 1991.

[21] See the arguments for the interpretation of ideology at these different levels put forward by John B. Thompson in his *Studies in the Theory of Ideology*, Cambridge, 1987; Paul Ricoeur, *The Rule of Metaphor: Multi-Disciplinary Studies of the Creation of Meaning in Language* (translated by Robert Czerny), London, 1978; Paul Ricoeur, *Hermeneutics and the Human Sciences. Essays on Language, Action and Interpretation* (translated by John B. Thompson), Cambridge, 1988; and John B. Thompson, *Critical Hermeneutics. A Study in the thought of Paul Ricoeur and Jurgen Habermas*, Cambridge, 1983.

[22] It is for this reason, perhaps, that Suranjan Das could find very little material on Hindu communalism in Bengal, despite 'no dearth of search for such material'. *Communal Riots in Bengal*, p. 15.

[23] By the late nineteenth century, the bhadralok increasingly spoke of themselves as '*sikkhito sampraday*' ('educated community'). See S. N. Mukherjee, 'Bhadralok in Bengali Language and Literature', p. 233.

[24] See, for instance, Nirad Chaudhuri's description of the cultural milieu of his boyhood, and his discussion of the 'torch race of the Indian Renaissance'. *Autobiography of an Unknown Indian*, pp. 179–217.

[25] Broomfield, *Elite Conflict in a Plural Society*, p. 13, Rabindra Ray, *The Naxalites and their Ideology*, New Delhi, 1988, pp. 62–64.

[26] Thus Rabindra Ray, for instance, treads carefully in his discussion of 'the sociological aspects' of Tagore's work, because 'to say anything about Tagore's art is a risky business'. *Ibid.*, p. 63. Tanika Sarkar also begins her discussion of Tagore and Saratchandra Chattopadyay with 'a defensive statement for what it is worth'. 'Bengali Middle-Class Nationalism and Literature: A Study of Saratchandra's "Pather Dabi" and Rabind-

itself has been studied exhaustively, the relationship between bhadralok Bengalis and the Renaissance has escaped academic scrutiny. This section has the less ambitious purpose of touching upon the processes by which 'culture' became a central symbol of 'Hindu' identity in the discourse of the Bengali bhadralok in the 1930s and 1940s.

The question of identity was arguably at the eye of the intellectual storm which raged in nineteenth-century Bengal. The central quest of much Renaissance thought was to evaluate Hindu society in the light of its encounter with western rationalism[27] and colonial domination. The Bengali response ranged from the Derozian infatuation with western culture to the extreme cultural chauvinism of men such as Pandit Sasadhar Tarkachudamani, which proclaimed the 'scientific' basis of Hinduism. Within this broad spectrum fell several more sober intellectual traditions, such as the Brahmoism of Raja Rammohun Roy and the more assertive Hinduism of Bankimchandra and Vivekananda. Their responses to the big issues of reform and revival were complex and ambivalent,[28] but at the level of popular appropriation, lost much of their subtlety.[29] It was at this level that, by the turn of the century Hindu 'revivalism', as it is somewhat loosely described, gained ascendancy. The Young Bengal movement attracted more censure than sympathy, and was always marginal in the bhadralok world; the Brahmo movement, beset by internal schisms since

ranath's "Char Adhyay"', in D. N. Panigrahi (ed.), *Economy, Society and Politics in India*, New Delhi, 1985, p. 449.

[27] It was, as Raychaudhuri points out, the rationalist Enlightenment tradition that most influenced the first generation of western educated Bengalis in their encounter with western civilisation. Tapan Raychudhuri, *Europe Reconsidered*, p. 4.

[28] Sumit Sarkar, for instance, has remarked upon the deeply contradictory nature of Rammohun Roy's reformist philosophy, which accommodated within it compromises with orthodoxy, while even the Derozians shared many 'traditional' assumptions. Sumit Sarkar, *A Critique of Colonial India*. Asok Sen's study of Iswar Chandra Vidyasagar underlines that the great 'liberal' educationist sought scriptural sanction for his reformist programmes. Asok Sen, *Iswar Chandra Vidyasagar and his Elusive Milestones*, Calcutta, 1977. The Brahmo leader Keshub Chandra Sen, the author of the controversial 1872 Marriage Act which fixed the minimum age for marriage at 14 years, gave his under-age daughter in marriage to the Maharaja of Cooch Behar. Meredith Borthwick, 'The Cuch Behar Marriage: British Interests and Brahmo Integrity', *Bengal Past and Present*, vol. 95, Part II, 181, July–December 1976. On the other hand, Bankimchandra Chatterjee's project to rediscover Hinduism in its 'purest form' was firmly grounded in the western tradition of scientific rationalism, and used tools 'derived from such disciplines as comparative philology, sociology, the study of myths, Christian higher criticism and the methology of "scientific history"'. Tapan Raychaudhuri, *Europe Reconsidered*, p. 148. Also see Partha Chatterjee, 'The Fruits of Macaulay's Poison Tree' in Ashok Mitra (ed.), *The Truth Unites: Essays in Tribute to Samar Sen*, Calcutta, 1985; and his *Nationalist Thought and the Colonial World*, pp. 54–84.

[29] The crudities of both popular Brahmoism and Hindu nationalism have been depicted in Tagore's characterisations of 'Mistress Baroda' and Haran Babu on the one hand, and Gora's disciple, Abinash, on the other. Rabindranath Tagore, *Gora*, London, 1924.

the 1860s, was increasingly the target of ridicule both in 'high' intellectual circles and in the pulp press. Brahmo values were parodied in popular novels,[30] and the anglicised Bengali 'babu' was the butt of much satire. Even Bankimchandra Chattopadhyay, who had served as a Deputy Magistrate in the colonial bureaucracy, saw the 'modern Bengali' as a figure of fun:

By the grace of almighty God, there has appeared in this world during the nineteenth century an unprecedented [kind of] animal called the modern Bengali. Specialists in zoology have determined through examination that this animal has human characteristics externally, there are five digits on each of its hands and feet, there is no tail, and its bones and skull are, in fact, the bimanus type. But there is still no certainty with regard to its internal character. Some say, 'These animals are human inside, also'. Others say, 'They are human on the outside, but inside they are animal'. It is the opinion of some red-bearded sages that the Creator, in the same manner He gathered bits of beauty from the gorgeous women of the universe and created Tilottima, has collected animal traits bit by bit and created this unprecedented modern Bengali character. [Taking] from the jackal knavery, from the dog flattery and a passion for begging, from the sheep cowardice, from the monkey a skill at mimicry, from the ass his braying, and mixing them all together, He has raised in the sky of society, that illuminator of the Universe, that repository of the hope of all India, that receptacle of the affections of the learned Max Mueller, [namely] the modern Bengali.[31]

As the rising tide of Hindu nationalism swept Bengal in the early twentieth century, 'revivalism' rapidly outstripped 'reform' in its popular appeal. Ridiculing the Anglicised Indian was a constant refrain in the down-market literature of Battala, the popular farces and plays produced in what Sumit Sarkar describes as the world of the unsuccessful bhadralok: obscure hack-writers, clerks, humble school teachers and pandits losing the support of their patrons.[32] The mood was a reflection of the increasingly widespread reaction against the indignities of being subjects not citizens. But high-brow literature quite as much as the gutter press and the bazaar paintings of Kalighat reflected unease about the passing of the old social order and the collapse of its traditional hierarchies. The 'modern' woman thus shared pride of place with the foppish Brahmo

[30] See, for instance, Jogindrachandra Basu's *Model Bhagini*, ('The Model Sister') Calcutta, 1886–87, which parodied Brahmo values, in particular their views on the role of women in society.
[31] From Bankimchandra Chattopadhyay's *Se kal ar Ekal* ('Then and Now'), in *Bangadarshan, Paus*, 1281 B. S. (1874). Cited in Rachel R. Van Meter, 'Bankimchandra's View of the Role of Bengal in Indian Civilisation', in David Kopf (ed.), *Bengal Regional Identity*, East Lansing, Mich., 1969. Another brilliant exposition of the *babu* theme is Pyarechand Mitra's *Alaler Gharer Dulal* ('The Spoilt Child of a Rich Family'), Calcutta, 1937.
[32] Sumit Sarkar, 'The Kalki Avatar of Bikrampur', p. 37.

'babu' as the butt of savage humour.[33] Failing to respect traditional bonds and duties, she epitomised the 'Kaliyuga', the era of darkness and disorder that had engulfed Bengal. The Kaliyuga theme recurred frequently in the pages of cheap novels and farces, conjuring up the spectre of insubordinate lower castes, disobedient women and corrupt and decadent Brahmins: the inversion of traditional caste and gender hierarchies and norms of behaviour.[34] 'The world of bhadralok high culture' as Sarkar points out, 'concerned itself little with Kaliyuga'.[35] But the anxiety about the loss of traditional values and the threat to social order which it represented, was equally pervasive in the up-market literary products of the time. Bankimchandra, for instance, defended the caste system as 'an equitable and wholesome arrangement', advised *bhakti* (devoted service) towards Brahmins and argued that if women failed to play their traditional roles this would erode the very basis of society.[36] Hindu nationalist thought was deeply conservative in its vision of society, of caste and the place of women in particular. Thus Gora, Tagore's radical Hindu nationalist, observes caste rules with fanatical zeal, arguing that 'since I owe allegiance to society, I must respect caste'.[37] On the role of women, Gora holds that

as time has its two aspects – day and night, so society has its two sections, men and women. In a natural condition of society, woman remains unseen, like night – all her work is done unobtrusively, behind the scenes. Where society has become unnatural, there night usurps the province of day, and both work and frivolity are carried on by artificial light. And what is the result? Night's secret functioning ceases, fatigue increases progressively, recuperation becomes impossible, and man carries on only by recourse to intoxication.[38]

And although Gora makes no reference to the myth, his language is strongly reminiscent of Kaliyuga themes. His impassioned defence of orthodoxy and traditional values reflected the spirit of militant Hindu nationalism: it also mirrored the mood of bhadralok Bengal. Surendranath Banerjee, describing bhadralok society at the start of the twentieth century, wrote that 'our surroundings being what they are, and what they have been for generations, every Hindu has in him a strong conservative bias ... Scratch a Hindu and you will find him conservative'.[39]

---

[33] *Ibid.*, p. 39–42. The 'modern woman' was also mocked at by the 'lower orders' of nineteenth century Calcutta, the modern wife beating her babu husband was a popular theme of the Kalighat *pats*. See Sumanta Banerjee, *The Parlour and the Streets*, p. 89.

[34] Over thirty popular farces of the period have '*kali*' in their titles, while many more refer to the theme of the *Kali yuga* in their texts. Sumit Sarkar, 'The Kalki-Avatar', p. 37.

[35] *Ibid.*, p. 36.   [36] Tapan Raychaudhuri, *Europe Reconsidered*, p. 152.

[37] Rabindranath Tagore, *Gora*, p. 42.

[38] *Ibid.*

[39] Surendranath Banerjee, *A Nation in the Making. Being the Reminiscences of Fifty Years of Public Life*, Calcutta, 1963, p. 367.

The debates of the late Bengal Renaissance encouraged a positive re-appraisal of traditional Hinduism, forcing writers to describe, rationalise and define Hinduism in order to defend it. In the process, Hinduism was 'constructed' anew, as an internally coherent, single and monolithic religion that could favourably be compared with other world religions. Bankimchandra insisted, for instance, that the Vedas 'are nothing less than the basis of our entire religious and social organisation',[40] an argument that gave them the status of revelatory texts, similar to the Bible or Koran.[41] Although he recognised that Hindus had many different beliefs and practices, Bankimchandra thought that it was possible to 'sweep [Hinduism] clean of the dross that had accumulated over the centuries' and reveal 'the great principles of Hinduism' that 'are good for all ages and all mankind'.[42] This essence was 'non-possessive and rational spirituality', and in this sphere, Hinduism was, for Bankim, the supreme religion. Bankim's definition of Hinduism deliberately centred upon Vedic high philosophy. He aimed to restore the pride of educated Bengalis in Hinduism, and to counter attacks by missionaries and other whites infected by racist misapprehensions upon 'Hindoo' barbarism. But it mirrored the world view of the bhadralok, both in its contempt of popular religious practices ('the rubbish of the ages') and in giving the pride of place to Brahminical and Vedic philosophy.[43] Similarly, his prescription of national regeneration through *anushilan* ('practice') was an agenda for the bhadralok, who, as the intellectual and moral leaders of society, would awaken the masses, and inculcate in them a love of freedom.[44] In this sense, the debates of the Bengal Renaissance began to set out what 'being Hindu' meant to the bhadralok Bengalis.

The concern for national 'regeneration' that informed much Renaissance writing also prompted a search for a glorious national (Hindu) past. The new histories of the later nineteenth and earlier twentieth centuries were aimed primarily at inculcating a spirit of national pride and cultural confidence amongst middle-class Hindu Bengalis. As such, they were consciously political texts, deliberately selective in their choice of subjects, constructing for Hindu Bengal (and by extension India) a heroic history. As Meenakshi Mukherjee points out, Bankim's 'real concern was the identity of the Bengali people, and in order to arouse them, he did not hesitate to resurrect rumours of a colonizing past':

[40] Partha Chatterjee, *Nationalist Thought in the Colonial World*, p. 61.
[41] For a historical overview of this process, see Suvira Jaiswal, 'Semitising Hinduism: Changing Paradigms of Brahmanical Integration', *Social Scientist*, vol. 19, 12, December 1991, pp. 20–32.
[42] Partha Chatterjee, *Nationalist Thought in the Colonial World*, pp. 74, 77.
[43] *Ibid.*, p. 77.
[44] *Ibid.*, p. 79.

Truly, if not in any other respect, the Bengalis were like Athenians in their colonial enterprise. Simhala [Ceylon] was conquered by Bengalis and occupied by them for several generations. It has also been conjectured that the islands of Java and Bali were Bengal's colonies at one time. Tamralipti [in Bengal] was once a port from which Indians set out on voyages. No other race in India has shown such colonizing prowess.[45]

More frequently, the effort was to construct a tradition of patriotism and resistance in the 'national' past. These were primarily Hindu histories: their heroes were Hindu kings and chieftains who valiantly fought 'Muslim domination'.[46] Establishing a direct line of descent from Rana Pratap and Shivaji to modern Bengal, they allowed Hindu bhadralok Bengal to appropriate as its ancestors the lesser Rajput and Maratha chieftains who 'resisted' the Mughals.[47]

The driving sentiment behind these romantic historians was patriotic: past heroisms against 'alien' rulers were recalled or invented to inspire the Hindu 'nation' of the day to fight its foreign overlords. But they undoubtedly played a crucial part in the creation and popularisation of communal stereotypes, by depicting 'Muslim rule' as 'tyrannical', and Muslim rulers as cruel, violent, fanatical and sexually unlicensed. In the pages of these novels, Muslim kings invariably demolished temples, plundered cities and raped Hindu women. In his *Sansar* (or 'The Lake of Palms') – a novel less unequivocally anti-Muslim than others of this genre – Romesh Chunder Dutt casually conjures up the spectre of Muslim tyranny: 'The Moslem rulers of six centuries might sweep over this hoary town ay [*sic*], and demolish its towers and temples – but the faith of a nation lies not between the hands of an Iconoclast'.[48] Similarly, in his epic poem *Palasir Juddha* ('The Battle of Plassey'), Nabinchandra Sen portrays

[45] Meenakshi Mukherjee, *Realism and Reality. The Novel and Society in India*, New Delhi, 1985, p. 86. The excerpt from *Bangadarshan*, 1873–74, is cited on p. 86.
[46] Thus Bhudev Muhopadhyay's *Anguriya Vinimay* ('Exhange of Rings') projects Shivaji as the ideal Hindu hero, and his *Swapnalabdha Bharater Itihas* ('A History of India revealed in a Dream') 'assumes a contrafactual Maratha victory at the Third Battle of Panipat'. Tapan Raychaudhuri, *Europe Reconsidered*, p. 39. Bankimchandra's Rajput hero defends Mewar against Aurangzeb's armies in *Rajsinha* (1893). Also in this genre were Romesh C. Dutt's novels, *Maharashtra Jibanprabhat* (1878) and *Rajput Jibansandhya* (1879), and the plays of Dwijendralal Roy which celebrated the valour of Rajput and Maratha kings.
[47] For a discussion of this process, see Sudipta Kaviraj's mimeograph, 'Imaginary History', Occasional Papers in History and Society, 2nd series, No. 7, Nehru Memorial Museum and Library, 1988, pp. 16–17. Also see Partha Chatterjee, 'A Religion of Urban Domesticity: Sri Ramakrishna and the Calcutta Middle Class', in Partha Chatterjee and Gyanendra Pandey (eds.), *Subaltern Studies VII*, Delhi, 1992.
[48] Romesh Chunder Dutt, *The Lake of Palms: A Story of Indian Domestic Life*, London, 1902, p. 57. Cited in Şudhir Chandra, 'The Cultural Component of Economic Nationalism: R. C. Dutt's *The Lake of Palms*', *Indian Historical Review*, vol. 12, 1–2, July 1985–January 1986, p. 113.

Siraj-ud-daula as a vicious, cowardly and debauched young man, sur-rounded by a harem of dancing girls, torn between fear and lust .[49] These descriptions were doubly derivative: they took on board many of the assumptions of European imperial discourse on Islam,[50] as well as the paradigms of colonial and Indological writings on Indian history.[51]

The image of the 'Hindu' that emerges from Renaissance writings is, not surprisingly, more complex, more ambiguous, and has more nuances. On the one hand, the ideal Hindu character is portrayed as courageous and strong, willing to fight to the last for freedom, preferring death to the humiliation of conquest.[52] But on the other hand, Hindus as a race (or community) are presented as passive, caring little for political power or freedom.[53] For Bankimchandra, Sankhya philosophy had exercised a pernicious influence on the Hindu character, making it excessively other-wordly and fatalistic.[54] But at the same time, this other-wordliness reflects the inner grace of the Hindu religion. 'The character of a people is formed by their religion', he argues, and the inherent spiritualism of Hinduism fosters in the Hindu race a natural tolerance, 'a love for people':

Muslim kings followed Hindu kings, and the people did not object, Hindu and Muslim were equal [for them]. English kings followed the Muslims, and the people did not object. Rather, it was the Hindus who invited the Muslims and installed them in the kingdom ... For the Hindu had no hatred for the Englishman on the grounds of his different race.[55]

[49] Nabinchandra Sen, *Palasir Juddha* ('The Battle of Plassey'), (1876), Calcutta, 1984. See, in particular, pp. 53, 55–59. Also see the references to the tyranny of Muslim rule, p. 14, and temple-breaking, p. 63.
[50] The 'powerful sexual drive' of the Arab was a central theme in the Orientalist constuction of the Muslim character. Indeed, the origin of this stereotype may be traced back to the Christian view of the prophet Mohammed as the disseminator of a false revelation, and as 'the epitome of lechery, debauchery, sodomy, and a whole battery of assorted treacher-ies'. Edward Said, *Orientalism*, pp. 62, 311.
[51] For instance, Romesh Chunder Dutt's widely influential histories, *Maharashtra Jiban-prabhat* and *Rajput Jibansandhya* borrowed liberally from Tod's *Annals and Antiquities of Rajasthan* (1821) and James Cunningham Grant Duff's *History of the Marhattas* (1826). The chronology which divided up the subcontinent's past into a 'Hindu period' and a 'Muslim period' was James Mill's contribution. See his *History of British India*, 6 vols., London, 1858. When adopted by Renaissance writers, Mill's 'backward' and 'irrational' 'Hindu period' became the glorious epoch of India's past. Romila Thapar, Harbans Mukhia and Bipan Chandra, *Communalism and the Writing of Indian History*, New Delhi, 1987, p. 4.
[52] See, for instance, Dwijendralal Roy's portrayal of Rana Pratap in *Rana Pratapsingha* (1905) and Amarsingh in *Mewar Patan* ('The Fall of Mewar') (1908); and Bankimchan-dra's characterisation of Rajsinha in his historical novel, *Rajsinha* (1893), Prafullakumar Patra (ed.), *Bankim Rachanabali*, vol. I, Calcutta, 1989, pp. 503–597.
[53] Bankimchandra regards this absence of desire for freedom as the cause of India's subjection. Partha Chatterjee, *Nationalist Thought and the Colonial World*, pp. 54–84.
[54] *Ibid.*, p. 56.
[55] Bankimchandra Chattopadhyay, '*Dharmatattva*' ('Essentials of Dharma') (1894), in the collection entitled *Sociological Essays. Utilitarianism and Positivism in Bengal* (translated and edited by S. N. Mukherjee and Marian Maddern), Calcutta, 1986, p. 188.

Renaissance novels created an image of the ideal Bengali Hindu, who exemplified these generic Hindu qualities of gentleness, tolerance and spiritualism.[56] In his ideal incarnation, he was portrayed as being particularly gifted with the (Hindu) quality of high intellect. Amarnath, hero of Bankimchandra's novel *Rajani* is, for instance, 'an accomplished conversationalist. His mind [is] cultivated, his education complete, and his thought far reaching'. He speaks fluently about Shakespeare's heroines, comparing them with those of the Indian epics; his conversation, ranging from the classical histories of Thucidydes, Plutarch and Tacitus, the positivism of Comte and the philosophy of Mill, Huxley, Darwin and Schopenhauer, reveals a lightly carried burden of erudition.[57] But, on the reverse side, the Bengali Hindu was also depicted as the 'babu', that pusillanimous, craven and imitative creature upon whom Bankim pours the full weight of his scorn:

He who has one word in his mind, which becomes ten when he speaks, a hundred when he writes and thousands when he quarrels is a babu. He whose strength is in his one-time in his hands, ten-times in his mouth, a hundred times behind the back and absent at the time of action is a babu. He whose deity is the Englishman, preceptor the Brahmo preacher, scriptures the newspaper and pilgrimage the National Theatre is a babu. He who declares himself a Christian to missionaries, a Brahmo to Keshubchandra, a Hindu to his father and an atheist to the Brahmin beggar is a babu. One who drinks water at home, alcohol at his friend's, receives abuse from the prostitute and kicks from his boss is a babu. He who hates oil when he bathes, his own fingers when he eats and his mother-tongue when he speaks is indeed a babu.[58]

Here the babu is the mirror image of the 'bhadralok' Amarnath, whose conversational brilliance becomes in the babu pompous verbosity, whose sure understanding of western classics in the babu is mere aping, his

---

[56] For an interesting discussion of the relationship between novels, nationalism and imagined communities, see Benedict Anderson, *Imagined Communities*, pp. 30–37. Also see Clair Wills, 'Language Politics, Narrative, Political Violence', *The Oxford Literary Review*, vol. 13, 1991, pp. 34–36.

[57] Bankimchandra Chattopadhyay, *Rajani* (1880), *Bankim Rachanabali*, vol. I, pp. 418–419.

[58] Bankimchandra Chattopadhyay, 'Babu', in *Lokrahasya* (1874), *ibid.*, vol. II, p. 11. Also cited in Partha Chatterjee, 'A Religion of Urban Domesticity', pp. 62–63. The 'babu' stereotype, like that of the Muslim, was derived from colonial and orientalist thought. Macaulay, for instance, wrote that 'the physical organization of the Bengali is feeble even to effiminacy. He lives in a constant vapour bath. His pursuits are sedentary, his limbs delicate, his movements languid. During many ages he has been trampled upon by men of bolder and more hardy breeds. Courage, independence, veracity, are qualities to which his constitution and situation are equally unfavourable'. T. B. Macaulay, 'Warren Hastings', *Critical and Historical Essays*, 3 vols., London, 1843, III, p. 345. Cited in John Rosselli, 'The Self-Image of Effeteness: Physical Education and Nationalism in Nine-

mastery of English in the babu is slavish mimicry: all in all, a sarcastic indictment of the schizophrenia of the intellectual in British Bengal. The Bengali Hindu persona that emerges out of Renaissance writing is thus full of contradictory essences: it is simultaneously courageous and timid, vigorous and passive, other-worldly and venal, spiritual and hypocritical, cultured and imitative.

This dualistic identity lay at the heart of bhadralok nationalism, furnishing its dynamic and its particular idioms. It was expressed, first and foremost, in the preoccupation with physical culture. The attainment of physical strength and vigour, it was believed, through traditional forms of exercise – sword-play, *lathi*-play and wrestling – would exorcise the feeble and timid anglophile babu within and awaken the dormant strength and vigour of the Bengali nation. The earliest form of nationalist mobilisation in Bengal was thus the '*byayam samiti*' or the physical culture club. Nabagopal 'National' Mitra's gymnastic school, founded in 1866, served as a model for the numerous *akharas* ('physical culture clubs') and *tarun samitis* ('youth clubs') that sprung up at the turn of the century, which became both the front organisations and recruiting ground for the later terrorist secret societies.[59] The self-image of bhadralok Bengalis as a cultured but decadent people also informed the organisation of *palli samitis* ('village associations') during the Swadeshi period.[60] Going back to the villages was high on the nationalist agenda, not merely because the mobilisation of the peasantry was seen as being important in itself, but also to instil in the bhadralok the virtues of earthiness, hardiness and manliness that they lacked, and which were believed to spring from an association with the soil. In *Bande Mataram*, Aurobindo Ghosh bemoaned the fact that 'the Hindu community has lost possession of the soil, and with it the source of life and permanence':

Intellectual prominence often goes hand in hand with decadence, as the history of the Greeks and the other great nations of antiquity have proved, only the race which does not sacrifice the soundness of its rural root of life to the urban brilliance of its foliage and flowering, is in sound condition and certain of permanence ... If we train our young men to go back to the fields, we shall secure the perpetuation of the Hindu in Bengal which is now imperilled.[61]

The same dualism is evident in the structure of later nationalist

teenth-Century Bengal', *Past and Present*, 86, February 1980, p. 122. But it was a stereotype that bhadralok Bengalis made their own, using it as the basis for their exhortations to action.
[59] For a fuller treatment of this theme, see Rosselli, 'The Self-Image of Effeteness'.
[60] See Sumit Sarkar, *The Swadeshi Movement*, pp. 350–353.
[61] *Bande Mataram*, 6 March 1908.

literature.[62] Saratchandra Chattopadhyay's novel *Pather Dabi* ('Demands of the Road') is a classic in this genre. First serialised in the journal *Bangabani* between 1922 and 1926, *Pather Dabi* was banned soon after its publication as a full novel in 1926. Set in Burma, the novel describes the activities of a militant nationalist secret society named *Pather Dabi*.[63] Its leader, and the hero of the novel, is Sabyasachi, a *rajdrohi* ('enemy of the state') who works tirelessly, albeit in mysterious ways, for national liberation. Sabyasachi is, at one level, the bhadralok ideal: having trained as a doctor in Germany, as an engineer in France, and as a lawyer in England, and having picked up sundry academic qualifications in America, he has an enviable mastery of western knowledge. But, like Bankim's Amarnath, he wears his learning lightly: the reader is told that 'all this was for him mere recreation'.[64] He is exceptional in his physical strength and courage: although slight of build, he thinks nothing of swimming across the River Padma in full torrent or crossing over the Eastern Himalayas on foot to escape detection by British intelligence. As Tanika Sarkar has remarked, Sabyasachi is the first hero of serious Bengali fiction to be cast in the mould of a superman.[65]

The protagonist of the novel, Apurba, on the other hand, is unmistakably a babu in the pejorative sense of the word. Son of a deputy-magistrate, a Brahmin by birth, serving as a clerk in a Dutch firm, he is the archetypal bhadralok figure. As the novel unfolds, he is humiliated publicly at a railway station by a bunch of white youths, and, failing to get justice at British courts, he is drawn into the small circle of nationalist workers in Rangoon, led by the beautiful and brilliant Sumitra. A good-natured, impressionable and sentimental young man, often moved to tears at the thought of the servitude of his Motherland, he is also weak, indecisive and fearful. Unable to live up to the high expectations and ideals of Pather Dabi, he eventually becomes a police informer. The main narrative follows Apurba, his loves, his enthusiasms and his hesitations, while

---

62 The sociological and historical content of the works of literature discussed below is often not readily apparent, and may appear to have been imposed through this author's reading of the texts. But it will be argued here that the implicit structures that become apparent through a sociological reading of Saratchandra's novels not only reveal new layers of complexity within them, but also lead one to a clearer understanding of the cognitive structures that informed his political vision. The arguments for sociological readings of literature have been put forward convincingly by Paul Ricoeur in *Hermeneutics and the Human Sciences* and Pierre Bourdieu, *The Field of Cultural Production. Essays on Art and Literature*, Cambridge, 1993.

63 Saratchandra Chattopadyay, *Pather Dabi*, in Haripada Ghosh (ed.), *Sarat Rachana Samagra* ('Collected Works of Sarat Chandra Chattopadhyay'), III, Calcutta, 1989, pp. 9–190.

64 *Ibid.*, p. 36.

65 Tanika Sarkar, 'Bengali Middle-Class Nationalism and Literature', p. 453.

Sabyasachi comes and goes, appearing in the most unexpected places, and disappearing just as suddenly, without trace. The structure of the novel suggests, therefore, that Apurba is more than a foil to the character of Sabyasachi, indeed the author's chief concern is with the character of the babu. It is in Apurba's failings – his timidity, his cowardice and venality – that Saratchandra locates the cause of national subjugation. By overcoming these failings, the babu will become superman, and will liberate the nation.

Like Bankim before him Saratchandra regarded national liberation as the task of an enlightened elite, of whom Sabyasachi was the epitome.[66] But unlike Bankimchandra, who saw the task of this elite as the creation and imparting of the religious and cultural ideal of *anushilan*, Saratchandra's hero concerned himself little with matters of the spirit. Sabyasachi is a man of action: even his extraordinarily wide-ranging education is technical and pragmatic, rather than philosophical. Indeed, Saratchandra presents traditional Hindu culture as an obstacle in the path of nationalist action. Thus, Apurba's doubts about Pather Dabi concern its regular transgression of traditional Hindu mores: his obsessive concern with caste purity even in times of illness and danger is presented as pathetic, even paranoid. In contrast, the men and women of action who people the novel have all broken away from Hindu orthodoxy: Sabyasachi does not observe caste, and towards the end of the novel, makes a passionate plea for the destruction of 'all that is eternal (*sanatan*), ancient and decaying – [in] religion, society, tradition', because they are 'the greatest enemies of the nation'.[67] Sumitra and Bharati are women who despite their Hindu upbringing, live and work alongside men, caring little for the social conventions of the day: Sumitra, Portia-like, even makes a brilliant case for the right of a woman to leave a loveless marriage.[68]

Pather Dabi at one level presents a radical solution to the dilemma of the Bengali Hindu character. Like Renaissance thinkers before him, Saratchandra associates national servitude with the timidity of the babu. But he links national liberation with liberation from orthodoxy; it is through personal struggle against tradition and superstition, he suggests, that the bhadralok will overcome the weak babu within him to find the moral strength and courage to fight the colonisers. At another level, however, Saratchandra fails to challenge the inherent elitism of bhadralok nationalism. Indeed, he reinforces the notion that the bhadralok are the elect, chosen by virtue of their intellect and culture for the task of national

[66] Saratchandra Chattopadhyay, *Pather Dabi*, p. 167; Tanika Sarkar, 'Bengali Middle-Class Nationalism and Literature', p. 454.
[67] Saratchandra Chattopadhyay, *Pather Dabi*, p. 163.   [68] *Ibid.*, pp. 65–68.

liberation. Towards the end of the novel, Sabyasachi asks the poet Sashi to forget the peasantry, to sing instead of the glorious rebellion (*biplab*) of the community of the educated and cultured ('*shikkhita bhadra jati*'). When challenged by Bharati, he replies that while he does not believe in *varna*, he 'cannot but observe the caste difference between the educated and the unlettered'. These, he argues, are the 'true castes, fashioned by God'.[69] He thus underlines the separate and unique characteristics of the Hindu bhadralok, and reinforces the self-image inherited from the Renaissance – as educated, cultured, weak-yet-strong – but imbues this image with the heroism of a nationalist calling.

Culture and Identity: the shift from Nationalism

Questions of culture, religion and identity in bhadralok thought, emerged, therefore, as part of a wider preoccupation with nationhood. For Renaissance writers, the central question was to examine what in Indian culture and the Hindu personality made India so easy to subjugate, and, at the same time, to construct for (Hindu) India a cultural tradition which was equal, if not superior, to that of the West. Later full-blown nationalist novels like *Pather Dabi* were more unequivocal in their condemnation of British rule, yet at the same time more critical of Hindu orthodoxy. But 'culture' – in the sense of education and *bhadrata* ('cultivatedness') – retained a critical place in the self-image of the nationalist bhadralok: it was now regarded as the essential equipment of the class that would free the nation. The new definition reflected the heightened self-awareness of the bhadralok of their constituting a class,[70] with a specific political role and destiny. In both phases, questions of 'culture' were fiercely debated: it was recognised that culture was not something that was simply inherited: it had to be 'created'. For Bankimchandra, *anushilan* was a cultural synthesis of the best of past and present worlds that would be achieved only through the future intellectual endeavour of a vanguard intelligentsia, while for Saratchandra's Sabyasachi, a new culture of patriotism would have to be built on the ruins of the corrupt and decadent past.[71]

Changes in the social and political climate in the Bengal of the 1920s

---

[69] *Ibid.*, p. 163.
[70] See Pierre Bourdieu, *Distinction. A Social Critique of the Judgement of Taste* (translated by Richard Nice), London, 1986. Also see Bourdieu's discussion of 'the accomplished man' and 'cultural attainment' which he defines as legitimate competence in legitimate (and necessarily dominant) culture. Pierre Bourdieu and Jean-Claude Passeron, *Reproduction in Education, Society and Culture* (translated by Richard Nice), London, 1990, p. 34–35.
[71] Saratchandra Chattopadhyay, *Pather Dabi*, p. 167–8.

and 1930s perceptibly influenced this self-consciously political literary
tradition. The gradual erosion of the old world of unquestioned bhadralok social dominance and the growing anxiety about their political future
in the new era of mass politics, shaped bhadralok politics in ways that
have been examined in previous chapters, making it altogether more
inward-looking, more parochial, and more narrowly concerned with the
defence of established privilege. Some of the literary, political and
historical texts produced in this period reflected this mood. A critical
reading of some of these texts provides insights into the ways in which the
bhadralok themselves understood their predicament, and legitimised their
political response to it.[72]

In these writings, 'culture' continued to be a central concern. But the
way in which the question of culture was approached underwent a subtle
but unmistakable shift. Questions of nationhood and nationalism, which
had provided the frame of reference within which discussions of culture
had been situated, were no longer as central and were now set out rather
differently. This change is clearly reflected in the writing of Saratchandra
Chattopadhyay himself: in, for instance, the startling difference of theme
and emphasis between his later novel *Bipradas* (1933), and his nationalist
classic *Pather Dabi*. *Bipradas* is not one of Saratchandra's most famous
novels, nor, indeed, is it one of his best. But for the historian it has a
special significance because of its deliberate and sophisticated articulation
of the world view which growing numbers of bhadralok Hindus were
coming to share. The hero of the novel, Bipradas, is a noble zamindar,
who lives in his ancestral village, manages his estates, and is the moral and
spiritual leader of the local community. The scene of the novel alternates
between the two households he maintains – one in the mofussil, and the
other in Calcutta. He rules over both households and his estates with an
iron hand, but is scrupulously just: a patriarch who is revered not only by
his family but by his praja ('tenants').[73] The novel opens with the
description of a krishak meeting organised with the help of rabble-rousers
from Calcutta. But their revolutionary slogans fall comically flat, because
none of his tenants feel anything but the greatest regard for 'Bipradas-
babu'.[74] The picture painted of an orderly, harmonious rural society under
the firm but benevolent leadership of zamindars could hardly contrast

---

[72] The emergence of left-wing political groupings in the same period also coincided with the
rise of a consciously radical literary avant-garde, of whom Manik Bandopadhyay is only
the best known. But this chapter will concern itself only with texts which reflected a
communal and conservative view of the world.

[73] Bipradas strongly resembles the figure of the ideal 'traditional' zamindar invoked by
Satish Chandra Dasgupta in *Bharater Samyabad*, Calcutta, 1930.

[74] Saratchandra Chattopadhyay, *Bipradas, Sarat Rachana Samagra*, vol. III, p. 350.

more sharply with the image of rural life set out in Saratchandra's early and more famous novel, *Palli Samaj*, which presented corruption, greed, cruelty and ignorance as the keynotes of the zamindari order.[75]

As a hero, Bipradas is cast in a very different mould from Sabyasachi, and indeed from Ramesh, the idealistic reformer of *Palli Samaj*. Bipradas is neither a rebel nor a revolutionary: on the contrary, he shuns politics and nationalist action. In this novel, the author rejects political activism (particularly of the *krishak samiti* variety) as the pastime of immature and ineffectual (if well-meaning) youths. The only character in the novel actively involved in politics is Bipradas' younger brother Dwiju, who is an ardent believer in *swadeshi*, and is also a leader of the krishak movement. He is portrayed as a pleasant enough young man, but is clearly not a hero. He is an atheist, overly influenced by his western education (he has an M.A. degree from Calcutta), with too much time on his hands and no pressing need to earn his living.[76] Dwiju's 'nationalist' activism prevents him from becoming a responsible member of the family, and from shouldering his duties as a son.[77] Bipradas, on the other hand, takes little interest in politics. His heroism lies in his personal qualities, and in his spiritual quest. He is the ideal *grihastha* ('householder'): a dutiful son, devoted husband and father, guardian and provider of the whole zamindari establishment. But he is, at the same time, detached and other-wordly, searching for higher truth and self-knowledge through intense *dhyana* ('meditation').[78] The novel is centrally concerned with establishing the legitimacy (and indeed, superiority) of quietistic 'traditional' Hindu religiosity over modern, western, fashions. The message that emerges clearly is that noisy, boisterous nationalism and glib talk about peasants'

---

[75] *Palli Samaj* ('Village Society'), which appeared in 1918, tells the story of the idealist Ramesh, and his efforts to reform what the author depicts as the stagnant cesspool of village society. The zamindar in this novel, Beni Ghoshal, is as corrupt and greedy as he is cowardly, and his callous disregard for his tenants causes them untold hardship. Reprinted in Sukumar Sen (ed.), *Sulabh Sarat Samagra*, vol. I, Calcutta, 1991.

[76] Dwiju is not employed, but receives a stipend from his brother Bipradas, out of which he maintains an establishment in Calcutta. Saratchandra Chattopadhyay, *Bipradas*, pp. 352–353.

[77] Dwiju was disinherited by his father for his financial irresponsiblity; he refuses to accompany his mother on pilgrimage because he is too busy with nationalist work (*desher kaj*). *Bipradas*, pp. 353, 361–362.

[78] See the description of Biprodas' spiritual efforts, *ibid.*, p. 377. The influence of the philosophy of the rustic sage Ramakrishna Paramhansa is evident: Ramakrishna advised his bhadralok followers to live in the world, and fulfill their worldly obligations, but with detachment. See Sumit Sarkar, 'The Kathamrita as a Text: Towards an Understanding of Ramakrishna Paramhamsa', NMML Occasional Paper No. 22, 1985 and also his '"Kaliyuga", "Chakri" and "Bhakti". Ramakrishna and His Times', *Economic and Political Weekly*, vol. 27, 29, 18 July 1992; see also Partha Chatterjee, 'A Religion of Urban Domesticity'.

rights are little more than fads.[79] *Bipradas* thus closely mirrors the increasingly widespread mood of disillusionment with militant nationalism after the collapse of Civil Disobedience[80] and the growing bhadralok anxiety about the erosion of the zamindari order at the start of the Depression.

The novel returns to the themes of the Renaissance, comparing Hinduism with western doctrines. But unlike the writings of an earlier period, there is little attempt seriously to debate these questions. Modernity is introduced in the novel in the guise of a westernised young woman, Bandana. In the course of the novel, she is persuaded by the power of Bipradas' personality to recognise the folly of her ways, and to accept orthodox Hindu values. Bandana is presented as a bright but fickle young woman; all other 'westernised' characters in the novel are mere caricatures, all equally superficial and immoral.[81] *Bipradas* has a similar structure to Tagore's *Gora*, yet is radically different in its emphasis and conclusions. In both novels, the hero is an orthodox Brahmin who is confronted with an attractive and westernised young woman. But while both Gora and Sucharita continually and brilliantly debate the case for Hinduism and Brahmoism respectively, Bandana is rarely provided with any arguments to counter Bipradas. (The only exception is on the question of untouchability.) While Gora at the end of the novel embraces Tagore's liberal humanism, Biprodas attains sainthood through renunciation (*sannyas*). The passionate and often bitter debates of the Renaissance which come alive in Tagore's novel are rendered curiously flat and lifeless in *Bipradas*. Most significantly, while Gora's rigid Hindu orthodoxy is inspired by passionate nationalism, Bipradas' commitment to Hinduism derives from his strong sense of cultural identity. His nationalism is instinctive: an inherent character-trait rather than a conscious political choice. When faced with white racism, he reacts with natural dignity and courage: he thus deals summarily with the drunken and rowdy white mob who forcibly occupy his railway carriage, while the other western-educated and 'modern' bhadralok passengers cower in the background.[82] But in the course of the novel, Bipradas never once refers explicitly to British rule.

---

[79] A smartly-dressed foreign-returned barrister who has been holding forth on the emancipation of women and peasants rights is revealed to be a coward when confronted with the reality of white violence. Saratchandra Chattopadhyay, *Bipradas*, p. 367.

[80] Tanika Sarkar argues that the same mood is reflected in Tagore's novel *Char Adhyay*, which is an undisguised and bitter attack on the terrorist movement. Tanika Sarkar, 'Bengali Middle-Class Nationalism and Literature', pp. 456–459.

[81] See the portrayal of Bandana's 'modern' friends Sudhir and Hem. Saratchandra Chattopadhyay, *Bipradas*, p. 410–411.

[82] *Ibid.*, pp. 357–360.

Perhaps the most interesting feature of the novel is the portrayal of Bipradas himself, clearly intended by the author to be an image of the ideal Hindu personality. He is exceptionally tall and physically powerful, famed for his skill at sword and lathi-play, and a sure shot with the rifle. He is strikingly fair and handsome without any trace of effeminacy.[83] He is an orthodox Hindu Brahmin, who rigidly observes caste rules of hierarchy, purity and pollution. But he is, at the same time, tolerant to such an extent that he allows his younger brother to hold anti-zamindari meetings on his own zamindari. His tolerance is not, however, a sign of weakness: he commands awe, fear and unquestioned obedience from his family and dependants.[84] His altercation with the drunken mob proves that his is not a man passively to accept humiliation, and if circumstances demand it, is capable of swift, even violent, action. Nationalism for him is a natural instinct, as much a part of his personality as his religion. He is a rich man and responsible householder, but is not attached to property or worldly goods: at the end of the novel, he renounces the world and takes sannyas. And finally, he is a man of prodigious learning, well-versed in European literature and philosophy, but is, at the same time, deeply spiritual, and secure in his Hindu faith. He knows who he is, and is strongly and consciously rooted in his own 'culture'.

Saratchandra thus reconciles, in the person of Bipradas, the contradictory essences of 'Hinduness' inherited from Renaissance writing. The 'babu' plays no part in this novel, and the nationalist tension that this figure expressed is also absent. Whereas in *Pather Dabi*, nationalism was an actively chosen path, and a choice that separated the men from the babus, in *Bipradas*, nationalism is simply an essence, inherent in the ideal Hindu personality. The series of opposites that constituted 'Hinduness' are also apparently reconciled. Bipradas embodies, at the same time, manliness and passiveness, orthodoxy and tolerance, spiritualism and a love of freedom, other-worldliness and wordly responsibility, formal western knowledge and actual self-knowledge. The device by which the author resolves all these contradictions is 'culture'. It is his conscious commitment to his Hindu 'culture' – good or bad, right or wrong – that empowers Bipradas.[85] It makes him proud, dignified and courageous: it

---

[83] *Ibid.*, p. 360. He thus embodies both 'Aryan' (Brahmin) and 'Kshatriya' values. See Uma Chakravarty's discussion of the 'foregrounding' of 'Aryan' and 'Kshatriya' elements in the construction of the modern Hindu male identity. Uma Chakravarti, 'Whatever Happened to the Vedic *Dasi*? Orientalism, Nationalism and a Script for the Past', in Kumkum Sangari and Sudesh Vaid (eds.), *Recasting Women. Essays in Colonial History*, New Delhi, 1989, pp. 46–54.

[84] Saratchandra Chattopadhyay, *Bipradas*, pp. 369–370.

[85] The influence of Vivekananda's thought – particularly his 'manly' defence of Hinduism and his 'splendid scorn of apology for anything Indian' is much in evidence. See Tapan

makes him a nationalist in spirit even though he might shun nationalist action, it converts his tolerance, his spirituality and his other-worldliness into strength. At the same time, the debate about 'culture' is resolved. The Renaissance is invoked, and Hindu values are demonstrated as being vastly superior to the shallow superficiality of the West. But this is not crucially relevant, either to the structure or intention of the narrative. Saratchandra's argument in *Bipradas* is that Hindu/Indian 'culture' is a given; it is a single, unified inheritance that must be received as a gift. By embracing it uncritically and without hesitation, Hindus will find inner strength; because they know who they are, they will be invincible.

There is one question, however, that the author is unable to resolve effectively, and that is the question of caste. There are, interestingly enough, no low-caste characters in the novel. The issue of caste is introduced through the character Bandana, who belongs to a very wealthy and educated Brahmin family. But Bandana's parents have lost caste by going abroad, and have become *mlechha* ('untouchable') in the eyes of orthodox Brahmins. At the beginning of the novel, Bipradas' orthodox mother Dayamayee refuses to accept Bandana's obeisances, stepping back lest the girl's shadow pollute her.[86] Hurt and angered, Bandana responds to this 'insult' (*apamaan*) by leaving Dayamayee's house, where she was a guest, immediately, and without explanation. After a period of introspection, and with Bipradas playing mediator, both eventually learn to love and accept each other. Bandana gradually takes over the running of the household[87] (and significantly, the kitchen), and at the end of the novel, enters the family as Dwiju's bride. But first Bandana, under the influence of Bipradas, Brahminises herself: she gives up wearing shoes, bathes before entering the kitchen,[88] wears 'pure' clothes to prepare food,[89] and eventually participates in the evening prayers.[90] But more importantly, she accepts the higher values that, according to her *guru* Bipradas, lie behind these rituals: the sacred sense of duty, sacrifice and devotion of the Hindu woman.[91] Dayamayee, for her part, takes Bandana to her heart and treats her as she would her own daughter. But her acceptance of Bandana is influenced by the fact that Bandana is indeed a Brahmin – albeit a fallen one – by birth.

Raychaudhuri, *Europe Reconsidered*, p. 249, and Sarkar, '"Kaliyuga", "Chakri" and "Bhakti"', p. 1545.

[86] Saratchandra Chattopadhyay, *Bipradas*, p. 358.   [87] *Ibid.*, p. 383.

[88] *Ibid.*, pp. 381–382.

[89] *Ibid.*, p. 408.   [90] *Ibid.*, pp. 407–408

[91] *Ibid.*, pp. 371–382, 407–408. For a history of the construction of 'ideal' Hindu womanhood, see Uma Chakravarti, 'Whatever happened to the Vedic *Dasi?*'; Malavika Karlekar, *Voices from Within. Early Personal Narratives of Bengali Women*, Delhi, 1991,

The novel thus presents untouchability as a problem – but one that can be solved within the framework of Hinduism, provided that there is goodwill on both sides. It recommends the adoption by mlechhas not only of 'clean' Brahminical practices, but of higher Hindu cultural values. To the high castes, on the other hand, it preaches acceptance: based not upon scriptural sanction, but upon human generosity, the 'Hindu' spirit of tolerance and love. The problem of caste is resolved through the use of a familial metaphor – the marriage of Dwiju and Bandana is figurative of the reunion of the larger Hindu 'family'.[92]

Unlike the novels and essays of an earlier period, where the issue of caste was debated threadbare, in *Bipradas*, the controversial and divisive question of the justice of *varna* philosophy is not addressed.[93] The accent of the novel is on harmony. Both in its subtle and brilliant reconciliation of the opposite 'essences' of Hinduism, and its prescription on untouchability, the novel creates a picture of a harmonious 'Hinduness' that is waiting to be recovered. This 'Hinduness' is the cultural essence of an ordered society, where people attain greatness not by rebellious action but by fulfilling their pre-ordained social roles. 'Religious' values thus merge indistinguishably with the social values of the bhadralok–zamindari order. The novel expresses a sense of profound social disquiet at the threat to the old order, from within and without, from low-caste alienation, bhadralok radicalism, and spurious nationalism as much as from irreverent modernism and divisive peasant politics. By representing this disquiet as a matter of 'religion', it portrays the threat as a threat to the religious community. The novel thus constructs a meaning of 'Hinduness' which is strongly rooted in the social and cultural world of the bhadralok, and apparently, without any reference to Muslims. But, as will

---

and Samita Sen, 'Marriage, Migration and Militancy. Women Workers in the Jute Industry in Bengal', University of Cambridge, Ph.D. dissertation, 1992.

[92] The choice of metaphor is not accidental – expressions of ethnic (and communal) identity almost invariably draw upon the idea of fictive kinship. See G. Carter Bentley, 'Ethnicity and Practice', *Comparative Studies in Society and History*, vol. 29, 1, 1987, p. 33.

[93] *Palli Samaj*, for instance, repreatedly raises the question of the caste system and its injustices: the plight of Kulin widows, the corruption of Brahmins and the oppression of the low castes. But interestingly, these are regarded as being distortions, and the caste system as a whole is defended, again through a familial metaphor. Jethima, a widowed aunt thus tells Ramesh, 'In the villages, nobody bothers too much about whether their caste is high or low. A younger brother does not resent his elder brother simply because he is elder, the fact that he was born one or two years earlier does not worry him in the least. It is the same in the villages. Here Kayasthas care little that they were not born as Brahmins, nor do Kaibarttas try to attain the same status as Brahmins. A younger brother feels no shame at paying obeisances to his elder brother, in the same way, the low castes feel no slight when they touch the Brahmin's feet'. *Palli Samaj*, p. 164.

be seen, a definition of an opposite and opposing 'Muslimness' is implicit in the notion of 'Hinduness' that it sets out.

'Hinduness' and Hindu communalism

The ideal of 'Hinduness' presented in *Bipradas*, although profoundly conservative and patriarchal in its social implications, is not, at first glance, overtly 'communal'. Unlike the novels and epics of the Renaissance period, which abound with allusions to Muslim cruelty and tyranny, Muslims are conspicuous by their absence in *Bipradas*.[94] But in fact, its construction of Hinduness was informed by a specifically anti-Muslim communal political agenda. An examination of Saratchandra Chattopadhyay's extraordinarily polemical essay, *Bartaman Hindu–Mussalman Samasya* ('The Current Hindu–Muslim Problem')[95] throws light upon the close and complex relationship between the growing social conservatism of bhadralok society, its changing political preoccupations, and the emergence within it of a full-fledged Hindu communal ideology.

First presented as a speech at the Hindu Sabha conference in 1926, *Bartaman Hindu–Mussalman Samasya* argues strongly that nationalist vision of Hindu–Muslim unity is an idle and futile dream. Written in the aftermath of the Calcutta Riots of 1926,[96] and clearly influenced by the failure of Non-Cooperation, Khilafat and the Das Pact, it boldly declares that Hindus and Muslims are not only different, but are fundamentally unequal, and that 'unity can only exist amongst equals'.[97] Distancing himself completely from the composite nationalism that was Sabyasachi's creed in *Pather Dabi*, in which religious difference was subsumed within the *desh* ('nation'),[98] in *Bartaman Hindu–Mussalman Samsasya* Saratchandra makes a passionate case for accepting that there were irreconcilable differences between Hindus and Muslims. The crux of the difference between the two 'communities', he argues, is 'culture'. Here culture is loosely defined, as a quality of mind and heart that all Hindus naturally possess, but that Muslims lack, and have little hope ever of attaining:

[94] There is only one passing reference to a Muslim family in the entire novel. *Bipradas*, p. 384.
[95] Reproduced in Harihar Ghosh (ed.), *Sarat Rachana Samagra*, vol. III, p. 841. The complete and translated text of the essay is furnished in the Appendix.
[96] For a description of these riots, see P. K. Dutta, 'The War over Music'; Suranjan Das, *Communal Riots in Bengal*, pp. 75–91; and Kenneth McPherson, *The Muslim Microcosm*, pp. 90–97.
[97] Saratchandra Chattopadhyay, *Bartaman Hindu–Mussalman Samasya*, p. 843.
[98] Sabyasachi tells the poet Sashi, for instance, that he will become 'our national poet (*jatiya kabi*) – the poet neither of Hindus or Muslims or Christians but of the (Bengali) nation as a whole'. *Pather Dabi*, p. 167.

If learning is simply knowing how to read and write, there is little difference between Hindu[s] and Muslim[s] ... But if the essence of learning is width of the mind and culture of the heart, then there is no comparison between the two communities ... Many may hope to establish a parity of learning [between them] but I do not. A thousand years has not been enough time [to achieve this] – nor will another millennium suffice.[99]

It is their basic lack of 'culture' that, Saratchandra argues, accounts for the brutality, barbarism and fanaticism of Muslims. These are the age-old, universal and unchanging attributes of the Muslim community, as much in evidence among the first Ghaznavite conquerors, who 'were not satisfied merely with looting – they destroyed temples, they demolished idols, they raped women',[100] as any present-day Bengali Muslims, who were responsible for the 'monstrous events at Pabna'.[101] In this regard, moreover, there was little to choose between 'old Muslims' and recent converts. Unlike converts to Christianity, who retain their original (Hindu) 'culture', converts to Islam renounce their Hindu origins, and are immediately and irrevocably Islamicised. Saratchandra provides anecdotal evidence in support of this claim:

I had a Brahmin cook once. He sacrificed his religion in order to indulge his passion for a Muslim woman. One year later, he had changed his name, his dress, and even his nature. The very face that God had given him had changed beyond recognition. And this is not an isolated instance. Those who know a bit about village life know that this sort of thing happens frequently. And in the matter of aggression, these new converts put their Muslim co-religionists to shame.[102]

Islam has, in this construction, a mysterious power rapidly to transform even the physical and personal attributes of recent converts, so that they are indistinguishable from the Muslim mass. The uncultured and barbaric essence of Islam, it suggests, is able to transcend not only the barriers of space, time and geography, but also to cross the local *ashraf–atrap* frontier, so that these characteristics are as true of Bengali peasant converts as of the old Muslim aristocracy. Interestingly, this argument demonstrates that communal discourse must not only putatively unify the 'community' for which it claims to speak: it must also render the other, its

---

[99] Saratchandra Chattopadhyay, *Bartaman Hindu–Mussalman Samsasya*, p. 843.
[100] *Ibid.*, p. 842.
[101] *Ibid.*, p. 843. The reference is to the riots in Pabna, that were sparked off by an incidence of mutilation of deities in the home of a local Hindu zamindar. The violence that ensued left one dead and twenty-two injured. For details, see Suranjan Das, *Communal Riots in Bengal*, p. 82.
[102] Saratchandra Chattopadhyay, *Bartaman Hindu–Mussalman Samasya*, pp. 843–844. The voluntary conversion of Hindus to Islam, when discussed at all in the Hindu press, was invariably dismissed as the product of aberrant sexuality.

'opposite', as a single entity, united by a set of shared, abhorrent, characteristics.

The characteristics of Muslims are always the opposite of the attributes that are taken to constitute 'Hinduness'. Thus, Hindus may – like Bipradas – be 'orthodox' but they are always tolerant, while Muslims are invariably 'fanatics'. In Hindus, adherence to orthodox religion is a matter of culture and virtue (as in Bipradas, Dayamayee and the transformed Bandana), but in Muslims, 'obsession with religion' is a mark of their lack of culture, their innate barbarism. *Bartaman Hindu–Mussalman Samasya* argues that: 'The Muslims will never truly believe that India's freedom will bring them freedom too. They will only accept this truth when their *obsession with their religion* weakens. Then they will understand that whatever one's religion, to be proud of *fanaticism* is a matter of shame, there is no greater *barbarism*'.[103]

Even where Hindu 'passiveness' is contrasted with Muslim 'aggressiveness', this quality of the opposite religion can never be a virtue. It reveals itself in repeated acts of violence, cruelty and oppression (*atyachar*):

All that we do is compile lists of all instances of their cruelty, oppressiveness and hostility towards us and all we ever say is this – 'You have killed us, you have broken our idols, destroyed our idols and kidnapped our women. In this you have been very unjust, and have caused us great pain. We cannot continue to live like this'. Do we ever say more than this, or do more than this?[104]

Muslim 'strength', in the same way, is described as 'virility', with all its negative associations of lust, debauchery and excessive sexuality. Saratchandra makes repeated references to the 'rape', 'abduction' and 'kidnapping' of Hindu women.[105] The notion of the lustful Muslim, has, as we have seen, a long history, with its antecedents in European stereotypes of the Arab. In Saratchandra, it is a bogey that is raised not only to shame 'passive' Hindus into retributive action, but to stress that the threat to the chastity (*satitva*) of Hindu womanhood emanates from *all* Muslims, high and low:

When journalists raise the question of the abduction of Hindu women, why are the Muslim leaders silent? When men *of their community* regularly commit such grave crimes, why do they not protest? What is the meaning of their silence? To my mind, the meaning is crystal clear. It is only a sense of decorum that prevents them from

---

[103] *Ibid.*, p. 844. Emphasis added.   [104] *Ibid.*, p. 844.

[105] *Ibid.*, pp. 842–844. The figure of the Hindu woman – as a repository of the purity and traditional values of the community, – repeatedly raped and defiled by vile Muslim attackers, is a familiar symbol in Hindu communal discourse. See Gyanendra Pandey, 'Hindus and Others: The Militant Hindu Construction', pp. 3003–3004; and Tanika Sarkar, 'Woman as Communal Subject', p. 2058.

admitting openly that given the opportunity, they would commit the same crimes themselves.[106]

The implication is that the inherent 'Muslimness' which is expressed in these acts of criminal sexuality transcends class boundaries. At the same time, he argues that 'Hinduness' – or 'culture of the heart' – is shared by all Hindus, even the poorest and most illiterate. Saratchandra dismisses the arguments of apologists that Muslim peasant violence was a result of poverty and illiteracy. It is, he suggests, nothing more than a demonstration of their 'Muslimness':

Many argue that the monstrous events at Pabna were the work of mullahs from the west, who excited the innocent and uneducated Muslim peasants, and instigated these awful deeds. But if, in the same way, a party of Hindu priests were to arrive in a Hindu [majority] area and to try, in the same way, to excite the docile [Hindu] peasantry to burn the homes, loot the wealth and insult the women of their innocent Muslim neighbours, then the same unlettered Hindu peasantry would immediately declare them mad and run them out of the village.[107]

The difference between the level of education among Hindu and Muslim peasants may, he argues, be negligible. What makes the two peasant communities so different in their behaviour is that elusive substance, 'culture'. In this sphere, there can be 'no comparison between the two communities'.[108]

In this way, the symbol of 'culture', which emerged out of the bhadralok's historical perception of themselves as a class with a particular political destiny, now became a symbol of the communal identity of all Hindus. For the first time, 'Hindu' peasants and workers were (figuratively) extracted out of the mass of *chhotolok*, and incorporated into an extended Hindu 'community'. The unbridgeable gulf between the educated and the illiterate 'castes' – between the *shikkhita bhadra jati* and the

---

[106] Saratchandra Chattopadhyay, *Bartaman Hindu–Mussalman Samasya*, p. 843.
[107] *Ibid.*, p. 843.
[108] *Ibid.*, p. 843. The contrast drawn out here between Hindu and Muslim peasants reversed completely the picture of the two communities painted by Saratchandra in *Palli Samaj*. In this early novel, Muslim peasant society was presented as being as purposeful, peaceful, united and hard-working as Hindu peasant society was fractious, corrupt, superstitious and lazy. Observing the efforts of Muslim peasants to improve their lot by (significantly enough) building a school, the hero Ramesh reflected that 'these (Muslim peasants of Pirpur) do not argue all the time, as do the Hindu inhabitants of Kuanpur. Even if they disagree, they do not rush off to the Sadar to file a complaint. On the contrary, as a result of the teachings of the prophet, whether or not they are satisfied, they attempt to accept (each other). Particularly at times of hardship, they stand united to the last in a way that Ramesh had never seen Hindu villagers do, whether *bhadra* or *abhadra* ... He concluded that the religious and social inequality was the cause of this violence and envy amongst Hindus. All Muslims are equal in terms of their religion, therefore they are united in a way that Hindus can never be'. *Palli Samaj*, p. 163.

askhikhita chasha-bhusha kooli-majur (unlettered peasants and labourers) – proclaimed by Sabyasachi in *Pather Dabi* as the 'handiwork of God',[109] was now spanned. The bridge, for Saratchandra, was a redefined 'culture', which had little to do with acquired book learning and formal education. 'Culture' was now an ascriptive attribute. It was a quality that all Hindus, high or low, were born with: and one that Muslims could never attain, no matter how long or how hard they strove for it. The problem of class division in 'Hindu society' was thus resolved in an ingenious way: by attributing to *all* 'Hindus' the quality that had, in its perception, been a badge of the bhadralok: *bhadrata*, that is cultivatedness or gentility. The old class distinction between the bhadralok and the chhotolok now re-emerged in the guise of a 'communal' difference, between bhadra Hindus and *abhadra* or *itar* Muslims.[110]

The problem of caste, however, could not be resolved in the same way, as Saratchandra was well aware. In *Bartaman Hindu–Mussalman Samasya*, he took the position that certain 'practices' *vis-a-vis* lower castes were the chief obstacle to the realisation of Hindu unity. These 'practices', he argues, are 'follies' – mistakes or distortions – that have to be remedied immediately. This is the first job to which Hindus must attend:

the problem before Hindus is not to bring about this unnatural union between Hindus and Muslims. Their task is to achieve unity within their own community – and to bring an end to the folly of those practising Hindus (*Hindu dharmaablambi*) – who insult some people by calling them 'low caste'. Even more pressing is the need for Hindus to think about how they may let the truth within them blossom like a flower in their public behaviour. Those who think do not speak, those who speak do not act, and those who act are not accepted. If this evil is not checked, even God will not be able to cement the countless cracks in the structure of the community. This is the problem, this is the duty [before us].[111]

Caste is seen here in a way similar to the approach in *Bipradas*. It is addressed only at the level of individual practice (*dharmaablamban*) and individual character or behaviour (*acharan*): there is no discussion of the validity of the institution of caste as a whole, or of varna philosophy. To insult fellow-Hindus by calling them low-caste is a foolish mistake, similar to Dayamayee's folly in rejecting Bandana's obeisances. The answer, as in *Bipradas*, is inner reflection, through which the higher truths of Hinduism

---

[109] Saratchandra Chattopadhyay, *Pather Dabi*, p. 163.
[110] The range of meanings signified by the word *itarta* make it both enormously evocative and difficult to translate. It means, in its orginal sense 'otherness'. But more popularly, it conveys baseness, vulgarity, inferior status, commonness, crudeness, meanness and narrowness. *Abhadrata* conveys incivility, unculturedness, ungentlemanly conduct, and also vulgarity and meanness.
[111] Saratchandra Chattopadhyay, *Bartaman Hindu–Mussalman Samasya*, p. 844.

will be revealed, love and mutual tolerance will 'blossom like a flower' and the Hindu family will be united. The text implies that untouchability or bad behaviour towards low castes goes against the spirit of Hinduism, against its tolerant essence. But the relationship between this inner 'spirit' and the letter of Hinduism on the vexed issue of caste is left deliberately vague. To probe too deeply would, perhaps, raise too many uncomfortable questions, difficult to answer without undermining the edifice of 'Hinduness' constructed by the author. Another interesting and revealing aspect of this discussion is that it is directed exclusively at an upper-caste audience.

The forging of Hindu unity was, for Saratchandra, the first task that Hindus had to undertake. Once this was achieved, independence would automatically follow. The combined strength of the Hindu community would be enough to free the nation. Muslim support in this task was neither likely nor necessary, because

Hindustan is the homeland of Hindus. (*Hindustan Hindur desh*). Therefore, the duty of freeing this nation from the chains of servitude belongs to Hindus alone. Muslims look towards Turkey and Arabia, their hearts are not in India ... Today it is vital that we understand this point – that this work is the work exclusively of Hindus, and of no one else. There is no need to get agitated counting the Muslim population. Numbers are not the ultimate truth in this world ... When Hindus come forward and vow to free their country, then it will matter little whether a few dozen Muslims lend their support or not.[112]

The use of the word *desh* in this passage is particularly evocative, because it not only describes the modern nation-state but it also conveys the colloquial sense of a more local 'home-land', one's 'native place', and the emotional ties associated with it. The author is thus able to suggest that for Hindus, 'natural' feelings of attachment for their *desh* or birthplace are 'naturally' extended to include the wider *desh* – the more abstract entity of 'Hindustan'. Muslims, on the other hand, can never share this emotional bond. They are eternally 'foreign', because their spiritual home is the Islamic heartland of 'Turkey and Arabia'. Saratchandra thus cleverly turns the Khilafat movement into an act of betrayal, a proof of the extra-national loyalties of the Muslim community as a whole. The powerful anti-British and anti-imperialist sentiment that drove the Khilafat demand is completely denied.

Having established that Muslims are not nationalists, Saratchandra goes on to argue that they can never become nationalists. Once again, the discussion hinges upon the point of culture:

---

[112] *Ibid.*, p. 844. An almost identical case was made ten years later by Dhires Chakravarty, in an article entitled 'Hindu–Muslim Unity: Platitudes and Realities'. *Modern Review*, vol. 53, 1–6, January–June, 1936, pp. 284–289.

There are those who argue that there is no teacher like grief and despair, that when Muslims suffered continuous humiliation at the hands of the foreign bureaucracy, they would be awakened and would fight shoulder to shoulder with Hindus for Swaraj. But they are mistaken, because they have not taken into account the fact that the very ability to sense humiliation is itself a product of learning. ... Most importantly, [they forget that] those who feel no shame while oppressing the weak similarly feel no shame when they grovel before the mighty.[113]

The problem, the author suggests, lies in the Muslim personality. Nationalist awareness and patriotic feeling are born of a higher sensibility, a higher culture. All Hindus, being intrinsically cultured, are capable of being aroused to nationalist fervour. The 'quality' of nationalism lies within them, the problem is simply of awakening it. Muslims, in contrast, can never be awakened to nationalism because nationalism, as much as the higher sensibility from which it springs, is foreign to their essential nature.

Nationalism is thus appropriated into Hindu communal discourse as a specifically Hindu essence. It is represented as one among the constellation of attributes that make up the Hindu character and Hindu culture: including tolerance, *bhadrata*, and spirituality.[114] It is an attribute that Muslims can never acquire. As in every essentialising discourse, human agency and contingency are displaced:[115] 'nationalism', in this construction, conveys no sense of active political choice – of being a deliberately chosen political agenda dedicated to action against imperialism.

This re-definition of nationalism is arguably the crux of the difference between nationalist and Hindu communal ideologies. One author has recently challenged the notion of an inherent difference between nationalism and communalism, arguing that both 'were part of the same discourse', and rather more elliptically, that 'nationalism was nothing more than communalism driven into secular channels'.[116] Admittedly both ideologies shared the premise that the basic political unit of Indian society was the religious community. Both creatively deployed elements of the same discourse – derivative concepts of 'Indianness' (and Muslimness) in particular – to fashion national and communal identities. But there was a crucial difference that marked nationalist from communal discourse, a difference of political intention. The intention of Hindu communal discourse was to deny the possibility of Muslim participation in the

[113] Saratchandra Chattopadhyay, *Bartaman Hindu–Mussalman Samasya*, p. 843.
[114] These are precisely the characteristics that Saratchandra attributes to his later fictional character, the Hindu hero Bipradas.
[115] For a detailed critique of orientalist/Indological essentialism and its implicit denial of human agency and history, see Ronald Inden, *Imagining India*, pp. 1–48, 263–270.
[116] Gyanendra Pandey, *Constructions of Communalism*, p. 235.

process of national liberation: an argument that would later be extended
to assert that Muslims could never be true national citizens.[117] Further, by
distancing anti-imperialist action from the definition of nationalism, it
underwrote a political programme which claimed to be 'nationalist' but in
which opposition to British rule played no part.[118]

Communalism, nationalism and imperialism: reconstructions of the past

Later communal narratives projected this new definition of nationhood
and nationalism upon the interpretation of the past. The age of 'Muslim
tyranny' was recovered from Renaissance histories, but with a difference.
The conscious political intention of the earlier texts had been to arouse
patriotic feeling against British rule. Now the historical spectre of 'Muslim
tyranny' was raised in order to exhort Hindus to fight 'Muslim tyranny' of
modern times: the rule, in other words, of democratically elected Muslim-
majority governments. The changed political preoccupations of the
present-day led to new readings of history, in which new symbols were
invented and old ones invested with new meaning. The shift from
'nationalist' to 'communal' preoccupations is nowhere more evident than
in the symbolic reconstruction of the Battle of Plassey.

Plassey was first recreated in fiction as the historic point at which the
British embarked on their conquest of Bengal and India more than a
century after the event, in Nabinchandra Sen's epic poem *Palasir Juddha*,
first published in 1875. Like most of his contemporaries, Nabinchandra
was deeply ambivalent about what had come to be regarded in the
terminology of James Mill as the 'Muslim period' of history. *Palasir
Juddha* abounds with references to the cruelty of Muslim kings and to the
temple-breaking, looting, rape and plunder which characterised Muslim

---

[117] The 'statism' that Pandey attacks in modernist and 'liberal–rational' nationalist thought
inheres equally in the apparently more 'traditional' politics of communalism. *Ibid.*,
pp. 253–254.

[118] Pandey's formulation, in its eagerness to attack the 'liberal–rational' and 'statist'
premises of nationalist discourse, overlooks this rather obvious but nonetheless fundamental point. Its critique of 'constructions' of 'communalism' both in colonial and
nationalist writing is undoubtedly insightful. But Pandey's failure to examine communal
discourse in the same way leads him to the fallacious position that communalism and
nationalism are not simply overlapping categories, but are in fact, the same thing
('nationalism was nothing but communalism driven into secular channels'). The invention of a third category, 'sectarianism', which he uses in exactly the same way that other
writers use 'communalism', further detracts from the clarity and rigour of his arguments.
Nothing is gained by describing the Hindu Mahasabha and the Rashtriya Swayam
Sevak Sangha as 'sectarian organizations' (p. 234) rather than as 'communal' ones. *Ibid.*,
p. 234.

rule.[119] It was responsible, perhaps more than any other work, for immortalising the image of Siraj-ud-daula as a debauched lecher, filled with fear and doubt on the eve of the famous battle, but unable to stir himself out of his drunken lethargy to face Clive's challenge.[120]

Nevertheless, the poem is written in the form of a tragedy. It opens with a classic description of the eve of the infamous battle that never was, the overcast and oppressive night with its premonitions of impending catastrophe. From the opening verse, it is clear that the end of 'Muslim rule' was not for the poet a cause for celebration. At the outset, Rani Bhabani argues passionately against the conspirators plotting to betray Siraj-ud-daula to Clive and points out that there is a world of difference between the Muslims and the British. The Muslims (referred to throughout the poem with the pejorative term, *Jaban*) may have once been an alien people, as alien as the British. But after seven centuries in India, she argues, they have become one with the native people, and love and fellow feeling have replaced hatred and mistrust. By inviting the British to take over, the conspirators will bring upon themselves, upon Bengal and upon India a servitude far more total than anything they have yet seen.[121] Her forebodings prove justified. Siraj is betrayed on the battlefield, taken captive and summarily executed. The dissolute young Nawab emerges as a tragic figure; the treachery in the mango grove at Plassey becomes the first step in the enslavement of India by the unseen Empress of an unknown and distant island.[122]

Later, more self-consciously nationalist authors developed this theme. In 1891, with the publication of his *Sirajuddaula*, Akshaykumar Maitra began the process by which Siraj-ud-daula was reincarnated as a nationalist hero.[123] Indeed, Maitra took issue with Nabinchandra Sen for his 'false' and 'damning' portrayal of the Nawab's character.[124] In 1905, in the midst of the Swadeshi upsurge, the play *Sirajoddaula* by the celebrated playwright Girishchandra Ghosh opened at the Minerva Theatre in Calcutta. In this version, the Nawab was the hero, his betrayers were quislings, and Clive and his camp were indisputably the enemy.[125] By the time Jawaharlal Nehru wrote his *Discovery of India* in 1944, Plassey was firmly established in nationalist historiography as the first step in a process

---

[119] Nabinchandra Sen, *Palasir Juddha*, pp. 1, 14, 63, 94–95.   [120] *Ibid.*, pp. 53–59.
[121] *Ibid.*, pp. 24–25.   [122] *Ibid.*, pp. 93–99.
[123] Akshaykumar Maitra, *Sirajuddaula*, Calcutta, 1891. See, in particular, Part XXVII, entitled *Palasir Juddha* ('The Battle of Plassey').
[124] *Ibid.* Also see the introduction by Sri Sajanikanta Das to the 1984 edition of Nabinchandra Sen's *Palasir Juddha*, p. xvi.
[125] *Sirajoddaula*, in Rabindranath Ray and Debipada Bhattacharya (eds.), *Girish Rachanabali* ('The Collected Works of Girishchandra Ghosh'), vol. I., Calcutta, 1969, pp. 551–630.

which was to reduce Bengal, 'once so rich and flourishing', to 'a miserable mass of poverty-stricken, starving and dying people'.[126]

The nationalist version continued to have its votaries in Bengal in the 1930s and 1940s. In his autobiographical sketch, *An Indian Pilgrim*, written in Austria in 1937, Subhas Bose challenged the very notion of a 'Muslim period' of Indian history, and represented the Battle of Plassey as an instance of Hindu–Muslim cooperation against a common enemy:

History will bear me out when I say that it is a misnomer to talk of Muslim rule when describing the political order in India prior to the advent of the British. Whether we talk of the Moghul Emperors at Delhi, or of the Muslim Kings of Bengal, we shall find that in either case the administration was run by Hindus and Muslims together, many of the prominent Cabinet Ministers and Generals being Hindus. Further, the consolidation of the Moghul Empire in India was effected with the help of Hindu commanders-in-chief. The Commander-in-chief of Nawab Sirajudowla, whom the British fought at Plassey in 1757 and defeated, was a Hindu.[127]

This reading of history prompted Bose, in July 1940, to take up the demand for the removal of the Holwell Monument, a memorial to the British victims of the Nawab's alleged cruelty in the famous 'Black Hole' incident. For Bose, the Holwell Monument was an issue that, he hoped, would draw both Hindus and Muslims behind him in an agitation against the British government, and so give impetus to his wider political efforts to find a new non-communal basis for Bengali politics.[128] His success in uniting Hindu and Muslim nationalist opinion against this 'unwarranted stain on the memory of the Nawab' and 'the symbol of our slavery and humiliation' was the startling exception which proved the rule. A meeting

---

[126] Jawaharlal Nehru, *The Discovery of India* (1946), New Delhi, 1986, p. 297. Nehru, writing at the height of the tragic Bengal Famine of 1943–46, argued passionately that the sorrows of Bengal were the direct product of two centuries of British rule: 'Bengal had the first full experience of British rule in India. The rule began with outright plunder, and a land revenue system which extracted the uttermost farthing not only from the living but also from the dead cultivators ... It was pure loot. The 'Pagoda Tree' was shaken again and again til the most terrible famines ravaged Bengal. This process was called trade later on but that made little difference ... The outright plunder gradually took the shape of legalized exploitation which, though not so obvious, was in reality, worse. The corruption, venality, nepotism, violence and greed of money of these early generations of British rule in India is something which passes comprehension'. *Discovery of India*, p. 297.

[127] Subhas Chandra Bose, *An Indian Pilgrim*, in Sisir K. Bose (ed.), *Netaji Collected Works*, vol. I., p. 15.

[128] In his report on the affair, Governor Herbert was clear that the agitation, which 'makes a strong appeal to Muslim sentiment ... is only one phase of the consistent endeavours of Subhas Bose and the Forward Bloc to find some plank on which civil disobedience can be started with the assistance of the Muslims'. Herbert to Linlithgow, 4 July 1940, FR, Linlithgow Collection, IOLR MSS Eur F/125/40.

called at the Town Hall to pay homage to Siraj-ud-daula's memory and to condemn the 'falsity of foreign historians' was attended not only by Subhas's camp followers – left-wing Muslims and Hindus – but also by the Muslim League Students Organisation, and had the support of the strongly anti-Bose *Amrita Bazar Patrika*.[129] An anxious Governor recommended that the agitation 'be stopped', so as to 'remove the last of the immediate causes of conflict in which revolutionary Hindus and Muslims can be banded together' against Europeans. Bose was duly arrested on the morning of the Holwell satyagraha, and remained in prison until December 1940, against the wishes both of Nazimuddin and the Huq Ministry.[130]

But this type of political action was becoming more and more rare, and the ideology that inspired it was increasingly contested. In 1932, B. C. Chatterjee, in his *Betrayal of Britain and Bengal* had described Plassey as the moment when Bengal was liberated from Muslim tyranny, which ushered in a new age of 'the outflowering [sic] of the Bengali Hindu genius and culture'.[131] A decade of provincial government by Muslim-dominated coalition ministries brought a new meaning to the notion of Muslim tyranny, and by the mid-forties, his interpretation had found its way into formal historiography. In the 'Concluding Reflections' of his monumental *History of Bengal*, Sir Jadunath Sarkar posed, with characteristic flamboyance, this rhetorical question: 'When the sun dipped into the Ganges behind the blood-red field of Plassey, on that fateful evening in June, did it symbolise the curtain dropping on the last scene of a tragic drama? Was that day followed by "a night of eternal gloom", as the poet of Plassey imagined?'

His answer draws together, in a purple passage, the disparate strands of bhadralok communal discourse:

Today the historian, looking backward over the two centuries that have passed since then, knows that it was the beginning, slow and unperceived, of a glorious dawn, the like of which the history of the world has not seen elsewhere. On 23rd June, 1757, the middle ages of India ended and her modern age began. When Clive struck at the Nawab, Mughal civilization had become a spent bullet, its very life was gone. The country's administration had become hopelessly dishonest and inefficient, and the mass of people had been reduced to the deepest poverty, ignorance and moral degradation under a small, selfish, proud and unworthy ruling class. Imbecile lechers filled the throne ... and the women were even worse than the men. Sadists like Siraj and Miran made even their highest subjects live in

[129] Herbert to Linlithgow, Telegram R, 4 July 1940, Linlithgow Collection, IOLR MSS Eur F/125/40.
[130] Bidyut Chakrabarti, *Subhas Chandra Bose and Middle-Class Radicalism*, pp. 63–65.
[131] B. C. Chatterjee, *The Betrayal of Britain and Bengal*.

constant terror. The army was rotten and honey-combed with treason. The purity of domestic life was threatened by the debauchery fashionable in the Court and the aristocracy and the sensual literature that grew up under such patrons. Religion had become the handmaid of vice and folly. On such a hopelessly decadent society, the rational and progressive spirit of Europe struck with resistless (*sic*) force. In the space of less than one generation, in the twenty years from Plassey to Warren Hastings ... the land began to recover from the blight of medieval theocratic rule. Education, literature, society, religion, man's handiwork and political life, all felt the revivifying touch of the new impetus from the West. The dry bones of a stationary oriental society began to stir, at first faintly, under the wand of a heaven-sent magician.[132]

Perhaps the most striking feature in Sarkar's hyperbole is its unabashed depiction of the 'Muslim period' as a Dark Age of unrelieved tyranny, borrowing themes from different European views of India. From Mill, he has taken the idea of a 'Muslim period'; from the missionaries, the moral revulsion at the 'sensuality' of the Court and the 'degradation' of family life, and from Montesquieu, the theory of a static oriental despotism. The portrait of Siraj-ud-daula painted by 'the poet' – a reference to Nabin-chandra Sen – is not harsh enough for his purposes.[133] For him Siraj is nothing less than a sadist, a monster who strikes fear in the heart of his highest subjects. To back up this claim, he falls back, typically, on European sources: he quotes Jean Law's assessment that 'the character of Siraj-ud-daulah was reputed to be one of the worst ever known ... distinguished ... not only by all sorts of debaucheries, but by a revolting cruelty'.[134] The conspiracy with Clive against the Nawab (in which disgruntled Hindu worthies played a leading role) is thereby implicitly condoned.

The repudiation of nationalist historiography could hardly have been more vehement. The insistence on a 'Muslim period' flies in the face of Subhas Bose's rejection of this derivative communal periodisation. The improbably harsh characterisation of Siraj-ud-daula challenged the fifty-year-old tradition that began with Akshaykumar Maitra's biography of

[132] Jadunath Sarkar, *The History of Bengal. Muslim Period, 1200–1757*, Patna, 1973, pp. 497–498.

[133] Sarkar takes 'the poet' to task, in another passage, for 'redeeming' the memory of the Nawab: 'Ignoble as the life of Siraj-ud-daula had been and tragic his end, among the public of his country, his memory has been redeemed by ... a poet's genius ... The Bengali poet Nabinchandra Sen in his masterpiece, *The Battle of Plassey*, has washed away the follies and crimes of Siraj by artfully drawing forth his readers' tears for fallen greatness and blighted youth'. *Ibid.*, p. 497.

[134] *Ibid.*, p. 469. The Muslim aristocracy were all equally evil, according to Sarkar. Thus Siraj's cousin and challenger, Miran, 'had all the vices of his rival, the same ignorant pride, insane ambition, uncontrollable passions, looseness of tongue and addiction to drink'. *Ibid.*, p. 478.

the Nawab in 1891 and culminated in the Holwell Monument agitation of 1940, of projecting Siraj-ud-daula as a nationalist hero. The assertion that British rule brought immediate prosperity to Bengal is perhaps the sharpest break with nationalist history. For Nehru, the years of revenue farming between Clive and Warren Hastings were years of 'pure loot' and 'outright plunder', which resulted in the famine of 1770, 'which swept away over a third of the population of Bengal and Bihar'.[135] For Jadunath Sarkar, the same twenty years saw 'the land recover from the blight of medieval theocratic rule'. His reading denies the association between British rule and the economic exploitation of India: an association that was a key pillar of nationalist thought.[136] He represents colonialism, instead, as a cultural intervention: as the 'magic wand' of modernity that awakened Bengal from the cultural inertia induced by seven centuries of medievalism.[137]

'Culture' now enters the narrative in a novel way. It is placed at the very centre of history, it defines historical eras – the 'Muslim period' is a dark, barbaric age, while British rule is the harbinger of a new and enlightened cultural dispensation:

It was truly a Renaissance, wider, deeper, and more revolutionary than that of Europe after the fall of Constantinople ... under the impact of the British civilization, [Bengal] became a path-finder and light-bringer to the rest of India. If Periclean Athens was the school of Hellas, 'the eye of Greece, mother of arts and eloquence', that was Bengal to the rest of India under British rule, but with a borrowed light, which it had made its own with marvellous cunning. In this new Bengal originated every good and great thing of the modern world that passed on to the other provinces of India. From Bengal went forth the English-educated teachers and the Europe-inspired thought that helped to modernise Bihar and Orissa, Hindustan and Deccan. New literary types, reform of the language, social reconstruction, political aspirations, religious movements and even change in manners that originated in Bengal, spread like ripples from a central eddy, across provincial barriers to the furthest corners of India.[138]

---

[135] Nehru, *Discovery of India*, p. 297.
[136] Nehru thus argues that the wealth plundered from Bengal under-wrote the industrial revolution in Britain. *Ibid.*, pp. 297–298. His analysis contributed to a forty-year-old nationalist tradition of associating colonial rule with economic exploitation, a tradition that began with the publication of Dadabhai Naoroji's *Poverty and Un-British Rule in India* in 1901, and received fresh impetus and direction with the appearance of Rajani Palme Dutt's *India Today* in 1940. For a history of this tradition, see Bipan Chandra, *The Rise and Growth of Economic Nationalism in India*, New Delhi, 1966.
[137] This passage suggests that it was not, as Gyanendra Pandey suggests in *Constructions of Communalism*, only the liberal, secular nationalists (qua Nehru) who were uncritically enthusiastic about modernity and rationalism. It demonstrates also that a communal discourse need not necessarily use 'traditionalist' idioms, or even 'religious' ones.
[138] Jadunath Sarkar, *The History of Bengal*, pp. 497–498.

Here, the Bengal Renaissance is interpreted so widely as to incorporate practically the entire social, political and intellectual history of the bhadralok over two hundred years. In it, the varied and often contesting intellectual traditions of the nineteenth and twentieth centuries, the 'universalism'[139] of Rammohun Roy and the Brahmo Samaj, the Anglophile enthusiasms of Michael Madhusudan Dutt and the Derozians, the reformist spirit of Vidyaysagar and the liberal humanism of Tagore, the cultural nationalism of Bankimchandra, Bhudeb Mukhopadhyay and Vivekananda, the Hindu histories of R. C. Dutt and the nationalist histories of Akshaykumar Maitra, the plays of Dwijendralal Roy and Girishchandra Ghosh, the nationalist–revolutionary novels of the early Saratchandra and the anti-revolutionary novels of Tagore – all these and more, collapse into a single great tradition, a unified cultural heritage. By the 1940s, the intense and often bitter debates on the question of national culture and identity that had fuelled Renaissance thought were irrelevant. Thus the Brahmos and Derozians, reviled and ridiculed in the late nineteenth century by more aggressive 'revivalist' writers and marginalised in bhadralok society, could be recovered and reinstated as the founding fathers of Bengali Hindu 'culture'. The 'Renaissance', in this construction, was fathered by Rammohun Roy, and carried through a single unbroken line of descent through Derozio, Madhusudan Dutt, Vidyasagar and Bankimchandra down to Rabindranath Tagore, the 'sage' of Santiniketan.[140] In this version, the history of nationalism is subsumed within the history of 'culture'. 'Political aspirations' as Jadunath Sarkar describes them, are but one aspect of the 'glorious dawn' of a new culture, and the confrontation between nationalist aspirations and the British Raj is trivialised. The bitter debates that divided elite politics – nationalists from loyalists, moderates from extremists, terrorists from non-violent activists, left from right – are ignored. Popular protest – peasant uprisings, street agitations, strikes, riots and demonstrations – forms of organised and unorganised political action that fell outside the ambit of bhadralok 'political aspirations' – are simply written out of this history.

In writing of the Renaissance in this way, Jadunath Sarkar did not merely celebrate British rule, or simplify a complex history. He denied Muslims a place in the history of modern Bengal. The Muslims, his epilogue suggests, had had their 'period' (from 1200 to 1757), during

[139] David Kopf characterises the thought of Rammohun Roy thus, in his essay, 'Universal Man and the Yellow Dog: the Orientalist Legacy and the Problem of Brahmo Identity', in Rachel Van M. Baumer (ed.) *Aspects of Bengali History and Society*, Hawaii, 1975.
[140] R. C. Dutt's *Cultural Heritage of Bengal* (1896) included Rammohun Roy, Vidyasagar, Madhusudan and Bankimchandra; Nirad Chaudhuri speaks of 'the great Bengali reformers from Rammohun Roy to Tagore'. *Autobiography*, p. 179.

which time they brought upon Bengal nothing but bloody and unrelieved barbarism and tyranny. In the modern age, the age of culture and enlightenment, they had no place. Modern Bengal was the creation of the Hindu bhadralok. They had made Bengal what it was – albeit with the help of 'light' 'borrowed' from the British – the centre of India's civilisation. By rights, therefore, Bengal belonged to them. The Renaissance, from this viewpoint, became a symbol not only of a culture which was bhadralok, but also of a Hindu Bengal from which Muslims were excluded. It was a construction that also denied the Muslims any title to Bengali nationality. It also fuelled the Hindu bhadralok's sense of themselves as heirs dispossessed of their rightful patrimony: 'Muslim rule' was unjust because it robbed them of their birthright and reduced them to the position of 'helots in their own province'.[141]

The choice of the Renaissance, and 'culture' more generally, as the key idiom of 'Hinduness', also fed another argument with strong communal overtones, that of Hindu superiority. This claim was increasingly used in the late thirties and forties to demand the continuation of bhadralok or 'Hindu' dominance in Bengali society, and to counter the claims of the Muslims, based on their larger numbers, for political power. As early as 1926, Saratchandra Chattopadhyay had set out, in his *Bartaman Hindu–Mussalman Samasya*, the case for Hindu 'cultural' superiority. In the same essay, he also repeatedly challenged the notion that the will of the majority should rule: the essay begins with the argument that 'when large numbers of people support an idea, despite the strength of their numbers and the power of their combined voice, they are not necessarily correct'.[142] In 1932, when it became likely that Muslims would win a statutory majority in the new Assembly, a widely-circulated pamphlet, 'The Bengal Hindu Manifesto', put the case in unequivocal terms:

The claims of the Bengali Muslims [to statutory majority] are anti-national and selfish and [are] not based on any principles of equity or justice ... if conceded, it will keep Hindus in a perpetual state of inferiority and impotence ... We say that the Muslims of Bengal cannot claim any special importance as ... they have never served as soldiers or done anything for the defence of the Empire, while the superiority of the Hindu community in educational qualifications and political fitness, their contribution to the growth of civic and political institutions and the record of their past services to the state in every branch of the administration are too well known to need recapitulation. The achievements of Hindu Bengalis stand foremost in the whole of India in the fields of Art, Literature and Science, whereas

---

[141] Lead editorial in *Amrita Bazar Patrika*, 5 April 1939. The author urged Bengali Hindus to 'wake up' and 'to do a little thinking of (*sic*) their own account and decide for themselves their future line of action'.

[142] Saratchandra Chattopadhyay, *Bartaman Hindu–Mussalman Samasya*, p. 841. This theme is repeated several times in the essay. See Appendix I.

the Muslim community in Bengal has not so far produced a single name of All-India fame in these fields. Political fitness cannot be divorced from the larger intellectual life of the Nation, and in political fitness the Mussalmans of Bengal are vastly inferior to the Hindus ... Their apprehension of not being able to secure adequate representation in spite of their superiority in numbers is really tantamount to an admission of their political unfitness and to claim political predominance in the future constitution on the basis of present political backwardness, is illogical and absurd.[143]

This was an argument designed to appeal to the British, who had long justified their own position in India in terms of their intellectual superiority and the 'unfitness' of the Indian people to rule themselves.[144] The implicit loyalism of the argument is evident in, for instance, the daring assertion that 'the Muslims of Bengal have not done anything for the defence of the Empire', and in the reminders to the Government about services rendered in the past by Hindus which were, just as well, 'too well known to need recapitulation' so as to demand favours today. But the sharpest break from the nationalist tradition lies in its outright rejection of the principle of democratic rule, based upon the sovereign will of the majority of the people, on the grounds that the majority was culturally inferior. This was a viewpoint that had become respectable in bhadralok circles, and was repeatedly voiced not only in the editorial columns of the 'nationalist' Hindu press but in the pages of scholarly journals and literary magazines. One pseudo-academic article on 'public spirit in Bengal', published in *Modern Review*, concluded with an observation that ridiculed

the achievements of the Muslim community of Bengal, whose boast of numerical superiority sounds ludicrous by the side of their poor performance in the sphere of ... public work. From the community which demands a lion's share in the Governmental powers of the country, we might have expected greater and better work for the good of the country ... Instead of expending their energy in manoeuvring violent movements against Hindu landowners and moneylenders and organising the defence of such Muslims as are accused of crimes against defenceless Hindu women ... let Muslims turn their attention to work of real public utility so that ... they themselves may attain a position befitting the majority community of the province.[145]

[143] 'Bengal Hindu Manifesto', 23 April 1932. Reproduced in N. N. Mitra (ed.), *Indian Annual Register*, vol. I, January–June 1932, p. 323. Signatories included many of Bengal's biggest Hindu zamindars, including Maharaja Sris Chandra Nandy of Cossimbazar (who later represented the Congress in the 1946 elections), the president of the Bengal Mahajan Sabha, and several lawyers and professionals. Report in GB SB 'PM' Series, File No. 6218/ 31.

[144] It also echoed the demand of North Indian Muslims for a greater share of representation, on the grounds of the political and social importance of their community.

[145] Ramesh Chandra Banerjee, 'Hindu and Muslim Public Spirit in Bengal', in *Modern Review*, vol. 55, 1–6, January–June, 1934, p. 315.

Another article in the same vein accused the Muslim community of 'deliberately [lying] about the possession of a qualification such as literacy which it has not'.[146] Yet another asserted the superiority of Hindus in the sphere of public enterprise,[147] a fourth spoke of the greater Hindu contribution to the revenue.[148] The point of the argument was the same in each case: that Muslims were palpably inferior to Hindus, and they had no business to be 'ruling' over their superiors.

Bhadralok communal discourse never rid itself of the elitism which it had displayed from the start. Its key symbols – 'culture', 'learning', the 'Renaissance' – were born of the social world, the experience and self-image of the Hindu bhadralok. The idiom of 'superiority' derived from this self-image was enormously powerful in its appeal to many sections of bhadralok society. But it was an idiom that could not easily be adapted to the purposes of mass mobilisation of other less privileged members of this would-be band of brothers. Saratchandra Chattopadhyay may have argued that all Hindus, high and low, shared the superior sensibility of a cultured people. But it is doubtful that many bhadralok Hindus believed this. Nor is it likely that they accepted the 'Hindu' chhotolok, the workers and peasants (*chasha-bhusha kooli-majur*), the low castes and the tribals, as their cultural equals and brothers in arms against the tyranny of the 'inferior' Muslim community. Indeed, for many bhadralok Hindus (including Shyamaprasad Mookerjee), the sense of superiority in relation to Muslims was fed by the belief that Bengali Muslims were, by and large, 'a set of converts' from the dregs of Hindu society.[149] One learned article in the *Modern Review*, for instance, backed this belief with scholarly anthropometric 'evidence'. Quoting the authority of an anthropology derived from the school of British administrators in India, it pointed to the 'striking ... similarity of physical features between the Koches and Mohammedans of North Bengal', and the 'close resemblance between the Muhammedans of East Bengal ... and the Pods and Chandals on the other'.[150] Here, the open contempt for Bengali Muslims barely conceals

---

[146] Jatindra Mohan Datta, 'The Real Nature of the Muhammadan Majority in Bengal', *Modern Review*, vol. 49, 2, 1931.

[147] Jatindra Mohan Datta, 'Relative Public Spirit and Enterprise of Hindus and Muhammadans in Bengal', *Modern Review*, vol. 55, 1–6, January–June 1934, pp. 685–689.

[148] Jatindra Mohan Datta, 'Communalism in the Bengal Administration', *Modern Review*, vol. 49, 1, 1931. The same indefatigable author compared (with expected results) 'The Relative Heroism of the Hindus and Mohammedans of India', *Modern Review*, vol. 79, 1–6, January–June 1946.

[149] Undated note by Shyama Prasad Mookerjee in the Shyama Prasad Mookerjee Papers, II-IV Instalment, File No. 75/1945–46.

[150] Jatindra Mohan Datta, 'Who the Bengali Mohammedans Are?' *Modern Review*, vol. 49, 3, 1991.

an equal disregard for the 'Hindu' castes from which they were supposed to have come. The inherent contradiction between bhadralok claims of Hindu cultural superiority, and their disdain for low castes and tribals who formed a large part of this imagined 'community' was brought into the open when they tried to mobilise them as followers and pit them against the rival community.

5   Hindu unity and Muslim tyranny: aspects of Hindu bhadralok politics, 1936–47

In the late 1930s and 1940s, bhadralok politics underwent changes that corresponded, in interesting ways, with the ideological shifts that have been discussed in the last chapter. Most marked was the tendency to shun high nationalist endeavour and to focus instead on narrower, more immediate concerns. Perhaps the most ambitious scheme to attract the energies of the bhadralok in these years was the attempt to forge a greater Hindu political community, uniting the disparate castes and tribes of the putative 'Hindu family' into a single harmonious whole. But, generally, bhadralok politics grew more inward-looking and parochial, increasingly confined to the petty manoeuvrings of the localities and District Boards. This trend was particularly marked in traditional bhadralok strongholds in the west Bengal heartland where a growing Muslim influence had begun to erode established patterns of dominance. This chapter looks at these new orientations in bhadralok politics and examines their implications for communal relations in Bengal.

Caste and communal mobilisation

Since the turn of the century, ideologues of Hindu political unity had advocated programmes for the uplift of untouchables and the breaking down of caste barriers. Swami Vivekananda had looked forward to the coming of the age of Truth (*Satya-Yuga*) 'when there will be one caste (Brahman), one Veda, peace and harmony'.[1] But Hindu unity remained a distant dream to Sarat Chandra Chattopadhyay, writing in 1926. In his *Bartaman Hindu–Mussalman Samasya*, he had argued that the most pressing task before Hindus was to 'achieve unity within their own community' and to bring an end to the practice 'that has long distorted Hinduism – of insulting some people by calling them low caste'.[2] For although caste

---

[1] *The Complete Works of Swami Vivekananda*, vol. V, Calcutta, 1989, p. 167. Cited in Sekhar Bandopadhyay, *Caste, Politics and the Raj.* p. 123.
[2] Saratchandra Chattopadhya, *Bartaman Hindu–Mussalman Samasya*, p. 844.

hierarchies in Bengal were not as rigid as in some other parts of India,[3] high-caste Bengali Hindus shared the prejudices of their compatriots. The campaigns of nineteenth-century reformers against caste had enjoyed little lasting success. The response to the Untouchability Abolition Bill of 1933 and the Depressed Classes Status Bill of 1934, with 'the bulk of the opposition [coming] from ... Bengal',[4] suggests that by and large bhadra-lok Bengal had clung firmly to orthodoxy in matters of caste.

Caste (or *jati*) mobility had always been a feature of Hindu society in Bengal and there were instances of low-caste groups claiming higher ritual status long before the operations of the first decennial census.[5] In the 1870s, Chandals of Bakarganj and Faridpur boycotted caste Hindus when they refused an invitation to dine in the house of a Chandal headman, whose low ritual status did not match his secular authority. From this point onwards, the Chandals battled continuously to improve their ritual position and from the beginning of the twentieth century they claimed the more respectable title of 'Namasudra' and Brahmin status. Chasi Kaibarttas, a prosperous peasant community of west Bengal, had similarly claimed Mahishya status since the early nineteenth century. At roughly the same time, landowning Rajbangshi families in the northern districts began to claim Bratya Kayastha status and later launched a movement to encourage members of their caste to wear the sacred thread.[6] After the first census in 1891, the number of such claims increased dramatically and in 1911 petitions received by the census commissioner from different caste associations weighed over a *maund* (82 lb.). But census operations often sparked off caste friction, as high castes were irritated by the ritual pretensions of their social inferiors. In one instance, when the claims of Namasudras to Kayastha status were firmly rejected by the Kayasthas of East Bengal, Namasudras united to boycott all Kayasthas; and in another case, respectable Hindus preferred to buy their milk from Muslims rather than have any dealings with the Goalas, whose claims to Vaisya status they found difficult to swallow.[7] Well into the twentieth century, high-born Hindus of Bengal continued to view with suspicion all movements that challenged the established caste order.

From the late 1920s, however, some Hindu leaders began to recognise the need to 'reclaim' the low castes in order to create an unified Hindu political community. The Hindu Sabha movement, which grew out of a

[3] Some aspects of the peculiarities of the caste structure in Bengal have been examined in chapter 1.
[4] Legislative Council debates on the Untouchability Amendment Bill, in GOI, Home Political File No. 50/7/33.
[5] Sekhar Bandopadhyay, *Caste, Politics and the Raj*, pp. 98–99.   [6] *Ibid.*, pp. 98–99.
[7] *Ibid.*, p. 101.

perceived need to counteract Christian and Muslim proselytisation, under-lined solidarity among the different Hindu castes. At its provincial conference in 1924, the Sabha had declared that its chief focus would be on the removal of untouchability and the purification (*shuddhi*) of 'pol-luted' peoples. In 1931, one speaker at a Hindu Sabha meeting pointed to the 'dangers that were fast coming on the Hindus': 'He remarked that the cause of this danger lay in the attitude of the Hindus towards their own brethren which was full of indifference. He said that the Mahommedans actively sympathised with those Mahommedans who were oppressed and so seldom anyone dares to oppress Mahommedans.'[8] In 1925, a Congress-man from Malda, Kashishwar Chakravarty founded the 'Satyam–Shivam sect', whose object was to bring Santals into the 'Hindu community'.[9] With the support of other local Swarajist leaders, he launched a pro-gramme to 'reclaim' aboriginals and untouchables into the Hindu fold 'through ritual purification (*shuddhi*) and social reform'.[10] In 1929, Con-gress volunteers went on a satyagraha to press for the right of Namasu-dras to enter a Kali temple in Munshiganj.[11] While this may have been part of the Gandhian campaign for the betterment of Harijans, Satyam–Shivam activities were clearly part of a more deliberately political '*sanga-than*' movement to redefine the Hindu political community. 'Sangathan' (organisation) was a response to two distinct challenges: the British Government's policy of creating a separate political constituency for the 'depressed classes', and the efforts by Muslim politicians and preachers to persuade the low castes to give up even their nominal allegiance to caste society.[12] But after the Communal Award and the Poona Pact, sangathan took on a new significance. The Scheduled Castes in Bengal constituted roughly 11 per cent of the population of Bengal.[13] If they could effectively be 'converted' to Hinduism and be persuaded to have themselves entered in the census as Hindus, this would enormously strengthen the hand of

---

[8] Report of the speech of Narendranath Das at Albert Hall on 1 September 1931. GB SB 'PM' Series, File No. 6218/31.
[9] Tanika Sarkar, 'Jitu Santal's Movement in Malda, 1924–32: A Study in Tribal Protest', in Ranajit Guha, *Subaltern Studies IV*, New Delhi, 1985, p. 152.
[10] *Ibid*, p. 136.
[11] Tanika Sarkar, *Bengal 1928–1934*, p. 41. Also see Buddhadev Bhattacharya, *Satyagrahas in Bengal*, pp. 159–164.
[12] Namasudra caste associations, in particular, showed a willingness to cooperate with the British Government in return for special consideration. See chapter 1. There were occasional reports in the Hindu press that Muslim maulvis had converted *en masse* whole low-caste villages, which caused great concern among the Calcutta bhadralok. See, for instance, Prafulla Chandra Ray, *Life and Experiences of a Bengali Chemist*, pp. 529–530.
[13] The Census Commissioner in 1931 was unable to provide any firm figure for the Scheduled Caste population. But the Simon Commission placed their numbers at 11.5

caste Hindus in their bid for a greater share of provincial power. More and more, as the bhadralok gravitated politically towards the defence of specifically 'Hindu' interests, the need to construct a broader Hindu political base encouraged them to look with greater sympathy at the aspirations of the low castes for improved social status.

The idiom of 'cultural superiority' undoubtedly had great symbolic appeal for the bhadralok as a whole, whether urban professionals or the rural zamindars and taluqdars, the westernised intelligentsia or the more traditional gentry,[14] well-to-do notables or the more ordinary bhadralok clerics.[15] Indeed the middling bhadralok of Calcutta and the mofussil towns who staffed the lower rungs of the services – white-collar workers and small-town pleaders who depended for their livelihood on their education – were people who strongly identified with the cultural and intellectual pretensions of their superiors. But mobilising all segments of bhadralok society, even in its broadest sense, was no longer enough. The elections of 1937 had proved that caste Hindus would be able to influence the politics of the province only if they commanded wider Hindu support. The inability of the Congress to win more than 20 per cent of Scheduled Caste seats had revealed the narrowness of the social base of the party and its failure to win friends outside the little world of the bhadralok. Powerful political considerations pushed spokesmen for Hindu interests to woo those sections of the Hindu population which historically had shared little in these interests and which had long been excluded from bhadralok culture. The history of the abortive mass-contact initiative made it abundantly clear that any move to enlist the support of the depressed classes would not be based on agrarian radicalism: that Hindu unity could not be built by sacrificing bhadralok economic privileges. The consolidation of castes thus emerged as a significant instrument by which the sphere of the Hindu political community was sought to be expanded.

From the mid-thirties onwards, Bengal witnessed a flurry of caste consolidation programmes, initiated chiefly under Hindu Sabha and Mahasabha auspices. In 1931, the Mahasabha invited aboriginals to take on caste Hindu names and to register their caste as 'Kshattriya' in the coming census:

From the days of the Ramayan and Mahabharat there have been living in Bengal ... thousands of Santals, Garos, Dalus, Banias, Khasis, Oraons, Mundas, Mihirs,

million, and a report by the Bengal Government in 1932 at 11.2 million. See S. K. Gupta, *The Scheduled Castes in Modern Indian Politics*, New Delhi, 1985, p. 68.

[14] The *sahebi/boniyadi* distinction has been elaborated by Rabindra Ray, *The Naxalites and their Ideology*, p. 70.

[15] Rajat Ray has argued that bhadralok society was internally stratified between the 'notables' (*abhijata*) and the 'ordinary householders' (*grihasthas*). See Rajat Ray, *Social Conflict and Political Unrest in Bengal 1875–1927*, pp. 30–32.

Lushais, Kuhis, Lahungs, Kacharis, Rabhas and Meches. These inhabitants of Hindustan are fundamentally Hindus. In the census of 1921 they were returned as Animist instead of Hindu. By this a wrong has been done to our simple religious brothers and sisters. We hope that during the forthcoming enumeration the above Hindus, men and women, will rectify the mistakes made at the previous census. They should record 'Hindu' as their religion, and 'Kshattriya' as their caste and 'Singha' or 'Ray' as their family names.[16]

In March 1939, Savarkar himself formally relaunched the Mahasabha's programme in Bengal, which underlined the importance the Party placed on caste unity. At a public meeting in Monghyr, Savarkar received five Santal boys into the Hindu community. *Amrita Bazar Patrika* published an enthusiastic report of the occasion:

A thrill passed through the audience when Sj. Savarkar was found putting his hands on the head of five Santhal boys, who in Santhali, claimed that they belonged to Hinduism and sought Sj. Savarkar's lead to guide their destiny. When one of them garlanded him with a wreath of Sylvan blossoms, Sj. Savarkar embraced them in joy.[17]

Later that year, Dr Shyama Prasad Mookerjee visited Chandpur in Tippera to have the local Gaurnitai temple, owned by the Saha community, opened to worshippers from all castes. He held 'discussions with the proprietors of the temple and [was] successful in persuading them to throw open the temple to all castes of Hindus'.[18]

In some localities, such activities fed into politics of a different sort. In Malda district in North Bengal, where Muslim jotedars were particularly powerful, Mahasabha activists tried to persuade aboriginal labourers and share-croppers to stop working for Muslims. Their efforts caused 'the Santhals, Rajbangshis, Turies and other people of the same category' to stop 'working under the Muhammedans'.[19] Propaganda directed at share-croppers served two purposes: it would encourage aboriginals to make common cause with local Hindu politicians and break their connections with their Muslim employers, and might help to thwart the efforts of the left wing to win over share-croppers in the northern districts.[20]

Several new Hindu organisations now emerged, all aiming to unify Hindu society. In January 1939, the Bangiya Hindu Sanghati (the Bengal Hindu United Association) was set up 'to safeguard the rights and the

[16] *Lok Pranana O Banglar Hindu Samaj* ('Census and Bengali Hindu Society'), 5 Ashwin 1931, in *Census of India*, vol. V, 1931, p. 395.
[17] *Amrita Bazar Patrika*, 3 April 1939.   [18] GB SB 'PH' Series, File No. 501/39.
[19] Letter no. 1360/54–40 from S. P. Malda to Special Assistant, Intelligence Branch, 21 August 1940, in GB SP 'PM' Series, File No. 522/38.
[20] It is interesting that the Communist-inspired Tebhaga movement among sharecroppers in neighbouring Dinajpur and Rangpur districts did not spread to Malda.

legitimate interests and privileges of Bengal Hindus [and] to promote solidarity amongst all sections of the Hindu Community'.[21] In March of that year, its men in Calcutta underlined 'the necessity of aboriginal tribes being known as Hindus' and appealed to the Hindu zamindars of the province to join in its work. A 'Contact Board' was appointed with the express purpose of keeping all the different sects in Hinduism in touch with each other.[22]

Many low caste organisations responded eagerly to these overtures and were only too willing to accept an offer of membership of the Hindu community and recognition of their social aspirations. In April 1939 at a Mahishya Conference organised at Jalamutha in Midnapore,

The President in his address dwelt upon the glorious past of the Mahishya community. He said, 'The Mahishyas represented a large section of the Hindu Community like the similar other castes and in the matter of reorganisation and reconstruction of the greater Hindu Society the ... Mahishya Community was connected inseparably.'

He appealed to Mahishyas to do as the Bengal Hindu conference urged, 'viz. construction of Hindu temple in every village, introduction of Sarbojanin Puja Celebrations (combined worship by all castes) making themselves known as Hindu without mentioning the respective castes, introduction of inter-marriage among the various castes and sub-castes ... [and] attempt to preserve the interests of the Hindus in general'.[23] The Mahishyas were an intermediate *jalachal* caste whose economic standing and political weight had outstripped their low ritual status.[24] Unlike the Namasudras, they had played a part in nationalist campaigns, particularly in the boycott of Union Boards in Midnapore in the twenties. Now at least those Mahishyas who were represented by the Conference seemed willing to identify themselves with 'the interests of Hindus in general' if in their turn high-born Hindus accepted 'the glorious past of the Mahishya community'.

The caste consolidation programmes of the late thirties were part of a broader campaign to create a united and self-conscious Hindu political community in Bengal. Not surprisingly, these campaigns were an enormous irritant to Muslims. The Census of 1941, which as usual coincided

---

[21] GB SB 'PH' Series, File No. 505/39. Also see *Amrita Bazar Patrika*, 7 January 1939.
[22] See *Amrita Bazar Patrika*, 27 March 1939. The secretary of the Association also issued an appeal in *Ananda Bazar Patrika* on 16 May 1939, urging Hindu leaders to 'try to get the aborigines who profess religions of Indian origin and alien to Hinduism to be recorded as Hindus in the next census'. Memo dated 20. 5. 39 in GB SB 'PH' Series, File No. 505/39.
[23] *Amrita Bazar Patrika*, 3 April 1939.
[24] *Jalachal* castes were those intermediate castes whose touch was not deemed to be polluting, but who would not be served by any self-respecting Brahmin.

with a flurry of proselytisation by caste Hindus, was the occasion of much rancour between the communities and it dominated 'the political stage ... practically to the exclusion of everything else'. There were 'consultations between Ministers; statements [were] issued by the Chief Minister; counter-statements [were] published by the Hindu Press; and an atmosphere of mutual distrust [was] created between the two communities.[25] As the census operations got under way, 'attempts to record scheduled people as merely Hindus'[26] were reported from all over the province, and in some cases, these were accompanied by incidents of communal violence. In Rajashahi, 'the most important effect of the agitation [was] in connection with Santhals':

Attempts everywhere seem to have been made to get the Santhals to record themselves as Hindus ... In ... districts where Santhals are numerous, it will be interesting to see how much Hindu figures will be inflated by declarations of Santhals that they are Hindus. Santhals have been worked up in these districts to a state of some excitement.[27]

In Bankura, the District Magistrate noticed stenuous efforts in Mahasabha circles to get Santhals counted as Hindus. These prompted counter-efforts among the Santhals by the local branch of the Muslim League, which reportedly 'left no stone unturned to induce them to record their religion as aboriginal'. Shyamaprasad Mookerjee took a personal interest in this campaign, coming to Bankura from Calcutta to '[deliver] certain lectures in [the] district on the subject', and local Mahasabha leaders 'sent lecturers and agents to the Santhal inhabited localities'. The Muslim League, for its part, also stepped up its efforts and the Superintendent of Police reported that some Santhals were bought over 'by Muslim League by paying money and have been doing anti-Hindu propaganda'.[28]

There is not much contemporary evidence to suggest that the Scheduled Castes resisted this drive to bundle them into the 'Hindu Community'. In Jessore, a Scheduled Caste pleader by the name of Nagen Das 'submitted [a] scurrilous petition to the Ranaghat Municipality asking for beef stalls to be opened'. When this was rejected, he slapped in another petition 'citing alleged historical authorities to prove that Hindu women were

---

[25] Herbert to Linlithgow, 23 February 1941, FR. Linlithgow Collection, IOLR MSS Eur F/125/41.
[26] Report by the District Magistrate of Burdwan, LOFCR for the first fortnight in March 1941. GB HCPB File No. 13/41.
[27] Report of the Commissioner, Rajshahi Division, LOFCR for the first fortnight in March 1941. *Ibid.*
[28] Extract from Express Letter No. 246 C from the D. M. Bankura to the Additional Secretary, Home Political Department, Government of Bengal, 3 March 1941, in the report of the Commissioner, Burdwan Division, LOFCR for the first fortnight in March 1941, GB HCPB File No. 13/41.

fond of beef'.[29] But this was exceptional: more usually the lower castes, particularly those that were already demanding the recognition of a purer ritual status, gratefully accepted the 'Hindu' identity which was being offered to them.

Yet the caste consolidation campaign of the thirties and forties did not entail a change of heart about caste by the twice-born. The philosophy of the movement apparently inverted nineteenth-century Hindu nationalist thought, which defended the caste system and preached strict obedience to caste rules. But in fact a radical critique of the caste system formed no part of the programme and ideology of the Hindu Sabhas. Instead, movements to draw lower castes into the 'Hindu community' were intended to work within the acceptable framework of what might loosely be described as 'sanskritisation'.[30] Low castes were encouraged to take modest steps upwards in the caste hierarchy by being allowed to adopt some of the ritual practices of the twice-born, taking on respectable caste names, and by giving up some of the ritually 'impure' customs which had marked them out as degraded. The name chosen by the new Hindu proselytisers to describe their movement – 'shuddhi' ('purification') – itself suggests that the twentieth-century Hindu communal organisations con-tinued to be preoccupied with the very issues of purity and pollution that are arguably at the heart and centre of the caste system. [31] Thus Jitu Santal was encouraged by the Swarajist 'Sanyasi-baba' of the Satyam–Shivam sect to make 'the Santals into Hindus' by renouncing ritually impure pig and fowl meat[32] and in April 1932, 'week-long Hindu *melas* were organised all over Bengal' at which low castes were 'reconverted' through purification (*shuddhi*) ceremonies.[33] This strategy was well suited to Bengal, where many low castes were already trying to 'purify' or Brahminise their own practices. In the early twenties, for instance, the Rajbangshi leader Panchanan Barman had established a 'Kshattriya Sabha' in order to inculcate Brahmanical values and practices among his

---

[29] Report of the Commissioner, Presidency Division, LOFCR for the first fortnight in April 1941, *ibid.*
[30] The term 'sanskritisation' was first used by M. N. Srinivas to describe mobility by low castes within the caste hierarchy. See M. N. Srinivas, *Religion and Society among the Coorgs of South India*, Oxford, 1952; and 'A Note on Sanskritization and Westernization' in *Caste in Modern India and Other Essays*, Bombay, 1962. Some of the problems with this concept have been raised by David Hardiman in *The Coming of the Devi. Adivasi Assertion in Western India*, Delhi, 1987, pp. 157–163. Here, the term is used to describe the efforts by higher castes to encourage the adoption of high-caste rituals and practices by the lower castes so as to mobilise them behind the political interests of 'the Hindu community'.
[31] Louis Dumont, *Homo Hierarchicus.* p. 143.
[32] Tanika Sarkar, 'Jitu Santal's Movement in Malda', p. 137.
[33] *Ibid*, p. 143.

caste-fellows. The success of his movement was remarked upon twenty years later by settlement officer F. O. Bell who found in 1939 that even the poorest Rajbangshi cultivator wore the sacred thread of the twice-born castes. 'Questioned about the sacred thread', one cultivator told Bell that

Some years ago in 1329 B.S. (1922 AD), many of his caste men had entered the Kshattriya Sabha. Some thousands in the surrounding villages had been inducted, paying a fee of Rs. 2/8– for the services of a Brahmin and a barber to shave the head, at the time of initiation.... Since taking the sacred thread, he and his caste men did not eat pigs or fowl, or bear palkis. These things were done by the 'Palis'.[34]

Movements such as these among the low castes were often deeply ambivalent in their attitude to caste: they did not reject the caste hierarchy but sought only to improve the position of their own caste within it. Thus the peasant follower of the Kshattriya Sabha was quick to point out the difference between his own 'purified' caste and the 'Palis' who continued to adhere to degrading practices, just as Jitu Santal warned his Santal followers, 'Jitu says kill your hens and pigs, otherwise you will be domes, you will have to undertake the task of disposing dead bodies', and made several 'highly contemptuous references ... to lower castes and untouchables'.[35] Panchanan Barman himself opposed the Untouchability Abolition Bill in the Council in 1933, arguing that while he had 'every sympathy' with the object of the Bill, any clash with the religious rights of any individuals or of any particular community must be avoided ... [as] such measure will create divisions and dissensions within the Hindu community, which should be avoided to ensure its integrity.'[36] The campaign in the thirties and forties to bring the low castes into the 'Hindu community' built upon movements such as these, absorbing them into more overtly communal political battles. Jitu Santal's last stand was thus staged at the historic Adina Mosque in 1932, when he and his band of Santals stormed the derelict building and Jitu himself was shot dead by the police after enacting a 'debased' form of Kali worship in the ruins.[37] In the early forties, when the movement to draw the low castes into Hindu politics was at its height, there were many incidents of violence involving low caste groups and Muslims. Early in 1941 'there was local excitement over the passing of a Saraswati Puja procession with music in front of a mosque at

---

[34] F. O. Bell, 'Notes on Rural Travels in Dinajpur, 1939', pp. 10–11, in F. O. Bell Papers, IOLR MSS Eur D/733/2.
[35] Tanika Sarkar, 'Jitu Santal's Movement in Malda', p. 152. 'Doms' were an untouchable sweeping and scavenging caste.
[36] Debate in the Legislative Council on the Untouchability Abolition Bill, GOI, Home Political File No. 50/7/33.
[37] Tanika Sarkar, 'Jitu Santal's movement in Malda', p. 156.

Rajshahi'. Saraswati Puja, the worship of the goddess of learning, was celebrated every spring in most bhadralok Bengali homes. But on this occasion 'the presence of about two thousand Santhals in the procession with bows and arrows or lathis added to the excitement'. The involvement of Santals in the puja hinted at the methods by which bhadralok Hindus hoped to impose their 'culture' upon peoples whose allegiance to Hinduism was at best tenuous. It was also another instance of an ominous trend described by a local official as the 'utilisation' by Hindus of 'Santhals in communal disputes'.[38]

Two months later a violent confrontation was narrowly avoided at Narsinghbad near Burnpur when members of the Goala caste 'started objecting to the carrying of beef from Asansol to the Burnpur beef market though this [had] been done for many years without objection'.[39] That same fortnight Goalas were involved in another incident at Ahiran in the Suti thana area of Murshidabad district when 'high tension arose between Hindu Goalas and Muslim ryots as a result of various incidents'. [40] 'Purification' of 'polluted' peoples continued apace in North Bengal, where 'efforts [were] made to induce tea garden coolies to give up strong drink and beef-eating'. [41] In Tippera district in East Bengal, some Scheduled Caste groups took advantage of the prevailing climate to press their claims to a higher ritual status than they had previously been accorded. The local Superintendent of Police observed that 'under cover of the communal tension, scheduled caste Hindus of Bholahat, Nasirnagar and of Sarail, are urging caste Hindus to take food from them and not to treat them as untouchables'.[42]

This pattern persisted well into the mid-forties after the competitive proselytisation related to the census had come to an end. In January 1945 'trouble was apprehended between the Sonthals and the Muslims of Lalbag in Dinajpur district over a Kali Puja procession led by the former' past a local mosque during prayers.[43] That year, there was an ugly confrontation between Namasudras and Muslims at the Mithapur market in the Lohagara thana area of Jessore when

some Namasudras carried an image and sang and danced before a mosque in the *hat* during prayer hours. The Muslims of the mosque asked the Namasudras to go

[38] Report of the Commissioner, Rajshahi Division, LOFCR for the first fortnight in February 1941, GB HCPB File No. 13/41.
[39] Report of the Commissioner, Burdwan Division, LOFCR for the second fortnight of April 1941. *Ibid.*
[40] Report of the Commissioner, Presidency Division. *Ibid.*
[41] Report of the Commissioner, Rajshahi Division. *Ibid.*
[42] Weekly Confidential Report of the S. P., Tippera, enclosed in the report of the Commissioner, Chittagong Division. *Ibid.*
[43] Report of the Commissioner, Rajshahi Division, LOFCR for the second fortnight in January 1945. GB HCPB File No. 37/45.

away which they did. The following day about four thousand Namasudras came armed with *dhal*[s] [shields] and *sarki*[s] [arrows] and danced and sang in front of the mosque again. They went away without being molested as 'the Muslims were not prepared and ready'. After that, the Muslims organised the Muslims of other villages to come in force and attack the Namasudras next time they came there.[44]

Muslims and Namasudras in Jessore had battled violently in the past but these had been more in the nature of disputes between neighbouring villages over plots of land or over grazing rights. In 1911, two people were killed in a major riot that broke out when a Namasudra was dispossessed of his land for non-payment of rent and the land was given to a Muslim of the same village.[45] In 1936, in another incident, a fight broke out in Anandapur on the Jessore–Khulna border 'on a very petty matter, namely [a] quarrel amongst the cow boys in the field'.[46] Two years later, when Namasudras of several villages attacked neighbouring Muslim villages, killing at least one Muslim and injuring several others, police investigations revealed that the cause of the riot was 'a quarrel some time back between some Muhammedans and Namasudras ... over an *ail* (landmark between two lots of land)'.[47]

But the riot of 1945 was clearly different. The high turn-out of Namasudras at a Kali Puja procession was in itself significant. Namasudras, just as many other lower Bengali castes, had been influenced strongly by Vaisnavite heterodoxy, particularly after the establishment of the Matua cult by a Namasudra religious figure in the late nineteenth century.[48] Kali Puja, on the other hand, was a part of the Saivite great tradition of Bengal, and both Saivism and the Sakta worship of Kali were part of Bengali Hindu high culture.[49] By involving themselves increasingly in Kali and Durga Puja celebrations, low castes and tribals showed the extent to which they were beginning to identify themselves with the religion, culture and interests of the higher Hindu castes; this was also an index of the readiness of higher castes to include the lower castes into a redefined Hindu community.

[44] Report of the Commissioner, Presidency Division, LOFCR for the second fortnight in April 1945. *Ibid.*

[45] This riot is described in detail in Sekhar Bandopadhyay, 'Community Formation and Communal Conflict. Namasudra–Muslim Riot in Jessore–Khulna', *Economic and Political Weekly*, vol. 25, 46, 17 November 1990.

[46] Report of the Commissioner, Presidency Division, LOFCR for the first fortnight in April 1936. GB HCPB File No. 56/36.

[47] GB HCPB File No. 248/38.

[48] Sekhar Bandopadhyay, 'Community Formation and Communal Conflict', p. 2563.

[49] For a discussion of the respective social followings of Vaisnavism and Saivism in Bengal, see Barbara Southard, 'The Political Strategy of Aurobindo Ghosh', pp. 353–376.

In the late forties, more and more frequently, Namasudras and other low-caste and tribal groups fought communal battles over their 'religious' rights as 'Hindus'. The incident at Mithapur market was one such instance, where the Namasudras who marched past a mosque were noisily proclaiming their caste's new 'Hindu' identity. In another similar incident at Jalashi in the Narail subdivision of Jessore, 'tension arose between Namasudras and Muslims ... over the removal of the image of goddess 'Kali' by some unknown persons'.[50] In the same period, low castes played an increasingly visible role in communal riots. At Kulti in Burdwan Division, when a Hindu Mahabir Jhanda procession was prevented from passing a mosque by a Muslim crowd, the four who were shot dead by the police in the violence that ensued[51] all belonged to the Scheduled Castes.[52] The Dacca disturbances in 1941 were marked by 'violent clashes' in Khulna between Namasudras and Muslims in which 'the number of casualties [were] believed to be considerable. One Namasudra Hindu village and one Moslem village [were] burnt to the ground'.[53] In Dacca town itself, Goalas formed a visible contingent among the Hindu rioters.[54] Five years later, when Noakhali experienced one of the worst carnages in Bengal's bloody history of communal conflict, many of the victims were Namasudras, including 'one hundred and one poor Namasudra families of Chandipur, Police Station Ramgonj'.[55] The Santals of Midnapore were much in evidence in the partition riots. Describing his experience as District Magistrate in 1947, S. Rahmatullah recalls:

Trouble makers came down from Calcutta to incite local Hindus ... who were moneyed people and owned trucks in large numbers. They hired the militant Santhals who fired their arrows with tips carrying flames of fire at the huts of Muslims and roasted them alive ... [I faced] a mob of Santhals armed with big bows, arrows and spears, beating drums, performing the war-dance and shouting war-cries ... On a few occasions when, travelling by jeep or car, we noticed Santhals sending up lighted arrows to set fire to the house[s] of Muslim villages alongside the road to Kharagpur, I had no option but to bring the Santhals down with my personal 315 Mauser magnum.[56]

[50] Report of the Commissioner, Presidency Division, LOFCR for the second fortnight in May 1945. GB HCPB File No. 37/45.
[51] Herbert to Linlithgow, 8 October 1940, FR. Linlithgow Collection, IOLR MSS Eur F/125/40.
[52] The names of the deceased were entered as Samar Mahato, Anmal Tewari, Mohan Chamar and Kheali Koiri. GB SB 'PH' Series, File No. 543/44.
[53] Herbert to Linlithgow, telegram dated 20 March 1941. GOI Home Political File No. 5/25/41.
[54] Suranjan Das, 'Communal Riots in Bengal', pp. 286–288.
[55] Memorandum submitted by the Servants of Bengal Society to Dr S.P. Mookerjee. Shyama Prasad Mookerjee Papers, II–IV Instalments, File No. 82/1947, NMML.
[56] S. Rahmatullah Memoirs, IOLR MSS Eur F/128/14 (a).

By the mid-forties low castes and tribals were deployed in the vanguard of Hindu militancy.[57] The rhetoric of shuddi and sanghatan appears to have exerted a particularly powerful appeal on low castes and tribes such as the Namasudras of the east and the Rajbangshis and Santals of the north who had, of their own accord, been demanding for several decades that they be given a higher ritual status. The enfranchised minority, predominantly prosperous Namasudras and Rajbangshis, demonstrated their new willingness to identify themselves with the larger 'Hindu community' and with bhadralok political interests in the Assembly elections of 1946, when the Bengal Congress won overwhelmingly in all but three of the thirty Scheduled Caste seats, a striking improvement on its performance in 1936.[58] The poor, like Jitu Santal, increasingly took up arms on behalf of the 'Hindu community' which had given them membership. And all too often, like Jitu, they headed the lists of casualties. This is one extremely significant shift in the pattern of communal violence that has been overlooked in existing studies on Bengal, preoccupied as they have been with Muslim communalism.[59]

Power, precedence and communal conflict

Studies of communal violence in Bengal have tended to focus their attention on riots that occurred in the Muslim-majority, predominantly rural, areas of the eastern districts.[60] Yet one interesting feature of this

[57] The ways in which low-caste and tribal groups themselves interpreted and articulated the processes of their 'Hinduisation' are not clear from the evidence at hand (except, perhaps in the case of Jitu Santal), but form an interesting subject for further research.

[58] It is interesting that Bengal's Scheduled Caste voters, like their caste Hindu counterparts, showed little inclination to support the Hindu Mahasabha in the elections, and voted solidly for the Congress. The Mahasabha certainly had a higher profile in the caste consolidation campaign, though many of the leaders of the *shuddhi* movement had links with both organisations. For details, see Sekhar Bandopadhyay, *Caste, Politics and the Raj*, pp. 158–159. Yet the three non-Congress seats went to popular local leaders who had no known association with the Mahasabha. 'Franchise, Elections in Bengal, 1946'. IOLR L/P and J/8/475.

[59] Suranjan Das has, for instance, deliberately 'left out' an examination of riots between Namasudras and Muslims from his otherwise comprehensive survey of the major riots in Bengal in this period, because evidence of them is 'scanty'. *Communal Riots in Bengal*, p. 3.

[60] See, for instance, Sugata Bose, 'The Kishoreganj Riots'; Tajul-Islam Hashmi, 'The communalisation of the East Bengal peasantry, 1923–29', pp. 171–204; Tanika Sarkar, 'Communal Riots in Bengal'; and Partha Chatterjee, 'Agrarian Relations and Communalism in Bengal. Suranjan Das' more recent study examines communal conflict in Mymensingh, Patuakhali, Ponabalia, Dacca and Noakhali, all in East Bengal, including only Calcutta from the western districts. A glance at the first map in the book showing the 'districts principally affected by communal riots' clearly indicates the geographical/communal emphasis of the study. Suranjan Das, *Communal Riots in Bengal*.

period was the rising incidence of conflict in areas of Hindu bhadralok predominance, both in West Bengal and in the towns and cities of the north and the east where Hindu minorities held sway. Many of these localities experienced trouble between Hindus and Muslims for the first time in the 1930s and 1940s. An examination of shifting patterns of politics reveals the linkages between changes in the social and political balance of power and the rise of communal conflict in these localities.

After the Communal Award, a new urgency characterised bhadralok interest in local affairs and there was much jockeying for control over local bodies. The communal provisions of the 1935 Act did not apply to the districts and localities, where elections to local institutions – Local and District Boards, School Boards and Committees – continued to be held on the basis of joint electorates without the reservation of seats. Only a handful of seats were held by government nominees on District Boards and Municipal Committees. Local politics more accurately reflected social relations on the ground and were more sensitive to the changes in these relations. The electorate for local elections, perhaps 15 per cent of the adult population, was not defined by community but by wealth and education. Men who paid a minimum of one rupee in Cess or chaukidari tax and those who held graduate degrees or their equivalent had the vote; they represented the most prosperous and best educated people of the district.[61] For bhadralok Hindus, denied an effective role in provincial politics by the provisions of the Communal Award, local and district institutions remained one area where they could continue to exercise influence.

Yet even here, bhadralok dominance was being challenged by rising Muslim groups. Gallagher has drawn attention to the growth, albeit gradual, of Muslim representation in Local and District Boards in the Muslim-majority districts of East Bengal.[62] But he did not notice that there was also a marked growth of Muslim influence in institutions of local self-government in the western districts where Hindus were more numerous. This growing Muslim political influence in the localities derived from changes in the structure of mofussil society: the increasing wealth of a section of the Muslim peasantry and the emergence of a small but vocal Muslim middle class. As the better-off Muslim tenantry con-solidated their position on the land and as Hindu rentiers lost ground, the number and proportion of Muslim members in local bodies rose everywhere in the province. In Hindu-majority districts, Muslim repre-sentation often went well beyond what they might have achieved on a

[61] *Union Board Manual*, vol. I, Alipore, 1937. See, in particular, chapter II, section VII.
[62] J. A. Gallagher, 'Congress in Decline', pp. 601–607.

proportional basis.[63] It grew, however, at the expense of established Hindu bhadralok power.

This trend grew more marked after the coming of provincial autonomy, when measures taken by the Fazlul Huq ministry gave local bodies greater powers. Deploying the Bengal Agricultural Debtors Act of 1935, the Ministry set up three thousand and more Debt Settlement Boards in the localities,[64] which were to be controlled by existing local bodies. At a time when credit was short and debts were being repudiated, these Boards had enough power to make it worthwhile for creditors to combine to capture them through Union and Local Boards and so to ensure settlements in their favour. Touring Dinajpur in 1939, Bell observed that:

Union Board elections were now being fiercely contested, and at some ... recently, police had to be posted. The reason was that the Government was putting still more work upon Union Boards, or using them still more as agents of Government policy ... Debt Settlement Boards were frequently chosen from among Union Board members and the Debt Boards had great power. So people were realizing that if they wanted to get anything done, they should get control of the Union Board. A fiercely contested Union Board election might really be a struggle to get hold of the Debt Board.[65]

Union and Debt Settlement Boards became another field where zamindars and moneylenders did battle with their debtors, particularly with powerful jotedars. Where Boards fell into the hands of jotedars, zamindars and moneylenders knew that delays and obstructions would follow, which would encourage, in turn, the spreading 'non-payment mentality'. This was particularly evident in the northern districts such as Rajshahi, where jotedar influence was strongest, and where 'most of the members of Union Boards and Debt Settlement Boards belong[ed] to the jotedar (rent paying) class.' In these districts, Bell observed, 'the bias of members of Boards against landlordism ... makes them prone to delay disposals and to exaggerate inability to pay and induce persons who could pay to resort to the Boards ... The effect on collections has been disastrous'.[66]

Even wealthy and well-connected individuals found that when the decision of the Board went against them, they had little redress. Meeting

[63] See, in particular, the figures for Muslim membership of Local Boards in Howrah, Birbhum, Bankura, Midnapore, Hooghly and the 24 Parganas in Appendix G of *Resolutions Reviewing the Reports on the Working of District, Local and Union Boards in Bengal During the Year 1930–31 to 1936–37*. Alipore, 1931–37.
[64] Azizul Haque, *The Man Behind the Plough*, p. 169.
[65] F. O. Bell, 'Notes on Rural Travels in Dinajpur, 1939', p. 68. F. O. Bell Papers, IOLR MSS Eur D/733/2. Bell's tour diaries contain a wealth of detail on the working of Union Boards in Dinajpur district.
[66] 'Agrarian situation in the Balurghat Sub-Division', a note by A. J. Dash, Commissioner of Rajshahi, GB HCPB File No. 191/39.

the Commissioner in Balurghat, 'a prominent Congressman ... who had sunk all his life's savings in the Balurghat Banks and had probably lost them' sourly remarked that 'there is no need to worry about communist propaganda [because] the Government have brought about Communism themselves by their administration of the Bengal Agricultural Debtors Act'.[67] Where big money was at stake, capturing local bodies became a matter of vital concern to debtors and creditors alike and to the parties that represented them. Provincial leaders and parties now began to take an active interest in the composition even of the smallest local bodies. The Commissioner of the Chittagong Division noted with some annoyance that in Feni, 'local Members [of the Legislative Assembly] are demanding that all nominations to Union Boards should go to their own adherents ... [and] interfere in the case of Boards of which they have no local or personal knowledge'.[68] Many influential bhadralok Hindus had supported the Congress campaign against Union Boards, and had previously remained aloof from Union Board politics as a gesture of nationalist defiance. But now they began to take a keen interest in local elections. Without further ado the Bengal Congress dropped its anti-Union Board agitation. District Congress committees began to take an active part in local and municipal affairs. By December 1937, the Congress had begun to play an important role in local contests. In Hooghly, it was observed that 'the Congress party ... is active in the ... district particularly in connection with the forthcoming elections in the Serampore Municipality'[69] and in Dacca, local Congress workers made a determined attempt to capture the Municipality during the municipal elections that month.[70] Even the humblest Union Board elections were now taken seriously by the party: in Howrah, 'the Congress ... started two Election Committees to run candidates for the ... Union board elections' in the Uluberia and Sadar sub-divisions.[71] In Rajshahi, it put up candidates for several Local and Union Boards.[72] Even in Midnapore, which had been at the centre of its agitation against Union Boards, the Congress now enthusiastically joined the fray. In May 1937 the Raja of Narajole led the District Congress Committee to establish a 'Midnapore Local Bodies Election Sub-Committee' whose objective was 'to run candidates for the newly

---

[67] *Ibid.*
[68] Report of the Commissioner, Chittagong Division, LOFCR for the second fortnight of October 1937. *Ibid.*
[69] Report of the Commissioner, Burdwan Division, LOFCR for the first fortnight of December 1937. *Ibid.*
[70] Report of the Commissioner, Dacca Division. *Ibid.*
[71] *Ibid.*
[72] Report of the Commissioner, Rajshahi Division, LOFCR for the second fortnight of December 1937. *Ibid.*

formed Union Boards and control those already formed'. In the view of the District Magistrate, 'the reason probably is that [C]ongress now realise that by capturing Union Boards they capture a valuable weapon in rural politics'.[73]

As the competition for the control of local bodies became fierce, so the tension between communities grew more acute. In some cases, there was friction when the old guard in Muslim-dominated areas reacted against the new interest Hindus were showing in local bodies. In December 1937, 'voting in the Union Board [election]' in Tippera 'tended to go on communal lines. In Chandpur, Maulvis from Noakhali preached in mosques and elsewhere against voting for Hindus'.[74] A riot broke out in June 1937 at Betagiri in Mymensingh when local Hindus made a bid to enter the Union Board. According to the District Magistrate:

In the past Hindus of this village acting on the advice of their Congress friends took little interest in Union Boards, but when they found the value of it they attempted to get selected in the recent elections and succeeded in securing two seats. ... The Mahomedans are determined to prevent the Hindus [from] getting a majority. Any Mahomedan supporting a Hindu is threatened with ex-communication. There was a case of rioting between Mahomedans because one of them supported a Hindu.[75]

More often, however, trouble broke out in Hindu bhadralok strongholds, where Hindu parties were unable to check the growing influence of Muslims. In Howrah, for instance, despite the efforts of two election committees, the Congress campaign in 1937 to capture local bodies 'ended in failure',[76] and instead, the share of seats held by Muslims in Uluberia rose from 16.6 to 25 per cent in one year.[77] In the Midnapore Union Board elections, the Congress secured a majority only in thirty-nine out of a total of ninety-eight unions.[78] This trend grew sharper in the late thirties and early forties, when the Huq government introduced legislation which gave it control over nominated seats in the local bodies (one third of the total), a measure which inevitably led to a rise in the

[73] Report of the District Magistrate of Midnapore, LOFCR for the first fortnight of May 1937, GB HCPB File No. 10/37.
[74] Report of the Commissioner, Chittagong Division, LOFCR for the second fortnight of December 1937. *Ibid.*
[75] Report of District Magistrate of Mymensingh, enclosed in the report of the Commissioner, Dacca Division, LOFCR for the first fortnight of June 1937. *Ibid.*
[76] Report of the Commissioner, Burdwan Division, LOFCR for the second fortnight in December 1937. *Ibid.*
[77] Calculated from figures for Muslim representation in Local Boards in Appendix G of *Resolutions Reviewing the Reports on the Working of District, Local and Union Boards in Bengal*, for the years 1934–35 and 1936–37.
[78] Report of the Commissioner, Burdwan Division, LOFCR for the second fortnight in June 1937, GB HCPB File No. 10/37.

number of seats held by Muslims backed by the government. This caused bitter resentment amongst the local Hindu bhadralok. For instance, in the northern district of Rajshahi, where Muslims were more than three-quarters of the population but where, as in many parts of the province, Hindu influence was disproportionately strong, it was reported that

Hindus are in fact labouring under a sense of grievance ... [because] as a result of elections and long delayed nominations to the Rajshahi District Board, the Chairmanship, so long held for several years by Hindu zemindars, will pass into the hands of a fairly obscure Muslim pleader who is in support of the Government in the Assembly. When it is borne in mind that Rajshahi is a district where Muslims form the great majority of the population, while Hindus as zemindars and small taluqdars hold nearly all the property and have hitherto had a virtual monopoly of culture and influence, it is not unnatural that the threatened invasion of their preserve should give rise to deep ... resentment.[79]

The combined efforts of the Congress and the Mahasabha were not enough to keep local bodies under Hindu control in the early forties, particularly when the Ministry intervened by nominating Muslims to them. The Government's nominations could, and indeed frequently did, tilt the balance in favour of Muslims. Putting forward the claims for membership of a 'Hindu gentleman who is eminently suitable and is a champion of Hindu interests in the locality' for the Burrah Union Board in Nawabganj thana, a local Mahasabha man warned that 'if these nominations are interfered with by the Ministry in any way, a Muhammadan is bound to be elected President. Already most of the Union Board Presidents under Nawabganj P[olice]. S[tation]. are Mohammedans'.[80] This was happening in a district where Hindus were a majority of the population and the Mahasabha found to its dismay that it could

entertain little hope of justice from the League Ministry, who appear bent upon capturing the municipalities, even where the Hindus are in a large majority, as it has already done [in] the District and Union Boards. Even though in municipalities, the number of Hindu Commissioners may be greater than the elected Moslem Commissioners, yet nomination on communal lines by the League [can] always turn the scales in favour of the Muslims.[81]

In some Muslim-majority areas, Hindus were completely driven out of local bodies. A Mahasabha member from Bakarganj, a district where the bhadralok were strong, complained that 'very often no Hindus can get

[79] Reid to Linlithgow, 20 August 1939, FR. Robert Reid Papers, IOLR MSS Eur E/278/5.
[80] Intercepted letter from Niranjan Sarkar to N. C. Chatterjee, dated 20 April 1942. GB SB 'PH' Series, File No. 523/40.
[81] Sarat Chandra Guha to Shyama Prasad Mookerjee. 5 December 1944. Shyama Prasad Mookerjee Papers, II–IV Instalment, File No. 90/1944–45.

elected on account of Mahommedan majority who vote on communal lines' as the League Government's system of nomination was 'a hotbed of corruption and jobbery'.[82] A month later, the same correspondent informed Shyama Prasad Mookerjee that in Barisal 'the post of Chairman has been filled by a Hindu since the establishment of this town and this is now going to slip out of Hindu hands'.[83]

The changing composition of local bodies – Union, Local and District Boards and municipalities – reflected a significant shift in the balance of power between Hindus and Muslims. When groups that had previously been entrenched in power lost their control over these bodies, they were deeply resentful and it was usually the Hindu bhadralok who lost. The result, all too often, was communal conflict, sometimes violent. In Malda, for instance, the District Board election in 1941 was marred by fisticuffs when a group alleging 'communal bias' on the part of the presiding officer 'broke up the recording of votes by violence at the polling centre'.[84] In the same election there was 'rowdiness' at polling centres all over the Rajshahi Division. Union Board elections held that month in Rangpur district were reported as 'giving rise to an intensification of local communal ill feeling'.[85] Rangpur was a Muslim-majority district where the Muslim share of seats in local bodies had risen steadily during this period:[86] typical of a trend which fuelled communal bitterness in the localities of Bengal.

The same pattern was emerging in School Boards which in the past had been the preserve of the bhadralok. The loss of control over educational institutions was particularly intolerable for bhadralok Hindus since they saw themselves as the guardians of Bengal's intellectual and cultural heritage. Early in 1943, the Commissioner of Chittagong reported

local tension at Chaumuhani where the Begumganj H[igher]. E[nglish]. School, which was founded and largely financed by local Hindus, has been captured by Muslims with the result that the Hindus have started a rival H.E. School for Hindus ... The only danger is that either community may decide to burn down the school of the other.[87]

---

[82] *Ibid.*   [83] Sarat Chandra Guha to Shyama Prasad Mookerjee, 10 January 1945. *Ibid.*
[84] Report of the Commissioner, Rajshahi Division, LOFCR for the first fortnight in November 1941. GB HCPB File No. 13/41.
[85] *Ibid.*
[86] The percentage of seats held by Muslims on local boards in Rangpur district rose from 51.8 to 64.8 in the ten years between 1926–27 and 1936–37, and in the Kurigram subdivision, Muslims held 75 per cent of all seats in 1937. Calculated from Appendix G of *Resolutions Reviewing the Reports on the Working of District, Local and Union Boards in Bengal During the Year 1926–27 and 1936–37*. Alipore, 1927 and 1937.
[87] Report of the Commissioner, Chittagong Division, LOFCR for the second fortnight of January 1943, GB HCPB File No. 39/43.

Later that year, Hindus in Chittagong repeatedly complained of 'punitive transfers of District School Board officials'.[88] Even in Dacca, traditionally a bhadralok stronghold, Hindus could do little to prevent control over municipalities and schools from slipping out of their hands. At best, they were able to express their frustration in petty gestures of defiance. One Hindu merchant 'brought a case against almost all Government servants in the locality, who are presumably Moslem', and in another incident 'in a local H.E. School Committee election, the Hindus were in a minority and walked out, so all seats went to their opponents'.[89]

Control over school committees was a particularly emotive issue for Hindus at the time of Saraswati Puja, the yearly religious festival to the goddess of learning that was a peculiarly bhadralok tradition. School committees which were no longer under Hindu control were inclined to support Muslim teachers and students when they challenged the established custom of holding Saraswati Puja ceremonies in school compounds. This also led to friction between the communities, as demonstrated by an incident in Rajshahi district where

the Muslim students of K.D.H.E. School at Naogaon ... having objected to the performance this year of the Saraswati Puja which had been performed for sixty years at the school premises, it was resolved by the School Committee that no religious ceremonies should henceforth be allowed in the school premises ... This has frequently led to ill-feeling between the two communities.[90]

In Dacca, Muslim students threatened to perform *korbani* (cow sacrifice) in a school compound in retaliation against the performance of the Puja in a local school where it had regularly been performed in the past. 'Muhammedan students of the Teachers Training College'

objected to the celebration of the festival in the grounds of the attached school, and they issued an absurdly unreasonable threat that if the festival was celebrated there (as it had been done in the past) they would do 'Korbani' ... a screen was erected across the grounds of the school [during the ceremony] and there was no disturbance. There is, however, a possibility that a demand will be made for ... permission to do 'Korbani' on the occasion of the next Bakr-Id.[91]

Festivals were a benchmark against which the changes in the local balance of power between competing communal groups could be measured. Just as Muslim-controlled school committees refused to allow

88 Report of the Commissioner, Chittagong Division, LOFCR for the first fortnight of June 1943. *Ibid.*
89 Report of the Commissioner, Dacca Division, LOFCR for the second fortnight in May 1945. GB HCPB File No. 37/45.
90 Report of the Commissioner, Rajshahi Division, LOFCR for the second fortnight in January 1945. *Ibid.*
91 Report of the Commissioner, Dacca Division, LOFCR for the first fortnight in February 1941. GB HCPB File No. 13/41.

the performance of Saraswati Puja ceremonies in school compounds, so municipalities could refuse to sanction procession routes or could appropriate (for 'civic purposes') public spaces where festivals of particular communities were traditionally held. Thus in Kandi in Murshidabad

There has been some bad feeling ... regarding the decision of the Municipal Commissioners to acquire, ostensibly for a public street, that part of a house recently purchased by a Moslem Sub Registrar in which Thakur Rudradeb of the Jemo Babus used to rest during the ... procession: the real object is to prevent a Moslem from controlling a place where a deity used to rest and some Moslems resent this.[92]

This was an interesting case, where civic powers were used by Hindu Municipal Commissioners to re-capture 'sacred space'[93] which had passed, by secular processes, into Muslim hands. In another incident with similar overtones, again in Murshidabad,

the Chelam procession at Jangipore was not taken out owing to obstruction by the overhanging branches of a tree on a municipal road. The tree has objects of Hindu worship at its foot. ... there is now a certain amount of tension because the Chairman of the Jangipore Municipality has not taken any action on the letters of the Subdivisional Officer asking him to remove the obstructing branches.[94]

This particular dispute remained a cause of friction for several months, as both sides dug in their heels and refused to budge from their positions. Hindus rallied round the chairman of the municipality and would not allow the branches of the sacred *peepul* tree to be trimmed to enable the Muslim procession to pass under it, and the Muslims refused to go by a different route.[95] The dispute spilled over to other festivals and processions; as each community refused to allow the other to conduct its festivals in the customary way, sporadic incidents of violence broke out in the town.

In incidents such as these, where municipal authorities intervened to protect public places and objects that were sacred to their 'community', the performance (or non-performance) of festivals registered the local distribution of power between the two rival communities in a way

[92] Report of the Commissioner, Presidency Division, LOFCR for the second fortnight in March 1942. GB HCPB File No. 31/42.
[93] The concepts of 'sacred space' and 'sacred time' have been developed by Anand Yang and Sandria Frietag in their discussion of communal riots. See Anand A. Yang, 'Sacred Symbol and Sacred Space', pp. 576–596, Sandria B. Frietag, *Collective Action and Community. Public Arenas and the Emergence of Communalism in North India*, Berkeley, Los Angeles and Oxford, 1989, pp. 131–147.
[94] Report of the Commissioner, Presidency Division, LOFCR for the second fortnight in February 1945, GB HCPB File No. 37/45.
[95] See the reports of the Commissioner, Presidency Division, LOFCRs for the second fortnight in April and for the first fortnight in September 1945, GB HCPB File No. 37/45.

everyone could see. But even in cases where local politics did not impinge directly on the performance of religious rites, festivals were a way of gauging changes in the balance of power between different communities. Festivals were occasions for public display, not only of the strength and solidarity of the community concerned but also of the wealth it could command.[96] The economic power of the local Hindu community could, for instance, be measured by the lavish scale on which a particular festival was celebrated. Festivals were an expensive business: premises frequently had to be hired, *pandals* ('marquees') erected and decorated, idols and floats ordered from artisans, priestly services had to be rewarded and the whole community of worshippers had to be fed. Holding an annual puja thus involved the mobilisation of all the resources at the disposal of the community. In the countryside, a big zamindar might unaided shoulder the entire cost of a festival celebrated on his estate; in the towns, the burden was usually shared by the community as a whole. Urban bigwigs gave large donations for their own good reasons; their patronage won them religious merit and social recognition. Less well-to-do people gave smaller sums and the fund-raising by festival committees advertised not only the pecking order of donors within the community but also the wealth (and enthusiasm) of those who were active in mobilising the people.

Under the British, festivals also had come to have a relationship, albeit complex, with power and authority, because they were regulated on the principle of established 'precedence'. British policy on religious matters was dictated by the desire of the administrators not to interfere with 'traditional' religious practice. In effect, this meant that officials tried to establish what was 'customary' in the locality under their jurisdiction and conveniently assuming that the custom had been in place since time immemorial, elevated it to the status of traditional practice. In future, festivals had to follow what the officials deemed to be the established custom. Yet, in fact what was believed to be ancient 'custom' might have

---

[96] The role of festivals in integrating the multiplicity of identities within a religious group into an active and self-conscious 'community' has been underlined by various studies of community and communalism. Sandria Frietag, for instance, sees festivals as a 'metaphor' of community, and argues for their role in creating a sense of community through 'the juxtaposition of participants in a single location', the mobilisation of different client groups by a variety of patrons and the definition of 'sacred space'. Sandria B. Frietag, 'Religious Rites and Riots', pp. 88–89. Victor Turner has similarly argued for the role of festivals in creating the spirit of 'communitas', making those experiencing it think of themselves as a homogenous, unstructured and free community. Victor Turner, *Dramas, Fields and Metaphors*. Both these analyses, however, tend to concentrate on the significance of festivals within rather than between communities, underlining the dynamics of intra-communal integration rather than inter-communal conflict. Here, we will look instead at the role of the festival as an idiom of community power and rivalry.

been a recent innovation, reflecting some fortuitous compromise reached at a particular time between rival groups in local society. For example, the rules governing the passage of a Hindu procession by a mosque during prayer time was likely to simply reflect the balance of power between Hindus and Muslims at the time when the rules were made, and needed to be renegotiated when the structure of local power changed significantly.

Yet colonial administration was not designed to respond to such nuances. It codified the contingent as customary and gave permanence to temporary arrangements which merely reflected a status quo which was impermanent. But when the status quo was upset, if Muslims decided to build a new mosque or if Hindus decided to have a new procession, or an old procession along a new route, the system broke down.[97] Then, administrative decisions tended to be made by rule of thumb that placed the onus on those who wanted change either to establish factitious precedents or to persuade the authorities that their demand had merit. To get a licence, community bosses had to bring influence to bear upon the local magistrate or officer. Having charge over Local and Union Boards undoubtedly helped matters. This meant that even the most trivial change in religious practices entailed deep questions about who controlled the local power structures and brought with it noisy airings of public opinion and highly charged debates. The same was true of the apparently insignificant matter of the routes which processions took, which increasingly became a focus of dispute. Decisions by a community to hold a new procession, to build a new temple or a new mosque or to increase the number of cows that were sacrificed, were interpreted as symbolic public assertions of their authority and standing. The attempt to create new precedents for the conduct of festivals often lay at the roots of communal conflict in the localities during this period.

Conflicts of this sort were particularly evident in localities where Hindu groups had once been dominant, but now found that dominance being eroded. Burdwan, in the heart of West Bengal, was one such area. Described in the past as a 'stronghold of Hinduism', Burdwan was one of the last bastions of the Hindu bhadralok in the province. With much of its territory under the zamindari of the Maharajas of Burdwan, the district was the epitome of the bhadralok order which the Permanent Settlement had introduced.[98] Writing about bhadralok society in Burdwan town in the late twenties, Asok Mitra recalls that

[97] Some of the effects of the colonial administration of religion have been discussed in Katherine H. Prior, 'The British Administration of Hinduism in North India, 1780–1900', University of Cambridge, Ph.D. dissertation, 1990.

[98] Over 80 per cent of Burdwan's population consisted of Hindus, of which Burdwan's Rarhi Brahmins formed the third largest Hindu caste in 1910. Only 58.9 per cent of the

residents of Burdwan did not as a rule think as they would now of taking the money they earned in Burdwan to Calcutta and build and settle there. They believed in building in Burdwan and continuing to earn and invest there. In short, they expected to draw about as much satisfaction from the social, cultural and civic milieu of Burdwan as from Calcutta. The city was pretty proud of its wealth, enterprise and culture.[99]

The sense of security and self-congratulation which characterised the bhadralok of Burdwan was shaken in the following decade, when middle-class Muslims began to play a prominent part in Burdwan's public life. Muslim membership of local bodies grew, rising in the Katwa subdivision from approximately 28 to about 40 per cent between 1930–31 and 1936–37.[100] The Huq government's policy of filling the nominated seats on local bodies with its own supporters gave Muslims a powerful voice in municipal politics and upset the 'civic milieu' of which Burdwan's Hindus were so proud.[101] Nor was the Burdwan countryside immune to the developments of the Depression decade. Even the Maharaja felt the pinch as zamindari collections fell sharply: in a single year, the rental income from one of his largest estates fell from 42 to 24 per cent.[102] The power and prosperity that Burdwan's Hindu elites had long enjoyed suffered a serious setback in these years.

In the thirties, Burdwan, a district mercifully free of communal friction, began to show signs of tension. In Burdwan, the cause of communal conflict was invariably the result of one or other community attempting to establish new precedents in the celebration of festivals. The first such incident took place in February 1935, when Muslims of Deara town in Kalna subdivision celebrated Bakr-Id by sacrificing a cow. Korbani had never been performed in Deara before and the incident outraged Kalna's

district's population depended on agriculture for its livelihood in the same year. J. C. K. Peterson, *Burdwan District Gazetteer*, Alipore, 1910.
[99] Asok Mitra, *Three Score and Ten*, vol. I, *The First Score and Three*, Calcutta, 1987, p. 42.
[100] Calculated from *Resolutions Reviewing the Reports on the Working of District and Local Boards in Bengal*, for the appropriate years.
[101] Abul Hashim, in his memoirs, describes the growing influence of Muslims in Burdwan town and the refusal of local Hindus to accept it with grace. He recalls, for instance, the District Board election of 1941, when 'amongst the elected members of the [District] Board, the Congress Party was in a minority ... five Muslim League members held the balance'. Following protracted negotiations, the two parties agreed to elect a Hindu Chairman and a Muslim Vice-Chairman. But when the voting took place, 'the Hindu members of the Board expressed their unwillingness to vote for Maulvi Abul Hayat', despite the fact that he was a Congressman. Later that year, the local Muslim League was able to ensure the election of its candidate to the post of Chairman of the Burdwan Municipality. Abul Hashim, *In Retrospection*, Dhaka, 1974, pp. 24–26.
[102] Report of the Meeting of Local Officers on the No-Rent Campaign, GB HCPB File No. 283 /1938.

Hindus, who saw it as an act of provocation by the Muslim community.[103]
The performance of korbani by a minority community reflected not only
its prosperity but also indicated a new sense of confidence on its part.[104] It
was also undoubtedly designed as an aggressive show of strength, perhaps
inspired by pamphlets such as Ain-al-Islam's *Goru O Hindu-Mussalman*
('The Cow, Hindus and Muslims') which argued that cow-slaughter was
an essential religious duty and urged Muslims not to stop sacrificing cows
until Hindus gave up worshipping idols.[105] The incident led to much
tension throughout the district. Hindus in Burdwan town retaliated by
attempting forcibly to prevent Muslims from sacrificing a cow. This,
again, was a breach of local 'custom', since Burdwan Muslims traditionally performed korbani every year at Bakr-Id. In the event, a violent
clash was averted.[106] But bad feeling between the communities continued
to simmer, and the following year, the Kalna municipality split up into
two camps, as Muslim commissioners refused to take their seats on the
Municipal Board on which Hindus were a majority.[107] In 1937, relations
between the communities deteriorated rapidly when the League–Krishak
Praja Ministry took office. The Hindus of Burdwan reacted particularly
strongly against being placed under a 'Muslim Raj'. The District Magistrate predicted that

The way a group of people, specially in Kalna town, are vehemently protesting
against the present Ministry in Bengal ... will give rise to communal tension as
there is no denying the fact that the Mussalmans have complete confidence in the
Ministry and look upon attempts of a section of Hindus to denounce the Ministers
as inspired by malice.[108]

He was proved right the following year when riots broke out in the town
of Burdwan over the question of playing music before mosques during an
immersion ceremony at Durga Puja. The procession that led to the
trouble was organised by the '*Sarbajanin*' ('caste consolidation') groups.
Here again, it was precedence that caused the row: 'The Sarbajanin Durga
Puja was introduced in Burdwan town this year for the first time, by

---

103 GB HCPB File No. 143/35.
104 According to Koranic injunction, the choice of animal to be sacrificed – whether a
    camel, a cow or a goat, etc. – depended upon the wealth of the family or community
    concerned. Only the relatively wealthy were obliged to sacrifice a cow on the occasion of
    Bakr-Id.
105 Ain-al-Islam Khondkar, *Goru O Hindu–Mussalman* ('The Cow, Hindus and Muslims'),
    IOLR PP BEN D 6; PIB 53/1.
106 GB HCPB File No. 143/35.
107 Report of the Commissioner, Burdwan Division, LOFCR for the second fortnight in
    June 1936, GB HCPB File No. 56/36.
108 Report of the Commissioner, Burdwan Division, LOFCR for the first fortnight in
    August 1937, GB HCPB File No. 10/37.

following the practice of Calcutta ... It was organised by leading Hindus of the town, belonging to almost all shades of opinion'.[109] Caste consolidation campaigns, as has been seen, had strong communal overtones: and the fact that the new puja should have been organised by the Sarbajanin party was undoubtedly doubly provocative to Burdwan's Muslims. That evening at 8.40 pm, the procession arrived at the mosque area of Burra Bazar playing pipes and drums. Muslims at prayer inside the mosque were enraged and the two sides came to blows. The news spread rapidly to the Berikhana mosque, where a crowd of Muslims armed with sticks collected and refused to allow the idol to pass. After a heated argument, in which Muslims insisted that music must not be played in front of the mosque at any time, the Hindu processionists abandoned the idol on the roadside and went off in high dudgeon. After the local magistrate intervened, the Muslims eventually agreed to allow music outside the mosque after 10 pm and the procession went on its much-delayed way, late into the night.[110]

The Sarbajanin puja affair was an indication of new spirit of confrontation on both sides of the communal divide. Hindus and Muslims alike attempted to use the Durga Puja celebrations to establish new precedents in public worship. As the magistrate's report revealed, until that year processions with music had been allowed to pass the Burra Bazar mosque after 8.30 or 9.00 pm: yet on this occasion Muslims reacted to what they regarded as Hindu provocation by trying to enlarge their claims of 'sacred time', first refusing to permit music at any time and then agreeing to allow it only after 10 pm. In the whole affair, Burdwan's Muslim minority displayed new confidence and an unwonted readiness to take up the challenge of Hindu provocation. The Hindu procession, for its part, was intended to show off the newly discovered unity of all castes of the 'Hindu community'. By playing loud music in front of a mosque, Burdwan's Hindus intended, no doubt, to prove to all who could see and hear that they were still masters in their own house. But they were forced to back down by lathi-wielding Muslim mobs in a town they had long regarded as their bailiwick. Here was a clear case of the balance of power shifting in favour of Muslims, who, by forcing upon their rivals a further limitation of the hours during which music could be played before mosques, were able to stake out new and larger symbolic territories and claim them for their own.

Not surprisingly, a similar conflict broke out the following year at Kali Puja, which coincided with the Muslim celebration of Ramazan when 'there was considerable friction between the Hindu and Moslem public ... over the question of processions to be taken out by Hindus'. When it

[109] GB HCPB File No. 353/38.   [110] *Ibid*.

looked as if violence would result, the Chief Minister, Fazlul Huq, hurried to Burdwan to make terms with the Maharaja. It was agreed between them that the immersion of the goddess should be completed before 7 pm, so as not to disrupt Ramazan prayers.[111] Once again, Burdwan's Muslims had succeeded in cutting down the time allowed for Hindu celebrations. The following day, an editorial in the Hindu paper, *Dainik Basumati* protested against the role that the Chief Minister had played:

The Huq Government promptly took measures in regard to the sanctity of Ramzan prayers but they did not do so in matters relating to the religion of Hindus ... Does Mr Huq too think in the same way as the non-Hindu public that shouted jubilantly that Islamic rule had been established when the Huq ministry was constituted, that Islamic rule had really been established?[112]

The bugbear of 'Islamic rule' was well calculated to evoke an indignant reaction from the bhadralok, since this was one of the central themes of their communal ideology. For the Hindus of Burdwan, conscious that Muslims had become increasingly assertive under the protection of the Huq and Nazimuddin ministries, 'Muslim tyranny' was a chord resonating an ominously new meaning.

The same pattern was repeated in other Hindu-majority districts. In 1934, a major confrontation took place at Mollarchak in Kakwadip thana of the 24 Parganas. Lying close to the sprawling metropolis of Calcutta, the 24 Parganas shared with the capital city some of the characteristics of a bhadralok milieu. Like Burdwan, the 24 Parganas was a district more urban than others and it contained many educated Hindus.[113] But the hold of these educated Hindus over local politics was getting less secure every year. Indeed, Muslim membership of Local Boards rose faster in the 24 Parganas than it had done in Burdwan (see table 5). In two subdivisions, Basirhat and Baraset, there were many more Muslims on the boards than their population warranted.[114] By 1932, already Muslims had acheived parity on the Board of Baraset with Hindus who were a majority in the district.

In 1933, a fracas broke out at Behala, north of Calcutta, when 'a number of Hindus and Sikhs made a pre-arranged attack on a party of Muhammadans leading cattle to Shapore for sacrifice' on Bakr-Id.[115] In the fighting that followed, many persons were seriously injured. In 1934, another riot took place at Mollarchak near Kakwadip thana in the Diamond Harbour subdivision, when 'Muslims declared their intention

---

[111] GB HCPB File No. 3/39.   [112] *Dainik Basumati*, 12 November 1939.
[113] *Census of India*, 1931, vol. V, pp. 284–287.
[114] *Census of India*, 1931, vol. V, p. 389.   [115] GB HCPB File No. 117/34.

Table 5. *Muslim membership of Local Boards in the 24 Parganas: 1930–31 to 1936–37*

Local Board	Percentage of Muslim Members				
	1930–31	1931–32	1932–33	1934–35	1936–37
Sadar	25	25	30	30	30
Diamond Harbour	19	19	31.2	31.2	31.2
Baraset	40	40	50	50	50
Basirhat	33.3	33.3	41.6	41.6	46.6
Barrackpore	30	30	30	30	30

Source: Resolutions Reviewing the Reports on the Working of District, Local and Union Boards in Bengal, Alipore, 1931 to 1937.

to perform cow sacrifice ... and Hindus (in the majority) were determined to stop them'.[116] Once again, it was the issue of precedence that appears to have lit the fuse which exploded in a riot. In the view of the Commissioner, 'the trouble originated solely from religious sentiments, there having been no communal tension in the locality previous to this. The Hindus resented the idea of cow-sacrifice as an un-precedented act of sacrilege in a predominantly Hindu area and their zeal outran their discretion'.[117] A similar incident took place in the neighbouring district of Midnapore in 1935 when a minor scuffle broke out in Barhola thana in Kharagpur because local 'Hindu feelings [were] seriously injured by [a] new attempt of Mahomedans for cow korbani'.[118] Midnapore, like the 24 Parganas and Burdwan, was a Hindu-majority district and a stronghold of bhadralok politics.

The common pattern of events in these three districts suggests that at a time when bhadralok Hindu involvement in local politics was characterised by a new sense of urgency, the smallest change in the local balance of power could assume disproportionate significance. In the Hindu-majority districts in particular, bhadralok Hindus had hoped to compensate for their loss of provincial power with an increased voice in local affairs. But this had proved impossible, and instead, they found themselves losing ground to Muslims on all fronts. In these circumstances, Muslim attempts to establish new precedents in the conduct of festivals were particularly provocative. The vehemence of bhadralok resistance to the introduction of korbani for instance, was not so much a measure of religious outrage – it was an accepted practice in the town of

[116] GB HCPB File No. 117/34.   [117] GB HCPB File No. 370/38.
[118] GB HCPB File No. 143/35.

Burdwan and the Arya Samajist cow-protection movement had never been much of a crowd-puller in Bengal. It was rather a measure of their increasing political impotence. Korbani, when performed for the first time by a minority Muslim community, was a symbol both of its rising status and of its greater political influence. In the eyes of the Hindus, the performance of cow-sacrifice in localities which they traditionally domi-nated, represented a highly potent, if symbolic, challenge which they were determined to resist. During the Fazlul Huq and Nazimuddin ministries it became increasingly difficult to protect local bhadralok bastions from the interference of the 'Muslim' government in Calcutta. As a result, this determination hardened into a refusal to accept 'Muslim tyranny' in the province as a whole. It is not surprising, therefore, that it was in these three districts that the movement for the creation of a separate 'Hindu homeland' emerged most powerfully in 1947.

6   The second partition of Bengal, 1945–47

All-India imperatives and partition

The developments in Bengal with which this book has been mainly concerned were part of a larger canvas of all-India affairs which critically affected developments in Bengal and in their turn were affected by them. The all-India dimensions of this interplay have not been the focus of this study. Yet Bengal, in the last two years of British rule, cannot be studied in isolation from the dramatic changes which were taking place on the all-India stage. It is well known that the end of the Second World War and the coming to power of Attlee's Labour Government in July 1945 brought about a sea change in the policy of the British towards India. The first priority of the National Government under Churchill during the war had been to bring India effectively behind the war effort and to put the question of India's future into cold storage. Linlithgow's declaration of 8 August 1940 laid down as a precondition for constitutional advance that Hindus and Muslims must agree about the way forward; the failure of the Congress and the Muslim League to come to terms had justified the British in postponing consideration of the question of constitutional change until after the War. Cripps' mission in 1942 had been designed by his masters in London to be nothing more than a public relations exercise, which was not intended to succeed[1] and Wavell's dogged attempts to put back the constitutional question onto the metropolitan agenda also came to nothing.[2] But priorities changed when Attlee took office; the Simla Conference was rapidly followed by elections in India, the first since 1936–37, and by the arrival in India of the Cabinet Mission. It was no longer a question of whether the British would transfer power in India but how soon, to whom and on what terms.

[1] See R. J. Moore, *Churchill, Cripps and India, 1939–1945*, Oxford, 1979.
[2] For Wavell's own account of his efforts, see Penderel Moon (ed.), *Wavell: The Viceroy's Journal*, London, 1973.

Since the Lahore Resolution of 1940, the demand for Pakistan, unspecific though it was from start to finish, had proved to be extremely useful from the British point of view. After the war, however, the dangers that this ambiguous demand posed for British policy became increasingly evident. Jinnah and the League had been convenient allies while the British wanted to hold on to India; they became a serious embarrassment once the British decided to hand over power. London's priority was to find successors in India capable of defending British strategic and economic interests east of Suez. This pointed to keeping India united with a strong centre and an undivided army. Pakistan, princes and other divisive factors which had proved so convenient when it was a question of retaining power came, albeit slowly and confusedly, to be seen as obstacles once power was to be handed over. But the results of the elections of 1945–46, and the mandate given to the League by Muslim voters, made it impossible for London and Delhi to ignore Jinnah and the League in their negotiations at the centre about the transfer of power. For many reasons, London was anxious to transfer power as soon as possible.[3] Therefore, negotiations could no longer be drawn out according to the leisurely timetables of the past; and they had to exclude as far as possible those parties and interests which might delay a swift solution of the problem. This effectively meant a three-cornered negotiation, between plenipotentiaries speaking for the British, the Congress and the Muslim League. This had particularly important implications for Bengal. Previous chapters have shown how equivocal were the relations between the Bengal Congress and the all-India High Command. The rump of the Bengal Congress that had survived the power struggles of the late thirties had become very much the centre's poodle. The Muslim leaders in Bengal were also effectively shut out of the negotiations at the centre. Their poor record in the government of the province in the forties gave them little credit and less influence with Delhi.[4] And however important the Muslim-majority provinces were to Jinnah as a bargaining counter in his demand for parity for the League at the centre, his relations with Bengali Muslim

---

[3] These reasons have been dealt with in R. J. Moore, *Escape from Empire. The Attlee Government and the Indian Problem*, Oxford, 1982, and by the same author, in *Endgames of Empire. Studies of Britain's Indian Problem*, New Delhi, 1988. In a recent doctoral thesis, Indivar Kamtekar has analysed the imperatives that led to Independence and Partition from the perspective of the colonial state. Indivar Kamtekar, 'The End of the Colonial State in India, 1942–1947', University of Cambridge, Ph.D. dissertation, 1988.

[4] The vicissitudes of Bengali Muslim politics, the rise of the Muslim League and the fall of the Krishak Praja Party in these years, are in themselves a fascinating subject. But in view of the fact that these themes have been dealt with in some detail in several recent studies, they have not been touched upon in this book. See, for instance, Bazlur Rahman Khan, *Politics in Bengal*, and Harun-or-Rashid, *The Foreshadowing of Bangladesh*.

politicians were equivocal and as far as possible he kept his distance from them. It was simply not plausible to imagine that Jinnah would place Bengali Muslim interests and demands above his own plans and ambitions at the centre.

Nevertheless, provincial political pressures did play a part in shaping decisions that were taken at the all-India level. When the Congress High Command opted for Partition and settled for a truncated Pakistan, it did not ride roughshod over the Bengal Congress but rather had its strong support. Previous chapters have looked at the growing unwillingness of many Hindu Bengalis to countenance the idea of being permanently subjected to the rule of Muslim majority in what they regarded as their own province. Now, in late 1946 and early 1947, this reluctance hardened into a determination that Bengal must be divided and that Hindus must carve out for themselves a Hindu-majority province. This meant the creation of a new province out of the predominantly Hindu districts of western and northern Bengal in which Hindus would be the majority. Here was a determination clearly derived from the internal dynamics of Bengali Hindu politics; and yet its success, as will be seen, depended critically on the support of the Congress centre. It was this symbiotic relationship between provincial bhadralok politics and the priorities of the Congress High Command that shaped the partition of Bengal in 1947.

In 1937 when it took office in the provinces, the Congress High Command refused to accept the principle of coalition in the formation of ministries. Instead, taking a hegemonic view of its own role, the Congress insisted that in those provinces where it had won an absolute majority in the legislature it would form the ministry alone. Electoral allies who wished to share power would have to give up their separate party identity and merge with the Congress organisation. In the United Provinces, the Muslim League under Jinnah's leadership had won 27 seats against 134 which the Congress had won, but the Congress reneged on its electoral understanding and insisted that the provincial League, if it were to join it in office, should give up its separate organisation and become a part of the Congress. These terms were, not surprisingly, unacceptable to the Muslim League in the United Provinces and to Jinnah.[5] Similarly, in Muslim majority provinces, where the Congress had no chance of forming governments on its own, its provincial committees were forbidden to form coalitions with other local parties. This rule applied to Bengal, where the local Congress emerged as the largest single party in the Legislative Assembly,

---

[5] Ayesha Jalal, *Sole Spokesman* pp. 29–33. For a more detailed treatment of this theme, see Mukul Kesavan, *1937 as a Landmark in the Course of Communal Politics in the U. P.*

and although local leaders, notably Sarat Bose, pressed for the Congress to be allowed to form a coalition ministry with the Krishak Praja Party, they were rebuffed by the centre.[6] In the two-and-a-half years when Congress had held office in the provinces, Congress ministries faced problems which it avoided when it was in opposition and had bitter experience of how difficult it would be to please all the different interests that the party claimed to represent. Pressures for agrarian reform grew within the party and outside it and rival organisations emerged which questioned the party's claim to speak for the poorer and weaker sections of society. The Congress found its overarching claims to represent the people challenged by the emergence of the Kisan Sabha movement, by the growing number of labour organisations and by the parties of the left. In the forties, the party leadership reacted to pressure from the left by adopting a position that was more unequivocally on the right of the political spectrum than ever before. On the other hand, its claim to be the secular guardian of religious minorities was increasingly challenged by the Muslim League. On both counts, High Command responded by denying the legitimacy and sincerity of their opponents, and by questioning their commitment to nationalism. The arrogance of this response provoked the critics of the Congress to further extremes. The left, whether within the party or outside it, kept up an unrelenting attack on the claim of the leaders to speak for all classes, while Jinnah and the Muslim League became more and more uncompromising in their campaign against the Congress.

By the time it became clear that the British were minded to quit India, the claim of the Congress to be their rightful and sole successor had been challenged on all sides. In the general elections of 1945–46 the Congress did extremely well in the 'general' Hindu constituencies but it failed to substantiate its claims to represent the Muslims of India (see table 6). The Muslim League attracted 86.7 per cent of the total Muslim vote in the elections to the Central Assembly in contrast to the minuscule number of votes the Congress attracted, a mere 1.3 per cent. In the provinces, the League won 74.7 per cent of all Muslim votes while the Congress won only 4.67 per cent. In the last elections held in British India, both the Congress and the League markedly improved on their position in 1936. Both came to the negotiating table at which the end game was to be played determined to stick to their guns. Already at the first Simla Conference in 1945 Jinnah had insisted that he should be recognised as the

---

[6] Although, as we have seen, the BPCC negotiations with the KPP failed in 1937, some observers believe that Sarat Bose may have been able to pull off a reconciliation soon

Table 6. *All-India electoral results of the Congress and Muslim League: elections of 1945–46*

Province	Congress	Muslim League	Others	Total seats
N.W.F.P	30	17	3	50
Punjab	51	73	51	175
Sind	18	27	15	60
U.P.	154	54	21	228
Bihar	98	34	20	152
Orissa	47	4	9	60
Bengal	86	113	51	250
Madras	165	29	21	215
C.P.	92	13	71	12
Bombay	125	30	20	175
Assam	58	31	19	108

Source: N. N. Mitra (ed.), *Indian Annual Register*, 1946, vol. I, pp. 230–231.

'sole spokesman' of the Muslims, and that Muslims, as a separate nation, should be given parity of representation in any proposed federal government. The Congress, on the other hand, held on to its old position: its leaders insisted that they spoke for the nation as a whole including Muslims. As the Congress leadership turned to the question of the form that independent India would take, it was clear (as indeed it had been since the Nehru Report of 1928) that the Congress was committed to a strong and centralised unitary state. Leaders such as Vallabhbhai Patel had learnt from the experience of provincial autonomy and the growing rebelliousness of the provincial arms of the party that a strong centre was essential. Others with more left-wing leanings such as Jawaharlal Nehru came to the same conclusion; the economic crises of the thirties and forties underlined the need for the centre to have powers to plan and coordinate economic growth for the country as a whole. In 1946, when the Attlee Government sent the Cabinet Mission to India to negotiate a settlement between the two parties, the Congress president, Azad, informed the Mission that the

Federal Union must of necessity deal with certain essential subjects ... It must be organic and must have both executive and legislative machinery as well as the finance relating to these subjects and the power to raise revenues for these purposes in its own right. Without these functions it would be weak and disjointed

afterwards, if his hands had not been tied by the Working Committee. Author's interview with Amiya Bose, Calcutta, 4 March 1988.

... Thus among the common subjects in addition to foreign affairs, defence and communications, there should be currency, customs, tariffs and other such subjects as may be found on closer scrutiny to be intimately allied to them.[7]

This conviction grew stronger during the short but painful experience of a coalition with the League in the Interim Government which the Congress had in late 1946 and early 1947. The Interim Government was dominated by Congressmen: Jawaharlal Nehru and Sardar Patel were Prime Minister and Home Member respectively, but Liaqat Ali of the League was the Finance Member and by controlling the purse strings was able effectively to block the workings of government. Nehru complained that it had 'become impossible in the interest of good government and progress to have a Central Government which was divided and in which one group functioned as an opposition both in governmental activities ... and in the country'.[8] Patel, as Home Member, found it intolerable that

since the formation of the Interim Government, Lord Wavell had allowed such power to go to the Provinces that they could defy the Central Government, and by the introduction of the Muslim League members, against the advice of the Congress, had so weakened the centre that India was rapidly disintegrating into a lawless state.[9]

For Patel, the strong man of Congress, the need to impose law and order, control communal rioting and to stamp out labour unrest were powerful reasons why a strong centre was vital; he believed that 'those who commit acts of violence do so because they feel that there is no strong central power to check them'.[10] Vital concerns such as these encouraged the Congress High Command to look at Jinnah's demand for Pakistan in a new light. There had been a time when the idea of tearing the seamless web of the Indian nation had been anathema to every Congressman. Now they could see attractions in giving away those parts of the country that they could never hope to control and which in turn threatened their power at the centre. But they were determined to give away only the minimum. In other words, Hindu-majority districts in erstwhile Muslim-majority provinces would have to remain in India. This meant that if the Congress was to have its way, Bengal and Punjab inevitably would have to be partitioned.

---

[7] Maulana Azad to Pethick Lawrence, 26 April 1946, in N. Mansergh, E. W. R. Lumby and Penderel Moon (eds.), *Constitutional Relations between Britain and India: The Transfer of Power 1942–1947*, vol. VII, 'The Cabinet Mission, 23 March–26 June 1946', London, 1977. Document No. 153. [Henceforth TP, vol. VII, No 153, etc.].

[8] Nehru to Wavell, 24 February 1947, TP vol. IX, No. 456.

[9] Patel to Mountbatten, 25 February 1947, TP vol. X, No. 252.

[10] Patel to Wavell, 14 February 1947. Durga Das (ed.), *Sardar Patel's Correspondence*, Ahmedabad, 1972, vol. IV, p. 6.

For Jinnah and the Muslim League, on the other hand, the idea of being lesser partners in a centralised and unitary state controlled by the Congress party was equally unpalatable. It has been argued by Jalal that Jinnah favoured the establishment of a loose federation, one that would give the Muslim-majority provinces a considerable degree of autonomy from the proposed centre.[11] From this point of view, Jinnah is seen as deploying the idea of Pakistan as a 'bargaining counter'; Jinnah, it is argued, assumed that the Congress would be so anxious to avoid partition that it would make any concessions necessary to keep the Muslim-majority provinces within the Indian Union. Jinnah's willingness to consider the Cabinet Mission's 'Plan A', which provided for an India with a loose federal structure and a centre with limited powers suggests that it is likely that a federation of this sort was what Jinnah was really after.[12]

Jinnah, it is true, never clearly defined his demand for Pakistan, even to his closest colleagues, and the famed Lahore Resolution made no mention of partition. In fact, the very vagueness of the 'Pakistan' idea made it a slogan of inordinate power. It could mean different things to different people and there were almost as many images of Pakistan as Jinnah had followers. It was a slogan that drew on the increasingly bitter sense of grievance that an ever-larger number of Muslims harboured against the Hindus in general and the Congress Party in particular. Even if, as Jalal has argued, 'Pakistan' for Jinnah meant above all a greater degree of political power for Muslims (and perhaps for himself) within the Indian federation, for his followers it came to mean much more. Pakistan, for most Muslims who followed Jinnah, was a religious ideal, representing the dream of a *Dar-ul-Islam*, a promised land where Islam would flourish with its dignity restored. It was also a powerful political slogan, which promised Muslims liberation from their subservient minority position in India. Whatever Jinnah's motives might have been, his politics engendered a strong spirit of religious and communal nationalism among the Muslims of India: they encouraged a movement that inevitably contributed to the growing suspicion, hatred and violence between the communities. Even if Jinnah himself did not really want Pakistan, his followers certainly did and he encouraged them not only to demand it, but if

---

11 Ayesha Jalal, *Sole Spokesman*. Her case has been restated more recently in 'Azad, Jinnah and Partition', a review of Ian Henderson's *Abul Kalam Azad: An Intellectual and Religious Biography*, Bombay, 1988, and the new and controversial edition of Azad's own biography. Here Jalal argues that Jinnah's hopes for a federal structure closely resembled Azad's own vision of independent India. See *Economic and Political Weekly*, vol. 24, No. 21, 27 May 1989.
12 See Meeting of the Cabinet Delegation with Lord Wavell, 10 April 1946, TP vol. VII, No. 144.

necessary to fight for it. These are some of the aspects of the Pakistan movement that Jalal's study has not adequately addressed: a neglect that limits the scope of her powerful argument. Her analysis, by concentrating too heavily on the motives of individual politicians, fails to square up to the question of who wanted Partition and why. In this respect, it is in much the same tradition as most Partition studies, which focus exclusively on high politics and seek merely to assign responsibility, praise or blame to the handful of leaders who dominated the three-cornered negotiations during the end game. [13] This chapter will attempt to add another dimension to the story of Partition by looking deeper into the involvement and reaction of peoples of one province, Bengal. It will focus in the main on the role of Bengali Hindus in shaping the outcome in 1947 and will try to identify the parties and interest groups who wanted to partition the province. By doing so, it might help to correct the bias which a concentration on leaders at the top and on Muslim politics has given to studies of Partition. It will also challenge the conclusion emerging from such studies that Partition was exclusively a Muslim demand, opposed by the Hindus 'in every form'.[14]

Provincial roots of the partition of Bengal, 1945–46

There is evidence to suggest that Bengalis were not passive bystanders in the partition of their province; nor were they victims of circumstances entirely out of their control, forced reluctantly to accept the division of their 'motherland'. On the contrary, a large number of Hindus of Bengal, backed up by the provincial branches of the Congress and the Hindu Mahasabha, campaigned intensively in 1947 for the partition of Bengal and for the creation of a separate Hindu province that would remain inside an Indian union. It was a movement that undoubtedly had the support of the Congress High Command, yet its roots were located in the internal history of the province.

Previous chapters have shown how a notional 'Hindu identity' was first constructed and then given political expression in Bengal and how the assertion of the superiority of the 'Hindu community' was used to justify

---

[13] The partition and transfer of power have been discussed in terms of the wishes and idiosyncrasies of individuals, notably Mountbatten, Nehru and Jinnah. See, for instance, Philip Zeigler, *Mountbatten: the official biography*, London, 1985, and Mountbatten's own account in his pamphlet, *Reflections on the Transfer of Power and J. Nehru*, Cambridge, 1968. This version of the events of 1947 gained wide currency with the publication of Larry Collins' and Dominique Lapierre's *Freedom at Midnight*, London, 1975.

[14] Shila Sen, *Muslim Politics in Bengal*, p. 227.

Table 7. *Congress electoral results in Bengal: 1936–37 and 1945–46.*

Constituency	Total Seats	Seats won by Congress	
		1935–36	1945–46
General Seats			
Caste Hindu	48	39	47
Scheduled Caste	30	7	24
Special seats			
Commerce	4	0	4
Landholders	5	0	4
Labour	6	4	5
Women	2	2	2
Universities	1	0	0
Total	90	52	86

Source: Compiled from Public and Judicial Files, L/P and J/7/1142 and L/P and J/8/475, which give detailed breakdowns of the provincial election results in 1936–37 and 1945–46 respectively.

the refusal of a section of Hindus to accept the rule of the Muslim majority. It was an identity essentially of the bhadralok which, through its cultural and intellectual claims, served to unite the educated and well-to-do Hindus of Bengal, the rural landowning groups with the urban professional intelligentsia, the rich and powerful with the lower middle-class sections of the bhadralok. In the forties, this community sought to extend its boundaries so as to include non-bhadralok and nominally Hindu groups. Attempts were made to recruit the lower classes and so-called 'depressed' castes into Hindu political parties and the sanskritising aspirations of low-caste groups were encouraged in order to draw them into the ken of bhadralok politics. As popular religious festivals came to be an arena in which political battles were fought, ordinary Hindus in small mofussil towns of Bengal were increasingly drawn into the politics of a specifically Hindu communalism. And as the Bengal Congress came to present an unequivocally Hindu profile, the political differences between it and the Mahasabha became difficult for the untutored eye to discern.

The effectiveness of this unifying propaganda was demonstrated by the results of the general elections of 1945–46. In 1936–37, the Hindu vote had been split between Congress and Independents: in 1945–46, Hindus voted unambiguously for the Congress. In 1936–37, Congress had won only forty-eight of the eighty general seats and four of the special Hindu seats; in 1945–46, it won seventy-one general and fifteen special Hindu seats (see table 7).

In the 'General', or caste Hindu constituencies, the Congress victory was to all intents and purposes total. In 1945–46, the Party succeeded in wresting away the three general seats won in 1937 by the overtly Hindu organisations, namely the Hindu Sabha and the Hindu Nationalists. Similarly, it won back the five seats it had lost to independents in 1937. In each of its eight new general constituencies, the Party won by huge margins varying between 16,000 and 48,000 votes. The only caste Hindu seat lost by the Congress in 1946 was that of Darjeeling, which was won by a popular local man, D. S. Gurung, who had represented this constituency since 1936. By 1946, then, the Congress had become overwhelmingly the choice of the caste Hindu and had successfully won over the Hindu Nationalist and Sabha voter. Although the Mahasabha opposed the Congress in twenty-six general seats, it polled only 2.73 per cent of the total Hindu vote. Much to the surprise of Government House, the Mahasabha won only one seat, the special University seat, to which Dr Shyama Prasad Mookerjee was returned unopposed.[15]

Appearances notwithstanding, the very convincing defeat by the Congress Party of the Mahasabha was not a vote for secular nationalism against Hindu communalism. It reflected instead, the conviction of enfranchised Hindu Bengalis that the Bengal Congress was committed to protecting their 'interests', and was likely to do this more effectively than the Hindu Mahasabha. The two parties avoided a confrontation in the provincial elections, preferring, as has been seen, to cooperate through electoral understandings in different constituencies. So it was not surprising that the elections to the general seats went off without 'much excitement': '[There was] not one propaganda poster, no shouting of slogans, campaigning by volunteers. Everybody seemed sure that the Congress would sweep the polls and even rival candidates made no visible attempt to challenge Congress nominees. Polling therefore had no excitement'.[16] But the Congress had another, more remarkable, success. In 1945–46, the Congress won 80 per cent of the Scheduled Caste seats, whereas in 1936–37, it had won less than one in four of these seats. This time round, the party won all the Scheduled Caste seats in the West Bengal heartland by large margins of over 7,000 votes. Of the eleven Scheduled Caste representatives who were re-elected in 1945, five were Congressmen of long standing and another four were Independents who had subsequently

---

[15] These, and all other details of the electoral results in 1936–37 and 1945–46 are taken from IOLR, Franchise Files, L/P and J/7/1142, and L/P and J/8/475, respectively.
[16] *Amrita Bazar Patrika*, 21 March 1946.

joined the Congress. Taken as a whole, the Congress had succeeded in convincing over 90 per cent of Bengal's Hindu voters that the party was better equipped than any other, including the Mahasabha, to protect their interests. Its newfound supporters included not only the weaker 'out' groups among the Scheduled Castes and tribes, but also the rich and powerful, the big businessmen and large landholders, amongst whom the Mahasabha's influence had been strongest. It was an unanimity which not only reflected the extraordinary success of propaganda about a Hindu 'community' in creating a perceived unity of interest among Bengal's Hindu electorate but also showed how much the Congress in Bengal had changed in the forties, taking on a new, unequivocally Hindu colouring.

The elections also brought back the Muslim League into power in Bengal.[17] In April 1946, Huseyn Shaheed Suhrawardy formed a ministry and became the new Prime Minister of Bengal.[18] This was a prospect that filled Hindu Bengalis with dismay since Suhrawardy, as the Minister for Civil Supplies during the Famine, had become a demon in the eyes of Hindu public opinion for his corruption and was vilified in the columns of the Hindu press for being personally responsible for the huge number of deaths by starvation which the Bengal Famine had involved. As one Bengali reported to the Congress High Command, 'it is very painful to find the same person who is responsible for taking lives of about four million persons of Bengal in 1943 has again been seen as the Premier of Bengal'.[19] In the following months, Suhrawardy did little to allay fears shared by many Bengali Hindus about their prospects under Muslim rule. His first act as Prime Minister was to revoke the long-standing principle of Hindu–Muslim parity in the ministry. Reducing the total number of ministers from thirteen to eleven, he limited the number of Hindu ministers to three, and to add insult to injury, two of these were Scheduled Caste representatives. His announcement of a holiday on 16 August, the Muslim League's Direct Action Day, and his failure to deal with the civil war that followed in the streets and slums of Calcutta convinced Hindus that rule by a Muslim government would lead to the 'Pakistanisation of Bengal', a prospect which terrified most Hindus. Shyama Prasad Mooker-jee, once the champion of the unity of an indivisible Bengal changed his mind in 1946. In a private, handwritten note, he speculated on the future of Bengal under the rule of the Muslim League:

[17] The League's victory was no less spectacular: it won 114 out of 121 Muslim seats, polling over two million votes. The party won overwhelmingly in all 6 urban constituencies, in 104 out of 111 rural constituencies and in all 4 'special seats' reserved for Muslims. See 'Franchise, Elections in Bengal, 1946', IOLR L/P and J/8/475.

[18] For a detailed account of the rise of Suhrawardy within the Bengal Provincial Muslim League, see Abul Hashim, *In Retrospection*, pp. 89–112.

[19] Anonymous letter to the AICC President, AICC Papers, File No. G-53/1946.

If Bengal is converted into Pakistan ... Bengal Hindus are placed under a permanent tutelage of Muslims. Judging from the manner in which attacks on Hindu religion and society have been made, [this] means an end of Bengali Hindu culture. In order to placate a set of converts from low caste Hindus to Islam, very ancient Hindu culture will be sacrificed.[20]

The idea that partition might be preferable to Muslim rule had already occurred at least to some Hindus from West Bengal. When C. Rajagopalachari had argued in 1944 that Congress should accept a Pakistan comprising only the Muslim-majority districts, a handful of Calcutta Hindus had welcomed the proposal. Implicit in the Rajagopalachari Formula was the partition of the Punjab and Bengal. In 1944, when Shyama Prasad launched a campaign to denounce the 'C. R. Formula', one Bengali Hindu from Howrah wrote to him urging him to see the wisdom of the plan: 'What is the alternative that can meet the challenge to India held out by the Viceroy? ... [The Formula] has given a more natural and abiding solution on the basis of Independence for the whole of India'.[21] In the highly charged atmosphere of the summer of 1946, when talks between the Cabinet Mission and Indian leaders in Delhi raised speculation to a fever pitch, Hindus in Calcutta and in the West Bengal heartland began to look with favour on the idea of partitioning the province and in this way creating a new Hindu state of West Bengal. As the prospect of remaining under the 'permanent tutelage' of the Muslims grew increasingly intolerable in the months that followed this solution found favour with more and more Hindus in the Hindu-majority districts of western Bengal. More significant, perhaps, than Suhrawardy's declaration of 16 August as a public holiday (the proposed day of 'Direct Action' by the Muslim League) was his public statement less than a week before in which he threatened to declare Bengal's complete independence from the centre. Reacting to the creation of the purely Congress Interim Government at the centre, Suhrawardy warned:

A probable result of putting the Congress in power adopting the tactics of by-passing the League, would be 'the declaration of complete independence by Bengal and the setting up of a parallel government ... We will see that no revenue

[20] Undated note by Shyama Prasad Mookerjee in the Shyama Prasad Mookerjee Papers, II–IV Instalment, File No. 75/1945–46. This note is of particular interest because it reflects the bhadralok concern with 'Hindu culture' that, it has been argued, was a central idiom of Hindu bhadralok identity in these years. Also of interest is the disparaging reference to Muslims as 'a set of converts from low caste Hindus to Islam', which suggests that at least for Shyama Prasad, caste attitudes continued to remain ingrained despite the caste consolidation campaign and new 'Hindu togetherness' it claimed to engender.
[21] S. P. Shome of Howrah to Shyama Prasad Mookerjee, 18 August 1944. File No. 61/1944. *Ibid.*

is derived by such [sic] Central Government from Bengal and consider ourselves as a separate state having no connection with the Centre.[22]

The Hindu press reacted by interpreting this statement as a threat to 'Pakistanise' the whole of Bengal forthwith. 'Pakistan' had come to mean, for Hindu Bengalis, the permanent loss of political sovereignty and their subjection to the will of the Muslim majority. The crude and heavy-handed measures adopted by Suhrawardy's ministry in its first months in office ensured that this was a future that many Hindus were determined to avoid. Calcutta Hindus saw Direct Action, therefore, not as a mere tactic in the long drawn out and distant negotiations at the all-India level to do with interim governments and constituent assemblies, but a threat much closer to home against which they were ready to fight to the death.

This was the context in which the Great Calcutta Killing took place. The rioting, in which at least 5,000 died, was not a spontaneous and inexplicable outburst of aggression by faceless mobs. Both sides in the confrontation came well-prepared for it. Four days after the killing began, *The Statesman* informed its readers:

This is not a riot. It needs a word from mediaeval history, a fury. Yet 'fury' sounds spontaneous and there must have been some deliberation and organisation to set this fury on its way. The horde who ran about battering and killing with 8 ft lathis may have found them lying about or bought them out of their own pockets, but that is hard to believe.[23]

Another eye-witness saw that the Calcutta Killing was 'not a riot, but a civil war':

There was cold-blooded killing on both sides. The riot was well-organised on both sides. Suhrawardy organised the riot ruthlessly to show that ... [the Muslims] will retain Calcutta. *On the Hindu side, it was part of the campaign for the Partition of Bengal.* Its organisers included members of the Hindu Mahasabha and the Congress, particularly old terrorist Congressmen who had not joined the Communists. The Marwaris helped a lot, they gave finance and collected funds for the campaign for partition. The campaign hadn't then officially started, but everybody knew it was for that.[24]

Direct Action Day in Calcutta was not a flash in the pan but a product of developments which had long been coming to a head. In part it was the outcome of the growing arrogance of the leadership and rank and file of the Muslim League, heady with their success in the recent elections and confident of their ability to get for Bengal some form or other of Pakistan;

[22] Suhrawardy's statement as reported in *Amrita Bazar Patrika*, 10 August 1946.
[23] *The Statesman*, 20 August 1946.
[24] Nikhil Chakravarty, interview with the author, New Delhi, February 1989. Emphasis added.

and in part it flowed from the determination of Hindus to resist what they regarded as 'Muslim tyranny'. Suhrawardy himself bears much of the responsibility for this blood-letting since he issued an open challenge to the Hindus and was grossly negligent (deliberately or otherwise) in his failure to quell the rioting once it had broken out. By the time order was restored, thousands on both sides had been brutally slaughtered; ten days after the killings began, more than 3,000 bodies lay on the pavements of this City of Dreadful Night.[25] The city's normal burial and cremation services could not cope with the number of corpses, and the government had to hunt out low-caste Doms to collect bodies and dump them into mass graves.[26]

Suhrawardy's culpability is by now a well-established tradition.[27] But Hindu leaders were also deeply implicated, a fact which is less well known. More Muslims than Hindus died in the fighting, and in characteristically chilling style, Patel summed up the hideous affair with the comment; 'Hindus had the best of it.'[28] The preparedness of Hindus in 1946 for this ugly trial of strength is not surprising if it is recalled that since the late thirties and early forties, Calcutta and the mofussil towns had seen the establishment of a plethora of Hindu volunteer groups, whose professed aim was to unite Hindus but who devoted much of their energy to encouraging physical fitness and pseudo-military training among bhadra-lok youths. Perhaps the largest and best organised among these was the Bharat Sevashram Sangha, the volunteer wing of the Hindu Mahasabha. Ostensibly a society for social service, from the start the Sangha adopted a martial style and urged Hindus to train themselves in the arts of self-defence. At a meeting of the Sangha in September 1939, at which Dr Shyama Prasad Mookerjee presided and which was reportedly attended by 2,600 people,

the speakers referred to the Communal Award, which was designed to curb the Bengali Hindus and stated that they should organise Akharas with the help of Pulin Das and Satin Sen, ex-convicts, and develop their physique[s] and raise a thousand of lathis if the Hindus were attacked. ... Posters in Bengali were displayed of which one was entitled 'Give up the idea of non-violence now, what is required is strong manhood (*pourasha*)'.[29]

[25] By 27 August, the government itself estimated that 3,174 bodies had been collected in the cleaning-up operations.
[26] GB HCPB File No. 351/46 (part B).
[27] It is a tradition that lives on even today in popular Bengali fiction. Saradindu Bandpadhyay's detective novel, *Aadim Ripu*, for instance, set against the backdrop of Calcutta after the killings of 1946, holds Suhrawardy and his Punjabi police responsible for the cheapness of human life in the city at the time. Pratulchandra Gupta (ed.), *Saradindu Omnibus*, vol. II, Calcutta, 1980, pp. 1, 20.
[28] Patel to R. K. Sidhwa, 27 August 1946. In Durga Das (ed.), *Sardar Patel's Correspondence*, vol. III, p. 148.
[29] Memo dated 9 September 1939. GB SB 'PH' Series, File No. 510/39.

At another meeting of the Sangha two months later, Bengali placards with the inscription, 'Hindus, wake up and take up the vow of killing the demons', were displayed in the pandal.[30] The following year, this theme was developed with the use of Saivite religious imagery:

On the 7th [of April, 1940], a Hindu Sammelan ... was held at Maheshwari Bhawan under the auspices of the Bharat Sevashram Sangha. Mr B. C. Chatterjee presided. A large picture of Siva with a trident was exhibited ... Speeches were delivered urging the Hindus to develop a martial spirit ... Swami Bijnananda observed that Hindu gods and goddesses were always armed to the teeth in order to destroy the demons. Swami Adwaitananda ... remarked that he came with a lathi to serve the Hindus. The enemies of the Hindus should be beheaded, he said. Pointing to the picture of Siva with a trident he stated that his followers should come forward armed at least with lathis ... Swami Pranabananda wanted to raise a defence force of five lakhs ... he appealed to the Marwaris to help with money ... Harnam Das urged every Hindu to become a soldier. A resolution [was passed] approving the proposal of the Sangha to form a defence force of five lakhs of Hindus, noting with satisfaction that 12,000 had already been recruited.[31]

From the outset the Bharat Sevashram Sangha was closely associated with the Mahasabha. But in the forties, the Sangha, and other organisations like it, began to attract wider bhadralok support. Members of the Calcutta bhadralok intelligentsia, including Mrinal Kanti Ghose of the *Amrita Bazar Patrika*, Hemendra Prasad Ghosh, the editor of the vernacular paper, *Dainik Basumati*, and Ramananda Chatterjee, the editor of the *Modern Review*, were present at its meetings.[32] By 1947, even establishment figures made no secret of their association with the Sangha. It was announced that Sir Bejoy Prasad Singh Roy, who had been a member of the Indian Civil Service and a minister in government would open the session of the Hindu Sammelan organised by the Sangha and that P. N. Banerjee, Vice-Chancellor of Calcutta University, would preside.[33] The Congress Party, which had several volunteer organisations of its own,[34] often took part in the Sangha's programmes. In May 1946 when the Sangha organised a public meeting to 'protest against the desecration of the Chandranath Shrine', it was presided over by Sasanka Sekhar Sanyal, a Congress member of the Central Assembly.[35] The following year, at a procession organised by the Sangha to celebrate the birth anniversary of Swami Pranabananda, a Congress contingent was conspicuous 'clad in white shirts, shorts, Gandhi caps, ... they carried a

---

[30] Memo dated 11 November 1939. *Ibid.*   [31] Memo dated 9 April 1940. *Ibid.*

[32] Memo dated 9 September 1939. *Ibid.*

[33] *Amrita Bazar Patrika*, 18 February 1947.

[34] The police listed as many as thirteen volunteer bodies affiliated to the Congress in 1946. See Memo No. Dir. 101 in GB SB 'PM' Series, File No. 882/46 II.

[35] Memo dated 25 June 1946. GB SB 'PH' Series, File No. 510/46.

Table 8. *Some Hindu volunteer organisations in Calcutta: 1945–47*

Name	Strength	Area of influence	Financial positions	Threat to public order
RSS	100	North Calcutta	Moderate	None
Jatiya Yuba Sangha	200	North Calcutta	Moderate	None
Bagh Bazar Tarun Bya[ya]m Samity	25–30	Bagh Bazar area	Not sound	Potential
Deshabandhu Byam Samiti	25–40	BaghBazar, Shyam Bazar	Not sound	Potential
Hindusthan Scout Association	3000	Whole of Calcutta	Sound	None
Hindu Sakti Sangha[a]	300–500	Muchipara, Bowbazar	Sound	Potential
Arya Bir Dal	16	Park Circus	Sound	None
BPHM Volunteer Corps	250	Not known	Not known	None

[a] It is interesting that the Bharat Sevashram Sangha has not been listed in the police tables. The Hindu Sakti Sangha and the Hindu Mahasabha Volunteer Corps possibly overlapped with the Sevashram Sangha.
Source: Compiled from Special Branch memoranda on volunteer organisations, tabled in GB SB 'PM' Series, Files 829/45 and 822/47 I.

Congress flag [and] ... posters urging Hindus to unite and to gather strength following the ideals of Shivaji [and] Rana Pratap'.[36] Moreover, organisations such as the Sangha, with their programme of militant and aggressive Hinduism, were able to attract the remnants of the old terrorist organisations which had stayed outside the communist movement. Pulin Das and Satin Sen, both former Jugantar members who had been arrested in the past for 'terrorist' offences, now became the Sevashram Sangha's experts in 'martial' arts,[37] and in Madaripur the local branch of the Jugantar Party took over the training of the Sangha's volunteers in 1941.[38] Another prominent member of the Madaripur Jugantar group, Kalyan Kumar Nag, who later was known as 'Swami Satyanand' and founded the 'Hindu Mission' in 1926, was an active member of the Sangha and of the Hindu Mahasabha in the thirties.[39]

In the early forties, Hindu volunteer groups proliferated in Calcutta (see table 8). Some of these, such as the Hindu Sakti Sangha, another

[36] Memo dated 19 February 1947. *Ibid.*
[37] Memo dated 9 September 1939. GB SB 'PH' Series, File No. 510/39.
[38] Report of the Commissioner, Dacca Division, LOFCR for the first fortnight in March 1941. GB HCPB 13/41.
[39] Note on the Hindu Mission. GB SB 'PH' Series, File No. 502/42.

'active' wing of the Mahasahba,[40] were large and well organised, with over 500 members scattered in branches in different parts of the city, and were financially sound.[41] Others were smaller *para* ('neighbourhood') groups such as the 'Yuva Sampraday' of Behala

started in 1943 by Nirmal Kr. Chatarji with some young boys and girls at P.S. Behala. It functions as follows: 1. Bratachari and daggerplay for young boys and girls. 2. Dramatic section. 3. Football section. It also has a library. In all there are 50 members, 30 young school boys and girls and 20 young men. They also perform Durga Puja and Saraswati Puja. At the time of Durga Puja they stage dramas.[42]

Similar neighbourhood organisations included the Baghbazar Tarun Byayam Samiti with twenty-five members, and the Arya Bir Dal in the Park Circus area with sixteen members.[43] In greater Calcutta, active volunteer societies of this sort included the Entally Byayam Sangha (Physical Training Society), the Salkia Tarun Dal in Howrah, the Hindu Seva Sangha in Hajinagar in the 24 Parganas and the Mitali Sangsad in Serampore.[44]

The larger volunteer organisations were frequently well funded. The Bharat Sevashram Sangha, for instance, enjoyed Marwari support. In 1941, the Special Branch intercepted a letter from the Secretary of the Burdwan branch of the Bengal Provincial Hindu Mahasabha to Jugal Kishore Birla, thanking him for his offer to finance 'training and physical culture for the Hindus of Burdwan'.[45] Another organisation which enjoyed the patronage of the Birlas was the Bengal branch of the Rashtriya Swayam Sevak Sangha (RSS). The Calcutta headquarters of the RSS was reportedly housed in 'Mr Birla's Shilpa Vidyalaya at [the] Harrison Road and Amherst Street Crossing'.[46] By the mid-forties, the RSS had expanded from Calcutta to the interior, where it had the support of at least one big Hindu zamindar. An intelligence department report revealed that

at Rajshahi, Pabna, Salap (Pabna district) Mymensingh, Susang (Mymensingh district) and in other parts of Bengal there are many branches. Babu Parimal Singha of [the] Susang Raj family is a staunch devotee of the Rashtriya Swayam

[40] Intercepted letter from Ashutosh Lahiry to S. K. Deb, 23 August 1944. GB SB 'PH' Series, File No. 550/44 B.
[41] Note on Volunteer Organisations dated 30 November 1945. GB SB 'PM' Series, File No. 829/45.
[42] Memo dated 11 September 1946. *Ibid.*, File No. 822/46 II.
[43] See note on Volunteer organisations dated 30 November 1945. GB SB 'PM' Series, File No. 829/45.
[44] AICC Papers, File Nos. CL-14 (B)/1946, CL-14 (C)/1946 and CL-14 (D)/1946.
[45] Intercepted letter from the Secretary, Burdwan District Hindu Mahasabha to Jugal Kishore Birla, dated 9 December 1941. GB SB 'PH' Series, 543/41. Anandilal Poddar was particularly close to the Sevashram Sangha, and addressed a Janamashtami meeting organised by it in 1944. *Ibid.*, File No. 510/44.
[46] Memo dated 22 August 1939. GB SB 'PH' Series, File No. 510/39.

Sevak Sangha. It is said that in Bengal there are about a lac [*sic*] of members of this Sangha.[47]

Organisations such as these were effective in mobilising large sections of the Hindu bhadralok youth of Calcutta and the mofussil towns behind the communal ideology and politics of the Hindu Mahasabha and the Hinduised Congress of the forties. Although the authorities regarded most of them as harmless (see the last column in table 8), this was more a reflection of the Government's curiously tolerant attitude towards communal politics and organisations than a measure of the seriousness of their intentions.[48] The 'physical training' that the Rashtriya Swayam Sevak Sangha offered its young recruits included training in the use of firearms. In 1939, V. R. Patki of the Bengal branch of the RSS wrote to a friend in London:

The charts of the Lee En-field Bayonet etc. sent by you were received ... There is a well known firm in London known as 'Parker Hale' where Arms requisites are sold. Can you get an 'Aiming Rest' in that firm? This instrument is used for taking aim by resting the gun on it. This can be utilised by recruits before they are allowed to fire.[49]

After the War, demobilised servicemen and military employees were induced to procure firearms and ammunition for Hindu communal organisations.[50] A police report in May 1946 revealed that both the Anushilan and Jugantar groups were involved in collecting arms and it was rumoured that their activities were being financed by the Hindu Mahasabha:

Members of the Anushilan Party are reported to be trying to obtain arms through military employees ... On May 11, the house of Shyam Sunder Pal, a member of the Anushilan party was searched at Calcutta and 108 rounds of ammunition were discovered. The Jugantar Party, also engaged in obtaining illicit arms, is said to be

[47] CID Report dated 19 April 1943. GB SB 'PH' Series, File No. 511/42. This may well have been a liberal estimate, but it is clear that the organisation had expanded well beyond the 100-odd members it reportedly started out with.
[48] It is interesting that the Government regarded the tiny Byam Samitis which were associated with the Forward Bloc as 'potentially dangerous', while sticking to the view that the RSS held no threat to public order (see table 8), despite the fact that the Special Branch was aware that the latter organisation was collecting arms. This was another instance of its curious position with regard to communal politics, by which, for instance, men such as Shyama Prasad Mookerjee, Sir Nazimuddin and Suhrawardy were never arrested or detained after delivering speeches which were designed to incite communal violence, while others such as Sarat Bose spent years in British jails.
[49] Intercepted letter from V. R. Patki to R. V. Kelkar, undated. GB SB 'PH' Series, File No. 510/39.
[50] Saradindu Bandopadhyay in *Aadim Ripu* describes the free availability of firearms in Calcutta after the Second World War and refers to the sale of arms by demobilised soldiers to underworld bosses. *Saradindu Omnibus*, vol. II, p. 2.

financed by a prominent leader of the Hindu Mahasabha in their efforts to obtain arms and ammunition.[51]

The Mahasabha had been active amongst demobilised soldiers since the end of the war, attempting to organise soldiers 'and released INA men under the banner of the Mahasabha and also to arrange for the military training of Hindu youths by ex-servicemen'.[52] And at least in Burdwan, these efforts paid off. In an impassioned letter to Shyama Prasad Mookerjee, the 'Hindu Ex-Army Personnel of Panagar' declared that

We the Ex-Army Hindu Personnel of Burdwan District look forward eagerly for a retaliation against our dangerous enemy the Muslim in the Hindu majority district ... We are prepared and will follow your commands ... We have taken oath and will not refrain from fulfilling our heartiest desire. We are armed and are fully aware of the war tactics ... We consider that by this way of revenge we can stop the uncivilised moslim of this province and their leader the halfcast notorious Suhrawardy and Nazimiddin will understand the Hindu spirit of taking revenge [sic].[53]

Given that the Hindu Mahasabha had fought the 1945–46 elections quite openly on the platform of resisting Muslims tooth and nail, it is hardly a matter of surprise that Hindu volunteers a few months later were ready for this test of strength in Calcutta. B. R. Moonje, firing the first shot in the electoral campaign for the Mahasabha, had declared:

Hindu Mahasabha wants Independence but does not believe that it can be achieved through non-violence. It therefore wants to organise violence on the most up-to-date western scientific lines ... It would be wise if Congress were to take up ... to meet the [Muslim League] threat of a Civil War, the Mahasabha slogan of 'Train the Youths in Horse riding and Rifle Shooting'.[54]

When civil war became a reality in Bengal, Mahasabha volunteers were ready and eager to act upon their leader's advice, even if bamboo staves, knives and crude country pistols had to do service for cavalry and artillery. Hindus, as much as Muslims, were prepared for battle on 16 August; both sides were armed and Hindus appear to have had the bigger battalions.

An analysis of Hindu rioters reveals the extent to which volunteer organisations had been successful in mobilising middle-class Bengali Hindus of Calcutta behind the increasingly virulent communalism that

[51] Memo on Hindu organisations in possession of firearms. GB SB 'PH' Series, File No. 507/46.
[52] Memo dated 5 February 1946. GB SB 'PM' Series, File No. 829/45.
[53] Intercepted letter from the Secretary, The Hindu Ex-Army Personnel of Panagar to S. P. Mookerjee, dated 7 November 1946. GB SB 'PM' Series, File No. 937/46.
[54] Shyama Prasad Mookerjee Papers, II–IV Instalment, File No. 75/1945–46.

characterised bhadralok politics in the forties. While the Muslim rioters consisted mainly of up-country migrants, a surprisingly large number of bhadralok Hindus were arrested on charges of rioting. Discussing the composition of the Hindu crowds in the riots, Suranjan Das observes

Bengali Hindu students and other professional or middle-class elements ... were active. Wealthy businessmen, influential merchants, artists, shopkeepers ... were arrested on rioting charges. In central Calcutta, *bhadraloks* joined others to disrupt a Muslim meeting being addressed by the Chief Minister himself. Again, a large portion of the crowd which killed Dr Jamal Mohammed, an eminent eye-specialist, consisted of 'educated youths' ... It was not surprising that many of them spoke English with police officers.[55]

Indeed, one of the Hindus arrested for hurling a bomb into a Muslim crowd in the unrest that continued after the Killing was a prominent doctor, Dr Mahendranath Sarkar of Burdwan, who admitted, 'I am now a Congressman. I was previously a member of the Hindu Mahasabha. I joined the movement favouring the partition of Bengal'.[56] Also involved on the Hindu side were released INA soldiers and Marwari business-men.[57] It was this improbable alliance between students, professional men, businessmen and ex-soldiers, Congressmen, Mahasabhaites, shop-keepers and neighbourhood bully boys, that led the Hindu crowd to its bloody victory in the streets of Calcutta in 1946. It was also to be the basis of the Hindu movement for the partition of Bengal and for the creation of a separate Hindu homeland.

But Hindu culpability was never acknowledged. The Hindu press laid the blame for the violence upon the Suhrawardy Government and the Muslim League, and the Killing was held up as a dreadful portent of the fate of Bengali Hindus if they remained under 'Muslim rule'. In the months that followed, the Calcutta Killing – cloaked in recrimination by the Hindu press – became a powerful symbol which was used to rally Hindus behind the demand for a separate Hindu state in West Bengal. The riots in Noakhali and Tippera, in which local Muslims, reacting slowly but ferociously to rumours of how their fellow-Muslims had been massacred in Calcutta and Bihar, killed hundreds of Hindus in reprisal, gave Hindus the excuse they wanted to put themselves unashamedly on a war footing:

[55] Suranjan Das, *Communal Riots in Bengal*, p. 183. Perhaps the most interesting finding of Das' research is the extent of bhadralok participation in the major communal riots in Bengal, from the Dacca riots of 1930 to the Calcutta Killing in 1946, a finding that lends strong support to the main arguments of this book.

[56] Statement of Dr Mahendra Nath Sarkar of P. S. Ondal, Burdwan. GB SB 'PM' Series, File No. 62/47.

[57] Suranjan Das, 'Communal Riots in Bengal', pp. 327 and 339.

Make Shurawardy (I hate to utter his name) [know] that Hindus are not yet dead and that neither he nor his vicious lieutenants can terrorise the Hindus ... Shurawardy has sown the wind and must reap the whirlwind very soon. It is he who has made the Hindus rebel. Rebel and take revenge is our only motto from now on. Come and let us fight with the Muslim League brutes. We should not cease fighting so long as Bengal is not partitioned and Leaguers are kicked out from the homeland of the Hindus.[58]

Sentiments such as these fed a growing determination among many Hindus that, come what may and regardless of the cost, Bengal must be partitioned.

The partition campaign, 1946–47

In the last months of 1946 and early in 1947 these fears fuelled an organised and well-supported campaign among the Hindus for the partition of the province. The campaign for partition was inaugurated officially only in March 1947, when the *Amrita Bazar Patrika* announced that it was holding a poll to 'make a correct estimate of public opinion' on the question.[59] But it was in fact already well under way before the end of 1946, with the establishment of the 'Bengal Partition League', the declared object of which was 'to demand a separate province in the district of West Bengal to safeguard the Hindu interest in West Bengal where they are in a majority'.[60] The Partition League began to enrol members before the end of the year. The Special Branch in Calcutta happened to intercept three completed application forms from would-be members of the League. Each form contained the statement, typed in English: 'As I agree with the aims and objectives of the Bengal Partition League, please enrol me as a member', followed by the name, age, and profession of the applicant. All three applicants were members of the Calcutta bhadralok;[61] the first, N. N. Ghosh, aged thirty-seven years, was a teacher at a well-known school in Calcutta, the Hare School; the second, G. N. Ghosh, aged twenty-five years was an accountant; and the third, P. Ghosh, aged twenty-nine years, was an auditor at the Jehapur Gun Factory.[62] As will be seen, it was the Hindu bhadralok of the Hindu-majority districts of western Bengal, determined to be once again

[58] Intercepted letter from Mrinmoyee Dutt to the Editor, *Amrita Bazar Patrika*, dated 19 April 1947. GB SB 'PM' Series, File No. 938/47 III.
[59] *Amrita Bazar Patrika* , 23 March 1947.
[60] Memo No. 286/87/ SB on the Bengal Partition League. GB SB 'PM' Series, File No. 822/46 II.
[61] Intercepted letters from N. N. Ghosh, G. N. Ghosh and P. Ghosh to the Bengal Partition League. *Ibid.*
[62] *Ibid.*

masters in their own house, who formed the core of the partition movement. And it was the bhadralok to whom the propaganda for partition was addressed:

The hour has now struck. Sisters and Brothers, I appeal to you to give up soft sentimentalism and to come down from the giddy heights of dreamland to the realities of the *terra firma*. It is not patriotism to repeat old slogans and to be slaves of catch words. The most glorious chapter in the history of Bengal is the agitation against the Partition imposed by British Imperialism. Traditionally and sentimentally the people of Bengal are against any move of dividing the province. But we shall be guilty of treason to the motherland if we merely quote old slogans without understanding their implications. The Anti-Partition movement in the Swadeshi days was a fight against Imperialism which wanted to cripple the greatest nationalist force working for the Independence of the country by making the Bengal Hindus minorities in both the provinces. Our demand for partition today is prompted by the same ideal and the same purpose, namely, to prevent the disintegration of the nationalist element and to preserve Bengal's culture and to secure a Homeland for the Hindus of Bengal which will constitute a National State as a part of India.[63]

These clarion calls drew upon many of the now familiar idioms of the Hindu bhadralok's communal identity: images of Bengal's glorious past, claims that partition would protect Bengal's unique 'culture' and would provide a secure Hindu 'Homeland', dreams that in the security of their new Homeland, they would cease to be a hopeless minority but rather a confident majority, restored to its rightful dominance. Couched in such terms, the appeal was irresistible. In April 1947, *Amrita Bazar Patrika* was able smugly to report that in its opinion poll partition had gained a virtually unanimous vote of confidence, 98.6 per cent voting yea, with those raising their voice in favour of united Bengal being a tiny minority on the wrong side of a decimal point.[64]

The poll, however, was only one part of a much wider campaign, which mobilised Hindus of Calcutta and the mofussil by organising petitions and signature campaigns all over the province. If the campaign for partition was to have an impact upon the negotiations under way in distant Delhi, its leaders realised that it would have to demonstrate wide popular support. And to achieve this, those who led the movement saw that they would in turn have to convince large numbers of Bengali Hindus that living in a Muslim-majority province was a fate worse than death. In the months that followed the Calcutta Killing, Hindus were subjected to

[63] Presidential address by N. C. Chatterjee at the Tarakeswar session of the Bengal Provincial Hindu Conference, 4 April 1947, in the Hindu Mahasabha Papers, File No. P 107/47.
[64] Only 0.6 per cent were reported to have favoured a united Bengal. *Amrita Bazar Patrika*, 23 April 1947.

a continuous stream of virulently communal propaganda that was designed to keep emotions at fever pitch. One leaflet entitled *Sangram* ('Struggle'), circulated in Calcutta in November 1946, egged Hindus on to 'brutally murder one hundred League *goondas* (criminals) in revenge for the molestation of every Hindu woman'. It demanded:

In these days of extreme calamities on the Hindus in India, will the Hindus remain quiescent like cowards in the confines of their houses? ... Will they not organise themselves at once in order to destroy the enemy and defend themselves? Will not the Hindu youths of Bengal avenge the molestation of their mothers and sisters? ... You shall have to take the vow of self-sacrifice this very day! Deterrent action must be taken! ... the League gangsters will have to be wiped out and the Pakistani regime terminated by the destruction of the League ministry!

Urging Hindus to shed their inherent 'peacefulness', the pamphlet harked back to the glorious revolutionary tradition of violence and self-sacrifice:

The path along which the young revolutionaries of Bengal advanced in ordered array with the valour and ferocity of lions is the only path – there are no alternatives. Listen to the call of those heroic Bengalis who have blazed the trail and stained it with their own life blood![65]

Communal violence was thus given a specious legitimacy by likening it to the patriotism of the revolutionary terrorists and nationalism itself was deployed as part of the armoury of Hindu communal propaganda. The title of the pamphlet, '*Sangram*', was a term borrowed from the nationalist vocabulary, except that now the 'struggle' was not against the British but against 'Muslim tyranny'. The British were now regarded as mere accomplices in Muslim crimes and the Governor and Viceroy took second place to Suhrawardy in the new demonology of Hindu communalists. In October 1946, for instance, a poster was prominently displayed on Rash Behari Avenue which declared:

We want the head of that dog Suhrawardy
We want the blood of the white skins!
(*Kukur Suhrawardyr mundu chai*
Sada chamrar rakta chai!)[66]

Wild rumours of Government-planned genocide did the rounds in Hindu neighbourhoods in the city, feeding communal suspicion and paranoia. One pamphlet discovered early in 1947 made this astonishing claim:

[65] *Sangram*, undated, anonymous. Attached to memo dated 12 November 1946. GB SB 'PM' Series, File No. 506 Part IV/46 A.
[66] One 'Hindu sufferer' thus advised Gandhi to punish all three: 'Let the Viceroy's wife be abducted and married to a Muslim Leaguer. Let the Governor's wife be abducted and married to a Pathan. Let the Bengal Premier's wife be abducted and married to a Hindu Cobbler. Let there be forcible conversions to Mohammedanism of wives of viceroy ... and Governor of Bengal ... Let there be rapes on [all] their wives'. Memo dated 2 November 1946. *Ibid.*, File No. 937/46.

Do you know what is happening today in the name of Law and Order behind the screen of curfew in a city like Calcutta? They have set up a Secret Slaughter House in Calcutta, and people arrested for violation of Curfew Orders are Taken in Police Lorries by the Punjabi Police and Handed over to the Murder Gangs Living or quartered in those Slaughter House, then you know what happens to most of the arrested persons, they are butchered, their bodies chopped off and packed in wooden crates and taken out of the city for some unknown destination – this is the 'Mystery of Disappearance of Arrested Persons in Calcutta'. So resist with all your might, when you know death is certain, to kill the Punjabi Police however strong and snatch his gun, if possible, or even bite him and raise the neighbourhood where you are arrested to come to your assistance. Thus can you have a chance of escape from such mysterious disappearance, well-planned by the Muslim League aided by the Goonda Muslim Ministers of Bengal. DOWN WITH PAKISTAN AND THE METHODS TO ACHIEVE IT![67]

The story of Direct Action Day was told and retold and with each telling the account of Muslim 'atrocities' against the 'peace-loving' Hindu population of Calcutta grew wilder and wilder. One pamphlet found in a tram car on Lower Circular Road in April 1947 urged Hindus not to forget the events of 16 August:

let us always remember without allowing to be obliterated from our memory the atrocities committed by those who deem it to be their religious duties to erect mosques on Hindu lands, to ravish Hindu women, destroy and defile Hindu places of worship and to interfere with Hindu rituals and religious functions and who, while celebrating their Direct Action Day on 16 August lost in a religious frenzy converted into one channel by ripping open with a sharp cutting instrument the vaginal passage and the anus of our dear mothers and sisters having raped them before and maimed the mothers breasts to suck the milk of which we, as Hindus, feel so proud ...

Described by the Special Branch as 'a hymn of hate', the pamphlet ended with an appeal to Hindus to 'wipe out' all those who opposed the partition of the province.[68]

Another account in the same vein of the Calcutta Killings, a poem entitled *Soula August Unnis-sau Chhe-challis* ('Sixteenth August 1946')[69]

---

[67] *Rise Up All Hindus Wherever You Are and Get Ready to Return Blow for Blow*, anon. undated. GB SB 'PM' Series, File No. 937 (4)/47 II. The influence of this type of propoganda can be guaged from the fact that decades later, the brutality of Suhrawardy's police was a recurrent theme in popular (and ostensibly non-communal) Bengali fiction. Saradindu Bandopadhyay's novel *Aadim Ripu* thus opens with the description of corpses littered on the Calcutta streets, and adds that 'when Suhrawardy Saheb's police was called in to rule the Hindus, the number of corpses would rise'. *Saradindu Omnibus*, p. 1.

[68] *Hindu! Jagrihee* ('Hindus! Awake'), anon., undated. GB SB 'PM' Series, File No. 938/47 III.

[69] Dwijendranath Bhaduri, *Soula Agasto Unnis-sau Chhe-challis*, Calcutta, 1946. GB SB 'PM' Series, 937/46.

by a well-known Hindu poet, Dwijendranath Bhaduri, was circulated
among Hindu schoolchildren to be memorised as a recitation piece for a
competition to be held at Saraswati Puja early in 1947. The competition
was organised by one of the many neighbourhood volunteer groups, the
Sinthi Chhatra Sangha. Several copies of the pamphlet were found in the
possession of 'one Babu Sourendra Kumar Chatarji, a head clerk in the
Dispatch Section of James Finlay and Co.', who described himself as the
Assistant Secretary of the Uttar Palli Milan Sangha, 'an organisation for
the promotion of physical culture'. Chatarji also admitted to being the
general secretary of the 'Jatiya Krira Sangha', a volunteer group established in 1940 with the proclaimed aim of 'promoting physical culture and
Indian sports'. He told the police that he received the pamphlets from a
member of the Sinthi Chhatra Sangha 'for distributing them among the
clubs I knew to enable them to participate in the essay and recitation
competition'.[70] Sourendra Kumar Chatarji's evidence suggests that the
complex network of volunteer organisations in Calcutta played a central
role in disseminating communal propaganda that was designed to mobilise Hindu support for the demand for partition. In Entally for instance,
seven different clubs worked side by side to organise public opinion in
favour of partition.[71] In the same way, a substantial number of partition
meetings and petitions were organised by different volunteer groups all
over Bengal.[72]

But the partition movement was not limited to the city of Calcutta. Its
organisers were able to whip up strong support from towns and villages
throughout the province. Not unexpectedly, the Hindu-majority districts
were at the forefront of the movement, but even in the Eastern districts,
Hindus signed petitions which if they succeeded in getting what they
demanded, would make them strangers in their own land (see table 9).
Petitions came in all manner of forms: resolutions by local bodies which
were often accompanied by several hundred signatures, and in one or two
cases, pages of thumb impressions of those who supported the demand.
Here was a wider cross-section of Hindu society than had been mobilised
for any political cause in the history of Bengal. Everyone favoured

[70] Statement of Sourendra Kumar Chatarji. *Ibid.*, p. 113.
[71] These were the Entally Kheyali Sangha, the Entally branch of the National Athletic
Club, the 'No Club', the Entally Young Athletic Club, the Entally Boys Library and the
Entally Orchestra. Each of these clubs sent separate petitions to the AICC demanding
partition. AICC Papers, Files No. CL-14 (B)/1946 and CL-14 (C)/1946.
[72] The Congress files contain records of such meetings and petitions from Khulna, Howrah,
24 Parganas, Hooghly, Faridpur, Chittagong, Bakarganj and Jessore. *Ibid.*

Table 9. *Distribution of petitions demanding the partition of Bengal and the proportion of the Hindu population, by district, 1947*

District	Number of petitions	Hindu population (%)
Burdwan	43	78.62
Birbhum	2	67.17
Bankura	34	90.99
Midnapore	34	89.23
Hooghly	18	82.93
Howrah	37	78.3
Calcutta	94	68.71
24 Parganas	23	64.2
Murshidabad	5	43.1
Nadia	18	37.53
Jessore	3	37.55
Khulna	15	50.22
Rajshahi	3	22.81
Dinajpur	6	45.22
Jalpaiguri	12	67.53
Darjeeling	6	74.12
Malda	12	42.17
Rangpur	1	28.77
Bogra	–	16.35
Pabna	1	22.99
Dacca	6	24.14
Mymensingh	6	22.89
Faridpur	3	35.86
Bakarganj	14	26.42
Tippera	1	24.14
Noakhali	2	21.47
Chittagong Hill Tracts	1	17.27

Source: Compiled from AICC Papers, Files Nos. G-54 (I)/1947, CL-14 (B)/1946 and CL-14 (D)/1946; and from Hindu Mahasabha Papers, II–IV Instalment, File Nos. 82/1947, P-107/1947, and 138/1946–47. Figures for the Hindu population are taken from the *Census of India*, 1931, vol.V.

partition; in all the files there are letters from a lonely quartet of individuals who dared to voice their dissent.[73]

The great majority of petitions came from Hindu-majority areas in

[73] The greatest irony of this demonstration of support for the partition of Bengal is that the records are filed in the All-India Congress Committees archives under the title of 'Anti-Partition Petitions'. See AICC Papers, Files G 54 (I)/1947, CL-14 (B)/1946, CL-8/1946 and CL-14 (D)/1946.

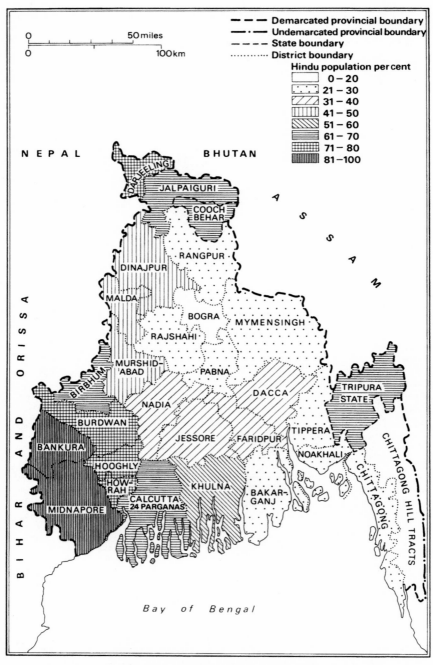

Map 3. Distribution of Hindu population, by district. *Number of Hindus per hundred of the total population, Census of 1931*

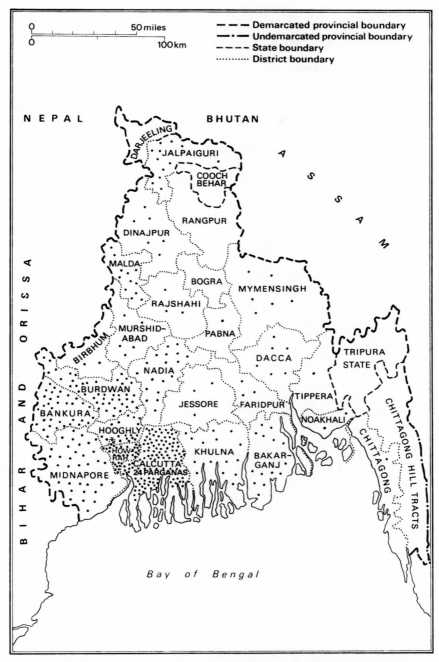

Map 4. Geographical spread of the campaign of partition. *Distribution of petitions, by district*

West Bengal (see maps 3 and 4). The six districts of the Burdwan Division together with Calcutta and the 24 Parganas accounted for over 70 per cent of the total number.[74] Of these, Burdwan, Midnapore, Calcutta and the 24 Parganas alone sent in almost 60 per cent. In those parts of Bengal where the Muslims were in a large majority, only Bakarganj provided more than ten petitions.[75] This distribution is hardly surprising since the proposed new Hindu state was to include only those districts which had Hindu majorities. The movement was specially strong in the districts that had experienced a marked rise in communal tension during the late thirties and forties, notably Burdwan, Midnapore, the 24 Parganas, Hooghly and of course Calcutta itself. In each of these districts, it has been argued, the local balance of power had shifted in the thirties and forties away from Hindus, and each had witnessed outbreaks of what has been described in this study as 'precedence' rioting. These were the areas where the 'tyranny' of Muslim rule was felt most acutely by bhadralok Hindus, who were forced to accept a Muslim government despite having a local majority in numbers.[76]

The partition movement was not a spontaneous expression of local grievances by Hindu groups in the districts. It was, on the contrary, a well-orchestrated campaign. Most petitions were framed in an identical way and followed an identical format:

Subject: Demand for the formation of a separate West Bengal Province. With respectful prayers: We wish to remain subject to the Independent Indian Federation. We inform you of the demand for a proposed 'West Bengal Province'. This province will remain within the Independent Indian Federation.[77]

This was invariably followed by the assertion that government under the Muslim League had made life intolerable for Bengali Hindus by failing to protect their property, life and liberty. Finally, the signatories demanded that the province be partitioned so as to save them from the unacceptable humiliations of living under a 'Muslim Raj'.

In most cases, the demand was printed, as were the sheets on which each signatory was expected to fill in his full name, address, post office, zilla, district, age and occupation. In all but four cases, the petitions were addressed to 'Rashtrapati' J. B. Kripalani, the President of the All-India

[74] A total of 400 petitions clearly indicate the thana and/or district from which they were forwarded. Of these, 285 were from the Burdwan districts, Calcutta and the 24 Parganas.

[75] All details and figures are derived from the analysis of over 400 petitions contained in AICC Papers, Files G-54 (I)/1947, CL-14 (A)/1946, CL-14 (B)/1946–47 and CL-14 (D)/1946–47.

[76] On the other hand, Birbhum had been remarkably free from communal conflict of this sort. Its minor role in the campaign for the partition is thus not entirely inexplicable.

[77] See, for instance, the petitions in AICC Papers, File No. G 54 (I)/1947.

Congress Committee and were sent directly to the central Congress office. Only the four remaining petitions, all from Barisal branches of the Hindu Mahasabha, were sent to Dr Shyama Prasad Mookerjee. The implication clearly is that local Congress groups were deeply involved in the organisation of the campaign. This is a fact that is not well-recognised. On the contrary, the campaign is widely and incorrectly believed to have been the brainchild of Shyama Prasad Mookerjee (certainly an advocate of partition) and organised by Mahasabha volunteers.[78] In fact, the Bengal Congress was the chief organiser of the campaign for the partition of Bengal.

The role of the Bengal Congress in the partition movement will not come as a surprise if it is recalled that, after a series of bruising battles with the left wing and the Bose brothers, the party had been reconstructed in the forties and that party policy shifted in these years towards an unequivocal defence of Hindu interests. In the process, the Bengal Congress became a more unified and streamlined organisation, under the firm control of its new leaders, Dr Bidhan Roy and Nalini Ranjan Sarkar, with the notorious fractiousness of the party a thing of the past. At the same time, the Congress shed its social radicalism, as one former Congressman noted with regret:

The Congress of Bengal, which, by consistent revolutionary urge of its leadership and workers had in the past been to some extent instrumental in influencing the orientation of some of the past historic decisions of the Congress and had acted as a check to the mere reformist tendencies occasionally exhibited, has in the past few years completely faded out of the picture ... The organisation is generally being kept in certain limits ... to be easily conducive to the attainment of [the] objects [of] the persons in power.[79]

Now that the leaders had decided that partition was the only way in which their power within the party could be translated into political power outside it, they used their newly disciplined cohorts to achieve this end, working closely with the Mahasabha where necessary. The distinctions between the Congress and the Mahasabha had been rubbed away during the forties, both in membership and in policy. On the communal question, little divided the Mahasabha and the Congress in Bengal. The Mahasabha in Bengal generally avoided the cruder rhetoric and style that characterised their movement in other parts of India. This owed much to the sophisticated leadership of Shyama Prasad Mookerjee and is as much a

---

[78] See, for instance, Harun-or-Rashid, *The Foreshadowing of Bangladesh*, p. 275; and Leonard A. Gordon, 'Divided Bengal: Problems of Nationalism and Identity in the 1947 Partition', *Journal of Commonwealth and Comparative Politics*, vol. 16, 2, July 1978, p. 156.
[79] N. C. Mitra to J. B. Kripalani, 30 April 1947, in AICC Papers, File No. CL-8/1946.

commentary on the extremism of the Bengal Congress as on the suave restraint of Mookerjee.[80] And increasingly, the relationship between the two parties was one in which the Congress led and the Mahasabha followed. In the early forties, the Mahasabha had been able to draw away a significant section of the Congress' traditional constituency. But when Congress policy turned towards a more businesslike defence of Hindu interests, many Hindus renewed their allegiance to the Congress and voted for it in the 1945–46 elections. The Congress in Bengal emerged from the War greatly strengthened in two important respects: it now enjoyed the unequivocal support of the Congress High Command and also the confidence of the increasingly powerful business community in Calcutta. The Mahasabha, for its part, was a demoralised organisation by 1946. Humbled by the Congress in the elections, it had failed to win a single seat in open contest. If, in the early forties, the Mahasabha tail had tended to wag the Congress dog, the roles were now reversed. While the two organisations worked closely together in the cause of partition, the Congress unquestionably took the lead in orchestrating the campaign.

In April 1947, when the Working Committee of the Mahasabha 'decided to observe a one-day *hartal* (strike) to protest against [the] atrocities' of the Punjabi Police as the 'first step in the partition movement', it was reported that 'the Mahasabha leaders are consulting the Congress leaders to chalk out a joint plan of action', and that 'the final decision with regard to the proposed hartal will be taken in the BPCC Executive Council'.[81] In May, the Congress and Mahasabha jointly convened a mammoth public meeting in Calcutta to press for partition which was presided over by the historian Sir Jadunath Sarkar.[82] This pattern of cooperation between the executives of the two parties at the provincial level was replicated in the localities. In Serampore town in Hooghly district, for example, a procession calling for partition turned out to be a joint operation by the local branches of the two parties. But even in the humble affairs of Serampore, the Congress called the shots and the Chairman of the procession was the local Congress boss, Babu

[80] On occasion, Shyama Prasad was found urging a more conciliatory attitude to Muslims than the Congress, and put his prospectus into practice when he agreed to form a coalition with Fazlul Huq's Progressive Coalition Party in 1941, and in 1943 announced conditions subject to which the Mahasabha was prepared to join Muslim League ministries. Shyama Prasad to Veer Savarkar, 22 July 1943, Shyama Prasad Mookerjee Papers, Subject File No. 57/1942–43.
[81] Report of the Working Committee meeting of the BPHM on 17 April 1947. GB SB 'PM' Series, File No. 938/47 II.
[82] AICC Papers, File No. CL-14 (C)/1946. Jadunath Sarkar's involvement in this movement will not come as a surprise if his role in popularising a deeply communal vision of Bengal's history is recalled. See chapter 4.

Kalipada Mukhopadhyay.[83] At Jhalakati in Bakarganj and at Kalma in Dacca, the subdivisional branches of the Congress and Mahasabha jointly held a public meeting to press for partition. In other cases, resolutions demanding partition passed by local Mahasabha committees were forwarded to Congress leaders rather than to Shyama Prasad Mookerjee. This was particularly true of the West Bengal Sabhas, such as those in Calcutta, Hooghly, Howrah and the 24 Parganas and, above all, in Burdwan.[84] Even local Mahasabha activists seem to have realised that it was the Congress leaders, and not Shyama Prasad, who were in command. In July 1947 when it became clear that Bengal would, indeed, be partitioned, Bengal's 'Khadi Group leaders', in an effort to formalise the working relationship between the two parties, invited Shyama Prasad Mookerjee to join the Cabinet of West Bengal as a Congressman. There were those in the Hindu Mahasabha who encouraged him to accept the offer. Shyama Prasad himself, it was reported, 'appears to be personally in favour of accepting the post of a Minister in West Bengal, but he is reluctant, it is understood, to comply with the top Congress leaders' wishes he should join the Congress party'.[85]

The Congress was clearly the senior partner in this joint campaign for partition. But its role in the partition movement was not limited to cooperation (albeit in a commanding position) with the Hindu Mahasabha. All over Bengal, the Congress independently of the Mahasabha organised public meetings to urge for partition. The meeting at Ballygunje in Calcutta presided over by Bengal's leading Gandhian, Dr Prafulla Chandra Ray, was only the most publicised of such meetings. Of the seventy-six partition meetings that are known to have been convened by a political party, no less than fifty-nine were organised by the Congress on its own. Twelve were held under the auspices of the Mahasabha and only five were joint ventures. There is, moreover, a clear overlap between those districts where the movement was most powerful (that is Calcutta, Burdwan, Midnapore, Howrah and Bankura) and those where the role of Congress was most marked (see maps 4 and 5). In Burdwan district, arguably the heart of the movement, Congress committees organised mass meetings in favour of partition not only in the towns such as Katwa, Kalna and Asansol but also in small villages such as Rayan, where public

---

[83] GB HCPB 224/1947.
[84] Nine different branches of the district Congress organisation forwarded petitions to the 'Rashtrapati', the Ketugram and Kalna Mahakuma CCs, the Rayan Union Congress Sevak Sangha, the Bantigram and the Barabanan Union CCs, the Khantaghosh Thana Congress Karmi Parishad, the Baidpur and the Nabagram CCS. AICC Papers, File No. CL-14 (B)/1946–47.
[85] Memo dated 1 July 1947. GB SB 'PH' Series, File No. 501/47 (A).

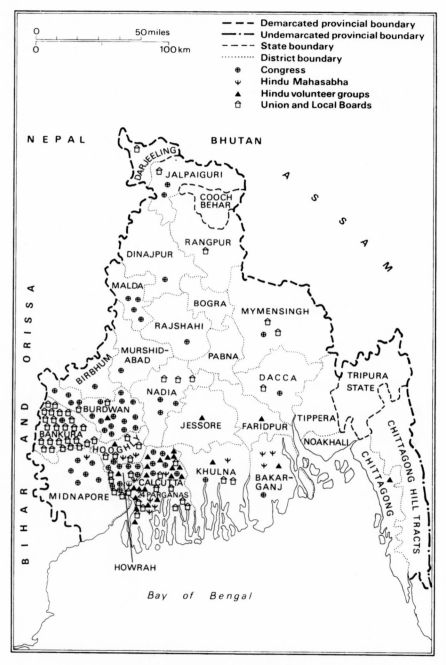

Map 5. The organisational basis of the campaign for partition.
Meetings organised by the Congress, Hindu Mahasabha and local bodies

petitions were backed by hundreds of signatures and thumb-prints.[86] It is clear, therefore, that the strength of the movement derived, in no small measure, from the organisational strength of the Bengal Congress.

That the bhadralok were the backbone of this movement should come as no surprise. Indeed, partition was the logical conclusion towards which the main currents in bhadralok politics had been flowing. Frustrated by their loss of power in provincial politics, shaken by the rapid collapse of the zamindari system, bhadralok groups had begun to devote their energies to the defence of their traditional privileges, moving away from the mainstream of nationalist politics in the process. Partition promised, in some measure, to restore their political hold over those parts of the province in which Hindus were in a numerical majority. It was in these areas that the prospects and experience of 'Muslim rule' had caused the fiercest resentment and it was here that the partition movement found its strongest support. In 1947, bhadralok Bengalis, once the pioneers of nationalism, used every available stratagem and device to demand that their province be divided. The Congress and the Hindu Mahasabha were by no means the only forums through which they expressed their demand for a separate Hindu province. Associations of Municipal Commissioners, Union Boards, Zamindars' Associations, Bar Associations, Trade Associations, Ratepayers Associations, local clubs (such as the National Athletic Club, Entally), volunteer organisations (such as the Kheyali Sangha in Calcutta) and even the Entally Boys Library sent in a flood of petitions. In Bankura, a bhadralok stronghold, as many as thirty different Union Boards sent in petitions[87] (see map 5). Where there was a significant Muslim presence on these bodies, the petitions usually included the caveat that it was approved only by the Hindu members, whose social profile was overwhelmingly bhadralok. The signatories, for instance, of the petition forwarded by the Jalpaiguri Municipality included three barristers, one pleader, two tea planters, two merchants (of whom one, Lachhmi Narayan Agrawal was a Marwari) and one zamindar.[88] In those districts where Hindus were in a minority and Muslims dominated the local bodies, professional associations controlled by bhadralok Hindus were pressed into service. The Bar Associations of Barisal,

---

[86] Other villages in Burdwan where Congress Committees were active in drumming up support for the campaign were Bhatar, Ketugram, Bantir, Bahumeria, Hajigram, Patuli and Santeswar. AICC Papers, File No. CL-14 (B)/1946–47 and CL-14 (C)/1946.

[87] These were the Union Boards at Chandar, Chiltore, Majigram, Lodgram, Layekhand, Khatia, Dheko, Arrah, Ghosergram, Barjora, Panchal, Radhamohanpur, Sashpur, Birsingha, Saltora, Neturpur, Gadaridhiti, Brindaban, Isulkusma, Chingani, Mandalgram, Kustor, Chhatna, Nabasan, Nadia, Seghari, Chhatua, Gandhapahar, Gopinathpur and Trakshabika. *Ibid.*

[88] AICC Papers, File No. CL-14 (A)/1946.

Pirojpur, Goalundo, Baruipore, Madaripore, Khulna, Suri, Behrampore and Nadia all sent in petitions, as did the Pleaders Association at Dinajpore and the Hindu Medical Practitioners Association in Nadia. Clerical and managerial staff of British and Anglo-Indian concerns – the so-called 'box-wallahs' of Calcutta – also shed nervousness about being seen to have political views and joined the movement. The files contain petitions from the Indian staff of Messrs. Jessop and Co., South British Insurance Co., Louis Dreyfus Co., Angus and Co., James Finlay and Co., Balmer Laurie and Co., and several other British and Marwari-owned concerns. The good and great of bhadralok Bengal – the ophthalmic surgeon, the professor of surgery, the barrister, the chief medical officer, the Chairman of the District Board, the zamindar, the babu mill manager and the executive engineer – all threw their weight behind the move to declare that 'as life, property, education and culture will be destroyed under the Muslim League Ministry' they had no alternative but to 'demand the immediate partition of Bengal'.[89]

There was a strong calculation of economic self-interest in this campaign which was not only well orchestrated but also well funded. Businessmen, whether Bengalis or outsiders, in Calcutta and up country, played a prominent role in organising the campaign. Birla, Ishwar Das Jalan, Goenka and Nalini Ranjan Sarkar – all the millionaires, the *lakhpatis* and *crorepatis* of Bengal – sat on the committee that planned the strategy of the campaign at the highest level.[90] Marwari traders from all over the province sent petitions to the All-India Congress Committee which declared that business in Bengal under the Muslim League ministry was 'absolutely crippled' and which were wholehearted in their support of the move to partition Bengal, describing it as a step that was 'necessary to restore peace and prosperity'.[91] Many of the public meetings organised in different parts of Bengal which passed resolutions demanding the immediate creation of a separate Hindu province were presided over (and of course paid for) by local business interests. Thus, for instance, the meeting in Dalimondalghat, Howrah, was presided over by a local mill-owner, while the pro-partition meeting in Siliguri in North Bengal was chaired by S. C. Kar, a well-to-do Bengali tea planter. And in Calcutta, Anandilal Poddar presided over

a meeting ... of the representatives of various religious institutions in Bengal, viz. the Arya Samaj, the Brahmo Samaj, the Mahabodhini Society, the Hindu Mission, the Sanatan Hindu Sabha, etc. ... [at which] speeches were made

[89] AICC Papers, File No. CL-14 (B)/1946.   [90] *The Statesman*, 1 May 1947.
[91] These included petitions from the Bengal National Chamber of Commerce, the Eastern Chamber of Commerce, the All-Bengal Traders and Consumers Association, the

demanding a separate Hindu province in Bengal comprising those areas willing to remain within the Indian Union.[92]

Indeed, G. D. Birla had been an advocate of partition for several years: he had admitted to Mahadev Desai as early as July 1942, that 'I am in favour of separation, and I do not think it is impracticable or against the interest of Hindus'.[93] Partition clearly made good economic sense to the Calcutta business community. The jute industry had never recovered from the traumas of the Depression, and although most Marwari families had made their fortunes through speculation in the jute fatka markets, they had rapidly moved out of jute in the thirties. Some, such as Anandilal Poddar, the Jhunjhunwallas, the Shethias and the Karnanis, made major investments in the collieries in these years, while others, including the Birla brothers, 'diversified into hitherto unknown and unfamiliar industries', such as sugar, paper, textiles and chemicals, banking and insurance;[94] investments that frequently took their interests out of Bengal, leading to the development of strong commercial links between Calcutta and other parts of the sub-continent. So if East Bengal and the jute-growing hinterland had once been vital to Calcutta business, this was no longer the case to important sections of that community in the forties. Nor were the markets of East Bengal, still reeling from the shock of the 1943 famine, an exciting prospect for Calcutta's entrepreneurs who had every reason to be confident of capturing the tiger's share of the all-India market in the wake of the British withdrawal.

But if the long-awaited harvest of Independence was to be brought in, Bengal would have to be partitioned. The Marwari community in Calcutta had no reason to believe that it would do well under a Muslim League government: indeed, the Bengal League, heavily dependent on the financial support of Hassan Ispahani, had made it clear that it intended to promote Muslim entrepreneurship after Independence.[95] A Congress government in Bengal, on the other hand, would be a friendly government, virtually in the pocket of the Marwari community. Partition was the only route by which the Congress could come to power in Bengal. A

Marwari Federation, the Calcutta Iron Merchants Association, and the Assam–Bengal Indian Tea Planters Association, among others. See, in particular, AICC Papers, File No. CL-14 (B)/1946.

[92] Memo dated 25 May 1947. GB SB 'PH' Series, File No. 507/46.

[93] G.D. Birla to Mahadev Desai, 14 July 1942. In G. D. Birla, *Bapu: A Unique Association. Correspondence, 1940–47*, Bombay, 1977, p. 316. Cited in Sumit Sarkar, 'Popular Movements and National Leadership, 1945–47', *Economic and Political Weekly*, Annual Number, April 1982, p. 679.

[94] Omkar Goswami, '*Sahibs, Babus and Banias*', pp. 300–301.

[95] M. A. H. Ispahani, *Qaid-i-Azam Jinnah as I knew Him*, chapters 7–9. See, also, Sumit Sarkar, 'Popular Movements and National Leadership', p. 679.

division on the basis of population, with Hindu-majority districts remaining in India, would keep Calcutta in the proposed Hindu province. Such a division was clearly in the interests of big business. The leading role played by Birla and members of his community in the Partition campaign made sound business sense.

Zamindars, professionals and Bengal's numerous tribe of respectable whitecollar (or rather *dhotied*) clerks, clearly dominated the movement along with business groups. But other less privileged sectors of Bengali Hindu society were also mobilised. The occupational breakdown of the signatories of petitions from four different rural areas include a surprisingly large number who entered their occupations as cultivation (*chash* or *chashadi*): the horny-handed tillers of the soil (see table 10). Of course, the number of cultivators who supported these petitions varied quite considerably from place to place. Even in the few cases outlined in table 10, they ranged from 80 per cent in Kashiara to 44 per cent in Tirol. Since those who signed (as opposed to putting their thumb-marks) were by definition minimally literate, in all probability they belonged to the upper strata of the cultivating classes. Nevertheless these petitions show that the organisers of the campaign were able to mobilise non-bhadralok Hindu opinion behind the demand for partition and point to the vigour and popularity of the movement. Particularly in Burdwan district, it is likely that this success owed much to the activity of local branches of the Congress Party. In Rayan village, for instance, the vigorous signature campaign owed everything to the activities of the local branch of the 'Congress Sevak Sangha', which sent in its own resolution supporting partition. But the extent to which persons who were not bhadralok joined in the campaign also reflected the success of the caste-consolidation campaigns of the forties in drawing less-privileged low caste and tribal groups into a Hindu political community. The Congress files include petitions from 'Scheduled Caste Hindus' of Baraset in the 24 Parganas, from the Adivasi Society of Paratal Union in Burdwan, the Islampur Harijan Seva Sangha in Mymensingh, the Khulna Scheduled Caste Association, the 'tribals of Jalpaiguri and Darjeeling', the Bangiya Sadgop Sabha, the Bangiya Mahisya Samity, the Bangiya Yadav Mahasabha at Khulna, and the 'scheduled caste Hindus' of Joyanagar in the 24 Parganas. It was in this area of mobilisation that the contribution of the Hindu Mahasabha, which had taken the lead in *shuddhi* and other caste-consolidation programmes, was most marked.

The Mahasabha also helped to drum up support for the partition campaign in East Bengal, particularly in Bakarganj, where its organisation was strongest. But the Hindus in the Muslim-majority districts who supported the call for partition all demanded, somewhat unrealistically,

Table 10. *Occupational breakdown of signatories of partition petitions (as returned from four different villages of Bengal)*

Occupation	No. of signatories	Occupation	No. of signatories
Kaiti P.O., Burdwan District:		**Kashiara P.O., Burdwan District**	
Business (vyavasa)	13	Business	2
Zamindari	2	Zamindari	—
Services (*brittibhogi/chakuri*)	6	Services	6
Cultivation (*chash/chashadi*)	125	Cultivation	44
Students	6	—	—
Miscellaneous	26	Miscellaneous	3
Total	178	Total	55
Rayan P.O., Burdwan District		**Tirol P.O., Hooghly**	
Business	3	Business	12
Zamindari	—	Zamindari	—
Services	20	Services	28
Cultivation	40	Cultivation	44
Miscellaneous	23	Miscellaneous	16
Total	86	Total	100

Source: Compiled from petitions contained in AICC Papers, File No. G-54 (I)/1947.

that their own subdivisions be somehow included in the proposed new Hindu state. Thus, for example, the memorandum prepared by the Barisal District Hindu Mahasabha, while supporting partition, argued for the inclusion of certain areas of Bakarganj and Faridpur districts in the new province:

It has become a well-recognised fact that in the interests of the preservation of communal harmony, peace and tranquillity, the creation of a Hindu majority Province in Bengal has become an absolute necessity of Hindu culture and religious, economic and political rights and privileges of the Hindus which have been seriously jeopardized by the Muslim League administration of Bengal during the last ten years, specially after the 16th of August, 'the Direct Action Day' declared by the Muslim League and the atrocities that followed.

It went on, however, to insist that a new 'Barisal district' should be created so as to include 'entire Gournadi, Wazirpur, Thalakati, Swaruphati, Nazirpur thanas and portions of Barisal (Kotwali) Babuganj, Nalchity, Bakarganj, Konkhali and Perojpur thanas', and that this district should be included in the new Hindu state.[96] None of those in East

[96] Memorandum of the Barisal District Hindu Mahasava, 17 May 1947. Shyama Prasad Mookerjee Papers, II–IV Instalment, File No. 82/1947.

Map 6. West Bengal and East Pakistan, 1947. *The Radcliffe Line*

Bengal who wanted to divide Bengal were ready to face the brutal fact that in the event of partition their own towns or thanas would go to 'Pakistan'. When it became clear in the middle of 1947 that there could be no special rescue plan to bring them into the new Hindu province, they had no choice but to join the endless stream of refugees who poured into Calcutta and West Bengal, leaving their homes, lands and jobs in East Pakistan in what became the largest transfer of population in recorded history.

The United Bengal Plan

The extraordinary success of the partition campaign in mobilising Hindu opinion did not, however, mean that it swept all before it. A handful of Hindu politicians, led by Sarat Chandra Bose, made a determined attempt to resist the tide. In January 1946 Bose resigned from the Congress Working Committee, to which he had made a brief return, on the issue of the Bengal Congress' 'acceptance' of the 6 December plan. The statement that it would not be 'party to any ... compulsion or imposition against the will of the people concerned' clearly indicated that the Congress had in fact accepted the principle of partition.[97] Similarly in March 1947 when the Congress Working Committee argued that the 'least amount of compulsion' would 'necessitate a division of the Punjab into two provinces, so that the predominantly Muslim part may be separated from the predominantly non-Muslim part',[98] Sarat Bose immediately saw the implications for Bengal: 'I think I ought to raise a voice of protest and sound a warning against the resolution ... to my mind a division of provinces on religious lines is no basis for a solution of the communal problem'.[99] He argued that the resolution was 'a violent departure from the traditions and principles of the Congress. And I am forced to say that it is the result of a defeatist mentality.'[100]

But it soon became evident that Bose did not have any backing in the provincial Congress. Within a fortnight, the Bengal Provincial Congress Committee passed a resolution formally associating itself with the partition demand, resolving that 'such portions of Bengal as are desirous of remaining within the Union of India should be allowed to remain so.'[101] A few days later, eleven Hindu members from Bengal in the Constituent Assembly approached Mountbatten with the demand for the creation of a

---

[97] Text of AICC Resolution, 6 January 1947. TP, vol. IX, No. 253.
[98] A. M. Zaidi (ed.), *The Encyclopaedia of the Indian National Congress*, vol. XIII, p. 127.
[99] Press Statement in *Amrita Bazar Patrika*, 15 March 1947.   [100] *Ibid.*, 19 March 1947.
[101] *Ibid.*, 5 April 1947.

'separate and autonomous province in West and North Bengal within the Indian Union'.[102] Nevertheless, Sarat Bose, with the support of Kiran Sankar Roy, attempted to come to an eleventh-hour agreement with Muslim leaders for the creation of a 'United and Sovereign Bengal'. In May 1947 Bose outlined the features of the proposal, which was seized upon enthusiastically by Suhrawardy and Abul Hashim, the powerful General Secretary of the provincial Muslim League. This unlikely alliance was based upon accepting the principle of joint electorates, adult franchise and reservation of seats according to population. The Government of the 'Free State' of Bengal would include an equal number of Hindu and Muslim ministers, with the exception of the Prime Minister, who would be a Muslim, while the Home Minister would be a Hindu. Muslims would be guaranteed an equal share in the services. And finally, it was agreed that the Free State of Bengal would be a 'Socialist Republic', as it was accepted that 'the solution of the communal problem lies ultimately in social justice'.[103]

However, the United Bengal Plan was never more than a pipe dream.[104] Even as Gandhi gave his conditional approval to the plan to keep Bengal united,[105] he was forced to withdraw his support, since, as he later confessed, his colleagues on the Working Committee had 'taken him to task for supporting Sarat Babu's move'.[106] The Congress High Command was by this time convinced of the need for a strong centre and a unitary India. Cutting out the Muslim-majority areas was necessary to ensure its unity and integrity, phrases that are now the cant of politicians but in 1947 were the keys to the future of independent India. Even Nehru and Patel, so often at odds, saw eye to eye on this matter. Nehru was vehemently opposed to what he described as the 'balkanization' of India[107] and was clear that individual provinces should in no circumstances be allowed the option of opting out of the Indian Union. Patel, for his part, appears to have been determined not to allow Jinnah an inch more territory than the Congress had to concede and therefore strongly supported Bengali Hindus in their demand for partition. He assured them that

[102] *Ibid.*, 12 April 1947.
[103] Associated Press Report, 22 May 1947. Cited in Sarat Chandra Bose, *I Warned My Countrymen: Being the Collected Works 1945–50 of Sarat Chandra Bose*, Calcutta, 1968, pp. 186–187. For fuller details on the plan, see Harun-or-Rashid, *The Foreshadowing of Bangladesh*, chapter 7; Shila Sen, *Muslim Politics in Bengal*, chapter 7, Leonard A. Gordon, 'Divided Bengal', and Amalendu De, *Independent Bengal: The Design and Its Fate*, Calcutta, 1975.
[104] This is something that has not generally been accepted by scholars of the plan, who have tended to study it as a realistic alternative to partition. See, for instance, Leonard Gordon, 'Divided Bengal'.
[105] Gandhi to Sarat Bose, 24 May 1947, *Ibid.*, p. 190.   [106] *Ibid.*, p. 192.
[107] Record of the Viceroy's meeting with Nehru, 11 May 1947. TP vol. IX, No. 405.

Bengal cannot be isolated from the Indian Union. Talk of the idea of a sovereign republic of independent Bengal is a trap to induce the unwary and the unwise to enter the parlour of the Muslim League. The Congress Working Committee is fully aware of the situation in Bengal, and you need not be afraid at all. Bengal has got to be partitioned, if the non-Muslim population is to survive.[108]

He soon made his views clear about the plans being drawn up by Sarat Bose and Kiran Sankar Roy who until recently had been a loyal ally of the centre in Bengal, describing the 'cry for sovereign Bengal' as 'a trap in which even Kiran Sankar may fall with Sarat Babu'.[109] Soon both gentlemen received a blunt warning from Patel, the party disciplinarian, who coldly advised them to stand united on the official policy of the Congress. There were precedents enough to show that his advice was not lightly to be ignored. Appeals by Bengal's few remaining Nationalist Muslims, begging the Congress to prevent partition, were given equally short shrift. Ashrafuddin Chaudhuri, heartbroken at the prospect of a communally inspired division that would leave him on the wrong side of the barbed wire, received no sympathy from the High Command. He was told that:

All that the Congress seeks to do today is to rescue as many as possible from the threatened domination of the League and Pakistan. It wants to save as much territory for a Free Indian Union as possible under the circumstances. It therefore insists upon the division of Bengal and Punjab ... I do not see what else the Congress can do under the circumstances.[110]

The Congress High Command's unbending hostility to the Sovereign Bengal Plan sealed its fate, for at this stage in the negotiations, Mountbatten, appearances notwithstanding, had to take his cue from the Congress bosses. But the plan to keep Bengal united was doomed even before it reached these olympian heights since it had failed to elicit support in Bengal itself. Despite the efforts of Abul Hashim and Huseyn Suhrawardy, the leadership of the Muslim League was deeply divided on the question. Every Muslim faction appears to have been opposed to chopping Bengal in two, but not all liked the idea that undivided Bengal should remain a free and independent state. In particular, Jinnah's most loyal followers, Akram Khan and Khwaja Nazimuddin, were convinced that Bengal should be a part of Pakistan or at least that it should maintain

[108] Patel to Binoy Kumar Roy, 23 May 1947, in Durga Das (ed.) *Sardar Patel's Correspondence*, vol. IV, p. 43.
[109] Patel to K. C. Neogy, 13 May 1947. *Ibid.*, p. 37.
[110] J. B. Kripalani to Ashrafuddin Ahmed Chaudhuri, 13 May 1947. AICC Papers, File No. CL-8/1946.

a close constitutional relationship with the new Muslim state in the West.[111] Others among the rank and file of the Muslim League, who had been enthused by the idea of Pakistan, were now unwilling to give up their promised land for the rather less Islamic 'Socialist Republic' of Bengal. Thus Abul Hashim was shouted down by his party-men at the League Conference in Delhi where he raised this possibility[112] while members of Jinnah's Muslim National Guard warned Congress leaders (and at the same time their own) that 'the loaded pistol is ready to correct them from the path of partition of Bengal and resistance against the creation of Pakistan'.[113] As for Jinnah's own views, typically he kept them close to his chest. Sarat Bose believed that Jinnah would support him[114] and appealed for his help.[115] Although Jinnah did not oppose the move, he did not openly support it either.[116] Yet for many of his followers in Bengal, the plan was a denial of the dream they believed the Qaid-i-Azam had shared with them, and so they rejected it in his name.

But the fatal weakness of the United Bengal Plan was its failure to attract any real support from the Hindus of Bengal. Sarat Bose appears to have been utterly unsuccessful in persuading them that a disputed share in the sovereignty over an undivided Bengal was preferable to partition and undisputed power. Only a tiny handful of Congressmen, including Kiran Shankar Roy, Akhil Chandra Datta, Nishitha Nath Kundu and of course Ashrafuddin Ahmed Chaudhuri, stood behind Sarat Bose in his last-ditch efforts: a commentary on the extent of Bose's isolation in Bengali politics by 1947. The Bengal Congress, which Sarat Bose had once dominated, was now firmly under the control of his rivals. It was a party that listened to its master's voice from the centre, and was run by men such as Dr B. C. Roy who owed their power mainly to the patronage of the Congress High Command. In March 1947 when the Congress declared that Bengal was to be divided, the provincial party was unlikely to have had the power to resist even if it had been minded to do so (which of course it was not). As for Suhrawardy's last minute change of heart, no Hindu was convinced by it and his backing for the plan made it all the more suspect and unwelcome in Hindu eyes. One pamphlet warned Bengal Hindus not to be

---

[111] For details of Muslim reactions to the plan, see Shila Sen, *Muslim Politics in Bengal*, pp. 223–245, and Harun-or-Rashid, *The Foreshadowing of Bangladesh*, chapter 7.
[112] Author's interview with Nikhil Chakravarty. New Delhi, 6 February 1989.
[113] Dutta Majumdar to Patel, 8 May 1947, in Durga Das (ed.), *Sardar Patel's Correspondence*, vol. IV, p. 36.
[114] Author's interview with Amiya Bose, Calcutta, 4 March 1988.
[115] Sarat Bose to Jinnah, 9 June 1947. Sarat Chandra Bose, *I Warned my Countrymen*, pp. 193–194.
[116] Shila Sen, *Muslim Politics in Bengal*, p. 243.

misled to-day by the wail of Suhrawardy. He is not lamenting of his concern over the fate of the Hindus or Muslims of Bengal. The real fact of the matter is that he is worried to think that it may not be possible for him and his colleagues to fatten their fortune by stealing any more. Do not forget that under the self-same Ministry ... [Muslims] have not only rested after committing murder, outrage on women and forcible conversion, but have rubbed off with their feet the vermilion marks from the foreheads of your mothers and have smashed the bangles on their hands with your shoes in order to humiliate the entire Hindu community ...[117]

Hindus in West Bengal had decided to plump for a Hindu state of their own rather than continuing to live under the premiership of a notoriously unreliable Muslim, and the Hindus of East Bengal were already reconciled to the bitter fact that they had to pack up their belongings and flee to the west.

So Sarat Bose waited in vain for Hindus from East Bengal to respond to his call. It was already far too late for that. Despite his assertion that only 'a section of the upper middle classes' in West Bengal favoured the decision to divide the province, he was unable to produce evidence to support his claim that 'the overwhelming majority of Hindus in East Bengal are dead against Partition'.[118] On the contrary, even the leading members of the Forward Bloc, the party he had inherited from his now-martyred brother Subhas Bose, denied him their support. In May 1947 the Police reported that

last week thirty-two members of the Executive Council of the Bengal Provincial Forward Bloc sent a joint memorandum to the President and Secretary of the All-India Forward Bloc urging the Forward Bloc High Command to reconsider its attitude in regard to the proposed partition of Bengal. If the Forward Bloc pursues its policy of opposition in spite of the growing support of the general public to the partition movement, it is urged, the Forward Bloc organisation will then perhaps disintegrate and eventually may collapse.[119]

Nor could Sarat Bose rely upon the support of Subhas' still significant rank and file following. In November 1945, when Calcutta's student and left-wing organisations had marched to Dalhousie Square in protest against the harsh sentences meted out to the INA accused, causing a panicky Governor to call out the army, Sarat Bose distanced himself from what was to become one of the largest popular uprisings that Calcutta had ever witnessed, declaring it to have been the work of *agents*

---

[117] *Banglar Hindu Sabdhan* ('Bengali Hindus, Beware'), anonymous, undated. GB SB 'PM' Series, 938/47 IV.

[118] Sarat Chandra Bose, *I Warned my Countrymen*, p. 198.

[119] Only eight of the Executive Council, including Leela Roy, Anil Baran Ray, Hem Ghosh, Jyotish Joardar and Satya Ranjan Bakshi, supported Sarat Bose's move. Memo dated 5 May 1947, in GB SB 'PM' Series, File No. 938/47 IV.

provocateurs.[120] The events of November 1945 had damaged Sarat Bose's image irreparably in the eyes of his brother's followers, and lost him his position as the rightful heir to 'Netaji's' new and volatile political constituency. In 1947 when Sarat Bose hoped to rally Subhas' followers behind him in the cause of United Bengal, he found them unamenable and hostile. One pamphlet spoke plainly of the revenge Subhas' followers could now take upon the brother who had let them down:

You will see how we will take our revenge. Let not the Bengal Partition movement stop. Today Sarat Bose and his blind satellites, both dogs and bitches, have stood against the Bengal Partition movement because they live in safe areas ... If his heroic brother Netaji remained today in our midst and had considered that the Bengal partition movement should stop he would have visited those [unsafe] places and inspired confidence in the minds of the sufferers ... On account of the cowardice which Sarat Bose displayed we would have silenced him for good and ever, had he not been a brother of Netaji ... We want a partition of Bengal or a Hindu-majority ministry, but such a Ministry should not be composed of men of Sarat Babu's type, who are satellites of the Muslims, there must be Hindus like Shyama Prasad in that Ministry.[121]

Shyama Prasad Mookerjee was close to the mark when he declared that 'Sarat Babu has no support whatsoever from the Hindus and he does not dare address one single meeting.'[122] The announcement of the June 3rd Plan and its acceptance by the Congress leadership sealed the fate of Bengal and Sarat Bose knew that he and all those who had dreamed of an united and sovereign Bengal had lost. His assertion that partition had been imposed upon the province without the support or consent of its people was mere wishful thinking:

I know that the Bengal Provincial Congress Committee and the Hindu members of the Bengal Legislative Assembly will not be asked to pronounce their own verdict of the Plan ... The democratic way would have been to leave them to exercise their own judgement after taking into consideration their electoral pledges and the interests of Bengal as a whole. But that is not to be. Bengal's voice has to be stifled and she is to continue to be a pawn in the all-India game.[123]

But Bengal had been in no sense a pawn in the game. The Bengal Congress had already chosen partition and over 90 per cent of the Hindu members of the Bengal Assembly were Congressmen. Sarat Bose's efforts notwithstanding, the decision to partition Bengal had a wide measure of

---

[120] GOI, Home Political File No. 5/8/1948. For further details, see Sumit Sarkar, 'Popular Movements and National Leadership', pp. 679–680.

[121] *Banglar Hindu Sabdhan.*

[122] Shyama Prasad Mookerjee to Vallabhbhai Patel, 11 May 1947. Durga Das (ed.), *Sardar Patel's Correspondence*, p. 39.

[123] Sarat Chandra Bose, *I Warned my Countrymen*, p. 198.

support among the Hindus and the Muslims of that unhappy province. Dropped by the official Congress, alienated from his own supporters and out of touch with the mood amongst his co-religionists, Sarat Bose was in 1947 a leader without a following. His 'movement' was in reality no more than the personal initiative of a man who no longer wielded influence among his people, and was, therefore, destined to fail.[124]

[124] The Congress files contain only four petitions opposing the partition, as against over four hundred in its support. Of these four petitions, three were the handiwork of Sarat Bose and his tiny coterie of supporters. The fourth, authored by Nishitha Nath Kundu, a low-caste peasant leader from Dinajpur, was phrased so equivocally as to be meaningless. While opposing partition, Kundu was quick to point out that 'we have not done and do not wish to do anything actively against the partition movement, for we are conscious that we may be mistaken in our beliefs'. Nishitha Nath Kundu to Acharya Kripalani, 3 May 1947. AICC Papers, F. No. CL-14 (B) / 1946.

Conclusion

The inwardness of Partition cannot be fully understood through a study of the motives of those in Delhi and in London who put the priorities of India and empire above the interests of Bengal. Nor do investigations into Muslim separatism tell the whole story. Partition, at least in one important province, was the considered choice of large and powerful sections of the Hindu population. When push came to shove, bhadralok Hindus preferred to carve up Bengal rather than to accept the indignity of being ruled by Muslims.

This book has attempted to challenge the prevailing wisdom about Partition on a number of counts. Partition is generally believed to have been a consequence of the separatist politics of Muslim minorities, but in the case of Bengal, Hindus evolved a parallel separatism of their own. The Congress High Command is widely (but wrongly) believed to have acquiesced only reluctantly to Partition. This study suggests that, on the contrary, not only was the Congress High Command ready to pay the price of Partition in order to strengthen its hold over an unitary India, but that the Bengal Congress campaigned successfully for the vivisection of its province on communal lines.

Many Bengalis believe that their province was a hapless pawn in the endgames of empire: that Bengal's aspirations were destroyed and her cultural integrity was sacrificed upon the altar of all-India imperatives. The United Bengal Plan is given as evidence that Bengalis actively fought against a second partition. But this version is far from the truth. In fact the United Bengal Plan had no takers on its home ground, culture was deployed as a mark of difference rather than evidence of traditional unity in the region, and bhadralok Bengalis, far from launching agitation against it, actually fought for the partition which gave them a separate homeland of their own. Partition was not imposed by the centre on an unwilling province. On the contrary, it reflected a symbiotic relationship between centre and province in which policy-makers at the centre encountered a reciprocal dynamic from Bengal. By focusing on the province rather than upon the centre, this study has tried to take his-

266

torical enquiry into Partition away from the smoke-filled rooms and negotiating tables where the men at the top played with the destinies of millions, into the towns and countryside of Bengal. It was here that the forces which led to the partition of that province mainly derived, and here that the harsh realities of vivisection, unprecedented even in the history of a province inured to calamity, were experienced in all their horror.

This book has placed the demand by the Hindus for the partition of their province and the communalism that drove it within the context of a rapidly changing society, where the balance had tilted against the erstwhile elites of the province. It has shown how the Communal Award and Poona Pact deprived the bhadralok of political power at a time when agrarian depression damaged their economic position and gave new opportunities and power to some Muslims. The measures enacted by successive Muslim governments demolished, step by step, the structures that had long sustained bhadralok dominance. Hindu communal mobilisation emerged as the most powerful of the competing political strategies that were evolved in response to this series of challenges. Secular strategies of a populist sort were also devised by an emerging left but these failed to carry the bulk of bhadralok opinion, which grew ever more parochial, more concerned with preserving narrow self-interest and more virulently communal. The 'Hindu' communal discourse of the bhadralok articulated the deeply conservative world view of an embattled elite, determined to pay whatever price it had to in order to cling to power and privilege. It was a discourse that was deeply communal in intention even when it did not invoke religious imagery or deploy sacred symbols.

The Hindu communalism of the bhadralok had little to do with primordial loyalties, popular cultures[1] or 'pre-bourgeois' modes of consciousness.[2] Nor was it an instance of deliberate and cynical manipulation of ancient ties and hatreds by an elite for their own ends. Neither the 'primordialist' nor the 'instrumentalist' approach, therefore, adequately explains the phenomenon of bhadralok communalism in Bengal.[3] By looking instead at the social and political challenges to which bhadra-

---

[1] Sandria Freitag's study of communal violence, for instance, situates it 'in a context provided by other collective activities – a world often labelled by scholars as '"popular culture"'. Sandria B. Freitag, *Collective Action and Community*, p. xii.

[2] See Dipesh Chakravarty, *Rethinking Working Class History. Bengal 1890–1940*, Princeton and New Delhi, 1989.

[3] For a detailed exposition of the 'primordialist' thesis, see Francis Robinson, 'Nation Formation: the Brass Thesis and Muslim Separatism', *Journal of Comparative and Commonwealth Politics*, vol. 15, 3, November 1977, pp. 215–234, and 'Islam and Muslim Separatism', in David Taylor and Malcolm Yapp (eds.), *Political Identity in South Asia*, London, 1979. The 'instrumentalist' case has been set out by Paul Brass in 'Elite Groups,

lok communalism was a response, and by examining the specificities of ideology that informed it, this book has attempted to 'de-mystify' this communalism by positing it with a history and rationale of its own, which enables it to be understood and more effectively challenged.

A history of Bengal on these lines may also provide clues to a clearer understanding of the more recent past: the relationship today between West Bengal and the centre, the history of the Bengal Congress since Independence, its ambivalent relationship with Delhi and its deep internal schisms; the strong regional base of the contemporary Bengali left; the proclivities of Bengali middle classes today and their characteristic impotence in all-India politics; the stark polarisation between the right and the left, and the unattractive cultural chauvinism which many bhadralok Hindus continue to share to this day. Finally, the arguments set out in this book may have some relevance to another debate which continues to dominate thinking about India's political future. A central theme of this work has been the idea of a *shift* from nationalism to communalism. Whatever similarities in style and idiom between nationalist rhetoric and Hindu communal posturings, the differences are critical. Nationalism was directed against imperialism, and gave top priority to anti-British action. The communalism of the bhadralok was directed against their fellow Bengalis.[4] History for the one was the struggle against British rule; for the other, it was the celebration of British rule as an age of liberation from the despotism of Muslims. Its key political objective was to prevent this 'despotism' from returning when the British left India, and to deny that Muslims could be Bengalis, and by extension Indians. The pernicious consequences of self-serving doctrines of this sort have gone much further than the division of a province; now once again they threaten the very future of the nation. If, by challenging the Hindu communalists' claim to the nationalist past,[5] this book has gone some way towards denying the legitimacy of their claims to India's future, it will have served a useful purpose.

Symbol Manipulation and Ethnic Identity among the Muslims of South Asia', in the same collection of essays.

[4] See Gyanendra Pandey, *The Construction of Communalism*, pp. 233–261.

[5] The Hindutva version of the history of the last decades of the Raj has it that Congress was 'anti-national' because it consented to Partition and surrendered to Pakistan the soil of the motherland; that Communists were 'anti-national' because they collaborated with the British during the war effort. Only the Hindu organisations, in this account, remained true to the cause of the nation.

Appendix I

Bartaman Hindu–Mussalman Samasya

Sarat Chandra Chattopadhyay

[*First presented as a speech at the Bengal Provincial Conference of 1926, the text of this essay later appeared in* Hindu Sangha, *19 Ashwin 1333. A translation is given below.*]

The current Hindu–Muslim problem

A notion need not be correct simply because large numbers of people assert it with great conviction. No matter what the strength of their numbers, and despite the clamour of their combined voice, what the crowds proclaim is not necessarily true. The unceasing cacophony of voices shouting in unison forces people into believing what they hear. But this is propaganda. In the last great war, both sides accepted as true the falsehood that killing each other is man's duty merely because much ink has flowed and many voices have been raised to persuade them of this untruth. The few who challenged this view and attempted to speak the truth were subjected to endless ridicule and humiliation. But times have changed. Having undergone much pain and sorrow, people today have realised there was little truth in much that was said at that time.

So it was some years ago in this country, at the time when Mahatma Gandhi launched his non-violent Non-Cooperation movement. Many leaders loudly proclaimed that Hindu–Muslim unity had to be achieved, whatever the cost. They wanted it not only because it was good in itself, but because without it, to dream of Swaraj and Independence was mere foolishness. If they had been asked why it was 'foolishness', who knows what they would have answered. But in speeches, through writing and shouting, it achieved the status of a self-evident truth. And nobody except a fool would dare to question it.

Then Hindus lost everything in an attempt to find the magic grail of togetherness. Countless time and energy was wasted in this pursuit. It resulted in the Mahatma's Khilafat Movement and in Deshbandhu's Pact, whose hollowness is unsurpassed in Indian politics. There was at least a semblance of an excuse for the Pact because willy-nilly it was a compromise suited to the times which aimed to defeat the Bengal

Government in Council. But the Khilafat movement, from the Hindu side, was not only pointless, it was false. Battles fought for a false cause can never be won. And the lie of Khilafat, like an unbearably heavy stone tied around the neck, dragged the Non-Cooperation movement to its destruction.

We want Swaraj. We want freedom from the yoke of foreign rule. The British may put up a case against this demand of the Indian people, but their case will not stand in the court of world opinion. Whether or not we succeed, the struggle for our birthright is noble, and those who lose their lives in this struggle will go to heaven. There is no one on earth who will not accept this truth.

But 'we want Khilafat'? What sort of talk was this? A country with which India had no connection – we did not even know what its people ate, wore or looked like – a country that was ruled by Turkey in the past! And once Turkey was defeated in the war and the Sultan was sent back, the colonised Indian Muslim community childishly insisted on his return. Was this reasonable?

In reality, this was also a pact. Or rather it was a bribe. 'We want Swaraj and you want Khilafat – so come, let us unite. We will offer our heads to be broken for Khilafat, and you will raise the slogan of Swaraj'. But to the one demand for Swaraj, the British Government paid no heed, and in reply to the other, the Caliph for whom the Khilafat movement had been launched, was expelled from Turkey. Thus, when the Khilafat movement proved entirely meaningless and insubstantial, in its hollowness it not only destroyed itself, but it also killed India's independence movement. Can one ever bribe, entice or delude people into joining a freedom struggle? And indeed if you can, will you ever win victory? I do not think this can ever be possible.

The one who laboured hardest for this [Hindu–Muslim unity] was Mahatmaji himself. No one else had as much hope, and no one else felt so cheated. In those days, Muslim politicians were at his right hand and at his left, they were his eyes and his ears. My goodness, was there ever such a spectacle? His last attempt for Hindu–Muslim unity was his twenty-one day fast at Delhi. He is a simple, god-fearing man: perhaps he thought that by showing a readiness to suffer, they would take pity on him [and relent]. Somehow his life was saved. His dearly beloved friend Mr Mohammed Ali was the one who was most disturbed, it all happened before his eyes. Shedding crocodile tears, he said, 'Oh, what a good man is this Mahatmaji! I want to do something really helpful for him. So let us first go to Mecca, then make an oblation to the Pir, then read the Kalma, and make him renounce the infidel religion'. On hearing this, the disillusioned Mahatma cried, 'Let the earth swallow me.'

The truth is that if Muslims ever say that they want to unite with Hindus, there is no greater hoax. The Muslims came to India to plunder it, not to establish a kingdom. They were not satisfied merely with looting – they destroyed temples, they demolished idols, they raped women. The insult to other religions and the injury to humanity were unimaginable.

Even when they became kings they could not liberate themselves from these loathsome desires. Even Akbar, who was famed for his tolerance, was no better than notorious emperors like Aurangzeb. But today it seems that their practices have become an addiction. Many argue that the monstrous events at Pabna were the work of mullahs from the West, who excited the innocent and uneducated Muslim peasants and instigated these awful deeds. But if, in the same way, a party of Hindu priests were to arrive in a Hindu-majority area and try to incite the docile Hindu peasantry to burn the homesteads, loot the property and insult the women of their innocent Muslim neighbours, then the same unlettered Hindu peasantry would immediately declare them mad and drive them away from the village.

Why does this happen? Is it simply the result of illiteracy? If learning is simply knowing how to read and write, there is little difference between Hindu and Muslim peasants and labourers. But if the essence of learning is breadth of mind and culture at one's very heart, then there is no comparison between the two communities. When journalists raise the question of the abduction of Hindu women, why are the Muslim leaders silent? When people of their community regularly commit such grave crimes, why do they not protest? What is the meaning of their silence? To my mind, the meaning is crystal clear. It is only a sense of decorum that prevents them from admitting openly that far from protesting, given the opportunity, they would commit the same crimes themselves.

Unity can only be realised among equals. Many may hope to establish a parity of learning [between Hindus and Muslims] but I do not. A thousand years has not been enough time to achieve this, nor will another millennium suffice. If to expel the British, this is our only resource, then Independence will have to wait. There is much else to do. Some hoped that with Khilafat and with the Das Pact, they might be able to sweet-talk Muslims into the freedom struggle, but the majority did not. There are those who argue that there is no teacher like grief and despair, that when Muslims suffered continuous humiliation at the hands of the imperialist, they would be awakened and would fight shoulder to shoulder with Hindus for Swaraj. But they are mistaken, because they have not taken into account the fact that the very ability to sense humiliation is itself a product of learning. While a man like Deshbandhu burned with humiliation, I [a lesser mortal] was unaffected. More importantly, those who feel no horror while oppressing the weak can feel no shame when they grovel before the mighty. So why are we deceiving ourselves? 'Hindu–Muslim unity' is a bombastic phrase. At different times, many such phrases have been bandied about, but they serve no purpose. We must sacrifice this illusion. It is useless for us to try to shame Bengali Muslims by saying that seven generations ago they were Hindus, therefore they are related to us by blood: fratricide is a sin, so show little pity. To my mind, there is nothing more dishonourable than begging for pity and grovelling for unity. In this country and abroad, I have several Christian friends. Either they or their forefathers adopted a new faith. But unless they tell you themselves that they are Christians, it is impossible to tell them apart from us, or to think that they are not still our brothers and sisters. I knew a Christian lady once. She died young, but even so, there are few who have earned as much respect in their lifetimes.

But Muslims? I had a Brahmin cook once. He sacrificed his religion in order to indulge his passion for a Muslim woman. One year later, he had changed his name, his dress and even his nature. The very face that God gave him had changed beyond recognition. And this is not an isolated instance. Those who know something about village life know that this sort of thing happens frequently. And in the matter of aggression, these new converts put their Muslim co-religionists to shame.

The problem before Hindus, therefore, is not to bring about this unnatural union between Hindus and Muslims. Their task is to achieve unity within their own community, and to bring an end to the folly of those practising Hindus (*Hindu dharmaablambi*) who insult some people by calling them 'low caste'. Even more pressing is the need for Hindus to think about how they may let the [religious] truth within them blossom like a flower in their everyday lives and public behaviour. Those who think do not speak, those who speak do not act and those who act are not accepted. If this evil is not checked, even God will not be able to mend the countless holes that are being punched into the fabric of the community.

This is the problem and this is the duty. There is no point in wailing or beating our breasts because Hindu–Muslim unity has not come about. If we stop our own crying, we may be able to hear crying from their quarters.

Hindustan is the homeland of the Hindus. Therefore it is the duty of the Hindus alone to free this nation from the chains of servitude. Muslims look towards Turkey and Arabia, their hearts are not in India. What is the use of bemoaning this fact? To appeal to them in the name of the Soil of Mother India is as pointless as talking to a brick wall. Today it is vital that we understand this point – that this work is the work only of Hindus, and no one else. There is no need to get agitated counting how numerous is the

Muslim population. Numbers are not the ultimate truth in this world. There are greater truths, in whose scale of values the arithmetic of counting heads has no place.

All that I have said about Hindu–Muslim unity may be a bitter pill to swallow. But this is no cause for alarm. Nor is there any reason to call me a traitor. I am not suggesting that I will not be pleased if ties of mutual respect and affection were to grow up between these two neighbouring communities. All I am saying is that if this does not come about, and if there are no signs that it is likely to ever come about, it is useless to weep. Nor is it helpful to believe that such a failure would mean the end of the world. It has been repeated so often that we have come to believe that it is the only truth, and that there is no other way. But are we actually achieving anything? No. All that we do is compile lists of all instances of the cruelty and hostility of Muslims towards us, all that we say is this: 'You have killed us, you have broken our idols, destroyed our temples and kidnapped our women. In this you have been very unjust, and have caused us great pain. We cannot continue to live like this.'

Do we ever say more than this, or do more than this? We have accepted without hesitation that it is our role to bring about 'togetherness' and their responsibility to stop oppressing us. But in truth, the roles should be reversed. It is our job to put a stop to their cruelty, and, if anything remains of 'Hindu–Muslim unity', it is their duty to bring it about.

But how can our country be freed? I ask you this – can our country be freed by fraud? When Hindus come forward and vow to free their country, then it will matter little whether a few dozen Muslims lend their support or not. The Muslims will never truly believe that India's freedom will bring them freedom too. They will only accept this truth when their obsession with their religion weakens. Then they will understand that whatever one's religion, to be proud of fanaticism is a matter of shame, there is no greater barbarism than this. But there is a long way to go before they will understand this. Unless all the people all over the world unite to educate the Muslims, it is doubtful that their eyes will ever be opened. Moreover, do all the people of a nation ever come forward together to fight for its freedom? Is it ever possible or even necessary? When America fought for her independence, the majority of her people supported the British. How many Irish people supported the Irish freedom movement? The Bolshevik government that is in power in Russia has not the support of even one per cent of the people. Human beings are not animals; crowds alone do not establish what is true. Intense spiritual endeavour alone can identify and establish the truth.

The burden of this single-minded devotion lies on the shoulders of the male youths of our nation. It is not their job to scheme for Hindu–Muslim unity. Nor is it their duty to waste their time applauding those political leaders who are howling hopelessly for this unity. There are many things in this world that can be attained only by sacrificing them first. Hindu–Muslim unity is one among these. I feel that if we sacrifice this hope and get down to work, we will see proof of this. In that event, unity will not be the outcome of the efforts of one side, but will be the result of a shared desire sincerely felt by both sides.[1]

[1] *Source:* Haripada Ghosh (ed.), *Sarat Rachana Samagra* ('Collected Works of Sarat Chandra Chattopadhyay'), III, Calcutta, 1989.

Bibliography

MANUSCRIPT SOURCES

PRIVATE PAPERS

John Anderson Papers (Indian Office Library and Records) (IOLR)
F. O. Bell Papers (IOLR)
Linlithgow Papers (IOLR)
Shyama Prasad Mookerjee Papers (Nehru Memorial Museum and Library)
    (NMML)
Pinnell Papers (IOLR)
Robert Reid Papers (IOLR)
B. C. Roy Papers (NMML)
Nalini Ranjan Sarkar Papers (NMML)
B. P. Singh Roy Papers (NMML)
Suamarez Smith Papers (IOLR)
Zetland Papers (IOLR)

MANUSCRIPT MEMOIRS

P. D. Martyn Memoirs (IOLR)
S. Rahmatullah Memoirs (IOLR)

ORAL HISTORY TRANSCRIPTS

Interview with Surendra Mohan Ghosh (NMML)
Interview with Nellie Sengupta (NMML)

RECORDS OF POLITICAL ORGANISATIONS

All India Congress Committee Papers (NMML)
Akhil Bharatiya Hindu Mahasabha Papers (NMML)

OFFICIAL RECORDS

Government of India
Public and Judicial Proceedings L/P and J (IOLR)

Private Office Papers L/PO (IOLR)
Home Political Proceedings (National Archives of India) (NAI)

Government of Bengal
(i) Home Department Records
Home Confidential Political Department, Political Branch (West Bengal State
    Archives) (WBSA)
Local Officers' Fortnightly Confidential Reports (WBSA)

(ii) Police Records
Special Branch 'PM' Series (Special Branch, Calcutta) (SB)
Special Branch 'PH' Series (SB)

PUBLISHED SOURCES

OFFICIAL PUBLICATIONS

District Gazetteers
Bengal District Gazetteer, Burdwan, by J. C. K. Peterson, Calcutta, 1910.
East Bengal District Gazetteer, Dinajpur, by F. W. Strong, Dacca, 1905.
Bengal District Gazetteer, Howrah, by L. S. S. O'Malley and M. Chakravarti,
    Calcutta, 1909.
Bengal District Gazetteer, Jessore, by L. S. S. O'Malley, Calcutta, 1912.
Bengal District Gazetteer, Murshidabad, by L. S. S. O'Malley, Calcutta, 1914.
Bengal District Gazetteer, Mymensingh, by F. A. Sachse, Calcutta, 1917.
Bengal District Gazetteer, Pabna, by L. S. S. O'Malley, Calcutta, 1923.
Bengal District Gazetteer, Tippera, by J E. Webster, Calcutta, 1910.

Survey and Settlement Reports
*Final Report on the Survey and Settlement Operations in the District of Burdwan,
    1927–34*, by K. A. L. Hill, Alipore, 1940.
*Final Report on the Survey and Settlement Operations in the District of Mymen-
    singh, 1908–19*, by F. A. Sachse, Calcutta, 1920.
*Final Report on the Survey and Settlement Operations in the District of Noakhali,
    1914–19*, by W. H. Thompson, Calcutta, 1919.
*Final Report on the Survey and Settlement Operations in the Districts of Pabna and
    Bogra, 1920–29*, by D. MacPherson, Calcutta, 1930.

Census of India, 1931 and 1941, report and tables on Bengal and Calcutta.
Report of the Land Revenue Commission, Bengal 1938–40 (Chairman Sir Francis
    Floud), vols. I–VI, Alipore, 1940.
*Resolutions Reviewing the Reports on the Working of District and Local Boards in
    Bengal*, Calcutta, 1931–35
*Resolutions Reviewing the Working of District, Local and Union Boards in Bengal
    During the Year 1934–35 and 1936–37*, Calcutta, 1936 and 1937.
Union Board Manual, vol. I, Alipore, 1937.
*Indian Round Table Conference (Second Session), Procedures of the Federal
    Structure Committee and the Minorities Committee*, Calcutta, 1932.

Report of the Indian Statutory Commission, vol. XVII, Calcutta, 1930.
Proceedings, Bengal Legislative Assembly, 2nd Session, vol. LI, Calcutta, 1937.

OTHER PUBLISHED SOURCES

Bose, Sisir K. (ed.), Netaji Collected Works, vol. I, Calcutta, 1980.
Collett, S. D., The Life and Letters of Raja Rammohun Roy, Calcutta, 1962.
Das, Durga (ed.), Sardar Patel's Correspondence, 10 vols., Ahmedabad, 1971–1974.
Mansergh N., Lumby, E. W. R., and Moon, Penderel (eds.), Constitutional Relations Between Britain and India: The Transfer of Power 1942–7, vol. I–XII, 1970–82.
Pandey, B. N., The Indian Nationalist Movement. Select Documents. London, 1979.
Munshi, K. M., Indian Constitutional Documents, vol. I: Pilgrimage to Freedom, Bombay, 1967.
Zaidi, Z. H., M. A. Jinnah – Ispahani Correspondence, 1936–48, Karachi, 1976.

NEWSPAPERS AND JOURNALS

Advance (Calcutta).
Amrita Bazar Patrika (Calcutta).
Bande Mataram (Calcutta).
Bengalee (Calcutta).
Dainik Basumati (Calcutta).
Forward (Calcutta).
Indian Annual Register (Calcutta).
Modern Review (Calcutta).
The Statesman (Calcutta).

INTERVIEWS

Bose, Amiya, Calcutta, 4 March 1988.
Bose, Sisir Kumar, Calcutta, 11 March 1988.
Chakravarty, Nikhil, New Delhi, 6 February 1989.
Hussain, Syed Sajjad, Dhaka, 12 February 1990.
Mitra, Ashok, Calcutta, 2 March 1988.
Rezzak, Abdur, Dhaka, 11–13 February 1990.
Sen, Ashit, Calcutta, 5 March 1988.
Sengupta, Rabindra, Calcutta, 14 February 1988.
Umar, Badruddin, Dhaka, 11 February 1990.

SECONDARY WORKS

MEMOIRS, JOURNALS AND BIOGRAPHIES

Ahmed, Abul Mansur, Amar Dekha Rajnitir Panchash Bachhar ('Fifty Years of Politics as I Saw It'), Dacca, 1970.
Banerjee, Surendra Nath, A Nation in the Making. Being the Reminiscences of Fifty years of Public Life, Calcutta, 1963.

Birla, G. D., *In the Shadow of the Mahatma – A Personal Memoir*, Calcutta, 1953.
Bapu: A Unique Association. Correspondence, 1940–47, Bombay, 1977.
Bose, Sarat Chandra, *I Warned my Countrymen. Being the Collected Works 1945–50 of Sarat Chandra Bose*, Calcutta, 1968.
Sarat Bose Commemoration Volume, Calcutta, 1982.
Bose, Sisir Kumar, *Remembering my Father*, Calcutta, 1988.
Bose, Subhas Chandra, *An Indian Pilgrim*, in Sisir Bose (ed.), *Netaji Collected Works*, vol. I, Calcutta, 1980.
Chaudhuri, Jamaluddin Ahmed, *Rajbirodhi Ashrafuddin Ahmed Chaudhuri*, Dacca, 1978.
Chaudhuri, Nirad, C. *Thy Hand Great Anarch! India, 1921–1952*, London, 1987.
The Autobiography of an Unknown Indian, London, 1988.
Chowdhury, Hamidul Huq, *Memoirs*, Dhaka, 1989.
Dutt, Kalpana, *Chittagong Armoury Raiders, Reminiscences*, New Delhi, 1979.
Gordon, Leonard A., *Brothers against the Raj. A Biography of Sarat and Subhas Chandra Bose*, New York, 1990.
Hashim, Abul, *In Retrospection*, Dacca, 1974.
Ikramullah, Begum Shaista, *From Purdah to Parliament*, London, 1963.
Ispahani, M. A. H., *Qaid-i-Azam Jinnah as I Knew Him*, Karachi, 1966.
Kamal, Kazi Ahmed, *Politicians and Inside Stories: A Glimpse Mainly into the Lives of Fazlul Huq, Shaheed Suhrawardy and Maulana Bhashani*, Dhaka, 1970.
Khalak, Khondokar Abdul, *Ek Shatabdi* ('One Century'), Dhaka, 1970.
Khan, Tamizuddin, *The Test of Time. My life and Days*, Dhaka, 1989.
Madhok, Balraj, *Dr. Syama Prasad Mookerjee. A Biography*, New Delhi, 1954.
Mitra, Asok, *Three Score and Ten*, Calcutta, 1987.
Moon, Penderel (ed.), *Wavell: The Viceroy's Journal*, London, 1973.
Purani, A. B., *The Life of Sri Aurobindo. A Source Book*, Pondicherry, 1964.
Rab, A. S. M. Abdur, *A. K. Fazlul Huq*, Lahore, 1966.
Ray Chaudhury, Prithwis Chandra, *Life and Times of C. R. Das. The Story of Bengal's Self-Expression*, London, 1927.
Ray, Prafulla Chandra, *Life and Experiences of a Bengali Chemist*, Calcutta, 1932.
Shamsuddin, A. K., *Atit Diner Smriti* ('Memories of Days Past'), Dacca, 1968.
Talukdar, M. H. R. (ed.), *Memoirs of Huseyn Shaheed Suhrawardy*, Dacca, 1987.
Ziegler, Philip, *Mountbatten: the official biography*, London, 1985.

CONTEMPORARY LITERATURE, TRACTS, AND PAMPHLETS

(Some of these publications are anonymous and undated, and their place of publication is uncertain. Where possible, the place and year in which the pamphlet was found, if known, is appended in square brackets.)

Ambedkar, B. R., *Gandhi and Gandhism*, Jullunder, 1970.
Bandopadhyay, Saradindu, *Aadim Ripu* ('Original Enemy') in Pratulchandra Gupta (ed.), *Saradindu Omnibus*, vol. II, Calcutta, 1980.
Banerjee, Bhavanicharan, *Kalikata Kamalalaya* ('Calcutta Abode of Lotuses'), Calcutta, 1823.
Banerji, Bibhutibhushan, *Pather Panchali* ('Song of the Road'), Calcutta, 1929.
Bangiya Prajaswatara Nutun Ain O Leaguer Bani ('The Bengal Tenancy Amendment Act and the League's Call'), Dacca, 1939.

Banglar Hindu Sabdhan ('Bengali Hindus Beware') (Anon.), undated.

Basu, Jogindrachandra, *Model Bhagini* ('The Model Sister'), Calcutta, 1886–87.

Bengal Anti-Communal Award Movement. A Report, Calcutta, 1936.

Bhaduri, Dwijendranath, *Soula Agasta Unnis Sau Chhe-challis* ('Sixteenth August, Nineteen Forty-six'), Calcutta, 1946.

Chakravarty, Dhires, 'Hindu Muslim Unity – Platitudes and Reality', *Modern Review*, vol. 59, 1–6, 1936.

Chatterjee, B. C., *The Betrayal of Britain and Bengal*, undated.

Chattopadhyay, Bankimchandra, *Anandamath* (1st English edn), Calcutta, 1938.

    Dharmatattva (1894) ('Essentials of Dharma'), in Bankimchandra Chattopadhyay, *Sociological Essays. Utilitarianism and Positivism in Bengal* (translated and edited by S. N. Mukherjee and Marian Maddern), Calcutta, 1986.

    Rajsingha (1893), in Prafullakumar Patra (ed.), *Bankim Rachanabali*, ('Bankim's Collected Works'), I, Calcutta, 1989.

    Rajani (1880), in Prafullakumar Patra (ed.), *Bankim Rachanabali*, ('Bankim's Collected Works'), I, Calcutta, 1989.

    Lokrahasya (1874), in Prafullakumar Patra (ed.), *Bankim Rachanabali*, ('Bankim's Collected Works') II, Calcutta, 1989.

Chattopadhyay, Sarat Chandra, *Palli Samaj* ('Village Society'), in Sukumar Sen (ed.) *Sulabh Sarat Samagra* ('Sarat's Collected Works'), 2 vols., Calcutta, 1989.

    Pather Dabi ('Demands of the Road'), in Haripada Ghosh (ed.), *Sarat Rachana Samagra* ('Collected Works of Sarat Chandra Chattopadhyay'), III, Calcutta, 1989.

    Bipradas, Sarat Rachana Samagra, III, Calcutta, 1989.

    Bartaman Hindu–Mussalman Samasya ('The Current Hindu–Muslim Problem'), *Sarat Rachana Samagra*, III, Calcutta, 1989.

Dasgupta, Satish Chandra, *Bharater Samyavad* ('Communism in India'), Calcutta, 1930.

Dutt, Romesh Chunder, *Maharashtra Jibanprabhat* ('The Dawn of Maharashtra'), Calcutta, 1878.

    Rajput Jibansandhya ('The Dusk of Rajput History'), Calcutta 1879.

    Cultural Heritage of Bengal, Calcutta, 1896.

    The Lake of Palms: A Story of Indian Domestic Life, London, 1902.

Effendi, Mohammad Ehsanul Huq, *Bartaman Rajnaitik Sankat O Muslamaner Kartabya* ('Current Political Dangers and the Duty of Muslims'), Rangpur, 1939.

Ghosh, Girishchandra, *Sirajoddaula*, in Rabindranath Ray and Debipada Bhattacharya (eds.), *Girish Rachanbali* ('The Collected Works of Girish Chandra Ghosh'), I, Calcutta, 1969.

Haque, Azizul, *The Man Behind the Plough*, Calcutta, 1939.

Hindu! Jagrihee ('Hindus! Awake') (Anon.) [Calcutta, 1947].

Hindur Sankatmoy Paristhiti: Netribrinder Ahaban ('The Difficult Situation of Hindus: The Leaders' Call') (Anon.) Calcutta, 1939.

Khondkar, Ain-al-Islam, *Goru O Hindu-Mussalman* ('The Cow, Hindus and Muslims').

Kirttana, Lakshmi Kanta and Bhattacharya, Kumud, *Ganer Bahi Loter Gan* ('Book of Songs, Songs of Plunder'), Mymensingh, 1930.

Mitra, Akshaykumar, *Sirajuddaula*, Calcutta, 1891.

Mitra, Pearylal, *Alaler Gharer Dulal* ('The Spoilt Child of A Rich Family'), Calcutta, 1937.
Naoroji, Dadabhai, *Poverty and Un-British Rule in India*, London, 1901.
Odul, Qazi Abd-al, *Hindu Mussalmaner Birodh* ('Hindu–Muslim Enmity'), Calcutta, 1935.
Rise Up All Hindus Wherever You Are and Get Ready to Return Blow for Blow (Anon.), [Calcutta, 1947].
Roy, Dwijendralal, *Rana Pratapsingha*, Calcutta, 1905.
    Mewar Patan ('The Fall of Mewar'), Calcutta, 1908.
Sangram ('Struggle') (Anon.) [Calcutta, 1946].
Sen, Nabinchandra, *Palasir Juddha* ('The Battle of Plassey') (1876), Calcutta, 1984 edn.
Swami Vivekananda, *Uthishtat! Jagrat! Hindu Rashtra ka Amar Sandesh* ('Arise! Awaken! The Immortal Message of the Hindu Nation'), Lucknow, 1972.
    The Complete Works of Swami Vivekananda, Calcutta, 1989.
Tagore, Rabindranath, *Gora*, London, 1912.
    Nationalism, London, 1917.
    Sahaj Path ('Simple Lessons'), Visvabharati, 1931.
Why Mr. Nalini Ranjan Sarkar left the Congress (Anon.) Calcutta, 1937.

PUBLISHED BOOKS

Ahmed, Rafiuddin, *The Bengal Muslims 1871–1906. A Quest for Identity*, New Delhi, 1981.
Ali, Hashim Amir. *Then and Now (1933–1958). A Study of Socio-Economic Structure and Change in Some Villages near Viswa Bharati University Bengal*, New Delhi, 1966.
Ambedkar, B. R., *Gandhi and Gandhism*, Jullunder, 1970.
Anderson, Benedict, *Imagined Communities. Reflections on the Origins and Spread of Nationalism*, London, 1990.
Bagchi, Amiya Kumar, *Private Investment in India 1900–1939*, Madras, 1972.
Bak, J. M. and Benecker, G. (eds.), *Religion and Rural Revolt*, Manchester, 1984.
Bandopadhyay, Gitasree, *Constraints in Bengal Politics 1921–41. Gandhian Leadership*, Calcutta, 1984.
Bandopadhyay, Sekhar, *Caste, Politics and the Raj. Bengal, 1872–1937*, Calcutta, 1990.
Banerjee, Sumanta, *The Parlour and the Streets. Elite and Popular Culture in Nineteenth Century Calcutta*, Calcutta, 1989.
Beteille, Andre, *Studies in Agrarian Social Structure*, New Delhi, 1974.
    The Idea of Natural Inequality, New Delhi, 1983.
Bhattacharyya, Buddhadev, *Satyagrahas in Bengal, 1921–1939*, Calcutta, 1977.
Bhattacharya, J. N., *Hindu Castes and Sects*, Calcutta, 1973.
Bose, Sugata, *Agrarian Bengal: Economy, Social Structure and Politics, 1919–1947*, New Delhi, 1987.
Bourdieu, Pierre, *Distinction. A Social Critique of the Judgement of Taste* (translated by Richard Nice), London, 1986.
    Homo Academicus (translated by Peter Collier), Cambridge, 1988.
    Language and Symbolic Power (translated by Gino Raymond and Matthew Adamson), Cambridge, 1992.

The Field of Cultural Production. Essays on Art and Literature, Cambridge, 1993.

Bourdieu, Pierre and Passeron, Jean-Claude, *Reproduction in Education, Society and Culture* (translated by Richard Nice), London, 1990.

Breuilly, John, *Nationalism and the State*, Manchester, 1985.

Broomfield, J. H., *Elite Conflict in a Plural Society. Twentieth-Century Bengal*, Berkeley, 1968.

Mostly About Bengal, New Delhi, 1982.

Buchanan-Hamilton, Francis, *A Geographical, Statistical and Historical Description (1908) of the District. A Zillah of Dinajpur in the Province, or Soubah of Bengal*, Calcutta, 1883.

Byres, T. J., *Charan Singh 1902–87. An Assessment*. Patna, 1988.

Cardechi, Guglielmo, *On the Economic Identification of Social Classes*, London, 1977.

Chakrabarty, Bidyut, *Subhas Chandra Bose and Middle-Class Radicalism. A Study in Indian Nationalism*, London, 1990.

Chakrabarty, Dipesh, *Rethinking Working-Class History. Bengal 1890–1940*, Princeton and New Delhi, 1989.

Chakrabarty, Ramakanta, *Vaisnavism in Bengal*, Calcutta, 1985.

Chandra, Bipan, *The Rise and Growth of Economic Nationalism in India*, New Delhi, 1966.

Communalism in Modern India, New Delhi, 1984.

Chatterjee, Bhola, *Aspects of Bengal Politics in the 1930s*, Calcutta, 1969.

Chatterjee, Partha, *Bengal 1920–1947. The Land Question*, Calcutta, 1984.

Nationalist Thought and the Colonial World: A Derivative Discourse, New Delhi, 1986.

Chatterjee, Partha and Pandey, Gyandendra (eds.), *Subaltern Studies VII*, Delhi, 1992.

Chattopadhyay, Gautam, *Bengal Electoral Politics and Freedom Struggle, 1862–1947*, New Delhi, 1984.

Clark, Gordon L. and Dear, Michael, *State Apparatus: Structures and Language of Legitimacy*, Winchester, Mass., 1984.

Cohen, Anthony P., *The Symbolic Construction of Community*, London, 1985.

Cohn, B. S. and Singer, M., *Structure and Change in Indian Society*, Chicago, 1968.

Collins, Larry and Lapierre, Dominique, *Freedom at Midnight*, London, 1975.

Das, Suranjan, *Communal Riots in Bengal, 1905–1947*, New Delhi, 1991.

Dasgupta, S., *Obscure Religious Cults*, Calcutta, 1969.

Davis, Marvin, *Rank and Rivalry. The politics of inequality in rural West Bengal*, Cambridge, 1983.

De, Amalendu, *Roots of Separatism in Nineteenth Century Bengal*, Calcutta, 1974.

Independent Bengal: The Design and Its Fate, Calcutta, 1975.

Dixit, Prabha, *Communalism: A Struggle for Power*, New Delhi, 1974.

Duff, James Cunningham Grant, *History of the Marhattas*, 3 vols., London, 1826.

Dumont, Louis, *Homo Hierarchicus. The Caste System and Its Implications* (translated by Mark Sainsbury), London, 1970.

Dutt, Rajani Palme, *India Today*, London, 1940.

Ewing, Katherine P., *Shari'at and Ambiguity in South Asian Islam*, New Delhi, 1988.

Foucault, Michel, *The Archaeology of Knowledge* (translated by A. M. Sheridan Smith), New York, 1972.

Fox, Richard, *Lions of the Punjab. Culture in the Making*, London, 1985.

Freitag, Sandria B., *Collective Action and Community. Public Arenas and the Emergence of Communalism in North India*, Berkeley, Los Angeles and Oxford, 1989.

Gandhi, Rajmohan, *Understanding the Muslim Mind*, New Delhi, 1988.

Geertz, Clifford, *The Interpretation of Cultures*, New York, 1973.

Giddens, Anthony, *The Class Structure of Advanced Societies*, London, 1973.

Gilmartin, David, *Empire and Islam. Punjab and the Making of Pakistan*, Berkeley, 1988.

Gramsci, Antonio, *Selections from Prison Notebooks* (translated by Q. Hoare and G. Nowell Smith), London, 1971.

Gopal, Sarvepalli (ed.), *The Anatomy of a Confrontation. The Babri Masjid-Ramjanmabhumi Issue*, New Delhi, 1991.

Gordon, Leonard A., *Bengal. The Nationalist Movement 1876–1940*, New Delhi, 1979.

Greenough, Paul, *Poverty and Misery in Modern Bengal. The Famine of 1943*, Oxford, 1982.

Guha, Ranajit, *A Rule of Property in Bengal: An Essay on the Idea of the Permanent Settlement*, Paris, 1963.

(ed.), *Subaltern Studies. Writings on South Asian History and Society*, 6 vols., New Delhi, 1982–89.

Gupta, S. K., *The Scheduled Castes in Modern Indian Politics: Their Emergence as a Political Power*, New Delhi, 1985.

Habelfass, Wilhelm, *Indian and Europe. An Essay in Understanding*, New York, 1988.

Hasan, Mushirul (ed.), *Communal and Pan-Islamic Trends in Colonial India*, New Delhi, 1985.

Hobsbawm, Eric and Ranger, Terence (eds.), *The Invention of Tradition*, Cambridge, 1984.

Holyoake, G. J., *The Origin and Nature of Secularism*, London, 1896.

Hunt, Alan (ed.), *Class and Class Structure*, London, 1977.

Hunter, W. W., *The Indian Mussalmans*, London, 1876.

Inden, Ronald, *Imagining India*, Cambridge, Mass., 1990.

Inden, Ronald B. and Nicholas, Ralph W., *Kinship in Bengali Culture*, Chicago, 1977.

Ionescu, Ghita and Gellner, Ernest (eds.), *Populism. Its Meaning and National Characteristics*, London, 1969.

Islam, M. M., *Bengal Agriculture 1920–1946, A Quantitative Study*, Cambridge, 1979.

Islam, Nurul Mustapha, *Bengali Muslim Public Opinion Reflected in the Bengali Press, 1901–30*, Dacca, 1973.

Jack, J. C., *The Economic Life of a Bengal District*, Oxford, 1916.

Jalal, Ayesha, *The Sole Spokesman. Jinnah, the Muslim League and the Demand for Pakistan*, Cambridge, 1985.

Joshi, Svati (ed.), *Rethinking English. Essays in Literature, Language, History*, New Delhi, 1991.

Kabir, Humayun, *Muslim Politics 1906–47 and Other Essays*, Calcutta, 1969.
Karlekar, Malavika, *Voices from Within. Early Personal Narratives of Bengali Women*, New Delhi, 1991.
Kawai, Akinobu, *Landlords and Imperial Rule: Change in Bengal Agrarian Society c. 1885–1940*, 2 vols., Tokyo, 1986 and 1987.
Khaliquzzaman, Choudhury, *Pathway to Pakistan*, Lahore, 1961.
Khan, Bazlur Rahman, *Politics in Bengal 1927–1936*, Dhaka, 1987.
Kumar, Nita, *The Artisans of Benares. Popular Culture and Identity, 1880–1986*, Princeton, 1988.
Kumar, Ravinder, *Essays in the Social History of Modern India*, Calcutta, 1986.
Kopf, David (ed.), *Bengal Regional Identity*, East Lansing, Mich., 1969.
Laclau, Ernesto, *Politics and Ideology in Marxist Theory. Capitalism, fascism, populism*, London, 1977.
Laushey, David M., *Bengal Terrorism and the Marxist Left. Aspects of Regional Marxism in India, 1905–1942*, Calcutta, 1973.
Leach, Edmund and Mukherjee, S. N. (eds.), *Elites in South Asia*, Cambridge, 1970.
Low, D. A. (ed.), *The Indian National Congress. Centenary Hindsights*, New Delhi, 1988.
Macaulay, T. B., *Critical and Historical Essays*, 3 vols., London, 1843.
Macpherson, Kenneth, *The Muslim Microcosm. Calcutta, 1918–1985*, Wiesbaden, 1974.
Majumdar, R. C., *Glimpses of Bengal in the Nineteenth Century*, Calcutta, 1960.
McGuire, John, *The Making of a Colonial Mind. A Quantitative Study of the Bhadralok in Calcutta, 1857–1885*, Canberra, 1983.
McLane, John R., *Indian Nationalism and the Early Congress*, Princeton, 1977.
Mill, James, *History of British India*, 6 vols., London, 1858.
Mitra, Ashok (ed.), *Essays in Tribute to Samar Sen*, Calcutta, 1985.
Momen, Humaira, *Muslim Politics in Bengal: A Study of Krishak Praja Party and the Elections of 1937*, Dacca, 1972.
Moore, R. J., *Churchill, Cripps and India, 1939–1945*, Oxford, 1978.
  Escape from Empire. The Attlee Government and the Indian Problem, Oxford, 1982.
  Endgames of Empire. Studies of Britain's Indian Problem, New Delhi, 1988.
Mountbatten, Louis, *Reflections on the Transfer of Power and J. Nehru*, Cambridge, 1968.
Mujeeb, N., *The Indian Muslims*, London, 1969.
Mukherjee, Meenakshi, *Realism and Reality. The Novel and Society in India*, New Delhi, 1985.
Mukherjee, Ramakrishna, *The Dynamics of a Rural Society. A Study of the Economic Structure in Bengal Villages*, Berlin, 1957.
Mukherjee, S. N., *Calcutta: Myth and History*, Calcutta, 1977.
Nanda, B. R. (ed.), *Essays in Modern Indian History*, New Delhi, 1980.
Nehru, Jawaharlal, *The Discovery of India*, New Delhi, 1986.
Omvedt, Gail (ed.), *Land, Caste and Politics in Indian States*, New Delhi, 1982.
Page, David, *Prelude to Partition. The Indian Muslims and the Imperial System of Control 1920–1932*, Delhi, 1982.

Pandey, Gyanendra, *The Ascendancy of the Congress in Uttar Pradesh, 1926–34. A Study in Imperfect Mobilization*, New Delhi, 1978.
The Construction of Communalism in Colonial North India, New Delhi, 1990.
Panigrahi, D. N. (ed.), *Economy, Society and Politics in India*, New Delhi, 1985.
Patnaik, Utsa, *The Agrarian Question and the Development of Capitalism in India*, New Delhi, 1986.
Poulantzas, Nicos, *Political Power and Social Classes*, London, 1975.
Classes in Contemporary Capitalism, London, 1975.
Pyarelal, *The Epic Fast*, Ahmedabad, 1932.
Rahman, Atiur, *Peasants and Classes. A Study in Differentiation in Bangladesh*, London,1986.
Rashid, Harun-or, *The Foreshadowing of Bangladesh. Bengal Muslim League and Muslim Politics 1936–1947*, Dhaka, 1987.
Ray, Rabindra, *The Naxalites and their Ideology*, Delhi, 1988.
Ray, Rajat Kanta, *Social Conflict and Political Unrest in Bengal 1875–1927*, New Delhi, 1984.
Urban Roots of Indian Nationalism: Pressure Groups and Conflict of Interests in Calcutta City Politics, 1875–1939, New Delhi, 1979.
Ray, Ratnalekha, *Change in Bengal Agrarian Society c. 1760–1850*, New Delhi, 1979.
Raychaudhuri, Tapan, *Europe Reconsidered. Perceptions of the West in Nineteenth Century Bengal*, New Delhi, 1988.
Three Views of Europe from Nineteenth Century Bengal, Calcutta, 1987.
Ricoeur, Paul, *Hermeneutics and the Human Sciences. Essays on Language, Action and Interpretation* (translated by John B. Thompson), Cambridge, 1988.
Risley, H. H., *The Tribes and Castes of Bengal. Ethnographical Glossary*, Calcutta, 1891.
Robb, Peter and Taylor, David (eds.), *Rule, Protest, Identity. Aspects of Modern South Asia*, London, 1978.
Robinson, F. C. R., *Separatism among Indian Muslims. The Politics of the United Provinces' Muslims, 1860–1923*, Cambridge, 1974.
Rothermund, Dietmar, *Government, Landlord and Peasant in India. Agrarian Relations under British Rule*, Wiesbaden, 1978.
Sangari, Kumkum and Vaid, Sudesh (ed.), *Recasting Women. Essays in Colonial History*, New Delhi, 1989.
Sarkar, Jadunath (ed.), *History of Bengal. Muslim Period, 1200–1757*, Patna, 1973.
Sarkar, Sumit, *The Swadeshi Movement in Bengal, 1903–1908*, New Delhi, 1973.
Modern India 1885–1947, New Delhi, 1983.
'Popular' Movements and 'Middle Class' Leadership in Late Colonial India: Perspectives and Problems of a 'History From Below', Calcutta, 1985.
A Critique of Colonial India, Calcutta, 1985.
Sarkar, Tanika, *Bengal 1928–1934. The Politics of Protest*, New Delhi, 1987.
Saville, John and Miliband, Ralph (eds.), *Socialist Register*, London, 1975.
Sen, Asok, *Iswar Chandra Vidyasagar and His Elusive Milestones*, Calcutta, 1977.
Sen, Asok, Chatterjee, Partha and Mukherji, Saugata, *Three Studies on the Agrarian Structure of Bengal, 1850–1947*, Calcutta, 1982.
Sen, Shila, *Muslim Politics in Bengal, 1937–47*, New Delhi, 1976.

Shaikh, Farzana, *Community and Consensus in Islam. Muslim Representation in Colonial India, 1860–1947*, New Delhi, 1976.

Singer, Milton, and Cohn, Bernard (eds.), *Structure and Change in Indian Society*, Chicago, 1968.

Singh, Anita Inder, *The Origins of the Partition of India, 1936–1947*, New Delhi, 1987.

Sisson, Richard and Wolpert, Stanley A. (eds.), *Congress and Indian Nationalism. The Pre-Independence Phase*, New Delhi, 1988.

Sperber, Dan, *Rethinking Symbolism*, Cambridge, 1975.

Srinivas, M. N., *Religion and Society among the Coorgs in South India*, Oxford, 1952.

Social Change in Modern India, New Delhi, 1977.

Taylor, David and Yapp, Malcolm (eds.), *Political Identity in South Asia*, London, 1979.

Thapar, Romila, Mukhia, Harbans and Chandra, Bipan, *Communalism and the Writing of Indian History*, New Delhi, 1987.

Thompson, John B., *Studies in the Theory of Ideology*, Cambridge, 1987.

Tod, J., *Annals and Antiquities of Rajasthan or the Central and Western Rajpoot States*, 3 vols., Calcutta, 1821.

Tomlinson, B. R., *The Indian National Congress and the Raj 1929–1942, The Penultimate Phase*, London, 1976.

James Tully (ed.), *Meaning and Context. Quentin Skinner and his Critics*, Cambridge, 1988.

Turner, Victor, *Dramas, Fields and Metaphors. Symbolic Action in Human Society*, Ithaca, 1974.

Van der Veer, Peter, *Gods on Earth. The Management of Religious Experience and Identity in a North Indian Pilgrimage Centre*, New Delhi, 1989.

Van M. Baumer, Rachel (ed.), *Aspects of Bengal History and Society*, Hawaii, 1975.

Viswanathan, Gauri, *Masks of Conquest. Literary Study and British Rule in India*, New York, 1989.

Williams, Raymond, *Keywords. A Vocabulary of Culture and Society*, New York, 1976.

Wilson, Bryan, *Religion in a Secular Society. A Sociological Comment*, London, 1966.

Wittgenstein, Ludwig, *Philosophical Investigations* (translated by G. E. N. Anscombe), Oxford, 1958

Yang, Anand A., *The Limited Raj. Agrarian Relations in Colonial India, Saran District, 1793–1920*, Berkeley, 1989.

Zaidi, A. M. (ed.), *Encyclopaedia of the Indian National Congress*, New Delhi, 1981.

ARTICLES

Addy, Premen, and Azad, Ibne, 'Politics and Culture in Bengal', *New Left Review*, vol. 79, 1973.

Ahmed, Rafiuddin, 'Conflict and Contradictions in Bengal Islam: Problems of Change and Adjustment', in Katherine P. Ewing, (ed.), *Shari'at and Ambiguity in South Asian Islam*, New Delhi, 1988.

Alavi, Hamza, 'India: Transition from Feudalism to Capitalism', *Journal of Contemporary Asia*, vol. 10, 1980.
  'India and the Colonial Mode of Production', in John Saville and Ralph Miliband (eds.), *Socialist Register*, London, 1975.
Ali, Hashim Amir Ali, 'Rural Research in Tagore's Sriniketan, *Modern Review*, vol. 56, 1–16, July–December 1934.
Asad, Talal, 'Anthropological Conceptions of Religion: Reflections on Geertz', *Man* (NS), vol. 18, 1983.
Bagchi, Jasodhara, 'Shakespeare in Loincloths: English Literature and Early Nationalist Consciousness in Bengal', in Svati Joshi (ed.), *Rethinking English. Essays in Literature, Language, History*, New Delhi, 1991.
Bandopadhay, Sekhar, 'Caste and Society in Colonial Bengal: Change and Continuity', *Journal of Social Studies*, vol. 28, April 1985.
  'Community Formation and Communal Conflict. Namasudra–Muslim Riot in Jessore–Khulna', *Economic and Political Weekly*, vol. 25, 46, 1990.
Banerjee, Ramesh Chandra, 'Hindu and Muslim Public Spirit in Bengal', *Modern Review*, vol. 55, 1–6, 1934.
Bannerji, Himani, 'The Mirror of Class. Class Subjectivity and Politics in 19th-Century Bengal', *Economic and Political Weekly*, vol. 24, 19, May 1989.
Baxter, Christine, 'The Genesis of the Babu: Bhabanicharan Bannerji and the *Kalikata Kamalalay*', in Peter Robb and David Taylor (eds.), *Rule, Protest, Identity. Aspects of Modern South Asia*, London, 1978.
Bhadra, Gautam, 'The Mentality of Subalternity: *Kantanama* or *Rajadharma*', in Ranajit Guha (ed.), *Subaltern Studies VI*, New Delhi, 1989.
Bhaduri, Amit, 'Evolution of Land Relations in Eastern India under British Rule', *Indian Economic and Social History Review*, vol. 13, 1976.
Bhattacharya, Jnanabrata, 'Language, Class and Community in Bengal', *South Asia Bulletin*, vol. 7, 1–2, Fall 1987.
  'An Examination of Leadership Entry in Bengal Peasant Revolts', *Journal of Asian Studies*, vol. 37, 4, 1978.
Bhattacharya, Neeladri, 'Myth, History and the Politics of Ramjanmabhoomi', in Sarvepalli Gopal (ed.), *The Anatomy of a Confrontation. The Babri Masjid–Ramjanmabhumi Issue*, New Delhi, 1991.
Borthwick, Meredith, 'The Cuch Behar Marriage and Brahmo Integrity', *Bengal Past and Present*, vol. 95, Part II, 181, July–December 1976.
Bose, Sugata, 'The Roots of Communal Violence in Rural Bengal. A Study of the Kishoreganj Riots, 1930', *Modern Asian Studies*, vol. 16, 3, 1982.
Bourdieu, Pierre, 'The Production of Belief: Contribution to an Economy of Symbolic Goods', in Richard Collins et al. (eds.), *Media, Culture and Society*, London, 1986.
Bruner, Jerome, 'The Narrative Construction of Reality', *Critical Inquiry*, vol. 18, 1, Autumn 1991.
Carter Bentley, G., 'Ethnicity and Practice', *Comparative Studies in Society and History*, vol. 29, 1, 1987.
Chakrabarty, Bidyut, 'Peasants and the Bengal Congress, 1928–38', *South Asia Research*, vol. 5, 1, May 1985.
  'The Communal Award of 1932 and its Implications in Bengal', *Modern Asian Studies*, vol. 23, 3, 1989.

'Political Mobilization in the Localities: The 1942 Quit India Movement in Midnapur', *Modern Asian Studies*, vol. 26, 4, 1992.

Chakravarty, Dipesh, 'Sasipada Banerjee: Bengali Bhadralok and Labour', *Centre for Studies in Social Sciences Series*, Occasional Paper No. 45.

Chakravarty, Uma, 'Whatever Happened to the Vedic *Dasi*? Orientalism, Nationalism and a Script for the Past', in Kumkum Sangari and Sudesh Vaid (eds.), *Recasting Women. Essays in Colonial History*, New Delhi, 1989.

Chandra, Sudhir, 'The Cultural Component of Economic Nationalism: R. C. Dutt's *The Lake of Palms*', *Indian Historical Review*, vol. 12, 1–2, 1985–86.

Chatterjee, Partha, 'Caste and Politics in West Bengal', in Gail Omvedt (ed.), *Land, Caste and Politics in Indian States*, New Delhi, 1982.

'The Fruits of Macaulay's Poison Tree', in Ashok Mitra (ed.), *Essays in Tribute to Samar Sen*, Calcutta, 1985.

'The Colonial State and Peasant Resistance in Bengal, 1920–47', *Past and Present*, vol. 110, February 1986.

'Agrarian Relations and Communalism in Bengal 1926–35', in Ranajit Guha (ed.), *Subaltern Studies I*, New Delhi, 1986.

'Transferring a Political Theory: Early Nationalist Thought in India', *Economic and Political Weekly*, vol. 21, 3, 18 January 1986.

'Caste and Subaltern Consciousness', in Ranajit Guha (ed.), *Subaltern Studies VI*, New Delhi, 1989.

'A Religion of Urban Domesticity: Sri Ramakrishna and the Calcutta Middle Class', in Partha Chatterjee and Gyanendra Pandey (eds.), *Subaltern Studies VII*, Delhi, 1992.

Chattopadhyay, Ratnabali, 'Nationalism and Form in Indian Painting. A Study of the Bengal School', *Journal of Arts and Ideas*, vol. 14–15, July–December 1987.

Chaudhury, B. B., 'The Process of Depeasantization in Bengal and Bihar, 1885–1947', *Indian Historical Review*, vol. 2, 1975–76.

Cohn, Bernard, 'Notes on the History of the Study of Indian Society and Culture', in M. Singer and B. S. Cohn (eds.), *Structure and Change in Indian Society*, Chicago, 1968.

Das, Suranjan, 'Towards an Understanding of Communal Violence in Twentieth Century Bengal', *Economic and Political Weekly*, 27 August 1988.

Das, Ujjwalkanti, 'The Bengal Pact of 1923 and its Reactions', *Bengal Past and Present*, vol. 99, Part I, 188, January–June 1980.

Dasgupta, Swapan, 'Adivasi Politics in Midnapur, c. 1790–1924', in Ranajit Guha (ed.), *Subaltern Studies IV*, New Delhi, 1985.

Datta, Jatindra Mohan, 'The Real Nature of the Muhammadan Majority in Bengal', *Modern Review*, vol. 49, 2, 1931.

'Relative Public Spirit and Enterprise of Hindus and Muhammadans in Bengal', *Modern Review*, vol. 55, 1–6, 1934.

'Communalism in the Bengal Administration', *Modern Review*, vol. 49, 1, 1931.

'The Relative Heroism of the Hindus and Mohammedans of India', *Modern Review*, vol. 79, 1–6, 1946.

'Who the Bengali Mohammedans Are?', *Modern Review*, vol. 49, 3, 1931.

Datta, Rajat, 'Agricultural Production, Social Participation and Domination in

Late Eighteenth Century Bengal: Towards an Alternative Explanation', *Journal of Peasant Studies*, vol. 17, 1, 1989.

Dutta, P. K., 'War over Music: The Riots of 1926 in Bengal', *Social Scientist*, vol. 18, 6–7, 1990.

'V. H. P.'s Ram at Ayodhya: Reincarnation through Ideology and Organisation', *Economic and Political Weekly*, vol. 26, 44, 1991.

Eaton, Richard M., 'Islam in Bengal', in George Michel (ed.), *The Islamic Heritage in Bengal*, Paris, 1984.

Freitag, Sandria B., 'Sacred Symbol as Mobilizing Ideology. The North Indian Search for a 'Hindu' Community', *Comparative Studies in Society and History*, vol. 22, 1981.

Gallagher, J. A., 'Congress in Decline: Bengal, 1930 to 1939', *Modern Asian Studies*, vol. 7, 3, 1973.

Gopal, Sarvepalli, 'Nehru and Minorities', *Economic and Political Weekly*, vol. 23, 45–47 (Special Number), 1988.

Gordon, Leonard A., 'Divided Bengal: Problems of Nationalism and Identity in the 1947 Partition', *Journal of Commonwealth and Comparative Politics*, vol. 16, 2, July 1978.

Goswami, Omkar, '*Sahibs, Babus* and *Banias*: Changes in Industrial Control in Eastern India, 1918–50', *Journal of Asian Studies*, vol. 48, 2, May 1989.

Hasan, Mushirul, 'The Muslim Mass Contacts Campaign. Analysis of a Strategy of Political Mobilisation', in R. Sisson and S. Wolpert (eds.), *The Congress and Indian Nationalism. The Pre-Independence Phase*, New Delhi, 1988.

Hashmi, Tajul Islam, 'The Communalization of Class Struggle: East Bengal Peasantry, 1923–29', *Indian Economic and Social History Review*, vol. 25, 2, 1988.

'Towards Understanding Peasants' Politics in Bangladesh: A Historical Perspective since 1920', *Journal of Social Studies*, vol. 42, October 1988.

Honneth, Axel, 'The Fragmented World of Symbolic Forms: Reflections on Pierre Bourdieu's Sociology of Culture', *Theory, Culture and Society*, vol. 3, 3, 1986.

Inden, Ronald, 'Orientalist Constructions of India', *Modern Asian Studies*, vol. 20, 3, 1986.

Jaiswal, Suvira, 'Semitising Hinduism: Changing Paradigms of Brahmanical Integration', *Social Scientist*, vol. 19, 12, 1991.

Jalal, Ayesha, 'Azad, Jinnah and Partition', *Economic and Political Weekly*, vol. 24, 21, 27 May 1989.

Johnson, Gordon, 'Partition, Agitation and Congress: Bengal 1904 to 1908', *Modern Asian Studies*, vol. 7, 3, 1973.

Kaviraj, Sudipta, 'Imaginary History', *Occasional Papers in History and Society*, 2nd series, No. 7, September 1988, Nehru Memorial Museum and Library, New Delhi.

Kesavan, Mukul, '1937 as a Landmark in the Course of Communal Politics in U.P.', *Occasional Papers in History and Society*, 2nd series, No. 11, November 1988, Nehru Memorial Museum and Library , New Delhi.

Kopf, David, 'The Universal Man and the Yellow Dog: the Orientalist Legacy and the Problem of Brahmo Identity in the Bengal Renaissance', in R. Van M. Baumer (ed.), *Aspects of Bengal History and Society*, Hawaii, 1975.

Kumar, Ravinder, 'Gandhi, Ambedkar and the Poona Pact', *Occasional Papers in History and Society*, No. 20, February 1985, Nehru Memorial Museum and Library, New Delhi.

'Class, Community or Nation? Gandhi's Quest for a Popular Consensus in India', in Ravinder Kumar, *Essays in the Social History of Modern India*, Calcutta, 1986.

Mandal, Archana, 'The Ideology and Interests of the Bengali Intelligentsia: Sir George Campbell's Educational Policy (1871–1874), *Indian Economic and Social History Review*, vol. 12, 1, 1975.

McLane, John R., 'The Early Congress, Hindu Populism and Wider Society', in R. Sisson and S. Wolpert (eds.), *The Congress and Indian Nationalism. The Pre-Independence Phase*, New Delhi, 1988.

Mukherjee, Nilmani, 'A Charitable Effort in Bengal in the Nineteenth Century. The Uttarpara Hitkari Sabha', *Bengal Past and Present*, vol. 89, 1970.

Mukherjee, S. N., 'Bhadralok in Bengali Language and Literature: An Essay on the Language of Class and Status', *Bengal Past and Present*, vol. 95, Part II, July–December 1976.

'Caste, Class and Politics in Calcutta', in S. N. Mukherjee, *Calcutta: Myth and History*, Calcutta, 1977.

Mukherji, Sugata, 'Agrarian Class Formation in Modern Bengal, 1931–51', *Economic and Political Weekly*, vol. 21, 4, January 1986.

Niranjana, Tejaswini, 'Translation, Colonialism and the Rise of English' in Svati Joshi (ed.), *Rethinking English. Essays in Literature, Language, History*, New Delhi, 1991.

Nugent, Helen M., 'The Communal Award: The Process of Decision-Making', *South Asia* (N S), vols. 2.1 and 2.2, 1989.

Pandey, Gyanendra, 'Rallying Round the Cow. Sectarian Strife in the Bhojpuri Region, c. 1888–1917', in Ranajit Guha (ed.), *Subaltern Studies II*, New Delhi, 1983.

'The Colonial Construction of "Communalism": British Writings on Banaras in the Nineteenth Century', in Ranajit Guha (ed.), *Subaltern Studies VI*, New Delhi, 1989.

'In Defence of the Fragment: Writing about Hindu–Muslim riots in India today', *Economic and Political Weekly*, vol. 26, No. 11–12, Annual Number, 1992.

'Hindus and Others: the Militant Hindu Construction', *Economic and Political Weekly*, vol. 26, 52, 1991.

Pant, Rashmi, 'The cognitive status of caste in colonial ethnography: A review of some literature on the North West Provinces and Oudh', *Indian Economic and Social History Review*, vol. 2, 2, 1987.

Patnaik, Utsa, 'Class Differentiation within the Peasantry', *Economic and Political Weekly*, vol. 11, 1976.

Prindle, Carol, 'Occupation and Orthopraxy in Bengali Muslim Rank', in K.P. Ewing (ed.), *Shari'at and Ambiguity in South Asian Islam*, New Delhi, 1988.

Ranger, Terence, 'Power, Religion and Community: The Matabo Case', in Partha Chatterjee and Gyanendra Pandey (eds.), *Subaltern Studies VII*, New Delhi, 1992.

Ray, Asim, 'The Social Factors in the Making of Bengali Islam', *South Asia*, vol. 3, 1973.

'Bengali Muslims and the Problem of Identity', *Journal of the Asiatic Society of Bangladesh*, vol. 22, 3, 1977.

'Bengali Muslim Cultural Mediators and Bengali Muslim Identity in the Nineteenth and Early Twentieth Centuries', *South Asia*, vol. 10, 1, 1987.

Ray, Rajat and Ratna, 'Zamindars and Jotedars: A Study of Rural Politics in Bengal', *Modern Asian Studies*, vol. 9, 1, 1975.

'The Dynamics of Continuity in Rural Bengal under the British Imperium', *Indian Economic and Social History Review*, vol. 10, 2, 1973.

Ray, Rajat Kanta, 'The Crisis of Bengal Agriculture, 1820–1927: The Dynamics of Immobility', *Indian Economic and Social History Review*, vol. 10, 3, 1973.

'Political Change in British India', *Indian Economic and Social History Review*, vol. 14, 4, 1977.

'Three Interpretations of Indian Nationalism', in B. R. Nanda (ed.), *Essays in Modern Indian History*, New Delhi, 1980.

'The Retreat of the Jotedars?', *Indian Economic and Social History Review*, vol. 25, 2, 1988.

Ray, Ratnalekha, 'The Changing Fortunes of the Bengal Gentry under Colonial Rule. The Pal Chaudhuris of Mahesganj', *Modern Asian Studies*, vol. 21, 3, 1987.

Raychaudhuri, Tapan, 'Permanent Settlement in Operation: Bakarganj District, East Bengal', in R. E. Frykenburg, (ed.), *Land Control and Social Structure in Indian History*, Madison, Wis., 1969.

Robb, Peter, 'The Challenge of Gau Mata. British Policy and Religious Changes in India, 1880–1916', *Modern Asian Studies*, vol. 20, 2, 1986.

Robinson, Francis, 'Nation Formation: the Brass Thesis and Muslim Separatism', *Journal of Commonwealth and Comparative Politics*, vol. 15, 3, 1977.

Rosselli, John, 'The Self-Image of Effeteness: Physical Education and Nationalism in Nineteenth-Century Bengal', *Past and Present*, vol. 86, February 1980.

Samuel, Raphael, 'Reading the Signs', *History Workshop Journal*, vol. 32, Autumn 1991.

Sanyal, Hitesranjan, 'Nationalist Movements in Arambag', *Annya Artha*, September 1974.

Sarkar, Sumit, 'The Kalki Avatar of Bikrampur: A Village Scandal in Early Twentieth Century Bengal', in Ranajit Guha (ed.), *Subaltern Studies VI*, New Delhi, 1989.

'Popular Movements and National Leadership, 1945–47', *Economic and Political Weekly*, Annual Number, April 1982.

'Rammohun Roy and the Break with the Past', in Sumit Sarkar, *A Critique of Colonial India*, Calcutta, 1985.

'The Kathamrita as a Text: Towards an Understanding of Ramakrishan Paramhansa', *Occasional Papers in History and Society*, No. 22, 1985, Nehru Memorial Museum and Library, New Delhi.

'"Kaliyuga", "Chakri" and "Bhakti": Ramakrishna and His Times', *Economic and Political Weekly*, vol. 26, 29, 1992.

Sarkar, Tanika, 'Communal Riots in Bengal', in Mushirul Hasan (ed.), *Communal and Pan-Islamic Trends in Colonial India*, New Delhi, 1985.

'Jitu Santal's Movement in Malda, 1924–1932: A Study in Tribal Protest', in Ranajit Guha (ed.), *Subaltern Studies IV*, New Delhi, 1985.

'Bengali Middle-Class Nationalism and Literature: A Study of Saratchandra's "Pather Dabi" and Rabindranath's "Char Adhyay", in D. N. Panigrahi (ed.), *Economy, Society and Politics in India*, New Delhi, 1985.

'Woman as Communal Subject: Rashtrasevika Samiti and Ram Janmabhoomi Movement', *Economic and Political Weekly*, vol. 26, 25, 1991.

Skinner, Quentin, 'Motives, Intentions and the Interpretation of Texts', in James Tully (ed.), *Meaning and Context. Quentin Skinner and his Critics*, Cambridge, 1988.

Smalley, Alan, 'The Colonial State and the Agrarian Structure in Bengal', *Journal of Contemporary Asia*, vol. 13, 1983.

Southard, Barbara, 'The Political Strategy of Aurobindo Ghosh. The Utilization of Political Symbols and the Problem of Political Mobilization in Bengal', *Modern Asian Studies*, vol. 14, 1980.

Torri, Michelguglielmo, '"Westernised Middle-Class" Intellectuals and Society in Late Colonial India', *Economic and Political Weekly*, vol. 25, 4, January 1990.

Upadhyaya, Prakash Chandra,'The Politics of Indian Secularism', *Modern Asian Studies*, vol. 26, 4, 1992.

Van der Veer, Peter, '"God Must be Liberated!" A Hindu Liberation Movement in Ayodhya', *Modern Asian Studies*, vol. 21, 2, 1987.

Van Meter, Rachel, 'Bankimcandra's View of the Role of Bengal in Indian Civilization', in David Kopf (ed.), *Bengal Regional Identity*, East Lansing, Mich., 1969.

Washbrook, D. A., 'Gandhian Politics', a review of Judith M. Brown's *Gandhi's Rise to Power*, Cambridge, 1972, *Modern Asian Studies*, vol. 7, 1, 1973.

'Law, State and Agrarian Society in Colonial India', *Modern Asian Studies*, vol. 15, 1981.

Wills, Clair, 'Language, Politics, Narrative, Political Violence', *Oxford Literary Review*, vol. 13, 1991.

Yang, Anand A., 'Sacred Symbol and Sacred Space in Rural India. Community Mobilization in the "Anti-Cow Killing" Riot of 1893', *Comparative Studies in Society and History*, vol. 22, 1981.

UNPUBLISHED SECONDARY WORKS.

DOCTORAL DISSERTATIONS

Das, Suranjan, 'Communal Riots in Bengal, 1905–1947'. University of Oxford, D.Phil thesis, 1987.

Freitag, Sandria B., 'Religious Rites and Riots: From Community Identity to Communalism in North India, 1870–1940', University of California, Berkeley, Ph.D. dissertation, 1980.

Goswami, Omkar, 'Jute Economy of Bengal 1920–1947: A Study of Interaction between Agricultural, Trading and Industrial Sectors', University of Oxford, D.Phil thesis, 1982.

Kamtekar, Indivar, 'The End of the Colonial State in India, 1942–47', University of Cambridge, Ph.D. dissertation, 1988.

Murshid, Tazeen M., 'The Bengal Muslim Intelligentsia, 1937–77. The Tension between the Religious and the Secular'. University of Oxford, D.Phil thesis, 1985.

Prior, Katherine H.,'The British Administration of Hinduism in North India, 1780–1900', University of Cambridge, Ph.D. dissertation, 1990.

Sen, Samita, 'Women Workers in the Bengal Jute Industry, 1890–1940. Marriage, Migration and Militancy', University of Cambridge, Ph.D. dissertation, 1992.

PAPERS

Guha Thakurta, Tapati, 'Orientalist Constructions of Indian Art at the Turn of the Century: The Polemics of "Tradition" and "Indianness"', presented at the seminar 'Orientalism and the History and Anthropology of South Asia', London, 1988.

Index

Act
    Bengal Agricultural Debtors' (1936),
    106, 205–206; Bengal Moneylenders'
    (1940), 106; Bengal Public Security,
    96; Bengal Tenancy (1885), 56; Bengal
    Tenancy Amendment (1928), 72, 114;
    Bengal Tenancy Amendment (1938),
    118, 121, 131; Bengal Village
    Self-Government (1919), 32; Calcutta
    Municipal Amendment (1939), 107;
    see also Government of India Act
    (1935)
agricultural labourers, 56, 57, 70, 76, 195
Ahmed, Abul Mansur, 45n, 73–74, 76,
    104n
Ahmed, Shamsuddin, 73, 123n
Ahmed Wasimuddin (Osimuddin), 88,
    98–99
Ali, Liaqat, 225
Ali, Syed Nausher, 73, 83, 113, 129
Ali, Yakoob, 88, 98
All-India Congress Committee, 69;
    all-India priorities of, 52; Bengali
    influence over, 43; 'betrayal' of
    Bengal's interests by, 45–46, 127;
    Communal Award and, 44, 48–53;
    constitutional question and, 224–25;
    High Command of, 16, 44, 95,
    124–125, 127–129, 137, 139, 221;
    Interim Government and, 225, 231;
    involvement in Bengal Congress of,
    46–51, 125–128; left-wing and
    124–125, 223; ministries, 103, 122, 223;
    minorities and, 223, 226; Muslim
    League and, 220, 222–223, 226;
    office-acceptance and, 44, 222;
    Parliamentary Board, 53; partition of
    Bengal and, 222, 225, 227, 259;
    partition of India and, 222, 225, 266;
    performance in 1946 elections,
    223–224; Poona Pact and, 35; Tripuri
    session of, 124, 130, 139; United
    Bengal Plan and, 260–261; Working

Committee of, 45–46, 48–49, 52, 54,
    104, 108, 124, 129–130, 259–260
Ambedkar, B. R., 34–35
Anderson, John, 21, 85
Aney, M. S., 46–47
Arambagh, 39
Arya Samaj, 219, 254
ashrams, Gandhian, 39, 89; Betur, 100,
    117; Abhoy, 117
Assembly elections, see elections
Attlee, Clement, 220, 224
Azad, Maulana Abul Kalam, 145, 224,
    226

Bakarganj, 69, 71, 84; Chandals in, 192;
    Krishak Praja Party in, 87; local
    bodies in, 208–209; partition campaign
    in, 244, 248, 251, 256–257
Bak'r-Id, 214–215, 217
Banerjee, Jitendra Lal, 26, 35, 43, 94
Banerjee, Surendranath, 4n, 12n, 158
Banerji, Bibhutibhushan, 9
Bankura, Gandhians in, 117; Hindu
    Mahasabha activity in, 197; local
    bodies in, 205n; partition campaign in,
    251, 253; praja samitis in, 101, 112;
    relations between landlords and
    tenants in, 91
bargadars, see share-croppers
Barisal, 30, 69; Congress committees in,
    45n; Gandhian ashram in, 89; local
    bodies in, 209; partition campaign in,
    249, 257; praja samitis in, 114
Barman, Panchanan, 198–199
Bengal Congress, 8, 17, 22, 26, 108,
    129–130; All-India Congress
    Committee and, 43, 45–54, 124–128,
    221, 250; Assembly elections and
    (1936), 83, 94–95, 99–102, 108,
    228–229; (1946), 203, 228–230, 250;
    big business and, 137, 139, 145, 148,
    250, 255; 'Big Five' and, 47; Bose
    group, purge of, 125–130, 139–140,

293

Cambridge South Asian Studies

These monographs are published by the Syndics of Cambridge University Press in association with the Cambridge University Centre for South Asian Studies. The following books have been published in this series:

29 Ian Stone: *Canal Irrigation in British India: Perspectives on Technological Change in a Peasant Society*

30 Rosalind O'Hanlon: *Caste, Conflict and Ideology: Mahatmas Jotirao Phule and Low Caste Protest in Nineteenth-Century Western India*

31 Ayesha Jalal: *The Sole Spokesman: Jinnah, The Muslim League and the Demand for Pakistan*

32 N. R. F. Charlesworth: *Peasant and Imperial Rule: Agriculture and Agrarian Society in the Bombay Presidency, 1850–1935*

33 Claude Markovits: *Indian Business and Nationalist Politics, 1931–39. The Indigenous Capitalist Class and the Rise of the Congress Party*

36 Sugata Bose: *Agrarian Bengal: Economy, Social Structure and Politics, 1919–1947*

37 Atul Kohli: *The State and Poverty in India: The Politics of Reform*

38 Franklin A. Presler: *Religion Under Bureaucracy: Policy and Administration for Hindu Temples in South India*

39 Nicholas B. Dirks: *The Hollow Crown: Ethnohistory of an Indian Kingdom*

40 Robert Wade: *Village Republics: Economic Conditions for Collective Action in South India*

41 Laurence W. Preston: *The Devs of Cincvad: A Lineage and State in Maharashtra*

42 Farzana Shaikh: *Community and Consensus in Islam: Muslims Representation in Colonial India, 1860–1947*

43 Susan Bayly: *Saints, Goddesses and Kings: Muslims and Christians in South Indian Society, 1700–1900*

44 Gyan Prakash: *Bonded Histories: Genealogies of Labour Servitude in Colonial India*

45 Sanjay Subrahmanyam: *The Political Economy of Commerce: Southern India, 1500–1650*

Printed in the United States
74733LV00004B/172-189